T0265734

CRITICAL ESSAYS
VOLUME 1

THE FRENCH LIST

Georges Bataille

CRITICAL ESSAYS
VOLUME 1
1944–1948

Edited by
Benjamin Noys and Alberto Toscano

Translated by
Chris Turner

LONDON CALCUTTA NEW YORK

Seagull Books, 2023

First collected and published in volume form in French as
Œuvres complètes, XI: Articles I, 1944–1949 by Georges Bataille,
edited by Francis Marmande and Sibylle Monod
© Éditions Gallimard, Paris, 1988

First published in English translation by Seagull Books, 2023
English translation © Chris Turner, 2023
Editors' Introduction © Benjamin Noys and Alberto Toscano, 2023
This compilation © Seagull Books, 2023

ISBN   978 1 80309 060 3

British Library Cataloguing-in-Publication Data
A catalogue record for this book is available from the British Library

Typeset by Seagull Books, Calcutta, India
Printed and bound in the USA by Versa Press

CONTENTS

At the Crossroads
The Postwar Bataille

Bataille's Dualities

This volume is the first of three that will gather hitherto untranslated articles by the French novelist, philosopher and essayist Georges Bataille (1897–1962), published between 1944–1961 and collected in volumes 11 and 12 of his *Œuvres complètes* with Gallimard. The bulk of these essays and reviews were published in the journal *Critique*, which Bataille founded in 1946 and which continues to publish today.

Readers for whom the name Bataille is synonymous with the eroticism and excess, the tumult and transgression of texts like *L'histoire de l'œil* (*Story of the Eye*) (1928), 'L'anus solaire' ('The Solar Anus') (1931) or *Madame Edwarda* (1941) may be confounded by the seeming equanimity of many of the texts collected here. Bataille's postwar articles seem to represent a new serenity and sobriety in comparison to the turbulent texts of the interwar years and the anguished texts of wartime, such as *L'expérience intérieure* (*Inner Experience*) (1943) and *Le Coupable* (*Guilty*) (1944). Although, in *Inner Experience*, Bataille had stated his ambition to combine rapture and rigour,[1] those wartime texts expressed themselves in disordered forms. The postwar essays reveal an exoteric Bataille, determined to contribute to public debate, in contrast to the esoteric Bataille of the Acéphale group and its 'sacred conspiracies'.[2] They also show a Bataille moving from an interwar

---

1 Georges Bataille, *Inner Experience* (Leslie Anne Boldt trans.) (Albany: State University of New York Press, 1988), p. *xxxiii*.

2 Georges Bataille, *The Sacred Conspiracy: The Internal Papers of the Secret Society of Acéphale and Lectures to the College of Sociology* (Marina Galletti and Alastair Brotchie eds) (London: Atlas Press, 2017).

antifascism so virulent as to be termed *sur*-fascist to a sui generis political philosophy of neutrality in the ambit of the Cold War.[3]

In his preface to *La Littérature et le Mal* (*Literature and Evil*) (1957), Bataille reflected on how the long review articles he penned for *Critique* were at the origin of that collection of studies of writers from William Blake to Jean Genet. The journal, he noted, 'owed its success to its serious character', but he added that 'turmoil is fundamental to my entire study'.[4] Bataille's suggestion is that the serious, even sober appearance of the postwar work is a conduit, perhaps even a screen, for the same turbulence that had always driven him. For a writer who had devoted considerable attention to Nietzsche—impelled by the 'feeling of community' that bound him to the German philosopher[5]—this donning of the mask of moderation might be taken as a kind of parody. But it is perhaps more fecund to see the non-partisan and encyclopedic mandate of *Critique*,[6] along with Bataille's capacious and apparently eclectic practice of reviewing and essay writing, as bearing its own subterranean affinity with the ambition to systematize, even if in the form of a 'non-system',[7] which animated his postwar studies

---

3 On Bataille's interwar antifascism see Michèle Richman, 'Fascism Reviewed: Georges Bataille in *"La Critique sociale"*', *South Central Review* 14(3–4) (1997): 14–30.

4 Georges Bataille, *Literature and Evil* (Alastair Hamilton trans.) (London and New York: Marion Boyars, 1997), p. *viii*.

5 Bataille, *Inner Experience*, p. 26. See Denis Hollier, 'From Beyond Hegel to Nietzsche's Absence' in Leslie Anne Boldt-Irons (ed. and trans.), *On Bataille: Critical Essays* (Albany: SUNY Press, 1995), pp. 61–78.

6 Georges Bataille and Pierre Prévost (who would serve as *Critique*'s chief editor in 1946–47) sent this project for the review to the publisher Maurice Girodias in December 1945: 'We propose the foundation under the title *Critica* of a journal of general information touching on all the domains of knowledge—history, sciences, philosophy, technics—as well as on current political and literary events. This journal will comprise substantial analyses of the principal works published both in France and abroad. The information thereby conveyed would therefore not represent merely the limited contribution of a small number of writers but a systematic extract of what is published across the world.' Quoted in Sylvie Patron, Preface to Georges Bataille and Éric Weil, *A en-tête de 'Critique': Correspondance 1946-1951* (Sylvie Patron ed.) (Paris: Lignes, 2014), p. 10.

7 Georges Bataille, *The Unfinished System of Non-Knowledge* (Michelle Kendall and Stuart Kendall trans, Stuart Kendall ed. and intro.) (Minneapolis: University of Minnesota Press, 2001).

like *La Part maudite* (*The Accursed Share*) (1949) and *L'Erotisme* (*Eroticism*) (1957), as well as the multiple texts that make up *La Somme athéologique*. If Nietzsche is one pole of Bataille's eccentric orbit then the other is always Hegel, and while mimicking Nietzsche's antisystemic fragmentation is one impulse in Bataille, so is the aspiration to system and completion that drives Hegel's *Phenomenology* and *Logic*. Bataille had long dreamt of a 'universal history', outlining the project to Raymond Queneau in 1934.[8] That ambition would dominate Bataille's own postwar research.

Bataille met the initial moment after the Liberation with a 'frenzy of publications'.[9] In 1945, he published *Sur Nietzsche* (*On Nietzsche*) and *Mémorandum*, the latter being a selection of Nietzsche's writings which he edited and introduced; *The Oresteia*, with Éditions Quatre Vents; *Dirty*, through Editions Fontaine; and a new edition of the novel *Madame Edwarda*, with Le Solitaire. While these efforts could be seen as a consolidation of his wartime meditations and an attempt to re-emerge as a writer, Bataille's subsequent labours for *Critique* as both reviewer and editor were formidable and consuming. As his editorial correspondence testifies, this thinker so widely associated with the derangement of the senses, with baseness and transgression, was also a tireless and punctilious organizer, mediating political dissensions on *Critique*'s board, commissioning, copy-editing and negotiating the precarious finances and paper shortages that beset postwar publishing.[10] Between 1946 and 1949, Bataille would write

---

8 Michel Surya, *Georges Bataille: An Intellectual Biography* (Krzysztof Fijalkowski and Michael Richardson trans) (London: Verso, 2002), p. 462.

9 Stuart Kendall, *Georges Bataille* (London: Reaktion, 2007), p. 176.

10 See especially Bataille and Weil, *A en-tête de 'Critique'*. See also Georges Ambrosino and Georges Bataille, *L'Expérience à l'épreuve: Correspondance et inédits (1943–1960)* (Claudine Frank ed.) (Meurcourt: Éditions Les Cahiers, 2018), and Sylvie Patron, *Critique 1946–1996: Une encyclopédie de l'esprit moderne* (Paris: Institut mémoire de l'édition contemporaine, 1999). For an insightful overview of Bataille's editing and writing in *Critique*, see Michèle Richman, 'Bataille Moralist?: *Critique* and the Postwar Writings', *Yale French Studies* 78 (1990): 143–68. Richman foregrounds the theme to which we will turn in the second half of this introduction, Bataille's crowning preoccupation in the postwar period, namely 'the reinterpretation of the instant of *dépense* as the basis for an alternative ethic' (p. 146).

over 600 pages for the journal. This was not simply the sign of a new maturity, a category of very little use when considering the French thinker. Kristin Ross, writing on Rimbaud, has noted how the poet's texts produce an 'adolescent body' that is 'too slow and too fast', a body torn between laziness and insurrection, and one that disrupts linear development.[11] Bataille could be seen as producing a body of writing, including in the postwar moment, that is similarly temporally disruptive and—to continue the adolescent theme—at once seemingly conformist and suddenly rebellious, driven by competing and unintegrated impulses.

Serious and turbulent, frenzied and systematic, it is difficult not to multiply dualities when considering Bataille in this period. In an interview, Bataille described an article by his friend the Hegel scholar Alexandre Kojève in the following terms: 'This article marks most clearly the intentions of *Critique*, which would like to be the crossroads of philosophy, literature, religion and political economy.'[12] This crossroads is a figure of mediation and of totality, as well as of the dualities that threaten to rend that totalization. *Critique* was a project that would reject the compartmentalization of consciousness and so remain true to the explosive Bataille of the 1930s, who sought a synthesis that would both encompass and exceed Marx, Freud and Hegel. Yet the crossroads is also the site of the burial of suicides (as in the case of the suspect in the Ratcliff highway murders of 1811, buried at a crossroads after hanging himself in his cell[13]). It is a figure of wrenching or tearing. It is difficult not to recall Bataille's favourite quote from Hegel's *Phenomenology of Spirit*, which he would include in his article 'Hegel, la mort et le sacrifice' ('Hegel, Death and Sacrifice') (1955), first published in the philosophy journal *Deucalion*, edited by Jean Wahl. We quote only the concluding lines:

---

11 Kristin Ross, *The Emergence of Social Space: Rimbaud and the Commune* (London: Verso, 2008), p. 55.

12 Surya, *Georges Bataille*, p. 369.

13 Thomas de Quincey, *On Murder* (Robert Morrison ed.) (Oxford: Oxford University Press, 2006), p. 141.

Now, the life of Spirit is not that life which is frightened of death, and spares itself destruction, but that life which assumes death and lives with it. Spirit attains its truth only by finding itself in absolute dismemberment. It is not that [prodigious] power by being the Positive that turns away from the Negative, as when we say of something: this is nothing or [this is] false and, having [thus] disposed of it, pass from there to something else; no, Spirit is that power only to the degree in which it contemplates the Negative face to face [and] dwells with it. This prolonged sojourn is the magical force which transposes the negative into given—Being.[14]

Spirit lives through tarrying with the negative and the dismembering encounter with death. It should be recalled that Hegel's *Phenomenology* is a very bodily text, driven by the passage of spirit through its various incarnations. Spirit's figures are so many bodily postures, experiences, disturbances, and ruptures.[15] The crossroads is not simply the tranquil confluence of various disciplines and forms of thought in a new unity, but also the site of a negativity that would contemplate and dwell with absolute dismemberment. As a figure, the crossroads attests to turbulence and division, as well as the desire to stabilize this negativity into a systematic form.

This duality is, as Michel Surya notes, something that marks Bataille in this postwar moment. Alongside the respectable and even serene articles for *Critique*, between 1947 and 1949 Bataille also published *La Haine de la Poésie* (*The Hatred of Poetry*), *L'Alleluiah*, and *L'Abbé C*, 'which are among the least respectable [texts] he wrote'.[16] Even during the 1920s and 1930s, we could contrast the duality of Bataille's daytime life as a librarian and his dissolute night-time life, transfigured in fictional works like *Le Bleu du Ciel* (*Blue of Noon*) (written in 1935–36, published in 1957). It seems irresistible

---

14 G. W. F. Hegel, cited in Georges Bataille, 'Hegel, Death and Sacrifice' (Jonathan Strauss trans.), *Yale French Studies* 78 (1990): 14.

15 For a parallel consider the bodily reading of Marx's *Capital* as a work of embodied satire proposed by Keston Sutherland, 'Marx in Jargon' in *Stupefaction: A Radical Anatomy of Phantoms* (London: Seagull Books, 2011).

16 Surya, *Georges Bataille*, p. 371.

to describe Bataille in terms of opposition, contrast and duality. This duality, in which life and the concept confront each other, is what Bataille called a lived experience. It is not just a matter of a duality *between* life and work or thought and existence, but a duality *within* life and work, thought and existence in Bataille's own work—a totality always haunted by the absence of the work, *l'absence de l'œuvre*.

Bataille at the crossroads, in which the seriousness of the scientific aims of *Critique* remains traversed by the subterranean currents of his own base materialism,[17] is a living embodiment of the duality of life and concept. This duality, as we have suggested, is not merely a standard contrast of the exoteric (*Critique*) and the esoteric (the 'unrespectable' or 'obscene' writings), but something that Bataille lives and tries to resolve. In the 1930s, duality and dualism had been the signs of a weaponized materialism. In 'Le bas matérialisme et la gnose' ('Base Materialism and Gnosticism') (1930), the Gnostics offer 'the most monstrous dualistic and therefore strangely abased cosmogonies'.[18] These are visible in the duck-headed Gnostic Archontes, incarnations of a bestial materialism that disrupts all idealization and ruins any philosophical ontology. These bestial hybrids mock the pretensions of thought,[19] as did Bataille's meditations on the big toe or the solar anus. They articulate what Denis Hollier has called Bataille's 'dualist materialism', understood as an 'attitude of thought', a non-systematic 'resistance to system and homogeneity'.[20] This articulation is further explored in the

---

17 Georges Bataille, *Visions of Excess: Selected Writings, 1927–1939* (Allan Stoekl ed.) (Minneapolis: University of Minnesota Press, 1985), pp. 45–52.

18 Bataille, *Visions of Excess*, p. 46.

19 Giorgio Agamben argues that these Gnostic images that mix human and animal articulate a remnant 'outside being' and separated from the 'anthropological machine' that structures Western biopolitics by dividing human from animal (and then casting some humans into the category of the animal). See Giorgio Agamben, *The Open: Man and Animal* (Kevin Attell trans.) (Stanford: Stanford University Press, 2003), pp. 89–92. This is a speculation which has considerable affinities with Bataille, but as Agamben's remarks on the sacred and sacrifice in *Homo Sacer* suggest, it also breaks with his thinking in significant regards. See Giorgio Agamben, *Homo Sacer: Sovereign Power and Bare Life* (Daniel Heller-Roazen trans.) (Stanford: Stanford University Press, 1998), pp. 112–15.

20 Denis Hollier, 'The Dualist Materialism of Georges Bataille', *Yale French Studies* 78 (1992): 127.

postwar writings, where the virulent dualism of the interwar years is transmuted by an orientation towards system and totality. Of special interest in this regard is the 1947 essay, included in this volume, 'On the Relationship between the Divine and Evil' (see below, pp. 122–31) discussing the work of philosopher and scholar of Gnosticism Simone Pétrement. Dualism is here explicitly linked by Bataille to one of his chief preoccupations in this period, namely morality, or what, in *Literature and Evil*, he would identify as the effort to delineate a 'hyper-morality'.[21] Reviewing Pétrement's 1946 book on dualism in the history of philosophy and of religions, Bataille declares: 'Morality is, in its essence, a questioning about morality; and the decisive move in human life is constantly to use all available sources of enlightenment to seek out the origin of the opposition between Good and Evil' (see below, p. 123). But this moral questioning is also indexed to the uncertainty, stasis and disorientation of the postwar. As Bataille reflects: 'It is probable that the rapid transformation of the world itself requires another morality today' (see below, p. 131).

Using Pétrement's treatment of Gnostic and Christian dualities to breach the confines of Durkheim's sociology of religion, Bataille will shift from the dualism between Good and Evil to that which opposes the sacred to the profane, as two contrasting ways of experiencing duality. His contention will be that the divine and the sacred are marked by an *inner, immanent* duality, and that—contrary to our Christian, theological prejudices—it is the profane that introduces transcendence into the world. This is what Bataille calls the 'fundamental paradox' that a theory of religion must confront:

> *if the divine is considered independently of its intellectual forms, it is not transcendent but sensible and, in the most undeniable way, immanent; transcendence by contrast (the intelligible sphere) is given in the profane world; in its classical form, which Pètrement's essay brings out clearly, religious dualism is therefore the inversion of its primitive form.* (see below, p. 127; emphasis in the original)

---

21 Bataille, *Literature and Evil*, p. *viii*.

The sensible immanence of the sacred, its in-separate character, also underlies the '*communion, communication* of unfettered, dangerous, *contagious* forces', which is in turn to be understood in terms of a dualism that will govern Bataille's system of non-knowledge, the dualism between *utility* and the *expenditure* that marks the limits of the useful (see below, p. 128; emphasis in the original).[22] Having framed dualism in terms of the moral discrimination between Good and Evil, and then displaced that dualism with the dualities between the sacred and the profane, the immanent and the transcendent, contagious expenditure and calculative utility, Bataille will advance his own (hyper-)moral definition of evil as the instrumental unleashing of the passions *by* reason, in other words as 'bestiality serving *raison d'État*'. Without this dimension, Bataille adds in a note, 'Buchenwald would not be the decisive, undisputed, irreducible mark of *evil*' (see below, p. 131n6).[23] Or, in a related formulation, 'evil lies in the fact that passion has grown servile, has placed itself in the service of a legal power that can only exert itself coldly. Pure passion is naturally in revolt and never wants legal power: generally, it does not even have power as its end but ruin, excessive expenditure rapidly destroying power' (see below, 'A Morality Based on Misfortune', pp. 165–66).[24]

Notwithstanding this postwar moral tone, the interwar virulence does not disappear, and texts like 'The Friendship between Man and Beast' (see

---

22 See Bataille's wartime notes for the project that would eventually become *The Accursed Share*: Georges Bataille, *The Limit of the Useful* (Cory Austin Knudson and Tomas Elliott eds) (Cambridge, MA: The MIT Press, 2023).

23 See also the remark in Bataille's review of Sartre's 1946 *Réflexions sur la question juive* (translated into English as *Anti-Semite and Jew*), on the anti-Semite as 'finding in exercises in loathing those moral prerogatives that entitle one to property ownership' (see below, 'Sartre', p. 151). In his essay on *The Plague*, Bataille will outline a reading of 'Camus *avec* Sade' precisely around this question of the rational instrumentalization of excessive violence, taking his cue from Sade's peroration against the death penalty in *Philosophy in the Boudoir*. In the end, evil just is the monopolization of violence by the state—further proof if proof be needed that the customary meaning of sovereignty is the opposite of Bataille's. See below, 'A Morality Based on Misfortune', pp. 153–67.

24 As Julia Kristeva observes, the Bataillean sovereign is ultimately *powerless*. See her 'Bataille, Experience and Practice' in *On Bataille: Critical Essays*, p. 251. Accordingly, Bataillean sovereignty can never be simply equated with a Nietzschean will-to-power.

below, pp. 107–11) retain some of the surrealist swagger and provocation of the 1920s and 1930s. The dividing line between rigour and excess can never be drawn once and for all, for the very precise reason that the rigour Bataille deploys is in the service of the pursuit of excess. Bataille carries forward his fascination for a writing of or at the limits of reason—no doubt buoyed by his friendship with Blanchot—and proposes a kind of discipline that can give shape to a thinking of literature and poetry as modes of useless and insubordinate excess. This concern with literature and rigour, already laid out in the early articles, will come to shape Bataille's writings for *Critique*.

Bataille's first article for *Critique*—on Henry Miller and the scandals surrounding his novels (see below, 'Miller's Morality', pp. 24–39)—will articulate hyper-morality through the vision of a life free from the demand to generate revenue, a life associated with childhood and marked by sovereign freedom in its lack of concern for risking death. Relating back to Bataille's analysis of Hegel—deeply informed by Kojève's teaching with its stress of the master/slave dialectic—this analysis also points forward to the essays from *Critique* that will be later collected as *Literature and Evil*. While concerned with familiar figures of transgression, Bataille's postwar writings on literature are also attentive to the limits that make sovereign poetic moments possible. They also emphasize the need for rigour, discipline, even a certain method in pursuing the dialectic of limit and excess. In the discussion of Henry Miller, we see the attention to the pursuit of excess as well as the sense that Miller remains a Nietzschean 'last man', falling within certain limits and failing to inhabit his own forms of transgression and expenditure. In a similar way, Bataille's discussion of the pursuit of abasement by Arthur Adamov also discerns a tendency to sentimentality that prevents the Franco-Armenian playwright from the full embrace of the defilement and dissolution of the self. In each case, Bataille is attuned to what, in a writer, makes them approach limits but also to what leads them to recoil or retreat from them.

This is the tension in thinking through excess that Bataille also likens to a dog chasing its own tail: trying to complete knowledge, trying to attain action, simply leads to more reading (and more articles!) (see below, 'The

Last Instant', pp. 56–65).[25] The paradox is expressed in Bataille's practice of extensive quotation and citation; in the act of letting the text speak for itself, admitting the excess into Bataille's text, we are still only making room for another text, and the experience itself remains elusive. The dog chases its tail, while the reviewer or reader chases yet another reading or book to find an experience that can only be imagined outside of books. As Bataille laments: 'We may speak, furtively, of Miller's "explosive perspectives," but no one explodes: and we continue to write, to publish, to read . . . ' (see below, 'Miller's Morality', p. 39). Such a problem is evident in the philosophy of the moment or instant that Bataille outlines—a moment of excess, an instant of rupture, a shattering of experience, which, once it comes to be written, retreats from excess and reverts to being merely one moment among others. Of course, this is a problem brought to light by writing but it is also true of experience itself. The 'pure' moment of presence, as Jacques Derrida never tired of noting, only exists through its differential relation to other moments and, in that way, is never pure.[26] Bataille captures this predicament in one of the few of the texts in this collection not originally published in *Critique*, a reflection on the myth and figure of Dionysus for a one-off 1946 special issue of a travel journal, *Le Voyage en Grèce*, which had been published between 1934 and 1939. What are we to make, and who are we to be, when excess only manifests through loss? When the instant of presence is also the instance of loss? As Bataille observes:

> The Christian priests who deprived us of Dionysus, acted on us like
> a social worker removing an unfit mother, taking care to ensure the

---

25 The terms of this discussion trace those of Sartre's own sardonic remark in the article on Bataille that set off a creeping dispute between the two thinkers: 'For, in the end, M. Bataille writes; he has a job at the Bibliothèque Nationale; he reads, makes love and eats'; Jean-Paul Sartre, 'A New Mystic' (1943) in *On Bataille and Blanchot* (Chris Turner trans.), The Seagull Sartre Library, VOL. 10 (London: Seagull Books, 2021), pp. 1–61; here, p. 43.

26 Jacques Derrida, *Edmund Husserl's 'Origin of Geometry': An Introduction* (John P. Leavey Jr trans., pref. and after.) (Lincoln: University of Nebraska Press, 1989). For Derrida's reading of Bataille, see Jacques Derrida, 'From Restricted to General Economy: A Hegelianism without Reserve' in *Writing and Difference* (Alan Bass trans.) (Chicago: Chicago University Press, 1978), pp. 251–77.

child retained not the slightest recollection of her. It is only with great difficulty that we rediscovered the traces that remain. And, if we wish to do so, we can gauge the extent of our loss, but it was effected with such thoroughness that we cannot truly feel it: we know that we should weep but we know it only with dry eyes. (see below, 'Dionysus Redivivus', p. 41)

Bataille's awareness of this difficulty is, in part, what also recommended his thought to Derrida. Even if the attempted resolutions remain problematic, Bataille's rigour lies in refusing the temptation to evade this predicament. In the articles for *Critique*, we witness a series of probes that try to remain faithful to a conception and an experience of freedom as an unleashing (*déchaînement*) of forces that overrides and exceeds the subject. The animal here insinuates an unbridling without bounds, but it does not abide in that relation to consciousness that marks the experience of human unleashing with anguish and ecstasy. In this way, Bataille at once erodes the boundary between human and animal, privileges the animal in this binary as a force against reification, but also retains multiple features of the classical distinction between the human and the animal. In a striking formulation, Bataille posits that:

> *humanity* in the *human, anti-animal* time of work is that within us which reduces us to things, and animality is then what preserves within us the value of an existence of the subject for himself. [...] *'Animality' or sexual exuberance is the element within us which prevents our being reduced to things. 'Humanity', on the other hand, in its specificity in working time, tends to make us into things, at the expense of our sexual exuberance.* (see below, 'The Sexual Revolution and the Kinsey Report', pp. 260–61)

It is interesting that Bataille should figure the relationship between the human and the animal—with special attention to the horse—in terms of *friendship*. This word, so central to the thought of Bataille's friend and *Critique* contributing editor Blanchot,[27] is now transmuted to figure a

---

27 Maurice Blanchot, *Friendship* (Elizabeth Rottenberg trans.) (Stanford: Stanford University Press, 1997).

relationship with the non-human. Once again, we can remark the nuance of Bataille's thought, as it develops from such seemingly simple conceptual starting points like 'the instant' or 'unleashing', into an effort to try to capture the complexity and fluidity of relations that may at first appear as rigid dualities.

While Bataille's thought tends to appear as a kind of phenomenology of irreducible presence opposed to a rational order of substances, categories and distinctions, this is ultimately deceptive. In fact—as we witness when Bataille discusses 'What Is Sex?'—everything can be reversed, and the privileges of immanence and immediacy cast into doubt. In the instance of sex and sexuality it is our everyday phenomenological experience that, according to Bataille, supposes the capacity to identify sex and impose a binary. Yet this is far from what science registers. In this case, our own experience—our 'intimate sense of difference' (see below, 'What Is Sex?', p. 135)—reifies sex into the fixed modes of male and female, while science dissolves this certainty. Recounting a series of experiments involving animals, and wryly gesturing towards Heideggerian ontology, Bataille concludes that:

> science makes this overall finding: it removes from the beings claimed as such the possibility of serving as the basis for the idea of being. It dissolves into interactions what primary experience represented as substances. The only image of things that it countenances is that of continuous communication, in which beings and sexes disappear (for example, love, if we give that name to the conjunction of living beings, is the primary fact—not *man* or *woman*). (see below, p. 145)[28]

In this instance—and it is fascinating to read this argument in counterpoint with contemporary debates over gender and sex—Bataille stresses how science supplants the primacy of substance with that of a generalized communication, such that 'the problem of being is dissolved in these shifts [*glissements*]'.[29] This not only suggests the fluidity of sex—which would go

---

28 For a broader reflection on the place of science and its outside (*hors-science*) in Bataille's thought and research, see Jean-Louis Baudry, 'Bataille and Science: Introduction to Inner Experience' in *On Bataille: Critical Essays*, pp. 265–81.

29 This might also be read as a reply to Sartre, who had criticized Bataille's turn to

some way to countering Bataille's own tendency to resort elsewhere to clichéd images of sexual difference—but also forces us to attend to how science can align with a practice of undoing common sense and its folk ontologies.

While Bataille might constantly have recourse to a phenomenological idiom, in oblique dialogue with Sartre, Merleau-Ponty, Levinas, Blanchot and others—in the back of whom stands the unsurpassable power of Hegel's *Phenomenology*—it is evident that we do not have here a simple opposition between, on the one hand, intimate excess figured in the experience of consciousness and, on the other, a reifying rationality that reduces the world to discrete objects. Instead, Bataille frames science as the dissolution of phenomenological myths of immediacy and—with reference to the biologist Étienne Wolff's study of sex changes—as the problematizing of stability in the form of sexual difference.[30] In his critical survey of the Kinsey Report—riffing off of a formulation from his erstwhile colleague at the Collège de Sociologie and member of *Critique*'s inaugural editorial board, Jules Monnerot—Bataille will come to the following conclusion, which also testifies to his manner of pushing the texts he reviews beyond their limits:

> it is even possible that the deep meaning of the Report lies in something that it demonstrates to be impossible: we would then have to read it against the grain and thereby see only a truth that its authors could not or would not see: they have put together an enormous piece of work, the very principle of which requires sexual acts to be regarded as things, but the clearest outcome of their research has been to show without a doubt that ultimately *sexual acts are not things*. (see below, 'The Sexual Revolution and the Kinsey Report', p. 255)[31]

---

science for treating people as things and denying phenomenological meaning (Sartre, 'A New Mystic').

30 The book was composed while Wolff was a prisoner of war in a German Oflag (prisoner camp for officers) between 1940 and 1945. See Emil Witschi, review of *Les Changements de Sexe*, *The Quarterly Review of Biology* 22(1) (1947): 84.

31 See Jules Monnerot, *Les faits sociaux ne sont pas des choses* (Paris: Gallimard, 1946). Bataille reviewed Monnerot's book in the first issue of *Critique*. See Georges Bataille, 'The Moral Meaning of Sociology' in *The Absence of Myth: Writings on Surrealism* (Michael Richardson ed. and trans.) (London: Verso, 1994), pp. 103–12.

The Russo-American War and the Morality of the Instant

Political facts, we could add, are not things either. This is one of the prisms through which we can view the postwar Bataille. The founding and editing of *Critique*, as well as the many essays that Bataille penned for it, weave a complex path beyond the deceptive alternative between the politics of commitment and the pretence to be above politics. An instrumental image of partisan literature is antithetical to Bataille's ethics and poetics, which rest on the key duality between utility and a sovereignty that aims neither to conserve nor to command.[32] Writing in the Resistance journal *Combat* mere months after the liberation of Paris, Bataille declares:

> This war is being conducted against a system of life for which propagandist literature provides the key. The destiny of fascism is to enslave: among other things, to reduce literature to mere usefulness. What does useful literature mean but treating men as so much human material? For that sorry task, literature is indeed necessary.
>
> This does not imply the condemnation of any particular genre, but of the political stance, of slogans. It is on just one condition that I write authentically: that I not give a fig for anyone or anything; that I take instruction from no one.
>
> What often sends things awry is a weak writer's concern to be useful.
>
> Every man should be useful to his fellows, but if there is nothing in him beyond usefulness, then he is their enemy.
>
> The descent into usefulness—from being ashamed of oneself, when divine freedom produces a guilty conscience—is the beginning of a desertion. The field is left free to the weathercocks of propaganda.
>
> Why not accept the fact, in these circumstances where every truth is coming out, that literature fundamentally rejects usefulness?

---

32 It is worth noting that Bataille sees this duality overcome in the aesthetic domain in Picasso's paintings in response to the Spanish Civil War, remarking that it is 'strange that the freest of the arts should have reached its peak in a political painting' (see below, 'Picasso's Political Paintings', p. 16).

Being the expression of man—of the most essential part of man—
it cannot be useful, since man in his essentials isn't reducible to
usefulness. (see below, 'Is Literature Useful?', pp. 6–7)[33]

Returning, again in the pages of *Combat*, to the vexed debate on Nietzsche
and fascism which he had tackled with characteristic intransigence before
the war,[34] Bataille sketches a defence of the 'impolitical' Nietzsche against
his prosecutors on the Left, one that also provides some insight into his own
perception of the sovereignty of thought and poetry.[35]

> The truth is that the field of Nietzsche's thinking lies beyond the
> necessary, common concerns that determine politics. The ques-
> tions he raised touch on tragedy, laughter, pain, and joy despite
> pain; on richness and freedom of spirit: in general, the extreme
> states to which the human mind may aspire. He spurned basic
> problems such as income levels and political freedom. His doctrine
> of dangerous life, of clear-sighted, unfettered, disdainful humanity
> is far removed from public struggles. It is a doctrine for solitaries
> secretly and tragically ruminating for themselves while the
> universe maintains its hostile silence. (see below, 'Is Nietzsche
> Fascist?', p. 5)[36]

---

33 In a review of Jean Paulhan which reflects on recent polemics on writers and the
Resistance, Bataille observes that literature 'is always to some degree the mockery of
politics (that is the reason why, if literature has some political meaning, it is revolutionary; but in that case the relationship is not a lasting one)' (see below, 'Jean
Paulhan—Marc Bloch', p. 268).

34 See Georges Bataille, 'Nietzsche and the Fascists' and 'Nietzschean Chronicle' in
Visions of Excess, pp. 182–96 and 202–12.

35 Bataille is a central reference in Roberto Esposito's important intervention into
political philosophy, *Categories of the Impolitical* (Connal Parsley trans.) (New York:
Fordham University Press, 2015).

36 Hitting a rare false note, the passage continues: 'Despite all the set dressing, the distance from Hitler to Nietzsche is the distance from the guardhouse to the summits of
the Alps. But doesn't the simplest of human beings, if he desires freedom, point to the
air of the mountaintops as his aim and distant goal?'

But this duality, between tragic solitude and public engagement, is far too simple, and perhaps not tragic enough, to account for Bataille's postwar relation to politics. As his editorial work for *Critique* testifies—but also articles like his survey piece on war and revolution in China (see below, 'The War in China', p. 72–85)—there is something like a *realist moment* in Bataille, a sense that it is necessary for him to know political, and especially economic, facts precisely in order to delineate their limits, what exceeds them, how they are not indeed things.

The postwar political fact was the onset of the Cold War. For Bataille the encounter with Communism is the encounter—missed by too many of his contemporaries—not just with an ideological doctrine but with 'the irruption of genuine [*réelle*] force into the systems of ideas' (see below, 'Political Lying', p. 238). While engaging—as his correspondence with Eric Weil and Georges Ambrosino testifies—in a complex editorial balancing act in the pages of *Critique* between pro- and anti-Communist voices, Bataille was elaborating a much more capacious vision, the one that would eventually find its provisional formulation in the pages of *The Accursed Share* on the Marshall Plan and the Soviet Union. In his 1948 essay on 'Political Lying', Bataille declares that the conflict between capitalism and Communism represents 'the keenest debate in the moral history of humanity' (see below, p. 238), ironically one that pits two camps both of which claim to be trying to stop men from treating other men like things. In a later essay on Raymond Aron, this epochal antagonism will be seen to attain a genuinely tragic level. The defining clash of the postwar reveals

> the capacity humanity has to oppose itself, to find within itself the fundamental opposition between two irreconcilable possibilities. As in tragedy, the antagonism comes to a high point of intensity; as in tragedy, we find an *exposition* of that moment. The present time seems, in fact, to share the tragic author's concern not to rush to the *dénouement* but first express the irreconcilable violence of the colliding forces. (see below, 'On the Meaning of Moral Neutrality in the Russo-American War', p. 275)

Bataille does not just appropriate Aron's reflections on the 'great schism' between the red East and the liberal-capitalist West, he explores Communism's own contradictory claims on humanity. Communism's own reality principle—its attachment to thinghood, concreteness, materiality, and force—is but the obverse of the reification that reigns in a capitalist society that must and yet cannot breach the bounds of utility. The moral challenge of the postwar also requires traversing Communism's own repudiation of morality, its practical antihumanism, so to speak. As Bataille observes, in the process of teasing out what he terms 'the unavoidable problem Marxism and the USSR pose today for humanity':

> if we reject individual escape and assert our shared humanity—if we accept not being things only at the same time and on the same basis as others—*we have first to accept being things.* It is only when the whole of humanity has stopped oppressing, when there are nowhere any commodity-human-beings for sale, that we shall ourselves escape reduction to thingness. Until then, it is at the level of useable thing, as members of a debased humanity, that we have to contribute, in a disciplined way, to an immense work of liberation. (see below, 'Political Lying', p. 242)

In answering what the young Lukács had termed 'the moral problem of Bolshevism',[37] Bataille comes to define something like the antinomy of Communism:

> Man cannot be regarded as a thing. And it is for that reason that he is a Communist. (But we must add: Communism can, at first, only render this reduction to a thing complete and general, and it is also for that reason that man fights Communism to the death.) (see below, p. 243)[38]

---

37 Georg Lukács, 'The Moral Problem of Bolshevism' (Judith Marcus Tar trans.), *Social Research* 44(3) (1977): 416–24. The article was originally published in Hungarian in December 1918.

38 In 1944, Bataille had tried to tackle the moral question of Communism, which represented for him 'the questioning of our social order and generally of the values and approvals linked to that order', in two drafts of articles provisionally entitled 'On Communism' and 'Communism and Freedom', for *Combat*. In the first of these two unfinished articles, Bataille announces the forthcoming publication of a book on the nexus of morality and Communism, *Nietzsche and Communism* (this would later serve as the title of a section in the unfinished third volume of *The Accursed Share*, *Sovereignty*). In the extant fragment of the piece on Communism and freedom he

Bataille's hyper-moral vantage on the clash between Communist and capitalist camps is also a strategy for breaking through 'the opacity without fear and without hope'[39] that he diagnoses as the lot of a postwar European condition marked by a critical lack of *imagination* (a predicament that echoes Robert Musil's balance sheet after World War One and Günther Anders's musings on the obsolescence of man in the atomic age).[40] It is also what subtends his effort to articulate a conception of neutrality from a reflexive position of *in*action—one that eschews fantasies of a 'Third Way' between capitalism and Communism, or postures of moral purity *super partes*. In his article on Aron and the 'great schism', Bataille—having declared the need for US economic growth as a precondition of human survival[41]—will argue for the urgency of 'the development and the *moral* predominance in the world of a *neutral* consciousness', adding, in a dense concluding note:

---

discusses the painful predicament of the Western man of freedom, affected by a kind of powerless indignation the more he understands 'the extent to which the solidarity between freedom and capitalism is harmful to the cause of freedom'. See Georges Bataille, *Œuvres complètes, Volume 11: Articles I, 1944-1949* (Francis Marmande and Sibylle Monod eds) (Paris: Gallimard, 1988), pp. 557–59.

39 Georges Bataille, 'Concerning the Accounts Given by the Residents of Hiroshima' (Alan Keenan trans.), *American Imago* 48(4) (1991): 497 (translation modified); originally published in *Critique* in 1947, now in Bataille, *Œuvres complètes*, VOL. 11, pp. 172–87.

40 See Robert Musil, 'Helpless Europe' and 'Mind and Experience' in *Precision and Soul: Essays and Addresses* (Burton Pike and David S. Luft trans and eds) (Chicago: University of Chicago Press, 1990); on Anders, see Alberto Toscano, 'The Promethean Gap: Modernism, Machines and the Obsolescence of Man', *Modernism/modernity* 23(3) (2016): 593–609.

41 Bataille's viewpoint on these questions was shaped by his dialogue with Jean Piel, whose book *La Fortune américaine et son destin* (Paris: Éditions de Minuit, 1948), was the first publication in the book series L'usage des richesses, directed by Bataille, whose only other volume would be the first part of *The Accursed Share: La Part maudite: Essai d'économie générale, t. I: La Consumation* (Paris: Éditions de Minuit, 1949). The discussion of the Marshall Plan in that volume fleshes out why Bataille's *sui generis* 'moral economy' would centre that key plank of US geopolitics in the early Cold War. In light of his remarks in these essays on (Soviet and Chinese) Communism, as well as his affinities for the Hegelian 'Stalinism' of his friends Weil and Kojève, we might hazard that rather than 'neither Washington nor Moscow', the perspective of Bataille's general economy on the postwar scene and its impasses took the improbable form of '*both* Washington *and* Moscow'. See also Richman, 'Bataille Moralist?': 152–55.

Neutrality undoubtedly means the rejection of any action, a determined distancing from any political undertaking, the sense of an inevitable pause, an inevitable moment when the onward rush of the driving forces of history ebbs (it is impossible, obviously, to know whether that ebbing will be the product of war itself or of fear of war). The deep sense of this paradox is that, in action there can be no *self-awareness*. (see below, 'On the Meaning of Moral Neutrality in the Russo-American War', p. 280n5)[42]

But this 'impolitic' moral distance from action is perfectly compatible in Bataille with a sober estimation of the moment of *realism*, and of struggle. This nuanced stance is best articulated in his 1948 essay on that *locus classicus* of disputes about political morality, the problem of lying.

I must say that the interest I take in action is not all that great; the supreme value attributed to it seems highly questionable to me (whatever may be said of it afterwards, action is, in a sense, just a necessity, of the same order as taking a bitter pill or paying a debt). But I cannot regard a man of action as leprous. Quite clearly, lying is no less necessary to him than speaking. And I might even say that, if he denied himself the right to lie, I could not look on him without an astonishment tinged with irritation: I should have to ask myself whether hypocrisy or foolhardiness were the stronger force within him. Those who *speak* of action *speak* of not lying. But those who act, and know how to act, lie insofar as lying is effective. Action is *struggle* and, insofar as there is struggle, there is no limitation on the various forms of violence; there is no limitation, other than effectiveness, on lying. Any other way of seeing is idealist and, as such, is the true leprosy of the soul: it is the inability to look things in the face, the weakness that diverts the eyes for fear of not being able to bear what they see. (see below, 'Political Lying', p. 239)

---

42 This emphasis on inaction recalls the notion of 'unemployed negativity' that Bataille had outlined in his 'Letter to X', a response to Kojéve's reading of Hegel. See Georges Bataille, 'Letter to X' in Denis Hollier (ed.), *The College of Sociology 1937–39* (Betsy Wing trans.) (Minneapolis: University of Minnesota Press, 1988), p. 90.

In a similar vein, Bataille will combine a plea for sensibility with a pitiless excoriation of political sentimentalism. As he writes in his review article on John Hershey's 1946 *Hiroshima*:

> the appeal to feeling is of negligible interest. [. . .] If, besides, as is human, we reject sentimentality and go resolutely to the limits of the possibilities of feeling, we find only the infinite 'absurd' of animal suffering. And in the meaningless world into which our reflection draws us, a cataclysm is limited to the instant it takes place—and its representation exceeds any concern for subsequent consequences. So much so that feeling cannot be the point of departure for action. And one can say with certainty that the most vivid imagination can place only a negligible force at the service of those who wish to ward off the return of misfortune.[43]

Across these essays, Bataille is seeking to define a thinking of the irreducible,[44] of experience in excess of utility and calculation, of what he insistently names *l'instant*—the instant or moment[45]—while refusing the posture of the mere mystic or the beautiful soul standing above the fray of human events.

> Thus at the very moment when the sovereignty of the instant appears to me to dominate utility, in no way do I abandon this enduring humanity: I will say that humanity is beautiful and admirable only to the extent that the instant possesses and

---

43 Bataille, 'Concerning the Accounts Given by the Residents of Hiroshima': 505.

44 See his letter to Georges Ambrosino on this theme in *L'Expérience à l'épreuve*, p. 230.

45 On the instant in Bataille, see Philippe Sollers, 'L'acte Bataille' in Philippe Sollers (ed.), *Bataille* (Paris: U.G.E., 1973), p. 19. Consider also Derrida's remark: 'And the *instant*—the temporal mode of the sovereign operation—is not a *point* of full and unpenetrated presence: it slides and *eludes* us between two presences; it is difference as the affirmative elusion of presence. It does not give itself but is *stolen*, carries itself off in a movement which is simultaneously one of violent effraction and of vanishing flight. The instant is the *furtive*: "Un-knowledge implies at once fundamental anguish, but also the suppression of anguish. Henceforth, it becomes possible furtively to undergo the furtive experience that I call the experience of the instant" (*Conférences sur le Non-savoir*)' (Derrida, 'From Restricted to General Economy', p. 263).

intoxicates it, but this does not imply on my part any neglect of a duration which the instant consigns, from beginning to end, to a vanishing splendor.[46]

This perspective is a continuation and modification of the project of *Inner Experience,* which had been oriented to the instant as the sovereign moment of that experience. Sartre had astutely identified this focus on the instant as crucial: 'Bataille wants to exist fully and immediately—this very instant.'[47] Sartre had also placed Bataille in a strange but illuminating lineage of thinkers of the instant—Descartes, Epicurus, Rousseau, Gide—who share 'the desire to exist right now and to the full.'[48]

If the postwar project of a 'general economy' can be understood as the unlikely conjunction of realism and excess, it demands an interpretation of what Bataille, in his acute critical engagement with the writing of Emmanuel Levinas, calls 'the economic meaning of the instant' (see below, 'From Existentialism to the Primacy of the Economy', p. 208). This is a meaning that transpires from a critical engagement with ethnology and the history of religion, and especially in Bataille's reflection on the question of *sacrifice.*[49] Sacrifice—which in general economy spans phenomena as disparate as martyrdom and the potlatch—is central to Bataille's thinking of *community, communion, communication* and *contagion.* But it must be thought beyond a horizon of functionality or calculation, namely as *expenditure.* Sacrifice is—Bataille writes in dialogue with Gabriel Marcel's preface to a play by Madeleine Deguy—'an expenditure on the present instant of resources that reason commanded us to reserve for the future' (see below, 'The Last Moment', p. 63). The denial of the future is crucial to the conception of the instant as the moment of excess.[50] For Bataille it is only *sensibility* and

---

46 Bataille, 'Concerning the Accounts Given by the Residents of Hiroshima', p. 497 (translation modified). In a note to this essay, Bataille remarks: 'It is interesting to note that the "man of sovereign sensibility", being the "man of the instant", may, by a play on words, also be called "the man of the atom", since the Greek word, "atom", served to designate the instant. (Aristotle and St. Paul used it in this sense)' (p. 514).

47 Sartre, 'A New Mystic', p. 6.

48 Sartre, 'A New Mystic', p. 36.

49 Bataille, *Limit of the Useful.*

sensuality—as opposed to sentimentalism or what he pejoratively terms *sensiblerie*—which escape the servitudes of utility and permit one to experience the sovereign intensity of sacrifice, its 'non-subordinate' character (see below, p. 62), with abandon.

If Bataille has an ontology it pivots around the idea of '*being in the moment*' (*être dans l'instant*), by contrast with any kind of *being-in-the-world* or even being 'towards' death (which would precisely implicate the dimension of futurity that Bataille rejects). It is an idea that he presents as shining forth from the letters of the Christian mystic Catherine of Siena,

> in which the tangible emotion is taken to such a degree that one cannot imagine a more intense orchestration of the possibilities of the human being and which, in its entirety, is the demonstration that, beyond any bargains, it is *emotion* that eliminates the concern with future time, giving decisive sovereignty to the *last instant* [*le dernier instant*] in which the perishable strikes down the powers of eternity. At that point, the *witness* that was borne to it depended on a disappearance of the concern to bear witness. (see below, p. 65)

This being-in-the-instant, which is the (impossible) vantage point from which Bataille will articulate his general economy, is one that he registers in the madness of Hölderlin and Van Gogh,[51] in Proust's prose (see below, 'Marcel Proust and the Profaned Mother', pp. 90–101), in Nietzsche's 'sovereign sensibility',[52] and in the figure of *revolt*, revolution's insubordinate

---

50 Bataille, *Literature and Evil*, p. 58.

51 'The fact is that mental health is the satisfactory operation of a machine that has efficient activity as its end-goal, *but to which the human element in us resists reduction*. [. . .] There is a constant fundamental conflict between the domain of the moment [*l'instant*]—of aesthetics and immediate seduction—and the domain of concern for the morrow—of ethics and the rules of action: to such a degree that if one of us suddenly and for no tangible reason rejects the rules, it seems to us, despite our fear, that we are falling under the spell of infinite seduction' (see below, 'Marcel Proust and the Profaned Mother', pp. 95–96).

52 'It is the instant, such as it is, without expression and without detour, that encloses being and, if one reaches an extreme state, can be neither balanced nor compensated for by anything that follows. Nietzsche was the first to experience this; or at least he was the first to express it with some degree of clarity.' Bataille, 'Concerning the Accounts Given by the Residents of Hiroshima', p. 509 (translation modified).

other.[53] It is also the inability truly to *experience* the instant—which is to say the effort to master, domesticate and reify it—which Bataille will present as the ultimate cause for the limitations of existentialism[54] and surrealism,[55] for their inability fully to acknowledge that '[h]umanity is the demand for an extreme possibility.' This demand calls upon both science (which is also to say *economy*) and poetry, though 'poetry is sovereign and can never be enslaved: extreme knowledge, by contrast, requires the recognition of poetry, which is never the means of its autonomous activity, but remains the end-goal of the one who knows—and the end of knowledge insofar as knowledge at its outer limit is the dissolution of knowledge' (see below, 'From Existentialism to the Primacy of the Economy', p. 205).[56]

The apparent paradox of the postwar Bataille is that of a thinker intimately invested in the production of 'extreme knowledge', while also trying to think beyond (as well as beneath) the great schism that marked the 'age of extremes', envisaging something like a neutrality based on excess and the instant.

Benjamin Noys and Alberto Toscano

---

53 'What always differentiates revolt from a revolutionary enterprise based on reason is that it attributes ultimate value to pride—that is to say, to insubordination. All life for revolt is sovereign, rebellious, not just the impossible objects that the priests keep apart from profane or servile activity' (see below, 'A Morality Based on Misfortune', p. 164).

54 Bataille's most biting criticism is perhaps that 'existentialist philosophy changes us into things more deeply than does science, which at least leaves *the intimate sphere* unchanged' (see below, 'From Existentialism to the Primacy of the Economy', p. 202). It is also around the instant that Bataille will organize much of his literary criticism in the essays collected herein, for instance in his appraisals of Joseph Conrad and Raymond Queneau.

55 See Jean-Louis Houdebine, 'L'ennemi du dedans (Bataille et le surréalisme: élements, prises de parti)' in Philippe Sollers (ed.), *Bataille*, pp. 153–91.

56 Passages such as this corroborate Jean-Louis Baudry's remarks about Bataille's 'ruptured anthropology' (*anthropologie déchirée*). See 'Bataille and Science', p. 279.

Bibliography

AGAMBEN, Giorgio. *Homo Sacer: Sovereign Power and Bare Life* (Daniel Heller-Roazen trans.). Stanford: Stanford University Press, 1998.

———. *The Open: Man and Animal* (Kevin Attell trans.). Stanford: Stanford University Press, 2003.

BATAILLE, Georges. 'Concerning the Accounts Given by the Residents of Hiroshima' (Alan Keenan trans.). *American Imago* 48(4) (1991).

—— and Georges Ambrosino. *L'Expérience à l'épreuve: Correspondance et inédits (1943–1960)* (Claudine Frank ed.). Meurcourt: Éditions Les Cahiers, 2018.

———. 'Hegel, Death and Sacrifice' (Jonathan Strauss trans.). *Yale French Studies* 78 (1990).

———. *Inner Experience* (Leslie Anne Boldt trans.). Albany: State University of New York Press, 1988.

———. 'Letter to X' in Denis Hollier (ed.), *The College of Sociology 1937–39* (Betsy Wing trans.). Minneapolis: University of Minnesota Press, 1988.

———. *The Limit of the Useful* (Cory Austin Knudson and Tomas Elliott eds). Cambridge, MA: The MIT Press, 2023.

———. *Literature and Evil* (Alastair Hamilton trans.). London and New York: Marion Boyars, 1997.

———. 'The Moral Meaning of Sociology' in *The Absence of Myth: Writings on Surrealism* (Michael Richardson ed. and trans.). London: Verso, 1994, pp. 103–12.

———. *Œuvres complètes, Volume 11: Articles I, 1944–1949* (Francis Marmande and Sibylle Monod eds). Paris: Gallimard, 1988.

———. *La Part maudite: Essai d'économie générale, t. I: La Consumation.* Paris: Éditions de Minuit, 1949.

———. *The Sacred Conspiracy: The Internal Papers of the Secret Society of Acéphale and Lectures to the College of Sociology* (Marina Galletti and Alastair Brotchie eds). London: Atlas Press, 2017.

———. *The Unfinished System of Non-Knowledge* (Michelle Kendall and Stuart Kendall trans, Stuart Kendall ed. and intro.). Minneapolis: University of Minnesota Press, 2001.

———. *Visions of Excess: Selected Writings, 1927–1939* (Allan Stoekl ed.). Minneapolis: University of Minnesota Press, 1985.

BAUDRY, Jean-Louis. 'Bataille and Science: Introduction to Inner Experience' in Leslie Anne Boldt-Irons (ed. and trans.), *On Bataille: Critical Essays*. Albany: SUNY Press, 1995, pp. 265–81.

BLANCHOT, Maurice. *Friendship* (Elizabeth Rottenberg trans.). Stanford: Stanford University Press, 1997.

DERRIDA, Jacques. *Edmund Husserl's 'Origin of Geometry': An Introduction* (John P. Leavey Jr trans., pref. and after.). Lincoln: University of Nebraska Press, 1989.

———. 'From Restricted to General Economy: A Hegelianism without Reserve' in *Writing and Difference* (Alan Bass trans.). Chicago: Chicago University Press, 1978, pp. 251–77.

ESPOSITO, Roberto. *Categories of the Impolitical* (Connal Parsley trans.). New York: Fordham University Press, 2015.

HOLLIER, Denis. 'The Dualist Materialism of Georges Bataille'. *Yale French Studies* 78 (1992).

———. 'From Beyond Hegel to Nietzsche's Absence' in Leslie Anne Boldt-Irons (ed. and trans.), *On Bataille: Critical Essays*. Albany: SUNY Press, 1995, pp. 61–78.

HOUDEBINE, Jean-Louis. 'L'ennemi du dedans (Bataille et le surréalisme: élements, prises de parti)' in Philippe Sollers (ed.), *Bataille*. Paris: U.G.E., 1973, pp. 153–91.

KENDALL, Stuart. *Georges Bataille*. London: Reaktion, 2007.

KRISTEVA, Julia. 'Bataille, Experience and Practice' in Leslie Anne Boldt-Irons (ed. and trans.), *On Bataille: Critical Essays*. Albany: SUNY Press, 1995.

LUKÁCS, Georg. 'The Moral Problem of Bolshevism' (Judith Marcus Tar trans.). *Social Research* 44(3) (1977): 416–24.

MONNEROT, Jules. *Les faits sociaux ne sont pas des choses*. Paris: Gallimard, 1946.

MUSIL, Robert. *Precision and Soul: Essays and Addresses* (Burton Pike and David S. Luft trans and eds). Chicago: University of Chicago Press, 1990.

PATRON, Sylvie. *Critique 1946–1996: Une encyclopédie de l'esprit moderne*. Paris: Institut mémoire de l'édition contemporaine, 1999.

———. Preface to Georges Bataille and Éric Weil, *A en-tête de 'Critique': Correspondance 1946-1951* (Sylvie Patron ed.). Paris: Lignes, 2014.

PIEL, Jean. *La Fortune américaine et son destin*. Paris: Éditions de Minuit, 1948.

DE QUINCEY, Thomas. *On Murder* (Robert Morrison ed.). Oxford: Oxford University Press, 2006.

RICHMAN, Michèle. 'Bataille Moralist?: *Critique* and the Postwar Writings'. *Yale French Studies* 78 (1990): 143–68.

——. 'Fascism Reviewed: Georges Bataille in "*La Critique sociale*" '. *South Central Review* 14(3–4) (1997): 14–30.

ROSS, Kristin. *The Emergence of Social Space: Rimbaud and the Commune*. London: Verso, 2008.

SARTRE, Jean-Paul. 'A New Mystic' (1943) in *On Bataille and Blanchot* (Chris Turner trans.). The Seagull Sartre Library, VOL. 10. London: Seagull Books, 2021.

SOLLERS, Philippe. 'L'acte Bataille' in Philippe Sollers (ed.), *Bataille*. Paris: U.G.E., 1973.

SURYA, Michel. *Georges Bataille: An Intellectual Biography* (Krzysztof Fijalkowski and Michael Richardson trans). London: Verso, 2002.

SUTHERLAND, Keston. 'Marx in Jargon' in *Stupefaction: A Radical Anatomy of Phantoms*. London: Seagull Books, 2011.

TOSCANO, Alberto. 'The Promethean Gap: Modernism, Machines and the Obsolescence of Man'. *Modernism/modernity* 23(3) (2016): 593–609.

WITSCHI, Emil. Review of *Les Changements de Sexe*. *The Quarterly Review of Biology* 22(1) (1947): 84.

Translator's Note

Critical Essays: Volume 1, 1944–1948 presents a selection of 41 articles in English translation taken from the eleventh volume of Georges Bataille's *Œuvres complètes: Articles I, 1944–1949* (Paris: Gallimard, 1988).

All footnotes without attributions within square brackets are Georges Bataille's own and were part of the original publications.

'[Trans.]' indicates a translator's note.

'[Eds]' indicates a note suppied by the editors of the original French volume, Francis Marmande and Sibylle Monod.

I would like to thank Dr. Leslie Hill, Professor Emeritus of French Studies at the University of Warwick, for giving so generously of his time to discuss Bataille with me and also the editors of the present volume for their valuable suggestions. Responsibility for the final translation is, of course, mine alone.

1944

Is Nietzsche Fascist?

The centenary of the birth of Nietzsche (b. 25 October 1844[1]) might simply be seen by us as the occasion to write: 'A German philosopher, whom some people regard as the precursor of fascism . . . '

And yet, were he a German fascist, Nietzsche would still remain what he is: if, as has been thought, his work is the symbol of deep aspirations, the aspirations it expresses have a meaning. And, if it could draw on him rightfully, fascism would not then be the empty thing we imagine it to be. But is Nietzsche fascist?

The question is worth asking. In any event, fascism is the doing of human beings, but we do not ordinarily think that an essential part of man is involved in the responsibility for it and its destructiveness. We see in it, rather, a combination of interests: those of a social class, a nation of slaves and a clique of adventurers. It would be otherwise if it were the expression of a dramatic philosophy that awakens people of all kinds to the life of the mind.

If we want to elucidate this problem—essential to the meaning of the current war—we must first look at the position National Socialism has chosen.

Nazism generally confines itself to appealing to simple sentiments and an elementary conception of the world: insofar as a National-Socialist philosophy exists, it is the philosophy of military patriotism, ignoring all else, scorning what cannot bring military strength. Of itself, National Socialism refuses to secure the human interest; it is the expression of German interest in opposition to the interest of all other human beings. Its own position calls attention to the fact that in destroying it, we are not

---

1 Bataille's text is in error here: Nietzsche was born on *15* October 1844. [Trans.]

3

eliminating an essential part of humanity, but a part that has cut *itself* off from the human totality.

Besides this, Nietzsche is recognized by the Nazis as one of the glories of Germany, but that, it seems, does not commit them to anything. There is no contention over his doctrine: isolated texts are used on occasion, but the whole of his work is never claimed by National Socialism. The doctors of the Nazi Church, who have nothing to do with him, are Paul de Lagarde and [Houston Stewart] Chamberlain. Nietzsche had no way of knowing Chamberlain's work, but if we want to gauge the distance between Nietzsche and Hitlerism, we have to take into account the contempt he felt for Paul de Lagarde: he expresses it scathingly.

National Socialism's position on Nietzsche is, ultimately, a propagandist convenience. The Nazi world can in no sense assimilate things that would separate it from chauvinistic vulgarity.

For its part, Nietzsche's position is more precise.

In his lifetime, Germany was home to a pre-Hitlerian, pan-Germanist, anti-Semitic tendency. It is the only tendency Nietzsche violently stood out against. Moreover, he declared himself far removed from all the political parties of his day, refusing in advance to be enlisted from any direction whatever. 'Does my life make it likely that I could allow anyone at all to "clip my wings"?'[2] But, more than anything else, anti-Semitic pan-Germanism drew his aggressive hostility. The violence of his feelings is condensed in this formula: 'Have no truck with anyone mixed up in this shameless fraud of race'. Nietzsche's thought is often ambiguous, even contradictory (that is why pacifists and libertarians can quote him, though with no more justification than fascists . . .), but on this it does not vary. That is because Nietzsche was the least patriotic of Germans, and, all in all, the least German of Germans. He claimed he was ethnically Polish, citing the Slavic origin of his name as evidence. He spoke of the Germans with disgusted contempt. (He had some respect for Jews and an overriding preference for the ways and wit of the French).

---

2 This passage (my translation) is cited from a letter Nietzsche wrote to Theodor Fritsch from Nice on 23 March 1887. [Trans.]

Thus, even the cautious position of the Nazis involves a great deal of mendacious commentary, clever silence and forgery. Admittedly, such things posed no difficulty in the Third Reich. The anti-Semitic writings of a hated brother-in-law are cited—precisely because of his political views— and phrases cited sardonically are taken out of context. The truth is that the field of Nietzsche's thinking lies beyond the necessary, common concerns that determine politics. The questions he raised touch on tragedy, laughter, pain, and joy despite pain; on richness and freedom of spirit: in general, the extreme states to which the human mind may aspire. He spurned basic problems such as income levels and political freedom. His doctrine of dangerous life, of clear-sighted, unfettered, disdainful humanity is far removed from public struggles. It is a doctrine for solitaries secretly and tragically ruminating for themselves while the universe maintains its hostile silence. Despite all the set dressing, the distance from Hitler to Nietzsche is the distance from the guardhouse to the summits of the Alps. But doesn't the simplest of human beings, if he desires freedom, point to the air of the mountaintops as his aim and distant goal?

Is Literature Useful?

Nothing is more common today than political poetry. It is spreading within the political underground and aims to outlive that clandestinity.

On this, I would like to state a first principle.

There is no human possibility that should not be tried, that doesn't deserve to be attempted and cannot be tested out felicitously.

I have before me an unpublished poem from the insurgency: everything that the rage for freedom puts into the mind of an eighteen-year-old cries out in these lines:

We're going to plunge our minds into the refuse tips, they say.

The remnant of an inspired outburst. Of a violence so true that I can only rejoice.

That said, I can see no reason not to highlight a second principle: it relates, in particular, to this war.

This war is being conducted against a system of life for which propagandist literature provides the key. The destiny of fascism is to enslave: among other things, to reduce literature to mere usefulness. What does useful literature mean but treating men as so much human material? For that sorry task, literature is indeed necessary.

This does not imply the condemnation of any particular genre, but of the political stance, of slogans. It is on just one condition that I write authentically: that I not give a fig for anyone or anything; that I take instruction from no one.

What often sends things awry is a weak writer's concern to be useful.

Every man should be useful to his fellows, but if there is nothing in him beyond usefulness, then he is their enemy.

The descent into usefulness—from being ashamed of oneself, when divine freedom produces a guilty conscience—is the beginning of a desertion. The field is left free to the weathercocks of propaganda.

Why not accept the fact, in these circumstances where every truth is coming out, that literature fundamentally rejects usefulness? Being the expression of man—of the most essential part of man—it cannot be useful, since man in his essentials isn't reducible to usefulness. Sometimes a writer, grown weary of solitude, demeans himself and lets his voice mingle with the crowd. Let him cry out with his people if he wants—as much as he can. If he does so out of tiredness or disgust with himself, there is only poison in him, but he imparts that poison to others: fear of freedom, need for servitude! His true task is the opposite: revealing to everyone in their solitude an intangible portion that no one will ever enslave. Only one political goal is commensurate with his essence: the writer can enlist only in the fight for freedom, proclaiming that free part of ourselves that can be defined not by formulas but only by the emotion and poetry of heartrending works. More, even, than fighting for freedom, he has to make use of it, at the very least embodying liberty in what he says. In many cases, his freedom even destroys him: that is what makes him strongest. What he then forces us to love is that bold freedom, limitless and proud, which at times leads to death, and even makes us love dying. What the authentic writer teaches in this way—by the authenticity of his writings—is the rejection of servility (primarily the hatred of propaganda). That is why he does not tag along with the crowd and why he knows how to die in solitude.

1945

The Will to the Impossible

I

The star-spangled night is the gaming table on which being is in play: tossed across this field of ephemeral possibilities, I fall from a great height, helpless, like an insect turned on its back.

No reason to regard this as a bad situation: it pleases, annoys and thrills me.

If I were of a 'static, given nature', I would be limited by fixed laws, some things necessarily bringing me pain and others joy. By putting me in play, nature pitches me outside of itself—outside the limits and laws that cause the humble to praise it. The fact of being gambled with makes of me a possibility that did not previously exist. I move beyond all that is *given* in the universe and I set nature in play.

At the heart of immensity, I am the extra, the exuberance. The universe could get along without me. My strength, my impudence derive from this superfluous character.

Were I to submit to what surrounds me, interpreting and changing the *night* into a children's fable, I would surrender that superfluity. As a part of the order of things, I would have to justify my life—on the mingled levels of comedy, tragedy and usefulness.

But in rejecting and rebelling, there is no call to *lose my head*.

It is too *natural* to rant and rave.

Poetic raving cannot fully defy nature: it justifies it, consents to embellishing it. Rejection is the act of a clear mind, gauging its stance with calm attention.

Distinguishing between the various possibilities—and hence being able to carry the remotest of them through to its fullest extent—is a prerogative of calm attention.

II

Everyone can, if so minded, heap blessings on a benign nature, bow down before God . . .

There is nothing in us that is not constantly in play—hence, abandoned.

The sudden harshness of fate proves humility and trust unfounded. Truth responds like a slap to the proffered cheek of the humble.

The heart is human insofar as it rebels. To be a human being, not a dumb creature, means rejecting the law (of nature).

A poet provides no justification for nature. Poetry is outside the law. However, *accepting* poetry turns it into its opposite, makes it the mediator of an acceptance. I weaken the coiled spring that keeps me tensed against nature, I justify the world as it is given.

Poetry spreads half-darkness, introduces ambivalence, distances us simultaneously from the night and the day—from questioning the world and from setting it in motion.

Is it not obvious? The constant threat of nature crushing us, of reducing us to the mere given—thereby putting an end to the game it plays above and beyond itself—prompts attention and cunning on our part.

Slackening of attention removes us from the game—as does excess of it. A joyous élan, reasoned leaps and calm lucidity are demanded of the gambler—up to the point when luck or life deserts him.

I approach poetry with an intention to betray: strongest in me is the spirit of cunning.

Poetry's power to overturn things is not to be found in its moments of beauty: by comparison with its failure, poetry is a dismal thing.

By common agreement, those two authors stand apart who added the brilliance of their failure to that of their poetry.

An air of dubiety generally hangs over their names. But both exhausted the poetic impulse—which ends in its opposite: in a sense of the impotence of poetry.

Poetry that does not rise to the level of the impotence of poetry is no more than the total absence of poetry ('fine verse').

III

The path man has embarked upon, if he questions nature, is essentially negative. It is one of endless contestation. It is a path that can be followed only in rapid bursts that are soon over and done with. Excitement and depression follow each other in quick succession.

The arc of poetry starts out from the known and leads to the unknown. If completed, it verges upon madness. But an ebbing begins when madness is near.

What is presented as poetry is, generally, only its ebbing: the movement towards poetry seeks humbly to remain within the limits of the possible. Whatever one does, poetry is a negation of itself.

The negation, in which poetry passes beyond itself, has more effect than an ebbing. But madness is no more capable than poetry of keeping itself in being. There are poets and madmen (and those who ape both): poets and madmen are merely stopping points. The poet's limit is like the madman's in that it applies only personally, not being the limit of human life. The moment of stoppage merely allows human flotsam and jetsam a way of keeping themselves in being. The flow of the waters is not thereby delayed.

Poetry is not self-knowledge, nor even less the experience of the remotest possible things (of what did not exist before), but the evocation through words of that experience.

Over an experience properly so-called, evocation has the advantage of an infinite facility and richness, but it distances us from experience (which is, initially, paltry and difficult).

Without the richness glimpsed in evocation, experience would be neither bold nor exacting. But it begins only if the void—the fraud—of evocation drives us to despair.

Poetry opens up the void to the excess of desire. Within us, the void left by the ravages of poetry is the measure of a refusal—of a will to go beyond what is given naturally. Poetry itself exceeds the given, but cannot *change it*. It substitutes the freedom of verbal association for the servitude of natural bonds—verbal association destroys any number of such bonds, but only verbally.

Rather than destroying it, fictitious freedom actually maintains the constraint of the naturally given. Anyone merely content with that freedom ultimately goes along with that 'given'.

If, seeing the wretchedness of those who content themselves with it, I persevere in challenging the given, I can only bear fiction for a time: I demand its reality and I go mad.

My madness may impact the outside world, demanding that it be changed to conform with poetry. If that demand is turned towards inner life, it calls for a power that belongs only to evocation. In both cases, I experience a sense of the void.

If I lie, I remain at the level of poetry—of going beyond the given only *in fiction*. If I persevere in obtusely disparaging that 'given', my disparagement is false (being of the same nature as the going beyond it): to criticize the real world on the basis of poetry is to pile one lie upon another. In a sense, consent to the given is deepened. But not being able to lie knowingly, I go mad (no longer seeing the obvious). Or, no longer knowing how to act out madness for myself alone, I still go mad, but inwardly: *I experience the darkness of night.*

IV

Poetry is just a detour: through it, I escape the world of discourse or, in other words, the natural world (of objects); through it, I enter a sort of tomb where, from the death of the logical world, infinite possibilities are born.

The logical world dies giving birth to the riches of poetry, but the possibilities evoked are unreal, the death of the real world is unreal; all is shady and elusive in this relative obscurity: in it I can pour scorn on myself and others. The whole of the real is valueless and all value is unreal. Hence the ease and inevitability with which I flounder around, not knowing whether I'm lying or have gone mad. From this treacherous situation comes the need for the darkness of night.

Night could not avoid this detour. Questioning is born of desire, which could not have the void as its object.

The object of desire is, first and foremost, the illusory and, only secondarily, the void of disillusionment.

Questioning without desire is formal and indifferent. It is not this desireless kind I am referring to when I say that questioning is synonymous with being human.

Poetry has to do with the power of the unknown (the unknown, an essential value). But the unknown is just a blank void if it is not the object of desire. The poetic is the middle term: it is the unknown rigged out in splendid colours and in the appearance of being.

Dazzled by a thousand figures, in which boredom, impatience and love combine, my desire has only one object: what lies beyond these thousand figures is the void destroying desire.

Remaining dazzled, knowing—having the vague awareness—that the figures depend on the ease (the absence of rigour) that gave birth to them, I can deliberately maintain ambiguity. The disorder then and the lack of satisfaction give me the impression that I am mad.

Poetic figures, deriving their brilliancy from a destruction of the real, remain at the mercy of nothingness; they must flirt with it, derive their shady, desirable aspect from it: they already have the strangeness, the sightless eyes of *the unknown*.

Rigour is hostile to those who love those figures; it betokens prosaic poverty.

What if I had maintained rigour within myself? Then I would not have known the figures of desire. My desire awoke to the glimmers of disorder, within a world transfigured. But with desire now awakened, what if I return to rigour?

As rigour dissipates the poetic figures, desire is at last *in the dark of night*.

Existence, in the dark night, is like a lover when their beloved dies (Orestes when he learns of Hermione's suicide). It cannot, in the form of darkness, recognize *what it was waiting for*.

Desire cannot know in advance that its object was its own negation. The night in which not only desire but every object of knowledge sinks into emptiness is an ordeal. In it every value is wiped out.

Picasso's Political Paintings

If free, antifascist Spain is full of meaning for us, then the Spanish painter Picasso, whose antifascism found an opportunity for expression during the Civil War, cannot be dissociated from that fact. Picasso isn't just the greatest of living painters, he is also the freest. He is so, it seems to me, in the most Spanish of ways: at one and the same time, tough, familiar and even, in a sense, excessive.

It was during the Spanish Civil War that Picasso first gave precise political meaning to his painting. The first aerial bombing massacre took place at Guernica. On 26 April 1937, German planes pounded the old town, the political capital of Euzkadi, whose ancient oak was the symbol of Basque freedoms. As everyone knows, Picasso exhibited an enormous canvas depicting Guernica's woes at the Spanish Pavilion of the 1937 Paris Exposition.

It is strange that the freest of the arts should have reached its peak in a political painting. Of all Picasso's pictures, *Guernica* is nonetheless the one that has moved us the most. Admittedly, this isn't the first time the Spanish people's struggle for freedom has prompted an artist to achieve his highest degree of inspiration. *El dos de Mayo*, in which a man is shot dead with his eyes wide open and a resounding cry on his lips, is probably Goya's master-piece. And that canvas in the Prado museum in Madrid, right at the heart of the last fascist 'redoubt', continues to glorify the 'resistance' of all ages and all lands.

The political meaning of *Guernica* is more complex, but perhaps also richer than that of *El dos de Mayo*. As in Goya's painting, the starting point is an extreme, unintelligible horror. But Picasso doesn't resolve the horror into a simple, fearsome defiance. It releases within him an excess that runs in all directions, drives the great pageant of life to extremes, spills out the unearthly content of things.

After *Guernica,* Picasso etched caricatures of Franco, but did not, for all that, become a political painter. He has in recent times simply set about registering the woes of current humanity on his canvas, in another large composition. *The Charnel House,* on which he is working and which exudes an overabundance of emotion, expresses the sacrifice of the concentration camp victims in a manner befitting their character . . .

Here the sufferings of Spain mingle with those of the whole of Europe.

On Ernest Hemingway's *For Whom the Bell Tolls*

I shall try to define what Spain means to us. In particular at a time when it has had more than its fair share of the ills that have beset us. To this end, I shall allow myself some digression—even drawing on personal memories.

I have before me a strange photograph of Blanquet, the *peón de brega* Pilar speaks of:[1] he is standing straight, facing the camera, his hands over his eyes in a gesture of horror. Of horror and even loneliness: the other characters in the drama are hurriedly carrying away the dying Granero after a bull has just staved in his head.

As Pilar says, the horn opened Granero's head. His face was, precisely, smashed, divided into red pieces: his eye was hanging out. That is what Blanquet saw and it was what drove his hands up to his face in horror.

I was at the other side of the *plaza* and only learned the details of the whole scene from the accounts—or photographs—that were published. But with this young man in his dazzling attire suddenly upturned and thrown against the fence, the bull goring him unrelentingly for a few seconds (as they slammed into the boards, the horns drew dull, macabre sounds from

---

1 In the article, the note refers to the extract from *For Whom the Bell Tolls* that was translated in *Actualité* ('L'odeur de la mort' [The smell of death], p. 115): 'When Blanquet, who was the greatest *peón de brega* who ever lived, worked under the orders of Granero he told me that on the day of Manolo Granero's death, when they stopped in the chapel on the way to the ring, the odour of death was so strong on Manolo that it almost made Blanquet sick.'

Manuel Granero, a former violin student at the Valencia conservatoire became, before he reached the age of 20, the most serious hope to replace Joselito (killed at Talaveira de la Reina on 16 May 1920). On 7 May 1922, at Plaza de Madrid, he died with a fractured skull and a horn through the eye. It is known that Bataille was present at this bullfight (see Georges Bataille, *L'histoire de l'œil* [translated as *Story of the Eye*] [Paris: Pauvert, 1928]). [Eds]

them, like the *three knocks* of death), then in the arena, where the numberless throng had sprung to its feet, at some indefinable moment there came a horrified silence; this theatrical entrance of death, with the fiesta in full flow and the sun beating down, had about it something self-evident, expected, unbearable.

Never, after that, did I attend a bullfight without anxiety straining my nerves intensely. But the anxiety in no way reduced my desire to be there. Quite the contrary, combining with a feverish impatience, it exacerbated it. I began to understand then that uneasiness is often the secret of the greatest pleasures. To refer to this kind of elation that underlies anxiety, the Spanish language has a precise word, *la emoción*: it is exactly the feeling produced when the bull's horns miss the *torero's* body by *an inch*. We are talking about a clearly determined category of sensations in which repetition, swiftness and elegance (in the movements of the body or the swinging of a cape) dice with danger. But the essence of that category is death, brought into play by an attitude of constant defiance, which is simply at the—barely avoided— extremity of a movement that goes all the more to the heart of things for being slow, slight and precise.

Having seen someone die before my eyes had made me, all at once, intimately familiar with such a game—to the point, indeed, where I could not bear it again.

Excessive as they were at that point, my reactions were in no way removed from those felt—and even sought—by the crowds in the arenas. Anyone who has lived in Spain is not in any way surprised by Hemingway's use of the strong word 'ecstasy' when speaking of the aims of all Spaniards watching a bullfight:

> If the spectators know the matador is capable of executing a complete, consecutive series of passes with the muleta in which there will be valour, art, understanding and, above all, beauty and great emotion, they will put up with mediocre work, cowardly work, disastrous work because they have the hope sooner or later of seeing the complete faena; the faena that takes a man out of himself and makes him feel immortal while it is proceeding, that gives him an ecstasy that is, while momentary, as profound as any religious

ecstasy; moving all the people in the ring together and increasing in emotional intensity as it proceeds, carrying the bullfighter with it, he playing on the crowd through the bull and being moved as it responds in a growing ecstasy of ordered, formal, passionate disregard for death that leaves you, when it is over, and the death administered to the animal that has made it possible, as empty, as changed and as sad as any major emotion will leave you.[2]

2 Ernest Hemingway, *Death in the Afternoon* (New York: Scribner's, 1932), pp. 206–7. In the French text, Bataille references the René Daumal translation, *Mort dans l'après-midi*, published by Gallimard in 1938. [Trans.]

1946

Klee

I take a great interest in the work of Klee, one of the contemporary painters who has most gained my loyalty. I have always felt an affinity with a discreet, forceful, obsessive, genuinely necessary and silent aspect of all his compositions. And I see that I have lived, more than I realized, in a sort of intimacy with ghosts that it was pleasant and yet a little dangerous to love. Klee, it seems to me, had more of the sweetness of a vice about him; there is something in his work that is less distant than is usually the case with painting, something I find difficult to distinguish from myself.

Miller's Morality

HENRY MILLER, *Tropique du Cancer* [translation of *Tropic of Cancer*] (Paul Rivert trans., Henri Fluchère pref.) (Paris: Denoel, 1946), 381 pp.

——, *Tropique du Capricorne* [translation of *Tropic of Capricorn*] (J-C. Lefaure trans.) (Paris: Éditions du Chêne, 1946), 508 pp.

——, *Printemps noir* [translation of *Black Spring*] (Paul Rivert trans.) (Paris: Gallimard, 1946), 271 pp.

Published in Paris in English in 1934 (the unexpurgated version is still unpublished in the US), *Tropic of Cancer* is, like *Tropic of Capricorn* (more lyrical and published later in English, also in Paris, in 1939), a sort of autobiography.[1] The subject of *Cancer* is the author's life in France, in Paris, at Montparnasse (and for a time in a provincial lycée where he taught English). *Capricorn*, for its part, is set in New York, where the author was born (on 25 December 1891; he is no longer young, it must be said, and when he published his first book, he was 43 years old, though he gained immediate notoriety). Part of *Black Spring* relates to adolescence, another part is mainly lyrical, dreamlike and rather whimsical (though, overall, Miller's work is down to earth; what he writes is simple and has a precise meaning).

The phrase *monstrous immorality* has been applied to Miller (Maurice Nadeau, *Combat*, 29 March 1946). But no doubt that is merely a superficial aspect, as Nadeau would willingly admit. These unusual books, which easily lend themselves to being misunderstood (their obscenity, which brings them readers, is barely more than a necessary void within them; to some, the 'elevated' moments seem facile and verbose), are worth going back over and taking slowly. This 'monster of immorality' is also a saint and his nimble

---

1 *Tropic of Cancer* was eventually published in the US by Grove Press in 1961, prompting an obscenity trial. [Trans.]

intelligence, which at times comes up with some very flabby truths, often penetrates the best-hidden secrets with lightning quickness. Deep down, these books are asking to be read as though the author had wanted them to go 'in search of lost moral value', but, just as in Proust, their quest is not in any way distinct from life. Their meaning lies in the fact that they boil down to the expression of life—from childhood to the days when they were written.

*

In *Capricorn*, Miller relates his earliest years in an immigrant district of Brooklyn, a little magical kingdom of violence and wonder in which gangs of children make fires on waste ground, cook French fries, endlessly discuss a host of stories that captivate them, fornicate in the cellars, and fight: 'The whole long summer, in fact, seems like an idyll out of the Arthurian legends.' (*Capricorn*, p. 214)[2] These gangs, with their naïve solidarity, form a bizarre little topsy-turvy world, whose laws are diametrically opposed to those of grown-up society. The adult accords value to the effort by which he earns his living. Everything that happens to him is evaluated by the profit he can take from it (is seen in terms of *revenue*). And so he lives in exile and in that exile children wrest him from his sadness, bring him news from the lost land.

> What I am thinking of, with a certain amount of regret and longing, is that this thoroughly restricted life of early boyhood seems like a limitless universe and the life which followed upon it, the life of the adult, a constantly diminishing realm. From the moment when one is put in school one is lost; one has the feeling of having a halter put around his neck. The taste goes out of the bread as it goes out of life. Getting the bread becomes more important than the eating of it. (*Capricorn*, p. 216)

---

2 This and subsequent page references are to the New Traveller's Companion Series edition of Miller's *Obelisk Trilogy: Tropic of Cancer, Tropic of Capricorn, Black Spring* (Paris: Olympia Press, 2008). [Trans.]

The event that marked Miller's free-roaming childhood most strongly is, according to *Capricorn*, the murder of the leader of a rival gang. In a 'rock fight', fought out amidst the rock pile by the river bank, Miller and his cousin Gene killed him with blows to the temple and stomach.

> [W]hen he went down he lay there for good and not a peep out of him. A few minutes later the cops came and the boy was found dead. He was eight or nine years old, about the same age as us. What they would have done to us if they had caught us I don't know. Anyway, [...] we hurried home [...] Aunt Caroline gave us our usual two big slices of sour rye with fresh butter and a little sugar over it and we sat there at the kitchen table listening to her with an angelic smile. (*Capricorn*, p. 213)

But Miller is not content merely to assert this innocence: he sets it aggressively against adult morality.

> The boy whom I saw drop dead, who lay there motionless, without making the slightest sound or whimper, the killing of that boy seems almost like a clean, healthy performance. The struggle for food, on the other hand, seems foul and degrading and when we stood in the presence of our parents we sensed that they had come to us unclean and for that we could never forgive them. The thick slice of bread in the afternoons, precisely because it was not earned, tasted delicious to us. Never again will bread taste this way. Never again will it be given this way. The day of the murder it was even tastier than ever. It had a slight taste of terror in it which has been lacking ever since. (*Capricorn*, pp. 214–15)

The child who lives naively and just for the sake of living has only one aim— *the savour of life*. He judges everything, in his naivety, by its taste. Wrongdoing, which his parents forbid, contributes to the taste of his food and the forbidden fruit is his Church's holy of holies.

> There is something about the rye bread which I am trying to fathom—something vaguely delicious, terrifying and liberating, something associated with first discoveries. I am thinking of another slice of sour rye which was connected with a still earlier

period, when my little friend Stanley and I used to rifle the icebox. That was *stolen* bread and consequently even more marvellous to the palate than the bread which was given with love. But it was in the act of eating the rye bread, the walking around with it and talking at the same time, that something in the nature of revelation occurred. It was like a state of grace, a state of complete ignorance, of self-abnegation. Whatever was imparted to me in these moments I seem to have retained intact and there is no fear that I shall ever lose the knowledge that was gained. It was just the fact perhaps that it was not knowledge as we ordinarily think of it. It was almost like receiving a truth, though truth is almost too precise a word for it. (*Capricorn*, p. 215)

The paradox here is more profound than common opinion. Parents have a responsibility—and an obligation—to introduce the child into the sphere of economic activity, in which one *has to* prefer usefulness to life's savour. The child one brings into this harsh world whether he likes it or not, clearly cannot love it: the truth of life, in these conditions, becomes bound up with throwing off constraints. On the one side there is the seduction of the immediate and, on the other, effort, merit and reward. Inevitably, our workaday world is initially foreign (and hostile) to the child's being: it tends to reduce the savour of life as much as possible; it subordinates life, making it bland and insipid. Unless he is a polished cog in the machine, the child confuses life with wrongdoing—with caprice, violence and sensuality. For him, its savour lies in evil.

A free-roaming child isn't immoral. Quite the opposite. He experiences the authentic test of morality in the gang he belongs to: generosity, devotion, loyalty, the sense of equality and justice are no less highly regarded by a gang of 'good-for-nothings' than they are disregarded in the Western organization of work. (The two conceptions of morality and law that clash here actually go beyond the current opposition between adults and minors: the Christian, bourgeois ideas of merit, work and hierarchy, based on the product of effort deployed, are foreign to the most ancient societies.) But there is nothing in the spontaneous virtues of childhood to counter 'the intense sense of the immediate'. However generous and upright children may be, this 'intense sense' cannot be stifled in the world they play in. It is the feeling Miller defines precisely when he writes: 'Murder is in the air, chance rules' (*Capricorn*, p. 260).

*

It is seemingly rare for the childhood phase of life to be experienced more intensely. Rare too that there should be so many lasting consequences. In no way did this prevent Miller from subsequently acquiring an education. But he continued to be affected by this initial experience and it apparently became his business in this world to see his childhood rebellion through to its end. The child's opposition must inevitably fail: it is possible to carry it on on the fringes and by cheating; but 'when the *grown-up* appears', the child falls silent. Neither materially nor morally can he hope, furtively, for anything more than a delay. The marvellous successes he pulls off *surreptitiously* are of a 'minor' character. He knows that sooner or later he will have to eat humble pie (as is shown by the pejorative sense of the word 'play'). It does, however, happen that one man in a thousand sticks to his guns, stands up for himself and refuses to submit. This is the case with those who prefer art, which is merely a game, to real work. Generally, it must be said, these latter continue to accept the 'minor' character of the childhood phase: they have no hesitation in agreeing that art is a luxury, that the serious business of existence lies elsewhere. But it is difficult to give freer rein than Miller to the desire to put the grown-ups in their place (he takes that desire to absurd lengths—to a point of unconcern). He is indeed so radically rebellious that he freely prefers abjection to servitude. It is, perhaps, a foolish course to take, but perhaps also, for him, the way to be entirely faithful to childhood.

The product of this unsustainable challenge is a being that's difficult to define. '[T]he confused man, the negligent man, the reckless man, the lusty, obscene, boisterous, thoughtful, scrupulous, lying, diabolically truthful man that I am'. It is in these terms that he paints himself in *Black Spring* (p. 338). What is difficult in adult rebellion is that, without seriousness, it retains the minor—humbled—character of childhood, while, if serious, it loses childhood's divine, capricious nature. Thus the rebel condemns himself to ambivalence, to the point where he becomes elusive even for himself. 'The man,' writes Miller,

> who raises the holy bottle to his lips, the criminal who kneels in the marketplace, the innocent one who discovers that all corpses stink, the madman who dances with lightning in his hands, the friar who lifts his skirts to pee over the world, the fanatic who ransacks libraries in order to find the Word—all these are fused in me, all these make my confusion, my ecstasy. (*Cancer*, p. 124)

There is something necessarily mad in this situation, and, at the same time, something shameful in the fact of not being mad. An exasperated Miller judiciously asked himself whether one of the ways of responding to these exaggerated difficulties wasn't to evade them. He renounced the concern to be human. 'I have nothing to do,' he says,

> with the creaking machinery of humanity—I belong to the earth. I say that lying on my pillow and I can feel the horns sprouting from my temples. I can see about me all those cracked forebears of mine dancing around the bed, consoling me, egging me on, lashing me with their serpent tongues, grinning and leering at me with their skulking skulls. *I am inhuman!* I say it with a mad, hallucinated grin [...] (*Cancer*, p. 123)

Madness is itself an escape and what are we to say of the language of a madman who, in spite of everything, flees madness more effectively than he flees sanity! This noisy, frantic hither-and-yon of a mind that cannot respond at the same time to the contradictory demands placed upon it, can only be represented cruelly. But it wouldn't be fair to speak of such a failure as though there were some alternative path and Miller were maladroit. One may naturally accept servitude—one knows that acceptance pays—but if, at the same time, one refuses the *possible*, then one accepts, in return, being torn and continuing to grapple with the *impossible*. In these conditions, one can only be what Miller is: the monster his books show him to be, books that are unbearable in every sense of the word.

*

Clearly, if it retains them, adulthood accentuates the indefensible characteristics of childhood. An adult can no longer lay claim to the insouciance that made things harmless and inoffensive. And since he must pay his way in life, he runs up against the reality of the social order. If he works, he just draws a wage while expending as little effort as possible. And the only satisfying way to respond to the employer's desires is with practical jokes. I am told that, in France, when he was put in charge of a weekly paper in a little racing town, he published articles in Chinese: it has an attractive script! Unfortunately, this could only be something of a flash in the pan: the imprudent proprietor sacked his wayward editor. Miller's life is made up of experiences of this kind, all of a nature to hone the awareness of a fundamental principle: *if you commit too much to the present instant, your future is compromised.* Education inculcates this awareness in the child, but the child would not be a child if it took effect from the word go. The child whose turbulence is constantly obeying the call of the present instant, leaving concern for the future to his parents, behaves that way because he doesn't have a clear enough awareness of the principle. In Miller, by contrast, painful experiences made one certainty 'clear and distinct': in living for the moment, he was condemning himself to a starveling's fate. But for once hunger, which he undoubtedly experienced, failed to do its job. The effect it achieved was the opposite of forcing him into line. Miller remained faithful to his childhood judgement. But as a child—he could not have asserted himself in that way: no child can—he became aware of the demand in him that he live for the present moment and not for the future, that he live his life and not earn his living. Pangs of hunger demonstrate fundamental truths in every sense, but it was the truth *opposite* to the commonly accepted one that made clear the cruel necessity within Miller. The experience of hunger speaks in him when he says: 'I am sitting at the Place Clichy in full sunshine. Today, sitting here in the sun, I tell you it doesn't matter a damn whether the world is going to the dogs or not; it doesn't matter whether the world is right or wrong, good or bad. *It is*—and that suffices' (*Black Spring*, p. 339). Or: 'At present I have no needs. I am a man without a past and without a future. *I am*—that is all' (*Black Spring*, p. 338). And even more to the point: 'To spit on the past is not enough. To proclaim the future is not enough. One must act *as if* the past were dead and the future unrealizable. One must act *as if* the next step were the last, which it is' (*Black Spring*, pp. 339–40). What was merely a child's behaviour provisionally tolerated by the world becomes an aggressive truth and rejects the values based on its negation:

> The hot sun is beating through the awning. I am delirious because I am dying so fast. Every second counts. I do not hear the second that has just ticked off—I am clinging like a madman to this second which has not yet announced itself . . . What is better than reading Vergil? *This!* This expanding moment which has not defined itself in ticks or beats, this eternal moment which destroys all values, degrees, differences. (*Black Spring*, p. 344)

For this consciousness born of hunger has not only stood the principle of adult societies on its head, it grants the derisory, laughable moments of play the prerogatives of ecstasy, which is the highest conceivable point, which is divinity and is also the destruction of consciousness.

> The type that represents this one and only way bears a head with six faces and eight eyes; the head is a revolving lighthouse, and instead of a triple crown at the top, as there might well be, there is a hole which ventilates what few brains there are. There is very little brain, as I say, because there is very little baggage to carry about, because living in full consciousness, the gray matter passes off into light. This is the only type of man one can place above the comedian; he neither laughs nor weeps, he is beyond suffering. We don't recognize him yet because he is too close to us, right under the skin, as a matter of fact. When the comedian catches us in the guts this man, whose name might be God, I suppose, if he had to use a name, speaks up. When the whole human race is rocking with laughter, laughing so hard that it hurts, I mean, everybody then has his foot on the path. In that moment everybody can just as well be God as anything else. In that moment you have the annihilation of dual, triple, quadruple and multiple consciousness, which is what makes the gray matter coil up in dead folds at the top of the skull.

At that moment you can really feel the hole in the top of the head; you know that you once had an eye there and that this eye was capable of taking in everything at once. The eye is gone now, but when you laugh until the tears flow and your belly aches, you are really opening the skylight and ventilating the brains. Nobody can persuade you at that moment to fake a gun and kill your enemy; neither can anybody persuade you to open a fat tome containing the metaphysical truths of the world and read it. If you know what freedom means, absolute freedom and not a relative freedom, then you must recognize that this is the nearest to it you will ever get. If I am against the condition of the world it is not because I am a moralist—it is because I want to laugh more. I don't say that God is one grand laugh: I say that you've got to laugh hard before you can get anywhere near God. My whole aim in life is to get near to God, that is, to get nearer to myself. That's why it doesn't matter to me what road I take. (*Capricorn*, pp. 307–8)

*

There is little danger of Miller's quite rare recourse to transcendent terms (describing states that others regard as immanent) throwing us off the scent. He isn't very logical: elsewhere he calls God the Father a 'worm-eaten son of a bitch' or 'old goat'! But if there is a God in the world, it might be him, Henry Miller.

Sailing down the river . . . Slow as the hookworm, but tiny enough to make every bend. And slippery as an eel withal. What is your name? shouts someone. *My name? Why just call me God—God the embryo.* I go sailing on. Somebody would like to buy me a hat. What size do you wear, imbecile! He shouts. What size? Why size X! (And why do they always shout at me? Am I supposed to be deaf?) The hat is lost at the next cataract. *Tant pis*—for the hat. Does God need a hat? [. . .] In this strange Capricornian condition of embryosis God the he-goat ruminates in stolid bliss among the mountain peaks. (*Capricorn*, p. 255)

Or it is, in fact, no big thing to be divine. Miller has something better:

> Every evening, after dinner, I take the garbage down to the courtyard. Coming up I stand with empty pail at the staircase window gazing at the Sacré Coeur high up on the hill of Montmartre. Every evening, when I take the garbage down, I think of myself standing out on a high hill in resplendent whiteness. It is no sacred heart that inspires me, no Christ I am thinking of. Something better than a Christ, something bigger than a heart, something beyond God Almighty I think of—myself. *I am a man.* That seems to me sufficient. (*Black Spring*, p. 339)

Miller is strangely attracted to the religious dimension, an attraction counter-balanced by a no less significant aversion for what tends towards perfection. The idea of God attracts him, it seems to me, as the greatest conceivable glory—perhaps for the 'moment', perhaps for himself—but if he describes the moment, he does so using images incompatible with an absolute that knows no randomness: 'Murder is in the air, chance rules' (*Capricorn*, p. 260). The idea of perfection bores him: '[W]hen you show me a man who expresses himself perfectly, I will not say that he is not great, but I will say that I am unattracted' (*Cancer*, p. 123). Thus the glory of imperfect man, with garbage—ordure—as his attribute, ultimately has greater seductive power than the glory of God. It is no doubt there in part that the sense of Miller's obscenity lies, which he lays before us without ceremony, evasion or excuse. If Miller is obscene, he is so in the same way as we breathe—hungrily, amply, fully (as though we were almost gulping in air). As though obscenity and obscenity alone, as a major object of our fears, had the strength to awaken us to what is hidden in the depths of things (which is equivalent to saying: at the level of illumination the author believes he himself has achieved). 'If anyone,' he says, 'knew what it meant to read the riddle of the thing which today is called a "crack" or a "hole," if anyone had the least feeling of mystery about the phenomena which are labelled "obscene," this world would crack asunder' (*Cancer*, p. 121). And it is logical for the extravagant Miller today to assume the tone of a religious preacher. First of all, he asserts, 'To discuss the nature and meaning of obscenity is almost as difficult as to talk about God,' but in conclusion, he writes, 'the real nature of the obscene lies in the lust to convert.'[3] The height of spiritual life is the acute—though, in one respect, unbearable—moment of seduction: that it should be bound up with the ambiguous moment of obscenity, in which the desire to be seduced takes the object of disgust as its preferred site, has in itself nothing surprising about it. Admittedly, it is not so simple as Miller says.

When it comes to sacrificing to the present moment reserves that are useful for the future, we have to distinguish between sacrifice *from excess,* which actively expresses potency, and sacrifice *from lack,* which has no other origin but impotence. Now, obscenity isn't just ambivalent between seduction and disgust, it is also ambivalent between excess and powerlessness. We might perhaps say that what is obscene is a sexual object without seductive power (the nudity of an obese woman): we can do nothing about it, but no matter, the object places us in a state of impotence. On the other hand, it also happens that a man attracted by a slender body may feel the desire to find in it the very aspect that disgusted him in another: at that moment, obscenity, far from having a chilling effect, increases the desirability of the object. If we are speaking of literature, a particular author may take pleasure in describing a repugnant aspect of fleshly life. He is thereby telling anyone who wants to know that the part of himself expressed in his books is far removed from the richness and potency of desire: and the aversion he manifests bespeaks at the same time the choice he has made to concern himself with the future, as opposed to the present moment (for he cannot be unaware that, in human terms, the flesh is seductive, not sordid or weak). That is not how it is with Miller who, in the *Tropics,* lets us know that he enjoys fleshly pursuits—even to excess. Generally, however, the *tangible* impression of them he conveys screens out the desirable element (this is represented, it is implicit, but it is not made *tangible*); that impression, by contrast, accentuates the vulgar, mindless element. His sensuality usually goes together with the abasement of its object. Desire and respect may not be mutually exclusive: attraction without respect is not true attraction (similarly, respect without attraction is not true respect). But the dissociation of the two, attraction without respect, lets in the ambiguous state of a sordid-looking obscenity.

*

---

3 Henry Miller, 'Obscenity and the Law of Reflection', *Tricolor,* February 1945, pp. 48, 55.

From all this we may pin down the weighty issues at play in Miller's attitude.

It is not that unusual for an adult man to live 'for the moment'. But it is rare for him to know it. His efforts are always directed towards some ulterior outcome (if he goes to the theatre, he does so in order to 'have seen' a play that really is a *must-see*; if he travels, he does so in order to have seen more countries: at least this is what he imagines). It is quite another matter to *know* that you are living for the moment. That implies an attention fixed on a current point, which must be attractive (otherwise, the moment could not be seized). In this concentration of one's whole being on a single point, an infinite respect is implied (conversely, in the infinite respect of love, the possibility of being wholly in the moment is at least available). But where there is ignorance or negation of the present moment, the mind is violently driven from the object of its interest. It has to disparage it in favour of something else *that does not yet exist*. Nothing is more conducive to the debasement of obscenity. It is laughable to *feel*, for one hasn't the requisite lucidity to tell oneself:

> I enjoy what I get, but it obviously isn't what I want: I *put up with it*, it's wretched; that's how it is, I love this object, I enjoy it, but at the same time, I spit on it. For I know that I belong to time-to-come, to the reserves that must be built up for that time. If, *for the moment*, I cast those reserves to the wind, that's quite annoying. Ultimately, I'm a swine.

There is no difference between this behaviour—where, far from being desired, being completely in the moment is something one *undergoes*—and equating the moment with badness. The equation bears within it the disparaged pleasures of obscenity. Those pleasures serve the underlying equation. If being in the moment is something willed and active, then the obscenity may continue to be there, but it changes: it now plays out against a background of veneration.

Nothing is clear in these matters in a confused body of work. But disparagement of the object means that there continues to be something stricken about the author's attitude. What situates the erotic scenes is, initially, a disruptive violent side and then a character of inevitability. At the same time as he disparages the victim, the hero of the scene seems to suffer, not to dominate, what he causes to occur. In my view, we may link this depressive element to a whole set of traits. Miller not only despises the women he desires, he may, in order to achieve his ends, take advantage of his prerogatives as a recruiter (an occupation he may perhaps have followed to some good end) and, in the process, rake off a little money. Otherwise, he readily accepts humiliating situations, begs in the street, cleans the shoes of a friend he scrounges from, works drumming up clients for a brothel. And, above all, he is eager to stay at the level of those who, like he does—*though without being aware of it*—live only for the moment (who, by their disparaging attitude, join him in a common—and not just Christian—condemnation of sensuality).

This preference Miller shows for vulgarity is perceptible in his choice of companions. The various characters in the *Tropics* have this in common: they live *childishly* at the whim of the moment (together forming a—dissolute—world apart, in which the only steady *truth* is the absence of money). But Van Norden, Fillmore, Hymie and Schnadig are prone to undeniably hideous, commonplace dissoluteness: colourful characters from a bad dream, horribly, sordidly alive. The women are, in general, no better, only the author usually whisks them away almost as soon as they arrive: they pass through the book at a fevered pace (they are barely glimpsed, and when they are, it is often below the belt). The sleazy, tacky, gutter-level aspects of human life no doubt have to do with this fact: what might have been *most* attractive has been viscerally rejected and is now only rubbish in the wastebin. For this reason, Miller's bias towards vulgarity had decisive significance. The empire of seduction hides not among the stars but in the mud. And Miller's most far-reaching truth might be expressed in this formula: *If you don't descend into the depths, if you remain attached to a heavenly purity, you forfeit forever the diamond of the present for a delusion.* It is only by paying this price—if you move among those who accept its denigration, *and indeed wallow in it*—that *lost time is regained.*

Thus, when Miller depicts himself 'stand[ing] among his own obscene objurgations, like the conqueror midst the ruins of a devastated city', realizing then 'that the real nature of the obscene resides in the lust to convert',[4] he must be taken literally. Only it is less simple than he says. This conqueror

---

4 Miller, 'Obscenity', p. 55.

of a lunar world had first to ruin himself and sink completely into his own devastation. This is the inner meaning of the sordid tales from which he crafts his books. In this light, these might be seen to assume a status that recalls myths of resurrection (unsurprisingly: the world in which Miller moves is located in the wake of the religions—it is in that respect that it is lunar). The descent into vulgarity is ultimately just the detour: at every moment, Miller—this is unexpected but it is how it is—comes back, like a capricious ghost, soiled like a winding sheet but 'in resplendent whiteness'.[5] Fired with the fullest, most elevated love for Mona. Inspired, ecstatic, crying out with the voice of a prophet. Being as crazedly ambitious as anyone has ever been in what he has to write.

His books do, in fact, exceed all intentions, all limits. They have this character of the moment, which all at once matches the immensity of the universe and reaches only to something elusive and explosive.

> [I]t is with a premonition of the end—be it tomorrow or three hundred years hence—that I feverishly write this book. So it is too that my thoughts sputter out now and then, that I am obliged to rekindle the flame again and again, not with courage alone, but with desperation—for there is no one I can trust to say these things for me. My faltering and groping, my search for any and every means of expression, is a sort of divine stuttering. *I am dazzled by the glorious collapse of the world!* (*Black Spring*, pp. 338–39).[6]

If one has the power of the moment within one, could one express anything less than a limitless collapse? In that case, one cannot see literary expression as something sustained over time, but only as the opposite. Little matter, even, that this human world should actually disappear. The moment grasped in its plenitude is, in any case, the crumbling of ordered affairs. And the only fitting language, if that is how things are, is the language of the 'last man': it has meaning only insofar as meaning fades, it changes the perspectives we are used to and substitutes for them the ecstatic vision of an elusive reality.

---

5 The phrase is from *Black Spring*. [Trans.]
6 The emphasis is Bataille's. [Trans.]

'The earth', writes Miller,

> is not an arid plateau of health and comfort, but a great sprawling
> female with velvet torso that swells and heaves with ocean billows;
> she squirms beneath a diadem of sweat and anguish. Naked and
> sexed she rolls among the clouds in the violet light of the stars. All
> of her, from her generous breasts to her gleaming thighs, blazes with
> furious ardour. She moves among the seasons and the years with a
> grand whoopla that seizes the torso with paroxysmal fury, that
> shakes the cobwebs out of the sky; she subsides on her pivotal orbits
> with volcanic tremors. She is like a doe at times, a doe that has fallen
> into a snare and lies waiting with beating heart for the cymbals to
> crash and the dogs to bark. Love and hate, despair, pity, rage, dis-
> gust—what are these amidst the fornications of the planets? What
> is war, disease, cruelty, terror, when night presents the ecstasy of
> myriad blazing suns? What is this chaff we chew in our sleep if it is
> not the remembrance of fang-whorl and star cluster. (*Cancer*, p. 121)

And how can we not see that nothing in this has any meaning beyond the
desire to cry out? Miller is aware of this, comparing his book to 'a last expiring dance' (*Cancer*, p. 125). But a *dance* is what it must be: 'A last expiring
dance. But a dance!' (*Cancer*, p. 125). No matter: he is wrong at this point
to wish for a definition. Nothing is definable in the moment, which has no
limit and which, though it is not 'all', is, at one and the same time, all that
one wants. And Miller knows this.

*

The trouble, if one has chosen this path, is that what necessarily subsists
does so, nevertheless, within the received limits; and that it is not a good
thing, on the pretext that one is essentially exceeding those limits, to ignore
them. For in that very moment, one continues, as one has to, to move and
speak within the field of those limits. Miller's lack of concern for them, however deeply justified it might be, is often disconcerting. It is no doubt natural,
if his cries are those of the 'last man'. But they are sold in bookshops! Given
that fact, they become part of time's flow, as measured by the works of man.

The Miller who cries out is still keen at times to judge those works in detail and though it is inevitable, judging things that don't concern him, that the 'last man' should talk nonsense, for those who remain those judgements are, nonetheless, nonsense. That he should regard Élie Faure as a genius, or Breton and Montherlant, Tzara and Unamuno as being on the same level, well and good! Nietzsche himself went overboard with Gyp, though that was exceptional, whereas Miller feels the need *generally* to deal off-handedly with things that should either be left alone or given due and proper attention. His political choices he makes frivolously, unwilling to see that accepting the established system as he does is, ultimately, to maintain the escapist attitude of the child. In the light of these facile attitudes, Miller's bias towards vulgarity is at times troubling. Finally, the ambiguity remains, inherent in the temptation to capture the moment: one can even see that there is no way to eliminate it. We may speak, furtively, of Miller's 'explosive perspectives', but no one explodes: and we continue to write, to publish, to read . . .

Dionysos Redivivus

This Satan, with his goat's head and feet, with his stinking cowshed rear, as a now fleeting imagination shows him in the gloomy, glimmering light of witches' Sabbaths (in this hideous form begotten by the sickly nervousness of the Christians)—is he not, so close to us, the emanation of Dionysus? Unlike creatures of flesh and blood, myths are not limited as individuals are, and there are many senses in which Dionysus lives on in the guise of the Archfiend. The life of a myth lies in the shared sensibility of minds to the words, images and stories that conjure it up, and that sensibility sometimes outlives belief. It is the association of an elusive feeling—similar to the feeling we have about a region which no other region would give us—with the complex of names, figures, legends, rituals and, on occasion, memories of rituals. Clearly, scepticism inevitably leads in the long run to the death of that sensibility: thus the name of Dionysus, and generally the names of the Greek gods, no longer connect with anything tangible for us. It is not the same with the Devil. This is doubtless of little consequence. The popularity of Mephistopheles is ultimately an unsavoury thing. But if he is represented in a guise that does not accord with our shared feeling, we do not recognize him: which means that we still *know* him. In *Les Visiteurs du Soir*,[1] Jules Berry was rather a bad Devil, for we could see that he *was* the devil but we had to learn the fact, feeling rather annoyed that we had not recognized him. The devil of the witches' Sabbath is rather less well known. And yet a responsive chord has only to be struck using one of the still accepted formulas and immediately miasmas, lightning and an ethereal gleam arise and we have a whiff of infernal air in our nostrils.

Clearly, nothing of the kind can restore Dionysus to us. We have to concede that the myth that binds us, draws us in and retains the greatest value in our eyes, is, for all that, a dead one: there is no longer any living human

---

1 Marcel Carné's film, released in France in December 1942. [Trans.]

being who is not dead now to a sense of Dionysus and I feel I may regard that as a genuine privation. None will ever imagine a richer figure; never will a figure be linked with such wonderful roistering. When, if we will only see it, there is nothing there that we can do without. The Christian priests who deprived us of Dionysus, acted on us like a social worker removing an unfit mother, taking care to ensure the child retained not the slightest recollection of her. It is only with great difficulty that we rediscovered the traces that remain. And, if we wish to do so, we can gauge the extent of our loss, but it was effected with such thoroughness that we cannot truly feel it: we know that we should weep but we know it only with dry eyes.

I do not want to bring archeological findings into the argument here, but I have to portray Dionysus as the deity that is the least concerned to burden the divine with authority (to convert immediate religious experience into ethics). He is, it seems, the divine in the pure state, unadulterated by the obsession with preserving a given order for all eternity. In Dionysus, the divine is at the opposite extreme from the Father of the Gospels: it is omnipotence, it is the innocence of the moment. It isn't the wine, but the intoxication. Dionysus, blind to consequences, is the absence of reason and the hopeless cry, instantaneous as a thunderbolt, of tragedy. And further, where tragedy is concerned, he lacks the individualization of the hero. He is the unrestrained, uncomplicated tragedy that erupts—harsh, flawed, inescapable. The poetry—and he embodies poetry—isn't the melancholy of the poet, nor is his ecstasy the silence of a solitary. He isn't the isolated individual, but the crowd, being not so much a being as a barrier over-turned. The air around him is full of shrill cries, laughter and kisses, when the smoky torch of night, concealing faces, throws its light on . . . !² *for there is nothing his demented retinue do not trample underfoot.*

But it is only from books that we learn all this now and what there was that was elusive and divine in the cries of the Bacchantes is beyond recovery. The image of the demon that has remained familiar to us is no doubt related and comes down to us from the image of the great god. Satan led the round of the witches, Dionysus the round of the Bacchantes and in each case it was lust that lent its venomous heat to the goings-on. But, to the very (small)

2 The omission by Bataille is deliberate and presumably made to anticipate the censors. [Trans.]

extent that he is the relic of the Thracian god, Satan is only an aged Dionysus. He has lost the innocent fury and laughter of the adolescent: his spite and impotence merely snigger. The clearest thing about the devil is that he is *old*; that he is shrewd, calculating and not at all given to impersonal ecstasy. The figures of the two divinities (for the devil is *divine*) embody the same—orgiastic, nocturnally frenzied—rites and, if there is not necessarily any continuity between those rites, there is at least contact and contagion. But even if I were to accept a fusional continuity between the two, still the earlier one is rich and the later poor. Though I can say that I know the devil, it is Dionysus that I glimpse through him, and I cannot conceal from myself that he is merely the sad afterlife of that god, a divinity fit for a *guilty* humanity.

And the impoverishment isn't only about a difference in the times. Satan isn't just a shrivelled old Dionysus, aware of his own guilt. He is only the half of Dionysus. The myth of the young Thracian divinity was a myth of the sacrifice of the God and of resurrection. Dionysus is a 'god that dies'. What he personifies is not just the erotic sacred, but the tragic sense of sacrifice. The Titans devoured the child born of a mother whom his father himself had just struck with a thunderbolt: he was reborn to the light only after being torn to pieces by the maenads, who performed on the new-born the furious sacrifice of omophagia. The 'mysteries' of Dionysus are thus akin to those mysteries of Antiquity that saw the passion of a god as the principle of life regenerated. So that the devil's mysteries are not the only ones that enable us still to *know* the figure of the god.

There can be little doubt that Jesus's passion and resurrection are a continuation of feelings associated with the legends of the slain divinities of Antiquity. In seeking after the lost god, we cannot limit ourselves, then, to the gloomy reminiscence of the goat-demon. The image, *living* within us, of a resuscitated Christ—I am thinking now, and this is just a way of immediately getting to the strongest aspect of a feeling, of Grünewald's Risen Christ—is perhaps no less faithful to Dionysus than is the image of a hairy devil. But what disappears in this adorable fusion is the curse cast on life, a curse common to both the devil and the god on the cross.

Mystical Experience and Literature

Louis Pauwels, *Saint Quelqu'un* [Saint Someone] (Paris: Seuil, 1946).

Louis Pauwels's novel has been warmly reviewed in the press[1] and one cannot deny its 'strong qualities': the critique which follows would be pointless if it were penned about a trifling work. The plot of the book alone grabs our attention. The wife of a man on obligatory work service for the German occupiers learns, during her husband's spell of leave, that he has cheated on her. The husband had merely given in to a passing desire and was happy, for better and for worse, to go back to his companion of fifteen years and his children. But that prospect is closed off for him: his wife tells him bluntly that he disgusts her. Seeing that it is pointless to insist, he makes his way back to his job on a North Sea coastal defence construction site. Suddenly, and for no reason, he has lost what tied him to life. He finds himself indifferent to the narrow range of prospects left to him, indifferent even to arrest by the Germans, a threat which hangs over him from a serious, though erroneous accusation. But, in spite of his torpor, he gradually begins to feel an unexpected sense of happiness and plenitude, or rather that feeling steals upon him like a thief in the night. *In a foreword, the author expressly compares the state that comes over his hero with the ecstasy of yogis.* In the end, his—decidedly vulgar—wife comes to his rescue, saves him at the last moment from arrest, takes him back home and hides him. But this man, having achieved an inhuman sainthood and detachment, cannot now love her physically, which she attributes, despite his protestations, to love of the other woman. This leads to a rather horrible state of malaise in which misery and (the mother's and daughter's) nastiness successively play their part. In the end, the little boy, obscurely affected by the horrible ordeal of this 'family life', falls ill and dies. At the sight of the corpse of the child, the only

---

1 'How to express the sense of plenitude we feel when reading such lines?' writes [Maurice] Nadeau.

human being who really loved him and whom he himself loved, the father feels a poignant sense of extraordinary *beauty* and *happiness* come over him. In his ecstasy he pays no heed to what his wife is up to, as she shuts herself in the kitchen and turns on the gas, no doubt expecting her husband to come in, throw open the window and effect a tear-filled reconciliation. But he does not come. She dies in her turn and, before the double funeral, the daughter, having refused to see her father again, is taken off to an uncle's in the Corrèze.

This curious story is served by expressive resources that are, in some ways, banal, though of genuine richness and not simple. But what is unacceptable in this realist book is the way it seeks to prove a point. The value of a novel that wishes to prove something, or at least attest to something, cannot be rejected out of hand. But it is not good when the outcome both lacks poetry and fails accurately to convey the truth that it aimed to serve.

If we have to speak of the singular experience of ecstasy, it is clear in advance that each possible course is insufficient, at least when taken in isolation: thus, known mystics drew not only on direct description but also on poetic allegory (the poetic element and allegory are, moreover, represented in all descriptions). Furthermore, the life stories of mystics are ordinarily bound up with the difficulty of communicating their experience (this is often the vivid part of the story). But Louis Pauwels's book is, all in all, devoid of the surpassing flights of allegory and poetry. And the story through which he communicates an experience to us has, for want of indications to the contrary, the gratuitousness of invention. Doubtless it cannot be wrong to link the theme of destitution, which acquires a 'horrible grandeur' here, with the ultimate possibility of ecstasy. But doesn't the legitimacy of the association actually lend it a merely conventional character? In the end, when considered attentively, the descriptive part of the book leaves one with a sense of great unease: it plays its part, whatever one thinks of it, in the gratuitousness of the narrative.

The convincing nature of the descriptions of ecstasy in Proust's *In Search of Lost Time* comes to mind, descriptions which do not, as here, fall under suspicion of being merely literary.

What gives substance to this suspicion—which the author has taken steps to allay—is not just the lack of emphasis (if one compares the descriptions of the ecstatic moments to other passages, though this reservation carries the weight of a personal impression only). This above all should give us pause: the only reference that situates the experience of the book's protagonist is this statement by Vivékânanda cited in the Foreword: 'It is possible that a man who does not know this science (yoga, the set of disciplines that mould the Blessed and Saints) may arrive by chance at that state in which the human creature is surpassed. *He stumbles, as it were, upon that state.*' So the author grants an essential value to the states described by Ramakrishna's wordy disciple—that is to say, in general, to the mystical experience of the yogis. But, taking that as his base, he latches on to a decidedly rare form of it: spontaneously achieved mystical experience. This is awkward in the sense that, where experiences of this kind are concerned—independent of any prior piety—there are no more precise references than these lines from Vivékânanda and . . . the story presumably invented by Pauwels. One might think, at least, that the author takes only a vague view of this question, that he is describing basic states irrespective of the ideas held about them by modern Hindus. But he puts the following words in the mouth of his protagonist (speaking of his ecstasy upon seeing the dead child): 'And what is it? Lowering my head, I see my chest through the opening of my collar. What is it? My skin is golden and drops of blood, like sweat, are burgeoning between the hairs.' We know that the colour of the chest, which can reach scarlet, is the sign, for Hindus, of an advanced practice of yoga. We may, then, be inclined to see this as something constructed by an author steeped in works on oriental mysticism.[2] And doubtless one cannot be sure of this without other information, but if the story has its origins in some real experience, it is hard to see why it assumed such a ponderously literary form, a form neither unadorned nor poetic.

---

2 In particular, the works of Romain Rolland. The author cites one of these (*La Vie de Vivékânanda* [Paris: Stock, 1930]) and could have taken the story of the chest from the other (*La Vie de Ramakrishna* [Paris: Stock, 1930], p. 162n): the drops of blood themselves are to be found in the latter book (p. 49).

For these reasons, the least one can say of this book's intent to demonstrate—or bear witness—is that it is a clumsy response to the primary requirement to separate the straightforward from the sham. The author cannot be surprised that one should protest against the way he mingles both the worst and the best here.

Without doubt, mystical experience—which one may describe directly or poetically—cannot with impunity be the subject of a realist novel or even of a novelized life. It is insofar as *In Search of Lost Time* is, without seeking literary effect, a record of daily life that Proust escapes criticism.

The Indictment of Henry Miller

> Whosoever produces or holds for commercial purposes [. . .], imports or exports [. . .], displays, exhibits or projects for public view, sells, hires out [. . .] distributes or makes available for distribution [. . .] any printed matter, writings etc. [. . .] that offend against public decency will be punished by imprisonment of between one month and two years and by a fine of [. . .]

So runs the wording of the law (article 119 of the Law of 29 July 1939) limiting the freedom of authors. This makes it possible today to prosecute Henry Miller, two of whose recently translated novels appeared to meet the definition stated in the law. It must be acknowledged that Miller expresses himself in these works with unusual freedom. To the point where the trial is said to be a foregone conclusion: the author, living in California, is beyond the reach of the indictment levelled against him, but one of the indicted publishers was told by the prosecuting magistrate, rather straightforwardly, that he would undoubtedly be found guilty.

In truth, nothing is straightforward in this matter. It remains the done thing in France not to laugh when freedom is at issue. And the question raised by this trial cannot in itself be taken lightly. We may doubt whether Miller's masterworks have met with a critical consensus, but they are widely admired. From the outset, they aspire to the first rank—and it is often conceded to them—but, at all events, the books strike a fresh note and what they say, with an eloquence at times sublime, is a response to the most elevated anxieties and concerns and not to a desire for a—difficult—arousal. And so what is being interrupted in the attack on Miller is not, as those who took the initiative of this prosecution[1] imagined, the trade in dirty books, but the activity of the human mind, a mind duty bound to express clearly and fully 'that which it is'.

---

1 The complaint was lodged in July by a 'Cartel of Social and Moral Action', led by a certain M. Daniel Parker.

In this country where writers can make their voices heard—precisely because its literature, the freest and the boldest, is one of its great claims to fame—it is surprisingly frivolous, for want of knowledge that could be easily acquired, to attack writings of dazzling literary quality. 'Offending against public decency'? Do those who brought this charge have any clear idea of what the phrase means? If they have any insights that might dispel the confusion around it, we would happily open the pages of this journal to them. Baudelaire's *Les Fleurs du Mal* offended against 'public decency' in 1857, but the judges who would be willing any day now to find Henry Miller guilty have that book on their shelves! Might not the legal category of 'offending against public decency' be introducing into the legal apparatus something which, from a legal standpoint, 'offends against the dignity of justice'—namely, mere whim? On this, the law has no other foundation than an *infinitely fickle* subjective judgement! And it would be easy for Miller to cite scripture in his defence: 'I know and am persuaded in the Lord Jesus that there is nothing unclean of itself: but to him that esteemeth any thing to be unclean, to him *it is* unclean' (Romans 14:14). So much do judgements vary on this point that the authorities in Britain and America which had imposed a ban on Joyce's *Ulysses* revoked it within the space of a few years. To rescind a judgement in this way, without any new evidence being adduced, reveals the nonexistence—perhaps even impossibility—of a legal system able to pronounce with authority what is lawful and what deserves to be condemned and banned.

Admittedly, French jurisprudence has apparently freed itself from pure arbitrariness. Before the law of 1939, legal custom denied the writer the right to depict the truth in precise terms. The author, who could not in those days be prosecuted personally (only the printer and the publisher were punishable), could in theory have known where he stood. But merely *could have* . . . In reality, this criterion made only for a furtive justice; the judges were not at ease with it and it was only meted out with the most extreme reluctance. As soon as a complaint was lodged, the justice ministry had no option but to prosecute . . . But it did not take the initiative: translations of *Ulysses* and *Lady Chatterley's Lover* were published in their turn: there was such a stir around them that the ministry cannot have been unaware of it, but it did not take the view that it needed to act. On the other hand, Robert Desnos's *La Liberté ou l'Amour* was met with an indictment. The 'By the Same Author' page of collections of his published since then, bears the following 'mark of distinction': 'Condemned and censored by order of the *tribunal correctionnel* of the département of the Seine.' It is distressing to note, then, that if the law that currently applies to us had existed earlier, a writer who honoured his country by producing works that are universally admired and *by dying as a political deportee* would have been imprisoned by the courts for expressing his thinking.[2] In reality, the justice ministry knows in advance that its action in these matters rests on no firm foundation and that the sentences it will call for embarrass itself more than they do those who are sentenced. For the latter regard them as a mark of honour, but does the ministry? It appears in practice that the clarity introduced by jurisprudence (which is, after all, jurisprudence, not law) is ineffectual: it has not been able to prevent the most unfortunate of judgements and obliges a judiciary *that doesn't like to act* to condemn itself more than the books it finds guilty.[3]

The decision of the British and American authorities on *Ulysses*—the licentiousness of which would seem to fall foul of French jurisprudence— in fact indicates clearly that the distinction between what is lawful and what is not cannot be based on the mode of expression. We know that the United States and Britain have generally shown themselves to be less liberal than France in the interpretation of what constitutes legally punishable literature.

---

2 Desnos died of typhoid in Terezin concentration camp on 8 June 1945, having been arrested by the Gestapo in Paris in February 1944 for resistance activity against Nazi occupation. [Trans.]

3 These conditions and the miscarriages that inevitably ensue from them are so appreciable that lawmakers have been moved to do something about them.

On a proposal by M. Georges Cogniot, the Constituent Assembly *unanimously* passed an act on 29 August 1946 establishing a procedure for the rehabilitation of the condemned works of art. The preamble to that act stated: 'Hypocrisy being one of the forms of the persecution of thought, it must be denounced and combatted [. . .]'

But, however felicitous its introduction might be, the law does not define what it means by 'offending against common decency': on the contrary, it underscores the impossibility of arriving at a distinction not only between unlawful and lawful, but also between ignominious and glorious.

And, indeed, *Ulysses* (a book no less bold than the *Tropics*) has been freely on sale in French bookshops for twenty years. We must very obviously regard *Ulysses* as an example of a piece of writing that does not 'offend against public decency' even though it is licentious. It is indeed not possible to regard as 'an offence against pubic decency' a work which shares no common aims with the publishers of pornography. Thus, ultimately, it is at the moral and literary levels that the question is posed. Let us be clear that it is not about saying: 'this book is beautiful, it cannot be immoral'; but, where appropriate, 'the author's intention was to produce a literary work, not to offend against public decency.'

Admittedly, it is perhaps difficult to prove an intention. But we cannot say that that is not the business of the courts. Where Joyce is concerned, the facts are glaringly obvious to everyone. As they are in the case of D. H. Lawrence. And if ambivalence is possible in Miller's case, it arises from the choice the author made to court it, though the doubt does not resist examination.

I freely admit that Miller expresses himself with unparalleled crudeness, but it has to be said that those who imagine themselves to be the guardians of moral rectitude will have to get used to it: we no longer mistake certain over-refined, prissy manners for purity. That human beings should one day have to express themselves with the worst vulgarity might even be seen ultimately as a necessary reparation for that betrayal of all morality that was over-refinement and prissiness. And it is only a counterfeit morality that will be offended at the foul-mouthed author of *Capricorn* himself expressing profound intentions in terms which, from the outset, raise the problem to supreme heights. Miller writes:

> Once [the artist] has made use of his extraordinary powers, and I am thinking of the use of obscenity in just such magical terms, he is inevitably caught up in the stream of forces beyond him. He may have begun by assuming that he could awaken his readers, but in the end he himself passes into another dimension of reality wherein he no longer feels the need of forcing an awakening. His rebellion over the prevalent inertia about him becomes transmuted, as his vision increases, into an acceptance and understanding of an order and harmony which is beyond man's conception and approachable only through faith. His vision expands with the growth of his own powers, because creation has its roots in vision and admits of only one realm,

the realm of imagination. Ultimately, then, he stands among his own obscene objurgations like the conqueror midst the ruins of a devastated city. He realizes that the real nature of the obscene resides in the lust to convert. He knocked to awaken, but it was himself he awakened. And once awake, he is no longer concerned with the world of sleep; he walks in the light and, like a mirror, reflects his illumination in every act. ('Obscenity', pp. 588–89)[4]

And Miller adds:

Once this vantage point is reached, how trifling and remote seem the accusations of moralists! How senseless the debate as to whether the work in question was of high literary merit or not! How absurd the wrangling over the moral or immoral nature of his creation! Concerning every bold act one may raise the reproach of vulgarity. Everything dramatic is in the nature of an appeal, a frantic appeal for communion. Violence, whether in deed or speech, is an inverted sort of prayer. Initiation itself is a violent process of purification and union. Whatever demands radical treatment demands God, and always through some form of death or annihilation. Whenever the obscene crops out one can smell the imminent death of a form. Those who possess the highest clue are not impatient, even in the presence of death; the artist in words, however, is not of this order, he is only at the vestibule, as it were, of the palace of wisdom. Dealing with the spirit, he nevertheless has recourse to forms. When he fully understands his role as creator he substitutes his own being for the medium of words. But in that process there comes the 'dark night of the soul' when, exalted by his vision of things to come and not yet fully conscious of his powers, he resorts to violence. He becomes desperate over his inability to transmit his vision. He resorts to any and every means in his power; this agony, in which creation itself is parodied, prepares him for the solution of his dilemma, but a solution wholly unforeseen and mysterious as creation itself. ('Obscenity', p. 589)

---

4 This and subsequent page references are to 'Obscenity and the Law of Reflection', *Kentucky Law Journal* 51(4). Reprinted in *Henry Miller on Writing* (New York: New Directions Publishing Corporation, 1964), pp. 175–88. [Trans.]

To accuse the author of these lines of having had the intention which the law is designed to punish clearly leads to the most grievous miscarriage of justice. As far removed from pornography as can be, we have here not the pure literary transfiguration effected by Joyce, but an effort by man to wrest himself from himself. What Miller was aiming for wasn't a gloomy wallowing in a sensual pleasure which he has not depicted favourably, but, as he says in a variety of ways, *religious ecstasy*. And he expressly proposes the ideal of the ascetic, which is not easily achievable and which he writes of in these terms:

> This quiet sort of triumph strikes a chill in the heart of the ordinary man, for not only does it make him visualize the loss of his meagre sex life but the loss of passion itself, passion as he knows it. This sort of liberation, which smashes his thermometrical gauge of feeling, represents itself to him as a living death. The attainment of a love which is boundless and unfettered terrifies him for the very good reason that it means the dissolution of his ego. He does not want to be freed for service, dedication and devotion to all mankind; he wants comfort, assurance and security, the enjoyment of his very limited powers. Incapable of surrender, he can never know the healing power of faith; and lacking faith he can never begin to know the meaning of love. He seeks release but not liberation, which is like saying that he prefers death instead of life.[5]
> ('Obscenity', p. 586)

These are the words of Henry Miller whom, if they had him in their custody, the French courts should, we are told, send to jail like a man peddling lewd photographs. And who remains, despite prosecutions of which those responsible cannot be proud, destined for the surest fame. His admirers are already legion; the action brought against him can only swell their number.

---

5 Bataille's original footnote reads: 'The passages cited here are from an important article by Miller himself on the rights of the author, which will appear very shortly in French translation in issue no. 55 of the magazine *Fontaine*.' [Trans.]

Gide - Baranger - Gillet

ANDRÉ GIDE, *Journal 1939–1942* (Paris: Gallimard, 1946), in 16°, 215 pp.

There is nothing in Gide's work which, when set alongside his *Journal*, doesn't look a little unsuccessful. Not that we don't also find affectation and stiffness there, but these are undercut—thwarted, as it were—by the brevity and rapidity of the entries. The section of the *Journal* just published—and this Parisian edition is more complete than the earlier ones that came out in America (June 1944), Algeria (September 1944) and Switzerland (April 1945)—isn't the densest part. But these notes, set down daily, run from 10 September 1939 to 6 May 1942 (the date the author reached Tunis) and derive their main interest from the events they run alongside. One of the virtues of the *Journal* is to present us directly not, as in other writings, with side issues but with the work that counts: this is the author himself ('Self-development' is still the reason he gives himself, wondering why, at the age of seventy, that process of enrichment still continues).[1] And Gide here faces up to the woes of his times.

What emerges is a peculiar *antihistoricity* (this is the word used in the *Journal* itself, p. 93[2]), a commanding need for order, harmony and serenity. The strange thing is that the author is clear sighted; and clear-sightedly— just as the words beneath his pen obey an ever-lively obsession with elegance—he *fearlessly* shuns what seems hazardous or unfathomable . . . Against the chaos that is the history of this age, in which there is nothing that is not in question, he pits a thorough humanism that is questioned only from the outside. He reads Kafka's *Trial* and cannot but know that he himself stands *accused*: 'That hunted creature,' he acknowledges, 'is I.' [28 August

---

1 This relates to the entry for 12 Sept 1940. [Trans.]

2 The reference is Bataille's to the French edition he is reviewing. For the full passage in English, see *The Journals of André Gide, Volume 4: 1939–49* (Justin O'Brien trans.) (London: Secker & Warburg, 1951), p. 50. [Trans.]

1940]. He nonetheless writes: 'There is much to be learned from it.' The kind
of humanity he embodies can be enriched: it cannot be destroyed, except
no doubt by material actions. True, he does not unreservedly accept the
limits Goethe placed on that humanity. 'We are not born to solve the
problems of the world, but to find out where the problem begins, and then
to keep within the limits of what we can grasp.'[3] I would surmise that it is
this sentence from the *Conversations with Eckermann* that is being referred
to in the passage in the *Journal* (p. 70) that regrets Goethe's decision to
'direct his curiosity away from what he judged human intelligence to be
incapable of ever achieving.'[4] But Gide saw that only as a limit to the scope
of scholarly research. In reality, a humble submission of human beings to
the conditions they find themselves in is required and, with it, the fact that
we are part of an unintelligible universe loses its importance. Gide is not
troubled by this (it isn't even something he sees). Current humanity in its
entirety is a ship weighing anchor but, in his cabin, someone is unconcerned
by this and believes himself at the end of the journey. He feels, he says, outside of time. He has, he supposes, arrived at the attainable limits.

Hopeless mediocrity. This isn't laughable, but distressing.

WILLIAM BARANGER, *Pour connaître la pensée de Nietzsche* (Paris: Bordas, 1946), in
8°, 127 pp.

An honest, conscientious work, conveying everything immediate analysis
provides. Like many others (such as Charles Andler, whose study he dubs
'admirable'), the author situates himself *outside of* Nietzsche. He ends on a
good thought: 'His main teaching, perhaps his only teaching, consists in
awakening people's personal consciousness, in bringing them a way of

---

3 The text here (*Œuvres complètes* VOL. 11, p. 114) reads: 'L'homme n'est pas né, pour
rechercher où commence le problème et ensuite se maintenir entre les limites de
l'intelligible', which omits a whole line from Goethe's remark to Eckermann. Since
Bataille's argument makes little or no sense without the omitted line, I have restored it
in the translation. [Trans.]
4 This is the entry for 25 July 1940, cited here from *The Journals of André Gide*, VOL. 4,
p. 38. [Trans.]

intensifying their individual existences, of living their lives more completely, since to philosophize, after all, should not exempt us from living, but, on the contrary, enable us to experience what we live more intensely.' What more is there to say?

MARTIN STANISLAS GILLET, *La Mission de sainte Catherine de Sienne* (Paris: Flammarion, 1946), in 16°, 262 pp.

Despite the serious scholarship expended on it by its author, who is Master General of the Dominican order, this little book is, in the end, a panegyric to the saint and through her, in some degree also to the order with which she wished to affiliate herself. Two chapters stress the consonance between the intuitions of an illiterate ecstatic (who, being unable either to read or write, had to dictate her words) and the teachings of Saint Thomas Aquinas. Even these somewhat conventional pages hint at the ferocity of her zeal, her unstinting passion. But in their unctuousness, perhaps the essential point is lost, the thing which, in this woman of such resolution, is astonishing, which is a sort of vehement, disembodied sensual delight that consumed her.

In fact, Father Gillet is so preoccupied with doctrine and intellectual definition, and sensibility so unsettles him, that when he cites the famous letter from the saint about the execution of a young condemned man whose head she received into her hands, he stops short just before these words:

'Now that he was hidden away where he belonged, my soul rested in peace and quiet in such a fragrance of blood that I couldn't bear to wash away his blood that had splashed on me.'

The Last Instant

MADELEINE DEGUY and GABRIEL MARCEL, 'Les Condamnés précédé' de 'La Parole est aux saints' (Paris: Plon, 1946), in 16º, 177 pp.

What does it mean to philosophize if not to raise thinking to such a pitch that ordinary existence seems like sleep and the philosopher's effort wakefulness? For even supposing that a solid written work on a subject could in the end establish the irrefutable truth, knowledge spread over many pages, not existing within me independently of a series of thought processes spread over several days of study, would—unless the only thing being aimed at were action—be the most empty comedy. The painful condition that sent me off down the long corridor of my research, the fact that incomplete knowledge leaves me feeling like a dog that goes round in circles chasing its own tail are things that definitely cannot be eliminated by subterfuge. My reading itself is more or less an acceptance of my wretchedness: my poor dog's tail just kept outstripping the pursuing teeth trying to bite it. I could at best tell myself that, by not philosophizing, I would at least have had the advantage of the dog that sleeps, eats, barks or gambols about, unconcerned with the opposite extremity of its being. But this does not tell us much about how human beings might have avoided these particular thought processes, though it must be admitted in the end that the enterprise leads further than was initially apparent. I will astonish no one today if I state it as a first requirement of thinking—adding this to the ones we already know—that it wrest me from the sleep of thoughtlessness. Who could still see its inevitable and long detours as anything other than an unwarranted prolongation of the state it exists to condemn?

For this reason, without lingering over the most contemporary positions of philosophy (which detain the mind in preliminary discussions that actually blur the unvarnished, material view of the world), we may quite properly direct our thinking to a particular object that excludes the possibility of that thinking being put to sleep. Following Gabriel Marcel, I shall, then, bring it to bear on the meaning that the instant of dying, of leaving his life, has for the condemned man.

M. Marcel started out here from a literary text whose author, Madeleine Deguy, is as yet unknown. I have every reason to imitate him in that approach, being surprised nonetheless that he grants such brief consideration to a starting point that he himself chose.

Mme Deguy has turned a dramatic episode in the life of Catherine of Siena into a three-act play. The episode is known from the letter the saint wrote to her confessor on the subject. For some rash remarks he had made, a young nobleman, Niccolo Toldo (he is called Felice Toldo in *Les Condamnés*), was sentenced to be beheaded. While awaiting death, he cursed God . . . but Catherine went to see him in his cell and converted him.

The document on which Mme Deguy based her work is so moving that I feel it necessary to supply the entire text here (*Les Condamnés* cites only a few lines):

Very loved and dearest father and my dear son in Jesus Christ,

I Caterina, servant and slave of the servants of God, send you my greetings in the precious blood of God's Son. I long to see you engulfed and drowned in the sweet blood of God's Son, which is permeated with the fire of his blazing charity. This is what my soul desires—to see you in this blood—you, Nanni and Iacomo, my Sons. Son, I see no other way of our attaining the most basic virtues we need. No, dearest father, your soul could not attain them—this soul of yours that has become my food. Not a moment passes that I am not eating this food at the table of the gentle Lamb who was slain in such blazing love. I am saying that unless you are drowned in the blood you will not attain the little virtue of true humility, which is born from hatred as hatred is from love, and so come forth in the most perfect purity as iron comes out purified from the furnace.

So I want you to shut yourself up in the open side of God's Son, that open storeroom so full of fragrance that sin itself is made fragrant. There the dear bride rests in the bed of fire and blood.

There she sees revealed the secret of the heart of God's Son. Oh tapped cask, you give drink and fill to drunkenness every loving desire. You give joy and illumine all our understanding. You so fill all our remembrance that we are overcome and can neither hold nor understand nor love anything other than this good gentle Jesus, blood and fire, ineffable love! Once my soul has been blessed with seeing you so drowned, I want you to act like a person who draws water with a pail. I mean, with a boundless desire pour the water over the heads of your brothers and sisters who are our members bound together in the body of the sweet bride. Watch that you don't pull back because of the devil's illusions (which have, I know, caused you difficulties, and will) or because of people's talk. No, whenever things seem most cold to you, always persevere until we see blood shed with sweet loving desires.

Up, up, my dearest father, and let's sleep no longer, for I'm hearing news that makes me no longer want either bed or pillow! I've already begun by receiving a head into my hands. It was sweeter to me than the heart can imagine or the tongue speak or the eye see or the ear hear. My desire for God went on along with the other mysteries that have happened earlier, which I won't recount because it would be too long.

I went to visit the one you know and he was so comforted and consoled that he confessed his sins and prepared himself very well. He made me promise for love of God that when the time came for the execution I would be with him. This I promised and did.

In the morning, before the bell, I went to him and he was greatly consoled. I took him to hear Mass and he received holy communion, which he hadn't received in a long time. His will was in accord with and submissive to God's will. His only fear now was of not being strong at the final moment. But God's measureless and burning goodness tricked him, creating in him such affection and love through his love for me in God that he could not do without God! He said, 'Stay with me; don't leave me alone. That way I can't help but be all right, and I'll die happy!' His head was resting on my breast. I sensed an intense joy, a fragrance of his blood—and it wasn't separate from the fragrance of my own, which I am waiting to shed for my gentle Spouse Jesus.

With my soul's desire growing, and sensing his fear, I said, 'Courage, my dear brother, for soon we shall reach the wedding feast. You will go forth to it bathed in the sweet blood of God's Son, with the sweet name of Jesus, which I don't want ever to leave your memory. I shall wait for you at the place of execution.' Just think, father and son! All the fear in his heart disappeared; the sadness on his face was transformed into gladness! He was happy, exultant, and he said, 'What is the source of such a grace for me, that my soul's sweetness will wait for me at the holy place of execution?' (He had become so enlightened that he called the place of execution a holy place!) And he said, 'I shall go all joyful and strong, and when I think that you will be waiting for me there, it will seem a thousand years until I get there!' And he said such tender words as to make one burst at God's goodness!

I waited for him at the place of execution. I waited there in continual prayer and in the presence of Mary and of Catherine, virgin and martyr. Before he arrived I knelt down and stretched my neck out on the block, but I did not succeed in getting what I longed for up there. I prayed and pleaded with Mary that I wanted this grace, that at his last moment she would give him light and peace of heart and afterwards see him return to his destination. Because of the sweet promise made to me, my soul was so filled that although a great crowd of people was there I couldn't see a single person.

Then he arrived like a meek lamb, and when he saw me he began to laugh and wanted me to make the sign of the cross on him. When he had received the sign I said, 'Down for the wedding, my dear brother, for soon you will be in everlasting life!' He knelt down very meekly; I placed his neck [on the block] and bent down and reminded him of the blood of the Lamb. His mouth said nothing but 'Gesù!' and 'Caterina!' and as he said this, I received his head into my hands, saying 'I will!' with my eyes fixed on divine Goodness.

Then was seen the God-Man as one sees the brilliance of the sun. His side was open and received blood into his own blood— received a flame of holy desire (which grace had given and hidden in this soul) into the flame of his own divine charity. After he had received his blood and his desire, he received his soul as well and placed it all-mercifully into the open storeroom of his side. Thus Supreme Truth showed he was receiving him only through grace and mercy and not for anything he had done. Oh how boundlessly sweet it was to see God's goodness! With what tenderness and love he awaited that soul when it had left its body—the eye of his mercy turned towards it—when it came to enter into his side bathed in its own blood, which found its worth in the blood of God's Son! Once he had been so received by God (who by his power was powerful enough to do it), the Son, Wisdom and Word incarnate, gave him the gift of sharing in the tormented love with which he himself had accepted *his* painful death in obedience to the Father for the welfare of the human race. And the hands of the Holy Spirit locked him in.

As for him, he made a gesture sweet enough to charm a thousand hearts. (I'm not surprised for he was already tasting the divine sweetness.) He turned as does a bride when, having reached her husband's threshold, she turns her head and looks back, nods to those who have attended her, and so expresses her thanks.

Now that he was hidden away where he belonged, my soul rested in peace and quiet in such a fragrance of blood that I couldn't bear to wash away his blood that had splashed on me. Oimé! Poor wretch that I am, I don't want to say any more! With very great regret I remained on earth! It seems to me that the first stone is already laid. So don't be surprised if I impose on you only my desire to see you drowned in the blood and fire pouring out from the side of God's Son. No more apathy now, my sweetest children, because the blood has begun to flow and to receive life! Gentle Jesus, Jesus love.[1]

---

1 *Le Lettere di S. Caterina da Siena*, VOL. 4 (Niccolo Tommaseo ed.) (Florence, 1860), in 16°, pp. 5–12. [I have, to a very large extent, followed the version of this letter in

In the introduction, which he entitles *La parole est aux saints* [Let the saints speak], M. Gabriel Marcel writes of the 'extraordinary facility', the author's tone that is 'so right, so firm'—and, to some degree, this is true. One cannot but praise that which, in these often lively pages, transcends the merely literary. And I must beg forgiveness for speaking of it so summarily. It is heavy-handed here to compare the work with the source. But what else can one do? If it is art's aim to transfigure, it must suffer if it leaves us hankering after the unvarnished expression of the very thing it is transfiguring. Yet in vain would one seek in *Les Condamnés* this severed-head-style transcendence and openness by which Catherine's letter lends the man's death both its insignificance and its clear sovereignty. It is painful, even, to read—rather than the death appearing in its tangible vividness—these words that are put into the mouth of the saint: 'Ah! Felice, sweet son! I take and offer up this young, strong blood, filled with the fragrance of life. I take your heart, Felice Tuldo, and lift it up with mine. I press it against our beloved Siena, against Tuscany and Italy . . . ' But once again, I must say, this painful comparison is unfair.

In his long Introduction, M. Gabriel Marcel connects *Les Condamnés* with the personal experience of the author, one of whose close relatives was shot by the Germans in 1942, and hence sets out the terms of a problem which I could describe as being, for all human beings, both the touchstone and the key: it is the problem which, in prison—and torture chambers— Resistance raised for martyrs of all faiths. 'One first point,' M. Marcel recognizes,

> must be placed entirely beyond dispute: there can be no question here of anything resembling a bargain—even if, at least in the religious sphere, a certain literature seems to accredit the idea that the soul renounces superficial, perishable things to achieve possession of a beatitude independent of all human vicissitudes. There is every reason to think that this is a distorting interpretation which

---

Suzanne Noffke's translation of *The Letters of Catherine of Siena*, VOL. 1 (Tempe, AZ: ACMRS, 2000), pp. 85–89. (Trans.)]

misses what is truly specific about the experience it is trying to express. Moreover, if we were genuinely talking about a bargain in the case of the believer, it would become literally incomprehensible that the nonbeliever, for whom no possibility of a similar bargain exists, should in fact turn out to be capable of performing acts of a similar nature. One is, therefore, justified in thinking that, even if the believer attempts to explain his sacrifice to himself by appealing to the idea of a such a bargain, he is deceiving himself and failing to grasp the true, hidden sense of his act.

In this way M. Marcel takes a decisive step and concedes two primary truths at the outset: 1) the idea of an afterlife (at least of an afterlife such that one could bring its profits and losses into the balance of the accounts of a living person) is of only superficial interest; 2) it is in the very instant when death occurs, not in a calculation involving future outcomes, that we must find the *raison d'être* of the martyr's stance. M. Marcel sees distinctly that the sacrifice of life, the gift of oneself cannot be subordinated, cannot be placed 'in the service of anything or anyone'. The *non-subordinate* character of the sacrifice—the word is to be understood here solely in the sense of a complete sacrifice, consented to by the victim—even underlies, as he sees it, any interpretation that is worthy of interest. He is keen to put 'the emphasis on the experience of relief felt by a soul suddenly freed from the weight of everyday life and the burdensome obligations it imposes. Perhaps, after all,' he goes on,

> we suffer infinitely more than we ourselves know from the continuous and, as it were, cutthroat pressure exerted on us not only by circumstances, but above all by the interplay of constraints to which they give rise for a person caught up in the web of social life. Sacrifice—or, more exactly, the indefinable act we refer to by that name—supposes a positive disinsertion.

The context indicates that he is not in any way alluding to 'the withdrawal of a human being isolating himself from the community in which he had previously played a part'. The very opposite is the case, and sacrifice is the rupture without which there is no communion. But it affords liberation from the connected sequence of acts in time that reduces this act I have just supposed to the role of means to an ulterior end. M. Marcel does not say this—sacrifice remains, in his eyes, *indefinable*—but he grants the point, as it were, in advance: he thus underwrites that definition of sacrifice in general which regards it as an expenditure on the present instant of resources that reason commanded us to reserve for the future.

But however boldly M. Marcel's wisdom sets off down this path, it soon judders to a halt. He fails to see clearly the necessary connections—necessary in the sense that total disinsertion is virtually impossible—between an act of disinsertion and shared notions *inserted* in the weft of time. And he sees even less clearly the ultimate necessity—since in the end he seeks to break these connections—of not just half-breaking them.

First of all, it is clear that in principle we can justify our disinsertions only on the plane of insertion; only by inserting them retrospectively; only by at least lending them meanings analogous to those of our acts that are acts of insertion. Otherwise, *sacrifice* would be openly an act without reason (which it is at a deep level). Animals, and sometimes human beings, are killed *on the pretext of ensuring a plentiful harvest etc.* Or further: a man is destroyed in intoxicated contemplation of the heavens, *in order to secure eternal life for himself* (or, at least, 'deliverance'). Or further: the religious, sacred, sacrificial operation—such as sacrifice on the cross—is necessary *to a moral order* (reducible to usefulness for society). Lastly, political sacrifices are demanded—in a more developed form—by the need to change the world, to eliminate the exploitation of man by man.

It is clear that the human mind inserts itself fully in *activity*—that is to say, that in it each thing has a meaning in relation to another (I shear sheep to clothe myself etc.—just as the sheep is covered in wool to keep it warm and eyes are there for seeing). Similarly, each operation of the intelligence has meaning only in the operations that follow, which it makes possible. Sensibility alone escapes this servitude: what I feel intensely, passionately in fact has value only in the instant. Poetic agitation, religious emotion, like laughter or sensuality, have in themselves a value detachable from the meanings assigned to them, a *sovereign* value which '*serves* nothing and no

63

one.' The material conditions of life sanction this and even demand it: those conditions themselves set an end to the subordination of efforts to results. Life needs energy to reproduce itself, but it normally harnesses more than is necessary for its maintenance and reproduction. Thus it has an excess available to it that cannot entirely be absorbed by a growth which is itself limited in advance, and moreover constantly subject to pauses, when excess energy abounds endlessly and must be expended but can never be expended usefully in its totality (usefully: that is to say, in the service of accumulation, of growth of the means of producing more energy). This is how, in various forms, human beings are led to expend certain quantities of energy that cannot ultimately be directed to 'the service of anything or anyone else' and have real meaning only in the instant—quantities of energy that are *sovereignly* squandered. Human beings dance, sing, get drunk, play—they work themselves up in a thousand ways irrationally to waste forces with which they are overflowing.

This fact is usually explained in terms of the pursuit of pleasure. But pleasure is the effect not the cause. We might even say that pleasure is simply the way sensibility, which is the realm of the instant, lets in the concern for future time. In the pursuit of pleasure, a basic concession is made, admittedly, to the principle of the instant. But the primacy of time-to-come is maintained: there is pleasure if the tumultuous expenditure of energy is not such that gloom is cast over the prospect of time-to-come. On the other hand, anxiety arises if, with the concern for the future continuing to be felt, expenditure (or even its possibility) seems to involve a threat in that regard. And there are indeed so many cases when the unleashing of forces exceeds both the limits of pleasure and anxiety that one cannot not linger there long. The various interpretations—religious, moral (transcendent) or utilitarian— show precisely the difficulty in which discursive thought then finds itself. It is therefore necessary to introduce a *simpler* (more elementary) notion than pleasure, moral purpose or utility: the notion of *being in the moment*, in which sensibility and the intensity of feelings intervene essentially in a negative way by eliminating—or, at a pinch, attenuating—the concern with future time. This reduction to *being in the moment* is clear, in particular, if we consider *the last instant*, when pleasure is impotent, when eternal life, moral purpose or utility are in play only *in a clouded way*—since they operate only in the form of a bargain and, as M. Marcel rightly notes, to see

things in terms of a bargain at the instant of death must, in spite of everything, be a 'distorting interpretation.'

Unfortunately, this notion of being *reduced to the interest of the moment
itself* isn't likely to satisfy a number of people. Despite his concern to detach
this *last instant*, which gives off the bright gleam of sacrifice, from any sort
of servitude, M. Marcel's solution is to argue that the virtue of sacrifice, for
the one who is sacrificing himself, is the virtue of *witness*. Clearly we cannot
just allow him this. Witness to what? To that which necessarily is articulated
in an order of actions based on bargains, which implies the subordination
to other instants that will follow from the present one—even if it is for other
people that they follow. What is striking here isn't the inadequacy of this
solution, in contrast to the clear posing of the problem, but the truly
blinding power of the motive that leads to that inadequacy: what is striking
in M. Marcel is this protest (which wholly undermines the praiseworthy
effort to get beyond the dead end of bargains) against 'pure tangible
emotion'. He has, he says, to 'transmute into intelligible content this inar-
ticulate experience that too often remains at the level of pure tangible
emotion'. He writes that,

> The sacrifice performed—or in the process of being performed—
> can doubtless not be equated with a felt state. One would doubtless
> be committing a grave mistake, not by imagining that there may
> exist an enjoyment in sacrifice—for that enjoyment is, in fact,
> possible—but by giving pride of place to that enjoyment in an
> experience that exceeds it in every way and does not involve it in
> all cases.

M. Marcel seems to have totally forgotten here that, in speaking of this work,
he was really addressing himself, through it, to the above-cited letter of
Catherine of Siena—in which the tangible emotion is taken to such a degree
that one cannot imagine a more intense orchestration of the possibilities of
the human being and which, in its entirety, is the demonstration that,
beyond any bargains, it is *emotion* that eliminates the concern with future
time, giving decisive sovereignty to the *last instant* in which the perishable
strikes down the powers of eternity. At that point, the *witness* that was borne
to it depended on a disappearance of the concern to bear witness.

Gide – Nietzsche – Claudel

ANDRÉ GIDE, *Thésée* (Paris: Gallimard, 1946), in 16°, 115 pp.

The myth of Theseus told by Theseus himself, more or less in the tone of *Gulliver's Travels*. This is how Ariadne speaks of the hero's projected expedition into the labyrinth:

> You came here, as I well know, to fight my half-brother, the Minotaur. I'm telling you all this for your own good, so listen carefully. You will win, I'm sure of it. To see you is to banish doubt. (Don't you think that's rather a good line of poetry—but perhaps you have no ear?) But nobody to this day has ever managed to get out of the maze in which the monster lives; and you won't succeed, either, my dear, unless your sweetheart (that I am, or shall presently be) comes to your rescue. You can't begin to conceive how complicated it is, that maze.[1]

It would seem that the author had some fun writing of this risky venture: it is at times very humorous (with a humour in no way reducible to the vulgarity of the passage just quoted) and it is, taken overall, dazzlingly executed. But when we lend the Ancients the language and reactions that are properly ours, it is no longer, as once it was, the most natural thing in the world, but a contrivance. Gide is quite happy to turn his back on exigencies that must surely be evident to him (perhaps he went furthest when he wrote the very insipid *Symphonie pastorale*). Is he a victim of perpetual affectation? Nietzsche one day called for a mask—*one more mask*! In the person of Gide, that wish would be met one hundredfold: there is something awkward and embarrassing in Gide that always gives his wisdom the superfluous character that definitely belongs to masks.

---

1 Cited from the John Russell translation: André Gide, *Oedipus and Theseus* (London: Secker and Warburg, 1950), p. 82. [Trans.]

FRÉDÉRIC [FRIEDRICH] NIETZSCHE, *Pages mystiques* (A. Quinot trans. and ed.) (Paris: Éditions Robert Laffont, 1945), in 8°, 297 pp.

M. Quinot is the founder, at Aix-en-Provence, of a 'French Society of Nietzsche Studies'. He has a touching admiration for Nietzsche, but he interprets him. He has published a large book in order to establish a truth which has, as he sees it, been neglected: Nietzsche was, above all, religious; we should see him as a St John of the Cross without the Christianity; a mystic, if not indeed a 'theosophist'. M. Quinot does not proffer this last term without hesitation, but that is because of the ridicule deservedly attaching to it. The sense of the term seems to him undeniably appropriate here: behind the interests of Nietzsche, M. Quinot divines the ceaseless search for God.

This standpoint leads him to publish some youthful writings that are Christian in inspiration (he opens his weighty tome with them). And he reminds us that Nietzsche, as an adolescent, was said to have had a vision of God. This youthful experience cannot be underestimated: Nietzsche's atheism is of a peculiar nature, it is the atheism of a man who *knows* God, who has had the same experience of God as the saints. Not the banal experience of childhood, but that of a young man of twenty—and a precocious one. This beginning is probably essential to the understanding of the Nietzschean experience as a whole. It would seem, in this connection, that if one has not had the same concrete—and overwhelming—experience of God as the saints, one is not a genuine atheist, but simply someone ignorant of a part of potential human experience. And, indeed, everything suggests that Nietzsche's teaching demands, if it is to be followed, the prior assimilation of Christianity (similarly, Christianity, for its part, does not exclude, but rather presupposes secular culture). And it is, in fact, the strength of Nietzsche's anti-Christianism that he doesn't combat faith for the limits it sets to other possibilities of the individual, but on the grounds of a surpassing of that faith on the plane of religion itself. And this is what has misled M. Quinot. Nietzsche was actually on the same plane as the mystics, but he had turned his back on 'mysticism'. Only late in life did he have an intense experience of states of ecstasy, but independently of any irrational revelation. He writes, very precisely: 'The new feeling of power: path to arrive at it' (*Écrits posthumes*, 1884).[2] And thus, in the mystical state,

---

2 It seems very likely here that a whole line has been missed in the setting of this article.

and with the clearest, boldest rationalism serving as a path to arrive at it, the sense of the *divine* is tragically linked to the sense of the *absence of God*. This gives rise to an unbounded disconsolateness that runs counter to any traditional consoling pity. Underlying the alleged religious experience of Nietzsche is the shattering of any possible respect—an explosive destruction of the transcendent: where the *divine* is concerned, he has provided the most necessarily atheistic expression of it: 'To see tragic natures go under and *be able to laugh about it*, in spite of the deep understanding, emotion and sympathy one feels—that is divine.'[3] The *divine* is the *sovereignty* of man, and hence his radical autonomy, a fundamental freedom that begins when one passes beyond a veneration that one continues to feel.

PAUL CLAUDEL's free translation of *Les Sept Psaumes de la pénitence avec un examen de conscience*, Le Buisson ardent (Pierre Legris series ed.) (Paris: Éditions du Seuil, 1945), in 16º, 70 pp.

Whatever objections one can or should level against the idea of God, it has at least the virtue of lessening the importance of the *self*. And it is the same with the workings of an established religion. Nothing is more oddly opposed to the principles of current literature. Literature has ceased to be a means of expression of social and religious truths laid down in advance. It is an entirely personal quest today, aimed at creating a world that does not yet exist. And there is perhaps nothing that quest aspires to more strongly than the effacement of a *self* which, so long as it is limited to its singularity, renders creation futile. But its existence is founded initially on the extreme audacity of the individual.

The actual passage in Nietzsche's *Nachlass* reads as follows: 'die Beschreibung das neue Macht-Gefühl: der mystische Zustand, und die heilste, kühnste Vernünftigkeit als ein Weg dahin' (*Nachgelassene Fragmente*, Summer–Autumn 1884, 26 [241]) and Bataille himself does indeed cite a French translation of the whole of this passage elsewhere (Bataille, *Œuvres complètes*, VOL. 6, p. 190). It therefore seems reasonable to assume that the phrase should probably read: 'The new feeling of power: the mystical state and the clearest, boldest rationalism serving as a path to it.' [Trans.]
3 *Écrits posthumes*, 1882–1884. My translation. [Trans.]

This is what renders so ludicrous the attempts to establish a *modern* Catholic art, offending, as it does, simultaneously against traditional religion and against the quest being pursued under cover of literature. That art which cannot resort to the deep, depersonalized source of the *sacred*, but which, from the same personal, whimsical source as a poetry with which it finds itself in competition, impudently duplicates—for want of being able to align itself modestly with it—the secular expression of religion.

By dint of an exaggerated assertion of his personality—and even of an undeniable literary genius—the would-be disciple of Rimbaud that is M. Claudel certainly stands on the horns of this ambiguity. And he seems intent on emphasizing the character of that ambiguity forcefully. He translates the Bible—the Penitential Psalms for example—but, as he tells us in a preface,

> in the depths of our spiritual captivity, the Hebrew of David and the Latin of Saint Jerome are not of a nature to produce an echo that we would find alien ... I translate God to myself and I translate myself to God, with the aid of this organ it pleased Him to implant between my teeth. Myself and not some prayer peddler. Myself—and too bad if you are not happy with my turn of phrase.

I will admit that certain lines of Saint Jerome's Latin, interpreting the admirable psalmist, have retained a distant *sacred* resonance for me. As far as I am today from inviting pity, I cannot read this lament of the generations without being a little overwhelmed by it: '*Miserere mei, Deus, secundum magnam misericordiam tuam* ... ', but when M. Claudel writes: 'Ayez pitié de moi, Dieu, dans l'énormité de Ta miséricorde' [Have pity on me, God, in the immensity of Thy mercy!'], the—undeniable—power of evocation of that crime represents *not so much* the terrible face of God as the enormous personality of M. Claudel. And why should we not see the opposition between the saint in the Christian sense and the poet in the modern sense as a very radical antinomy? In the extreme case, the poet, exasperated by an uncertain, unfathomable, unsettling illumination (I am thinking of Blake, Hölderlin, Lautréamont or Rimbaud), is the enemy but also the equivalent in the modern world of the saint. Insofar as M. Claudel is at once a failed saint and a poet *manqué*, his personality and writings help to clarify this healthy opposition.

Take It or Leave It

For René Char

I have the unshakeable conviction that, come what may, *what deprives man of value, his dishonour and his indignity*, wins out and must win out over all the rest, and deserves to have all the rest subordinated, and if necessary sacrificed, to it.

At any rate, what is *sovereign* is indefensible: in seeking to defend it, one betrays it. Giving rise to just so much pap: 'that which constitutes the value of man, his honour and his dignity', says André Gide.[1]

The only thing in me that is *sovereign* is my ruin. And my visible absence of superiority—my state of ruin—is the mark of an insubordination equal to that of the starry sky.

Who is not aware that the sovereignty of anyone among us—in that too, analogous with the starry sky—can find expression only in an impotent silence (a deliberate, inviolate silence can be marked down as mere chatter)?

The stupidest vanity: that silence which hides something other than the unavowable.

A sovereign silence: '*Dansons la capucine . . .* '[2] A *guilty* child: no obstacle any more between my mirror—the immensity of darkest night—and me (I, who . . .).

Friends: laughing up one's sleeve, the bum hole, ecstasy, absolutely black night.

---

1 'Ce qui fait la valeur de l'homme, son honneur et sa dignité'. These words are from a lecture by Gide at the Roxy Cinema in Beirut on 12 April 1946, reprinted in *Souvenirs littéraires et problèmes actuels. Avec deux présentations de G. Bounoure* (Beirut: Les Lettres françaises, 'Publications de l'École supérieure des lettres de Beyrouth', 1946), p. 58. [Trans.]
2 A children's round song at the end of which all the participants squat down. [Trans.]

Perfect *disorderliness* (giving in to the absence of limits) is the rule of an *absence* of community.

Poetry, written or figured, is the only sovereign cry: that is why it leads to these servilities of helots drunk on poetry.

It is not an option for anyone not to belong to my *absence of community*. Similarly, the *absence of myth* is the only unavoidable myth, filling the depths like a scouring wind.

The War in China

STUART GELDER, *The Chinese Communists* (London: Victor Gollancz, 1946), in 16°, 290 pp.

HARRISON FORMAN, *Ce que j'ai vu en Chine rouge* [Report from Red China] (Sabine Bernard Derosne trans.) (Paris: Éditions Pierre Seghers, 1946), in 8°, 277 pp.

ANDRÉ NOLDE, *La Chine de Chiang Kaï Chek* [Chiang Kai-Shek's China] (Paris: Corrêa, 1946), in 16°, 199 pp.

'We could become a Spain on a much larger scale, but we mustn't let it come to that.' So said Mme Sun Yat-Sen,[1] widow of the first president of the Chinese republic and sister-in-law of Chiang Kai-Shek, during the war against Japan. Looking beyond the war with Japan, Mme Sun Yat-Sen was, not without cause, contemplating the possibility of a conflict between the Kung Chang Tang (the Chinese Communist Party) and the Kuomintang (the nationalist party). Mme Sun Yat-Sen is a member of the Kuomintang which was founded by her husband. The Kuomintang spawned some very advanced tendencies but is dominated today by reactionaries, with Marshal Chiang Kai-Shek at the head of them. Like her stepson Sun Fo, Mme Sun represents the tradition of its founder within the Kuomintang. And many elements in the party remain discreetly in agreement with that tendency, though that does not change the policy of the government. Mme Sun herself has no influence, to the point where she cannot even speak. If we are able to cite her opinions today, that is because she asked the British journalist Stuart Gelder, in whom she confided, to publish them once he had left China. But, among her own people, she is reduced to silence. And when, in 1944, she spoke of the possibility of a war that would repeat in the Far East

---

1 Better known later as Soong Cing-Ling [Trans.]

the experience of Spain, she was despairingly aware, within her own party, of those who, like the *Caudillo*,[2] might act as enemies of their own people.

The war feared by Mme Sun Yat-Sen followed quite quickly on the heels of Japanese surrender. Admittedly, it is not yet an all-out conflict: it does not yet have that pitiless character, brooking no compromise, which the military struggle between the parties had from the outset in Spain. But armies of millions of men may join the conflict and the stakes cannot be underestimated: the Spanish business was mainly a premonitory sign; its outcome could not tangibly change the balance of forces. The Chinese question is of far greater importance: China has almost inexhaustible, though as yet unexploited, potential in terms of economic and military power. And the question at issue in the civil war is: 1) *who will equip it* (who will turn the potential into power) and 2) *who will benefit from that change* (which camp will have the future force of China on its side)?

First of all, it should be said that China seems, in theory, the obvious complement to American power. Only the United States can give it the industrial and financial assistance it needs, while, conversely, the Americans can find the markets that they need for their products as of today and the military resources in numbers of men that they would be lacking in a conflict tomorrow. Those who, after the defeat of Japan, control the Pacific must regard as decisive the possibility which now presents itself of arming vast contingents of Chinese allies with their resources and equipment. Given the extreme difference in the levels of their industrial development, such an operation would be to the advantage of both parties. The day is still far off when China in itself could be a danger to America. There is, nonetheless, a difficulty.

The essential problem concerns the changes time may bring—within such a brief period that they require immediate attention. The United States is the only country currently able to equip China industrially and militarily. But might not the USSR be able in the near future to see to the upkeep, for its own benefit, of the equipment that the US would have provided? The longstanding conflict that pits nationalists against Communists didn't arise out of this situation. But that conflict is currently subject to the interests

---

2 The reference is, of course, to General Francisco Franco. [Trans.]

governing that situation and it accentuates their dramatic character. In any event, they are fighting today in China to create the conditions in which 450 million human beings will get to use modern methods to exploit the resources of a region very rich in raw materials. But it must be said that things are far from clear.

There are few matters we know so little about as Chinese internal affairs: in particular, it is common not to have the slightest idea about the nature of Communist China. Information is extremely hard to come by. It is, at a pinch, possible to deduce from the daily news—of military operations or ongoing negotiations—a certain number of facts of a rather rudimentary kind. The Chinese Communists have an army that holds a vast territory to the north, to the southeast and also to the southwest of Peiping (formerly Peking). To the north, Harbin in Manchuria was occupied after the Russians left. To the South East, Yenan has since 1936 been the political organization's base. Between this region of Yenan and Shantung, both of them 'Red', the nationalists control the Peiping-Nanking railway that unites northern China and Mongolia with southern China (though the proximity of the Communist forces makes that connection hazardous). The 'regular' army of the 'government' of Yenan is said to comprise no fewer than eight hundred thousand men, backed up by even larger militias. But that revolutionary 'government' is not an autonomous power, recognized as such by its peers or seeking recognition from them. If one wishes to understand the internal politics of China, one has to take account of its semi-feudal character. Even though they are not hereditary, provincial governors in China have a kind of independence from the central government. The province's army is, in a sense, part of the Chinese national army, but it is normally under the command of its governor. And that official regards it as his own property: he maintains it at his own cost and, in fact, can do more or less as he likes with it (Nolde provides a great deal of interesting detail on this in *La Chine de Chiang Kai-Shek*). All in all, the autonomy of Communist China is similar to that of a provincial governor. The Communist forces are, in theory, part of the national army (of which they are the '18th army group', formed from the '8th route army' and the 'new 4th army'). And the war between Yenan and Nankin is comparable to a war between a vassal and his suzerain (with this difference: Communism is also a political party that has supporters outside the regions it controls). The Yenan Communists recognize the central power of Nankin, which they do not claim to supplant: they are simply asking to take the part in the government of Nankin which the normal operation of the democratic institutions makes rightfully theirs and they are calling for solid guarantees of that (such as a right to veto by one-third of votes cast). Similarly—in principle, just recently—Nankin was not demanding the surrender of the Yenan people, but only that they abandon part of the territory occupied by their army.

In addition, the press informs us that, after having registered successes early in the year (when they occupied a large part of Manchuria—China's only industrialized region), the Communists have recently suffered serious reverses: they have lost Kalgan to the southwest of Peiping and the important port of Andong[3] on the Yellow Sea. These cities had great strategic value and these reverses could have consequences. The loss of Harbin is already in prospect. A decisive—and even a rapid—victory for Chiang Kai-Shek is possible: the American 'observers' who, before the war was seriously underway, at least reserved their opinion on the outcome, have been shaken by these unexpected successes. The Marshal, who might once have negotiated only to gain propaganda advantage, is now sure of himself. He had accepted delaying the convening of the National Assembly, which will draw up the constitution. That assembly could not, in fact, have the democratic import it claims—and which meets the 'wishes' of the US— unless the Communists were present in it, after peace had been made. But its meeting on 15 November, in spite of last-minute interventions calling on the Marshal to grant a last, short delay, is seen as having burnt the bridges. In these circumstances, the Assembly is merely a sort of Kuomintang congress: it makes barely any more difference to the character of the regime, which is a single-party government, than Hitler's Reichstag did. Americans now regard the policy that Truman set out in December 1945—calling for every sinew to be strained to obtain an agreement between the parties—as having been overtaken by events. The mission of

---

3 Since 20 January 1965, this coastal city in Liaoning province has been known as Dandong. [Trans.]

Washington's extraordinary envoy, General Marshall, who had devoted almost a year to attempts at conciliation, seems to be at an end. Despite their great importance (perhaps because of a natural weariness, perhaps because France has lost the greater part of its positions in the Far East: it has had to withdraw from Shanghai, and Indochina is now not a source of rice but a source of concern), these events basically pass the French people by (the British press is not much concerned with them; only the Americans pay sustained attention). The above information is, nonetheless, available on a day to day basis in the same way as with other world events. By contrast, we have until recently been more or less unaware of the nature of this Communist China whose armies have successively foiled both Japan and Chinese government forces. This situation is remedied by the publication of the two books by Stuard Gelder and Harrison Forman, the first published in London, the second translated into French shortly after the appearance of the American edition.

Stuart Gelder, the *News Chronicle's* correspondent in Chungking has not been able to visit the Communist region himself. But his book presents us with copious documentation: political speeches and military, economic and political reports by the Communist leadership, extracts from the local and Japanese press, to which is added reporting by the *New York Times* correspondent Israel Epstein. Harrison Forman's book consists entirely of his reporting on a trip to Communist China in June–July 1944. All this information, revealing the real nature of Chinese Communism to the Western public, is, admittedly, quite old. The most recent of Stuart Gelder's documents is the Political Report of the Leader Mao Tse-Tung to the 7th National Congress of the Kung Chang Tang (Chinese Communist Party) dating from 24 April 1945: at that point, the American armies were still occupied in Europe and the Sino-Japanese war was at its height.

Stuart Gelder's introduction outlines how an 'iron curtain' separated Red China from the rest of the world. We are quite aware that Chiang Kai-Shek's government was barely democratic. It could not perhaps be described as fascistic, but that is mainly because it is far from having the efficiency and authority of the dictatorial governments of the West. Yet censorship in Chungking was careful throughout the war to ensure that nothing of the true situation in China got through to the outside world. Chiang Kai-Shek waged war on the Japanese, but not as resolutely as he might have. The Communists fought the enemy in a manner reminiscent of the French revolutionaries battling with the German invader. Having in mind the war he would have to wage a little later against these genuine defenders of China, wherever he could Chiang Kai-Shek conserved the military equipment he received from Lend-Lease. Out of an army of around two million men, he kept five hundred thousand back to blockade the Communists (who were, in these conditions, in an unequal struggle, more or less reduced to using such weapons as they could take from the Japanese). His government services confined themselves to representing the Reds as bandits. However, a semblance of democracy was maintained. The Communists were sent to concentration camps, but a Communist newspaper, which the censors gradually emptied of its content, continued to appear at Chungking. And a delegation from Yenan tried to negotiate an impossible agreement with Chiang Kai-Shek. While there was an 'iron curtain' in place with the rest of the world, Chinese liberal circles were not unaware that the Yenan Communists had—using democratic methods—set up a social, economic and military organization of undeniable efficiency: it was known that the Communist armies were resisting the Japanese quite outstandingly. The foreign correspondents were not unaware of this either, but censorship deprived them of the possibility of alluding to it. And they were not permitted to enter the Red zone.

Eventually, this situation actually came to seem scandalous. And Chiang Kai-Shek, aware of the power of the world's press, must have noticed that his behaviour was alienating it (without being able to hope that the truth would remain hidden indefinitely). His first concern being with American opinion, he felt compelled in late spring 1944 to permit a group of journalists to visit Yenan.

The Englishman Stuart Gelder was among those in Chungking battling to obtain that permission, though when it came he was not able to take advantage of it himself (at that point his newspaper sent him to Burma). Harrison Forman who, with Israel Epstein and some others, had the opportunity to pass through the blockade on this occasion, recounts the efforts of those in Chungking to forewarn the correspondents against the people at Yenan. But it isn't easy for representatives of an authoritarian government to convince Anglo-Saxon journalists. And in the end, their reporting, combined with the documents that the Communist delegation at Chungking obtained for Stuart Gelder, enables us to form an opinion of Communist China which, for want of more copious data, is necessarily provisional, but which, from the outset, involves a degree of admiration.

The Yenan region is a poor part of China. Irrespective of the blockade, the problem of feeding the sizeable army that came up from the South after a 1,500-mile march and occupied it in 1936 was an easy problem to solve . . . in the traditional Chinese style (a sickly army living off the backs of scrawny peasants). But that would have been a military and political dead-end. Textile resources were nonexistent: from 1939 onwards, the blockade cut off imports of cotton, which was not grown in the region. Lastly, the problem of armaments in this industry-free land, was clearly a desperate one.

When we entered the Communist area we expected to see the army and people hanging on grimly in the face of the economic and military blockade of their barren borderland, sustained mainly by conviction and determination. We found instead that cultivation was more extensive than in any other part of North-west China, that people were better fed and better dressed, and that a certain amount of industry had developed where there was none before. Five years ago the blockade cut off the importation of cotton cloth, none of which was produced locally. Since then the peasants, encouraged by tax remission and crop insurance, have come to grow 60% of the region's requirements. This is sufficient to provide each inhabitant and soldier with two summer suits and one winter suit (usually cotton padded) each year, and an equivalent amount of yarn is spun, mainly by the women's cooperatives, for weaving by many new mills. The importation of cane sugar from the south has been discontinued. Experiments have been made with sugar beets, which next year (1945) will yield enough for everyone, and in 1946 enough for export. Blast furnaces and machine-shops were

THE WAR IN CHINA

built out of captured Japanese equipment brought across the Yellow River, some knowledge and much enthusiasm.

There is no reason to contest this report by a correspondent on the biggest and probably best newspaper in the whole world. It chimes with what we can learn from other sources. Harrison Forman reports the same facts in some detail. And without these remarkable feats, it would not be possible to explain the role of Red China's armies in the war against Japan. '75% of the 15,000 engagements', reports *Asahi Shimbun* of Tokyo on 15 January 1944 (summarizing the operations carried out by the Japanese North China Army during 1943[4]),

> were fought against the Communist forces: more than half of the body count (109, 862) was Communist, whereas of the 74,000 prisoners taken, only 35% were Communist. This shows how weak and demoralized the Chungking army is and, at the same time, proves the moral resolution and fighting spirit of the Communist forces . . . It is clear that the commanders and men have undergone great hardships, which the adverse natural conditions—freezing winters and scorching summers—have made all the harsher. Moreover, the enemies that the North China Army are fighting against are the Communist forces, who are currently rousing a national consciousness and looking to fight decisive battles.

Other cuttings from the Japanese press run along these same lines. André Nolde, Chiang Kai-Shek's military adviser in the war against Japan, recognizes the 'vital role the Communists played in the guerrilla operations' (*La Chine de Chiang Kaï Chek*, p. 153). These precise reports generally confirm the detailed assertions of Gelder, Epstein and Forman.

For example, the widely recognized external—military—findings lend great weight to the American reporters' assertions about the internal—economic—evidence. And the discerning explanation of political, economic and military methods completes the impression that this information is authentic.

---

4 The [Japanese] North China Army held the greater part of occupied China (Peiping, Shanghai, Hangchow). The South China front (Canton, Hong Kong) was much smaller.

79

It is clear that the conditions which the Communists found when they first installed themselves in the region made economic organization a matter of life and death. The Kung Chang Tang leaders did not take the regions they controlled down the Communist path. Landed and industrial property continued to exist. There were, no doubt, expropriations in the early days, but the Yenan leadership wanted everyone united behind the drive to develop production. In the countryside, farm rents were—seriously—reduced, but, as substantial compensation, the landlords were guaranteed a regular payment (their only loss was of the political privileges they still enjoy in the rest of China, where the rural landowner is the unelected mayor of the village; there are, however, examples in Communist China of popular landowners freely elected by the peasant farmers).

Where industry is concerned, co-operatives exist in large numbers and are favoured (a January 1944 report records 260 such companies), but the Marxist Communists are in no doubt about the impossibility of creating industry from scratch without recourse to private capitalism: that is why they encourage individual initiative.[5]

The essential problem in need of solution was agricultural production. Exceptionally in China, the region had an excess of land in proportion to its population. That land, relatively fertile though it was, was still not sufficient to keep the population above the poverty line on account of frequent droughts and flooding. Coming on top of these commonplace threats were Japanese punitive expeditions, destroying installations and harvests. It was necessary from the outset to protect the social organization from possible famines. And individuals had to be won over to the cause by providing guarantees against personal ruin. The slogan 'three years harvests in two years' was laid down as a fundamental principle; a third of resources

---

5 This economic policy is summed up as follows by the party leader:

> It means enforcement of rent reduction and interest on the one hand and guarantee of the payment of rent and interest on the other; raising the wages of the workers and not opposing the legitimate increase in wealth of the capitalists. The standard of living of the peasants and workers should be raised, but meanwhile the full property rights of the landlords and capitalists should likewise be maintained. (Gelder, *Chinese Communists*, p. 188)

from the good years was held back for bad ones, and everything possible was done to extend the areas of cultivation and increase yields. A beneficial 'labour exchange' system was organized, covering groups of eight, ten or twelve farmers (though this is voluntary: no one is forced to join an exchange group). The devastated and abandoned regions were entrusted to peasant cooperatives. *The army itself was fully employed in agricultural production*: soldiers or, more exactly, units were allotted land and contributed appreciably to augmenting resources. In this way, the army managed to produce more than its own needs (this method had an additional advantage: hostility—deep seated in China—between soldiers and peasants was reduced). Moreover, the peasants were indemnified against the depredations of the Japanese: the government took care of farmers whose lands had been devastated. The elimination of usury, the introduction of rent relief, this indemnification policy and the propaganda from a *Production Movement* gave encouragement to the farmers. And the results, on which American reporters and the official reports are united, seem remarkable. In 1944, at a time when there were severe shortages in Europe, the meat rations of a tightly blockaded region for the civilian population were 300 grams per week.

The industrial effort is stranger: an arsenal visited by Harrison Forman is powered by a Soviet Zis truck and a Chevrolet engine, both driven by a gas generator. As raw materials, the establishment uses rails taken from the Japanese, pieces of temple bells, boilers, smoothing irons and old shells. Cartridges and grenade launchers are manufactured there. Elsewhere, 'I found exhibited considerable native ingenuity in compensating for the lack of proper machines,' writes Forman. 'The improvised machines made by the co-operators were of rough construction, but they worked.'[6] A host of indispensable products are made in improvised workshops: munitions, candles, soap, wire, ceramics, buttons, toothbrushes etc. An oil-well built by the Japanese thirty years before and almost immediately abandoned has been brought back into service despite terrible conditions. The most sizeable military production probably concerns explosives. Mines are manufactured

---

6 Forman, *Ce que j'ai vu en Chine rouge*, p. 79. This remark is made in reference to 'a co-operative spinning and weaving mill'. [Trans.]

in numerous locations, using earthenware pots, teapots and bottles. The most surprising production is of *wooden cannons*. These weapons are lined with metal and reinforced externally by being lashed with telephone cables (seized from the Japanese): they are loaded with iron debris.

Military methods have naturally adapted to this kind of weaponry. The Communist armies are, admittedly, not reduced to their own resources alone; they have taken quantities of weapons from the Japanese, even artillery pieces that are used in serious engagements. But however extensive this captured materiel might be, it is not sufficient to make for a modern army. Though they had a relatively organized force of around 800,000 men, the Communists' war was necessarily a guerrilla struggle, though probably one of the most large-scale ever fought. The region genuinely under Yenan's control, which runs to the southeast of Peiping, was tiny: two hundred kilometres, as it would seem, between the nationalist blockade line and the Japanese front. But, outside of Manchuria, the whole of occupied Northern China, from Manchuria to the Yangtze (the region of Shanghai and Hanchow) was more or less a guerrilla warfare zone. The Communist general staff divided this vast territory (1,200 kilometres from north to south, 700 from west to east) into three categories. Regular base: region controlled by the Yenan administration, out of reach of Japanese penetration (unless the enemy mobilizes its forces for a significant campaign). Guerrilla base: a region also controlled, but at the mercy of easy but transient Japanese incursions. Guerrilla territory: where the Japanese forces are in constant struggle with the Communist forces (and, at times, with the Chungking forces). Occupied territory: administered by the Japanese, where Chinese patriots are reduced to clandestine action. Within this framework 'guerrillas' operated: auxiliary corps made up of actual soldiers but ready to disguise themselves among the civilian population and popular militias, made up of peasants who did not leave their homes but were organized and armed to resist Japanese punitive expeditions in their own localities.

It would seem that the war has substantially enhanced the strategic options available to guerrilla armies. Seldom does the cunning employed in warfare behind enemy lines seem to have been so subtle. The abundant use of mines must have made the Japanese soldier's sojourn in northern

China a living hell. Added to this are the endless raids on the blockhouses and the traps of all kinds set for expeditions. In certain regions where the earth is easy to dig, peasant resistance took on a strange aspect. The inhabitants built enormous tunnels running from one village to the next: they were able to escape massacre, but an atrocious war ensued within the bowels of the earth. At times the Japanese attempted massive operations: in August 1940 they attacked in the Xi'an region, not far from Yenan, with forces around a hundred regiments strong. Three months of fighting ensued, but, achieving only disappointing results, the Japanese command was apparently thrown back on the defensive: building lines of blockhouses and engaging in local 'mopping-up' operations. Sizeable contingents of the Japanese occupying forces were reduced for years to a depressing impotence.

*

This outcome proves the success of the economic battle waged by the Communist leadership. At the same time, it attests to the popular support for the Yenan government. The picture is not entirely clear: politicians' speeches allude to resistance by spies and counterrevolutionaries. But it seems that Yenan has fought its opponents more through persuasion than by violent repression. It is curious that no reference is made to executions. Harrison Forman often reports cases of the Japanese forces and Chinese collaborators being dealt with very humanely. Japanese prisoners were either released or re-educated in a 'Japanese People's Emancipation League'. (Admittedly, if they availed themselves of the freedom they were granted, the Japanese command had them shot for surrendering when they returned; if they joined the League, they were used in the 'shouting war': armed with loudhailers, they would address their comrades in the Japanese lines, telling them how well treated they were and how pointless was the struggle into which the Japanese high command had dragged them.) This humane character of Communist policy is striking (though allusion is made in the reports to the imprisonment of traitors and it seems unlikely that such a harsh war was conducted without any violent repressive measures). Yenan claims to adhere fundamentally to the three principles of Sun Yat-Sen:

democracy, the expulsion of foreigners and freedom from want. And the Communists, by a convention struck with the central government, occupy only one post out of three in the leadership. Their methods have definitely gained them the trust of liberal circles in Chungking. (We must, admittedly, mention recent information from an American source that the same circles have lost some of that trust following incidents in which the Communists are said to have employed totalitarian methods in Shantung province. Much is also made of Li Lisan, leader of the Chinese Communist party in 1925,[7] returning in August 1946. Li advocated basing the movement on the urban proletariat, whereas Mao, who supplanted him, has relied on the poor peasantry. In the intervening years, Li Li-San has lived in Moscow. In reality, nothing can be deduced from these claims. If the Chinese Communists do have in their ranks elements hostile to Russian influence—something which the party's attitude of openness permits—the party has never been regarded as dissenting from Moscow. Moreover, with a treaty signed on 14 August 1945,[8] the Kremlin's policy has moved strongly towards an accord with nationalist China. There is nothing to indicate any marked change since. There is no indication the Russians are supporting the Communists in the civil war, whereas the Americans have helped the nationalists to protect their lines of communication.)

*

This is what we know of Red China, whose heroic action has deserved better than the silence that still surrounds it. And whatever it is truly like, whatever it may become, it must be said that it has a momentous destiny before it. After nine years of fighting the foreign invader, it is having to face the— more cruel—necessities of civil war. It would seem that Chiang Kai-Shek

---

7 It isn't entirely clear what Bataille is referring to here. Li Lisan was Director of the Central Committee of the Chinese Communist Party between March and August of 1930. [Trans.]

8 This was the so-called Sino-Soviet Treaty of Friendship and Alliance. The provision that the Soviet Union was not to give aid to the Chinese Communists is not widely believed to have been adhered to, though Bataille was not to know this in November 1946. [Trans.]

probably has no more chance of wiping it out than Japan had. But the Communists, who can now also draw on a section of Manchurian industry (Manchuria, equipped by Japan, is the only industrially developed region of China), no longer have the benefit of the inviolable union that was guaranteed by hatred of Japan. What we see now, in all its horror, is the excessive tension of that political tragedy depicted in André Malraux's *Human Condition*. And it is easier to imagine the conflict escalating than subsiding: an enormous region in which an excessive birth rate removes all hope of calm and equilibrium and where poverty is constantly increasing due to the arrival of ever more newborn children lays the groundwork for a perspective on life radically opposed to that which still undergirds a world where peace has seemed the norm and war the choice of a few mad souls. As of now, China is far from us but it promises storms ahead: there is no sense in our not being informed about it. Chiang Kai-Shek may, admittedly, bring peace to the country tomorrow, doing so by the most horrendous methods. That would first imply a continuation of Moscow's wise moderation, which runs counter to all reasonable predictions. But the immediate outcome is not so important (this is what justifies the Russians' dilatory policy, they being Marxists and not showing the same naïve interest as American politicians in temporary easings of tension). At stake in the war is the possibility of developing China's industry and hence its revolutionary proletariat. And that country's production cannot be developed fast enough to reduce the poverty of a political peasantry. In reality, China's problems, as posed today before our eyes by Communist Yenan at war, exceed the limited horizons and habits of sentimental chatter from which our worst misadventures have clearly not extricated us.

Cossery – Robert Aron

ALBERT COSSERY, *Les Hommes oubliés de Dieu* (Paris: Charlot, 1946), in 16°, 134 pp.[1]

The press has echoed the opinion of Henry Miller that, 'These stories will take their place alongside those of Gorky, Gogol and Dostoyevsky.'

It is more than a year now since the American magazine *Town and Country* offered this review by Miller of *Les Hommes oubliés de Dieu*, the first edition of which had been published in Cairo:

> 'When God forgets someone, my son, it is forever', says one of the characters to his young child. And these people who make up the unnameable world of Cossery are in truth forgotten by God and by man. They exist in a void where filth, oppression and misery reign supreme. They have lived this way for generation after generation, too stupefied to even dream of revolt, their only refuge being sex and drugs. Their only dream is of bread. To beg a bit of bread from those who had taken all from them was still, for them, a chance to live.
>
> There is one story called 'The Danger of Fantasy' which deals with a school of beggars run by one Abou Chawali who believes in the virtue of terror. In his opinion, 'the strength of the poor is in their rags and in their faces of men condemned. One could not wrest that strength from them; it remained the sole safeguard of their tragic destiny. It is with that that they defend themselves against the criminal world of the mighty, and it is with that too that they will succeed in making an impression on that world, ruining it in its security and well-being.' In Tewfik Gad, who has proposed a novel and completely fantastic way of begging, based on 'the science of psychology', he senses a dangerous rival. Gad tries to explain that he had simply wished to introduce 'a certain picturesqueness which

---

1 Translated into English by Harold Edwards as *Men God Forgot* (Berkeley: Circle Editions/George Leite, 1946). [Trans.]

would greatly facilitate the business.' To which the outraged Abou Chawali, a stern realist, replies: 'We do not want to serve as a picturesque element. We want to be a real people, a people that suffer and whose wounds are obvious and tangible.'

This danger of fantasy, elaborated by Cossery with diabolical humor and mockery, is precisely the danger which the disinherited have had to confront from time immemorial. It is a danger that makes itself felt only at the lowest level of existence, when the last scrap of human dignity is torn away and the great void of annihilation opens up to swallow the ghostly marionettes of life.[2]

It is true that another element dictates Miller's laudatory judgement (given in the conclusion that follows these lines). The sort of pungent sensuality that emanates from the book, which, uncompromising and without the slightest possibility of evasion, is to the conventional idea of sensuality what blood is to soap, places Albert Cossery in the vicinity of Henry Miller (though the former lacks the moral ease, health and passion, and the virtuosity of the latter). But when it comes to poverty, there is something I am uncomfortable with. As literature shows, poverty is not so simple. The extravagant attraction literature feels towards it is sufficient indication that it has the power to reveal a certain divine or sacred quality that touches on the nature of being: it is like the half of a human sacrifice. Its victims suffer it passively and yet there is in them a sort of diabolical consent. It is often the horrendous product of a lack of concern for the morrow and this, I believe, is what makes the poverty-stricken individual divine and the provident one contemptible. There is a strong affinity between sensuality and poverty—as there is between poverty and poetry—relating in each case to the rejection of the rules of propriety that are dictated by a concern for what tomorrow may bring.

And, in spite of everything, the mingling, in *Les Hommes oubliés de Dieu*, of a sort of Tolstoyan morality (without puritanism, admittedly, and without resignation) with the poetry of poverty troubles me (but who would have the heart to avoid it?).

---

2 These passages have been partially re-translated into English from Bataille's French rendering. [Trans.]

Robert Aron, *Retour à l'éternel* [Return to the eternal] (Paris: Albin Michel, 1946), in 16°, 251 pp.

Robert Aron is driven by poorly defined feelings which he calls religious. He is nostalgic for a state of harmony—of man with himself and man with nature: the medieval cathedral and Saint Thomas's *Summa* seem exquisite to him when espied from the chaos into which we are sinking. These sentiments already have the character of a belief: he accepts the existence of God, of transcendence, and of divine Providence: and, without over-committing himself, he is at least attracted by Catholicism. But he is firm on one point: between faith and reason—as between man and nature—he can accept no disharmony. He calls for a science whose results corroborate the faith that drives it. 'It ought to be the case that (the) beliefs of the scientist on religious topics should not appear devoid of all logical relation with his scientific conceptions.' In the past Descartes had seen 'great differences between Acquired and Revealed Truths,' and that is precisely what Robert Aron holds against him: a passage in a medieval Mystery Play enables him, for this reason, to equate Descartes with Judas. Descartes is charged with succumbing, like Arnould Gréban's Judas, to the mutual hatred between body and soul.[3]

This does not mean, however, that Robert Aron wishes to introduce a doctrine of immanence. He does not. We may say that he is tempted, but the presupposition of a transcendent reality is a stubborn one . . . There is little coherence in the way the principles of the book relate to one another. The aim of establishing a syncretism in which everything combines harmoniously is affecting: the desire for emancipation, the submission to God, the dignity of the person (Communism, Christianity, bourgeois individualism). This time there would be only *one* religion, *the* definitive religion. And in harmony with science. But the wish for harmony is not harmony.

Today however, the relation—and absence of relation—between science and religious sentiment—are openly visible to us. There is never anything in the truths science asserts that goes further than what it states specifically. Science establishes constant limits on distinct elements (though the constancy of the limits and the distinguishing of the elements cannot be regarded as absolute). A truth of science can never range wider than simple assertions: the sun emits light rays, roots sink themselves into the

---

3 Arnould (or Arnoul) Gréban, sometime organist and choirmaster of Notre-Dame Cathedral in Paris, was the author in 1453–54 of a famous passion play. [Trans.]

COSSERY - ROBERT ARON

earth . . . Science encroaches only negatively on the province of religion: a) insofar as the particulars of a religion involve crass factual judgements containing easily demonstrable errors (that the sun revolves around the Earth etc.); b) insofar as a *critical* knowledge of comparative religions exists; c) insofar as, proving to be the only thing that does not deceive us, science remains silent and abandons us to our anxiety if the scope of investigation is not properly circumscribed. All that science brings to religious disquiet is to encourage it not to be satisfied with easy answers any more, to move beyond dogmatic presuppositions and ask questions in the definitive darkness that is our lot. To the point where, so far as the established religions are concerned, that disquiet retains only their mystery, though it extends that mystery, inescapably, to the impenetrable totality of the world. In the strange times we are living in, there is no other 'syncretism' imaginable.

The rest is mere chatter, a *return* to today's *eternal* verity and tomorrow's error. The rest is a contempt for the rigorous foundations on which science is based. And Robert Aron takes things a long way here: 'Who, in our day,' he writes (p. 56), 'would still believe in the materialism of history after seeing the free intervention of an isolated, banished individual on 18 June 1940 change the course of events and the destinies of a people?' And he shows naively what he wants from scientists when, writing of the findings of modern physics, he ascribes to the photon within certain limits the freedom to 'locate and orient its position in space' (p. 55). To confuse Heisenberg's principle of indeterminacy with the philosophical idea of freedom! . . . But why call on science to underwrite something it cannot, and which (no doubt this is troubling) no one is asking for?

In reality, before our eyes, the 'chariot' of knowledge (I don't say of the sciences in the narrow sense) 'is riding a volcano'[4] and, in these conditions, it is quite a creditable thing to attempt, like Robert Aron, to take stock of the situation. But it is no surprise to see the result limited to regret for the time when all was apparently going well for the 'chariot'. All in all, you have to have a strong stomach to assert that you joyously prefer to 'ride the volcano', as the only course worthy of humanity, rather than enjoy this cathedral sleep.

---

4 When Bataille's writes le 'char' des connaissances . . . navigue sur un volcan, this is probably a conscious allusion to the famous phrase in Henry Monnier and Gustave Vaez's play *Grandeur et décadence de Monsieur Joseph Prudhomme* (1852): 'Le char de l'État navigue sur un volcan'. This was widely taken up as an example of windily pompous political language and is used to that end in the famous 'Comices agricoles' scene in Flaubert's *Madame Bovary*. [Trans.]

89

Marcel Proust and the Profaned Mother

Dr André Fretet, *L'Aliénation poétique. Rimbaud, Mallarmé, Proust* (Paris: J.-B. Janin, 1946), in 8°, 333 pp (with an original drawing by D. Galanis as cover illustration).

Denis Saurat, *Tendances. Idées françaises: De Molière à Proust* (Paris: La Colombe [Éditions du Vieux Colombier], 1946), in 16°, 152 pp.

I am not one of those who believes the world is misbegotten. That means: 'the world is different from me . . .' or 'the way it is is not to my taste . . .'; and I know that where these sorts of ideas are in play, no thinking amounts to any more than a mark of the powerlessness of thought. However, of the many minor woes that commonly cause me to groan at the state of the world, there are few that inflame me more than the prejudice in favour of the 'specialist'. If intelligence—without any imaginable end-goal or awakening—remains at the mercy of problems of a clearly subordinate interest, is confined to them and sees no further, that is because there is within it a principle of servility. Specialization reveals a sort of docility inherent in thought, the first victim of which is the man who thinks (or who at least relies on thought). There are, however, discreet specialists who know the limits of their field, know that there are in the world objects of interest beyond their own, and retain an ambiguous respect for what lies beyond their scope. The very worst thing is the happy specialist who, in proud possession of the little bit of science that has fallen to his lot, uses it as a basis for wide-ranging explanations.

To relate literature to the categories of psychiatry, as Dr André Fretet attempts to do, is no doubt of the most limited interest. The author of *L'Aliénation poétique* stresses the clinical character of these categories. And rightly so: psychiatry comprises a rather rudimentary catalogue of illnesses or sets of symptoms; that catalogue is based on a great wealth of experience and methodical observations. But, though experience has enabled practitioners to recognize distinct states, form ideas about their possible evolution and, in well-defined cases, intervene effectively, the notions it introduces explain nothing. (Psychoanalysis did, admittedly, attempt to provide an account based on a theoretical psychology, but even if its theory were proven to be true, it would bring only faint glimmers of light into what remains almost total darkness). And if a medical man goes to great lengths to explain the work of Mallarmé in terms of a fundamental 'schizoid state' and bouts of 'melancholy' (to be understood in the technical sense the word possesses in the vocabulary of the asylum), we shall not be surprised to be put in mind of Molière.

But let us allow the doctor himself to speak:

Thus Nothingness, which fascinates both Mallarmé and Rimbaud, the end-point of their tendency towards the absolute, of their inadaptedness, attests in Mallarmé to an episode of stuporous depression, and in Rimbaud to a state of quietude in the mystical sense of the term, that is to say, mindlessness [abêtissement]. Thus the masochistic need for expiation that leads Rimbaud to fall silent causes Proust to bemoan his fate and accuse himself. In the one case, reticence, in the other, prolixity.

Just as Mallarmean absence is the expression of a melancholy experience by a schizoid, so Proust's anxious questioning betrays psychasthenic tendencies and Rimbaud's stenographic productions and subsequent silence attest to an illness: dissociative delusional disorder. (Fretet, l'Aliénation poétique, p. 183)

As we can see, the patients 'S. Mallarmé, A. Rimbaud and M. Proust' are serving the learned doctor as 'clinical examples' here. In fact, it has not proved sufficient merely to describe them as patients; the word 'clinical' refers to the experience the doctor has of an illness that has been treated: a slippage of meaning familiar to us from the comic authors who have represented ludicrous 'specialists' in wildly exaggerated form (misers, learned women, doctors . . . [1]). It is, however, remarkable that Dr Fretet finds

---

1 But obviously the distorted view Dr Fretet advances is not representative of medical

these 'clinical examples' exclusively among the dead. He cannot be unaware that it is questionable to treat a human being as a thing, in the way that the clinician teaching at the bedside *is forced to* do with hospital patients (though, in that case, the teaching is not public or, if observations are published, names are withheld). 'Many,' he tells us, 'are the masters—and indeed the very great masters—whether impressionists, intimistes, Cubists or Surrealists, whose vision suggests a precise diagnosis. But they are contemporaries. Or else they have a daughter, a grandson, nephews. They will thank us for not engaging in the public consultation that the works nonetheless call out for' (*l'Aliénation poétique*, p. 21). The doctor describes Rimbaud as 'cowardly' (*l'Aliénation poétique*, pp. 140–46), but, out of delicacy, levels his criticisms only at the dead.

I do not in fact see anything wrong with naming the miseries—and, if need be, the cowardice—of those who were broken by the human limits their temerity ran up against. I might even say that the only interest of *L'Aliénation poétique* lies in its harsh frankness. But this does not excuse a slightly unhinged tone of rage that proves nothing except the doctor's vulgarity. Nothing removes us from the rigours of science—to which the author appeals to overcome our resistance—more surely than a certain disorderly shoutiness:

> Money! So that was all it was! That was the price for Rimbaud's betrayal, for his renouncing of the absolute and his silence. God on the one side, eight kilos of gold on the other, and, after striking out wildly for so many years, the terrible scourge that was Rimbaud's soul is at last stilled. (*l'Aliénation poétique*, p. 140)

men in general. On the contrary, with the exception of Dr Laforgue, the author of a regrettable volume on Baudelaire, the psychiatrists I have met have been wary of studying dead people who have not undergone any sort of 'clinical' observation. (They are not always right to take that stance: leaving aside Freud's 'Leonardo Da Vinci' study, which is perhaps unduly ingenious, the fine work devoted to Poe by Princess Marie Bonaparte shows that psychiatry—or at least psychoanalysis—can bring depth to a biographically based criticism.) The idiosyncracies of a Dr Fretet pose a potential threat to the 'specialists' of all professions; conversely, specialist activity doesn't always tie us down and there is nothing to prevent a 'fully rounded individual' from engaging in a restrictive occupation if he feels so inclined.

But this sums up quite well the doctor's intention. The materialist assumption is randomly tacked on to the psychiatric one to explain entirely (to reduce to nothing, to bring down to the level of a rudimentary intelligence that reduces what it touches to a thing, an object) such phenomena as we can have access to only by ceasing to explain them. It is, in fact, a virtue of literature that it 'presents things to be seen'. Scientific—or pseudoscientific—criticism turns its back on that and it is unsurprising that a stupefying effect ensues—even a ragingly stupefying effect—with all concern for objectivity abandoned.

But a curt dismissal will not rid us of a tendency inherent in the human mind that is ridiculous only in its excesses. We cannot really deny that the literary men cited were psychologically abnormal. The present state of knowledge with regard to mental anomalies does not permit of a sure diagnosis of illnesses that have not been observed directly; and the current notions of psychiatry would at best allow us to find similarities between the psychological traits of writers and others generally observed in the clinical setting that are *unexplained*. But explanation that is impossible today might be possible tomorrow. And one fact remains undeniable here and now: that Mallarmé, Rimbaud and Proust—and we should say a great many writers— were genuine neurotics (it didn't take Fretet to tell us that). If that is the case, should we not doubt the significant value of works that are the expression of defective states, of states *that are treated medically*, and which ought, if possible, to be eliminated as soon as they are detected?

*

In a collection of essays[2] mainly devoted to Proust, a man whose mind is as far removed from vulgarity as Denis Saurat devotes close attention to this doubt. In his eyes, Meredith can be said to enjoy the superiority of health over the sick genius Proust. Proust's genius drew Saurat to him, but he is hesitant: at the very least, he puts us on our guard against the tainted character of Proust's experience of love. In the end, he feels some embarrassment: 'It is up to us,' he says suddenly, as though in the grip of a strong emotion,

---

2 Written in 1925.

'to withdraw the accusations of sickness, vice and abnormality . . . with which we have, on occasion, assailed him'. Yet, all the same, he maintains a high regard for health against a negative 'disorderliness' of feeling. In his eyes, 'If one has not had prolonged experience of marriage,' one misses the general truth of love. 'And even childless marriage is an insufficient experience . . .' (*Tendances*, p. 102). He twice quotes 'old Tolstoy' saying 'The man who knows his wife knows more of women and love than the man who knows a hundred mistresses'. And the author to whom he grants pride of place at the beginning of the book is Molière (Shakespeare might be said, at a pinch, to be greater, 'but Shakespeare is not so supremely elegant in his laughter, nor so subtly intelligent in the light-hearted criticism of humanity . . .'). This declaration seems eminently reasonable to me. When it comes to condemning the literary expression of deficient states, we grant Molière pride of place. But we must, with Saurat, put the whole of literature on trial. For, as *Tendances* asserts (pp. 13–14),

> literature has somewhat deceived humanity. We have not forgotten that it began by celebrating the gods and those *demigods that were sons of men*. From the beginnings of human intelligence, then, it evinced an admiration for heroism, grandeur and the tragic that has done humanity a bad turn. The raging bull within man has been only too indulged and exalted by 'great' literature. There is in reality too much heroism, too much grandeur, too much force, just as, in the opposite direction, there is too much vice, too much shabbiness. What is missing more than anything else is common sense, the average man, the bourgeois, if you like. Molière's bourgeois: Ariste, Clitandre, Philinte. The man who doesn't take himself seriously and yet, at the appropriate moment, knows how to do 'the done thing'. Socrates, for example, who was irony incarnate, and was a good soldier. The fact is that this cheerfully sensible mental equilibrium, which is Molière's ideal, isn't so easy to achieve. Ultimately, it takes greater willpower, greater sustained strength to maintain this reasonable happy medium than to give in to the extreme temptation of the soul, whether into violence—and the sublime is ultimately merely violence—or into vice. It is not by literary convention that

tragedies end badly; it is because that extraordinary tensing of the human spirit collides too violently with things and goes against the way of the world.

In actuality, nothing that seduces is healthy and it is, crudeness and excess aside, a reaction of the same type that has Dr Fretet say (about the interest Mallarmé took in the choice of furniture and draperies, a clear sign of being unbalanced!) '[Is that not a] rare concern in France, where the first, sure indication of a man's mental health is the ugliness of his house, given over to his wife's taste and his children's vandalism? The opposite is a worrying sign and hints at some flaw' (*l'Aliénation poétique*, p. 77).

At this point, it will not be very surprising to see me turn all this on its head: if the health of the mind is contrary to the tragic, to the sublime, to vice and, in general, to those raptures in which we are elevated—or simply carried—beyond our limits, would there not be some antinomy between art, which wants only to move and entice us, and health? In reality, we know it is not poets alone that have their place in the known classification of 'mental pathology'. The gods and demigods, according to myth, the heroes and the saints—and all those whose unhealthy lives impassioned masses that were weary of a concern with health—share many features with the psychiatrists' clients. The fact is that mental health is the satisfactory operation of a machine that has efficient activity as its end-goal, *but to which the human element in us resists reduction.* And doubtless what halts that operation or impairs it is a danger: the machine, once wrecked, removes from us the possibility of living. But the reduction of man to a cog in a machine leads to the limited, domestic state which Dr Fretet, like a drunken helot, has sought sadly to exemplify. Those things which attract us and lead us astray, move us and intoxicate our senses—wine, sensuality, poetry, and beyond poetry *that sovereign disposition of self* that verges on madness— are dangers: we cannot know, as we risk them, whether we are not going to break the machine. *But we can be free and proud only if we allow ourselves to be seduced.* The defective states enumerated by psychiatry are, admittedly, diverse in nature, but in all of them the machine has gone awry. There are some purely negative ones, and the positive affective disorders that skew the machine are most often significant only for the sufferer. But these latter

95

are not clearly distinct from those that trouble most human beings. There are few obsessions, few sickly states of anxiety that poetry or the novel cannot express. Even the mere breaking of the bounds imposed by our functioning, the powerlessness—of no definite significance—of a sudden bout of madness itself exerts a sort of agonizing seduction. There is a constant fundamental conflict between the domain of the moment—of aesthetics and immediate seduction—and the domain of concern for the morrow—of ethics and the rules of action: to such a degree that if one of us suddenly and for no tangible reason rejects the rules, it seems to us, despite our fear, that we are falling under the spell of infinite seduction.

What essentially connects art to unreason (to 'mental pathology') is that both yield us up to the power of the instant, and that unreason, being the danger which art runs, is not simply a failed counterpart to it, but is also the mark of decisive rigour and necessity. Hence the overwhelming, intimate sense of enormous victory represented by the madness of Hölderlin, or Van Gogh or Nietzsche. And, from this point of view, we have to grant a similar order of value to the empty silence, the definitive stupefaction of Rimbaud. Proust's pathological abyss is less dark: his reason remaining inviolable, he seems even to have entered death with a sense of victory. Nevertheless, one cannot underestimate the gravity of anomalies that doubtless left him, right to the end, with a life that was somewhat awry. Not to mention the respectful reserve of Denis Saurat here, Dr Fretet's harsh frankness might itself fall short of the truth on this point. Apart from a constantly odious tone, his account in *L'Aliénation poétique* of the vices of the author of *À la recherche du temps perdu* is acceptable at a pinch (if he sins, he does so by omission,[3] though it is omission of what is essential). It is absolutely correct, it seems to me, to relate the anomalies of Proust's behaviour to the adoration he felt for his mother. But we are subject to a certain law: while believing that we want 'what pleases us', we in fact seek out what impinges most vividly on our sensibility. In so far as we can endure it, we provoke in ourselves the liveliest emotions—those which are most painfully

---

3 Dr Fretet does not seem to be interested in the fact that, though *attuned to* the very worst, Proust surmounts it and elevates a form of mental health to the level of the comprehension of its opposite.

unbearable. By paying that price, we cease to be part of the servile concern for the morrow. By paying that price, we do not put off living, and time, the moment, no longer escape us. Thus, only powerlessness and fear set a limit to the desire to defile what we love: love, on the other hand, incites us, and the emotion in an act of sacrilege is all the stronger for our loving the more. We cannot, admittedly, reduce the role of fear, all the greater itself as the love is great: this is how those terrible compromises are imposed in which the Christian believer is sent into ecstasies imagining the sufferings on the Cross or the lover weeps as he strips bare the woman he loves. It is sometimes the same with fear in the pursuit of strong emotion as it is with anxiety in laughter: at the very instant when the idea sets in that the laughter is absolutely senseless, indecent, impossible, it redoubles and becomes mad. Naturally, health is at the opposite pole from such a strange pursuit (and not only mental, but moral health). We regard as 'ill' those who—not being subdued by fear (concealed beneath the name of various 'moral sentiments')—give in, and cannot but give in, to the appeal of 'evil'. Clearly, it can come as no surprise if Dr Fretet sees the signs of a pathological disturbance in the association in Proust's mind of the absolutely holy image of the mother and images of murder or defilement. 'As the feeling of pleasure gripped me more and more,' the narrator of À la recherche tells us, 'I felt an infinite sadness and desolation stirring deep in my heart; it seemed to me that I was making the soul of my mother weep . . . '.[4] At a certain point, the mother of the story disappears, without there being any further mention of her death or herself; and only the death of the grandmother is related. As though the death of the mother herself had retained too momentous a meaning for the author, it is only of his grandmother that he tells us: '[T]hinking at once of my grandmother's death and Albertine's, it seemed to me that my life was stained with a double murder'. I can barely doubt that with this idea of moral murder was associated the idea of profanation. And Dr Fretet is right (*l'Aliénation poétique*, p. 239) to focus on the passage in *Sodom and Gomorrah* in which it is said that, 'sons not always taking after their fathers . . . may consummate the profanation of their mothers in their faces,' and the narrator adds, 'But let us here leave what would merit a

---

4 The passage is from Proust's *Les Plaisirs et les jours* (1896). [Trans.]

chapter on its own: the profanation of mothers'.[5] Doesn't the key to these elements of tragedy manifestly lie in the episode in which Vinteuil's daughter, whose behaviour had caused her father to die of a broken heart, only a few days afterwards—and in the period of deep mourning—enjoys the caresses of a homosexual lover who spits on the dead man's photograph (*Swann's Way*, part 1)? What Dr Fretet does not say is that bringing the female lover to live in the house during the father's lifetime also parallels exactly Albertine (or Albert) being brought to live in the narrator's parents' flat. Nothing is said—which leaves us hanging—of the mother's reaction to the interloper's presence (just as her death goes, no less oddly, unmentioned). There is no reader, I imagine, who has not noticed that the story leaves a blank at this juncture. By contrast, the suffering and death of Vinteuil are conveyed emphatically. But if we accept the possibility that may be said to have been given to us to fill the void that was left in this way, it is heartbreaking to read:

> Anyone who, like ourselves, had seen M. Vinteuil at that time, avoiding people whom he knew, turning away as soon as he caught sight of them, growing old within a few months, brooding over his sorrows, becoming incapable of any effort not directly aimed at promoting his daughter's happiness, spending whole days beside his wife's grave, could hardly have failed to realise that he was dying of a broken heart, could hardly have supposed that he was unaware of the rumours which were going about. He knew, perhaps he even believed, what his neighbours were saying. There is probably no one, however rigid his virtue, who is not liable to find himself, by the complexity of circumstances, living at close quarters with the very vice which he himself has been most outspoken in condemning— without altogether recognizing it beneath the disguise of ambiguous behaviour which it assumes in his presence; the strange remarks,

---

5 Proust, *Sodom and Gomorrah*, quoted here from John Sturrock's translation (London: Penguin Classics, 2003), p. 306. A translation of the same passage can be found in Marcel Proust, *Remembrance of Things Past*, VOL. 2 (C. K. Scott Moncrieff and Terence Kilmartin trans) (London: Penguin Books, 1989), pp. 938–39. References to *Remembrance of Things Past* have been added by me. [Trans.]

the unaccountable attitude, one evening, of a person whom he has a thousand reasons for loving. But for a man of M. Vinteuil's sensibility it must have been far more painful than for a hardened man of the world to have to resign himself to one of those situations which are wrongly supposed to be the monopoly of Bohemian circles; for they occur whenever a vice which Nature herself has planted in the soul of a child—perhaps by no more than blending the virtues of its father and mother, as she might blend the colour of its eyes—needs to ensure for itself the room and the security necessary for its development. And yet however much M. Vinteuil may have known of his daughter's conduct it did not follow that his adoration of her grew any less. The facts of life do not penetrate to the sphere in which our beliefs are cherished; they did not engender those beliefs, and they are powerless to destroy them; they can inflict on them continual blows of contradiction and disproof without weakening them; and an avalanche of miseries and maladies succeeding one another without interruption in the bosom of a family will not make it lose faith in either the clemency of its God or the capacity of its physician.[6]

What is most astounding here is that no room is left for despair. The mother did not doubt, and the son does not succumb to fear of the mother's doubt. And this certainty transfigured the inevitable abjection. This will to limitless horror reveals itself in the end for what it is: the measure of love. And there is hardly any doubt, a little further on, that Proust was referring to himself when he wrote (*Swann*, part I):

But, appearances apart, in Mlle Vinteuil's soul, at least in the earlier stages, the evil element was probably not unmixed. A sadist of her kind is an artist in evil, which a wholly wicked person could not be, for in that case the evil would not have been external, it would have seemed quite natural to her, and would not even have been indistinguishable from herself; and as for virtue, respect for the dead, filial affection, since she would never have practised the cult

6 Proust, *Remembrance of Things Past*, VOL. 1, p. 161.

of these things, she would take no impious delight in profaning them. Sadists of Mlle Vinteuil's sort are creatures so purely sentimental, so naturally virtuous, that even sensual pleasure appears to them as something bad, the prerogative of the wicked. And when they allow themselves for a moment to enjoy it they endeavour to impersonate, to identify with, the wicked, and to make their partners do likewise, in order to gain the momentary illusion of having escaped beyond the control of their own gentle and scrupulous natures into the inhuman world of pleasure.[7]

In *Time Regained*, he adds: 'there exists in the sadist—however kind he may be, in fact all the more the kinder he is—a thirst for evil which wicked men, doing what they do not because it is wicked but from other motives, are unable to assuage.'[8] Thus, as horror is the measure of love, so the thirst for evil is the measure of good. And no doubt in the depths of this quiet conscience a searing, manly pain persists, akin to despair, but in the abyss of evil into which he descended it is clear that, inescapably opening his eyes, he found himself worthy of being loved.

Loved by his mother and by those who, later, reading him, would guess what degree of horror he reached. And he was totally right in that. For few written works open up as much to their readers the inaccessible domain of the instant. The profound disturbance of mind we glimpse is merely the warning sign. And no doubt the machine might have been broken by it, but the opposite occurred: the gift made to us in an incomparable sacrifice is in no way the abandonment of reason; it is not illness, it is the cure, or at least the justification of the evil. The 'Search' conducted through vice—which had to be conducted through it insofar as concern for the morrow seemed contemptible—leads to the exact triumph of *Time Regained*. Nothing is further removed from pathology (for on this point there is agreement: reason is no longer in danger, no profanation is necessary to the intense sense of the present). And nothing is further from servile responses to the needs of the morrow either. It is curious that Denis Saurat should

---

7 Proust, *Remembrance of Things Past*, VOL. 1, p. 179.
8 Proust, *Remembrance of Things Past*, VOL. 3, p. 856.

draw a parallel between the flashes of insight of *Time Regained* and Platonic illumination: 'These intense moments of particular joy,' he writes (*Tendances*, p. 113), accompanied by intellectual illumination, either of a whole lost past or a great metaphysical intuition, are the *Ideas*.' But, outside of the notion of *sovereign good* and *ecstasy*, which Plato associated with the Idea (Plato was perhaps initiated into some experience akin to yoga), and the sense of *eternity*—in *Time Regained*—of the instant, these extremes of human possibility do not meet. Though it is true that Proust, in order to grasp the present, resorted—thus lending it eternal value—to the past, the operation takes place in the *sensible*, not the *intelligible* world. If we bring to mind the emotion which the sight of a historic city affords us, we can easily see that it is different from the sense we have of the modern city, in that this latter lies before us, broken down into the future possibilities its elements potentially have in store for us (offices, shops, itineraries . . .), whereas we see the medieval city as it might have been seen by someone, in his time, who had no purpose there and with time suspended for him. So that it is, above all, in memory—not unlike these moments that speak to us of the past, moments when its beauty is free of any useful meaning— that we live in present time. But, in this way, what memory extracts from the intelligible world is purely sensory experience, coming to life again without having to disrupt the machine.

Adamov

ARTHUR ADAMOV, *L'Aveu* [The confession] (Paris: Éditions du Sagittaire, 1946).

Arthur Adamov confesses to sickness, neurosis, vice. And perhaps no one ever went so far in terms of confessions, or at least never admitted having *abased* himself to such a degree. Adamov seems like someone who has come straight out of a dark imagination eager for a multi-coloured horror show, which would be mitigated only by the grotesque element, by something grandiloquent that wrings one's heart. Dostoyevsky—and perhaps also Ribera (in his weird figures made what they are by the majesty of rags and tatters)—have evoked the attraction of these viscid possibilities. The physical personage is himself menacing from the outset, clothed in an ugliness that smacks firmly of wretchedness. The sexual strangeness he confesses is of the kind usually met with a heavy silence. Adamov the masochist is in no way satisfied with the limited forms of his vice: the humiliation he craves is *infinite* humiliation.

He is in a squalid dive at the end of a blind alley in the Les Halles district of Paris. His entrance, the 'mere sight of him, had the knack of producing a general outburst of laughter'. He is taken for an invert and a hostess in an apron offers to make up his face. 'And all the men present stamp their feet with joy, burst out in such laughter as I'd never heard before. I let her do it to me, paralyzed by horror. The girl paints my face comically with rouge and black liner, as sarcastic remarks and jeers rain down all around.' He then asks the prostitute to take off her shoes and publicly kisses her bare feet. Then since, having paid for his drink, he hasn't the money for anything more, he begs her to hit him in the face. 'I didn't have to ask her twice,' he says.

The combination of this need for abasement and an emphatic idealism is painful to behold. It is more than a mistake to speak of the 'ancestral grandeur of the night of the flesh': it is laziness of mind. Strange as it may be, there is no nudity in this *confession*. The author is attached to too many ideal 'powers' and he expresses such contempt for the run-of-the-mill and the hideous materiality of this world—in short, he has such a passion for *escape*—that he seems to me rather to shy away from the resoluteness he calls for. Adamov is mystical, sentimental, eager for religiosity and human unity. He is not unaware of the painful quest pursued by others with a concern for rigour that he lacks. But mysticism and laziness of mind still open up many 'viscid possibilities'.

1947

The Friendship between Man and Beast

The animality of a barrack room; the boredom, laden with lamentable silliness, of offices; the artfully concealed self-satisfaction of human beings; the cowed, shameful element contained in the expression 'lapdog'; in a word, the *flight*, dispersed but general, into the merest semblances of escape—is this what all our enormous efforts have achieved? . . . We have bent the most intractable forces to our will; animals and bodies of water, plants and rocks have complied with our desires. But at the height of our power, we succumb to an undefined malaise and flee; the whole work of the nature we have at our disposal is lost in the affected crudeness of some, the boredom and playacting of others. What is the significance of these accumulated resources: these shops, these buildings, these utilities? We want to be protected not just from need but from all that disturbs, awakens or rouses; we want to avoid shocks which, suddenly revealing us to ourselves, would bring us up against the immensity of the universe. We have reduced nature to a thing that obeys our power, but we ourselves move at the pace of diminished things: we are like turkey-hens, sweetmeats, dusty old account books. We may snigger, swagger and feel superior to the common herd, but what we have have come to call noble is no less devious than the rest: if to be 'common' means to turn away from a possible way of being that is adopted by the nobility, nobles have shied away from the work performed by the lowly, and what they take for pride is merely the fear of getting their hands dirty. This is like a nightmare ballet: the hooligan and the venerable old lady are united in a common anxiety about *what is*.

Might this 'being'—or, better, this unknown—within us, which we prefer to squint at only furtively (as we might with the light of the sun), be horrible or embarrassing in itself? It is possible. The 'I am', the 'being' of the philosophers is the most neutral thing, the most lacking in meaning, having the innocent blankness of paper. And yet a slight shock turns it to frenzy: this 'being' that sees red, impervious to the clear, distinct calm of objects it knew how to name, and for which a sudden indifference raises the possibility of a torrent, an explosion, a crying out *that it is*, is *both* the energy that can discharge itself like lightning *and* the awareness of the lethal dangers ensuing from these discharges of energy. To *be*, in the strong sense, is not in fact to contemplate (passively), nor is it to act (if, by acting, we forego the possibility of free behaviour, keeping our eye, rather, on future outcomes), but it is precisely to *unleash oneself*. Thus we prefer, most of the time, to know nothing and to distance ourselves timidly from ourselves, as we would with a primed explosive charge. But, for the same reason, we are affected by the unleashing of forces that we see—an unleashing which is not ours but tells us that it could be.

*

The dumbfounded child who sees a runaway horse fly off like a raging storm across the cobblestones, white foam dribbling from its mouth and hooted at by a crowd of mothers, has had imprinted upon him an indelible image of how creatures might unleash themselves. That image clearly has about it little that is meaningful. The child cannot make it a part of the world of ordered action and efficiency that will be imposed on him. But ever after, dimly in his consciousness, the din of horses' hooves as it makes the ground shudder will summon up the dark possibilities of senselessness. These animal possibilities will neither attract favourable comment nor be condemned as dangerous: for the coruscating aspect of the unleashed beast lies beyond the limits of the human. This boundless discharge belongs, rather, to the sphere of dreams: it defines a *divine* possibility. In deepest antiquity, did not the gods pit their animal mystery against human measure? The essence of that divine possibility is *sacred*, terrible and elusive: it is based in a tragic wholeheartedness that provokes and leads to death and beyond. Only the majesty of a storm and the total frenzy of a horse have this power to take things to the limits of light and brilliance and boundless loss.

Runaway horses do not generally have this pronounced dignity in human life. The horse is usually reduced to the condition of a domestic servant harnessed to a cart . . . Whatever degraded state it has fallen into, man nonetheless retains a lingering regard for the horse, which is his *most noble* conquest. It is the least humiliated, most restive of the animals he has subjugated; even its master often lends it a part in his own glory. The Bible has God say, in His desire to show man—to show Job—the extent of His power: 'Did you give the horse its strength and courage. Did you clothe its neck with a floating mane? It leaps as lightly as the grasshopper and its snorting is the voice of terror . . . '[1] What assures the horse of a nobility that the burden of its servile condition can do nothing to diminish is this tremulous and, as it were, demented sensibility which, at the sight of a mere shadow, can turn to frenzy. To such an extent that it occupies pride of place in the human world. The taming of animals leads, overall, to their dejection. And wildness places them beyond our knowledge. The horse has the privilege of keeping alive, in the midst of human beings, an essence of animality— or, more precisely, an essence of the living being—which consists in being ungovernable. To the very extent that we have subjugated it, the truly domesticated animal has become virtually a thing and the wild animal is inhuman. The horse is itself degraded. It derives its dignity neither from a power it possesses nor, even less, from a moral value: it is on the bottom rung of the ladder. But even if it were harnessed, like men bound to their jobs, it can, out of foolishness, shaking off what holds it, break free of its chains. Its rebellion is then totally uncompromising: it isn't the product of some calculation of labour and reward (such errors can be rectified) but of a difference in nature between a cog and the machinery that governs it. Were this truth to have only mythic significance (similar to the truth of a work of art), a horse is fundamentally a dangerous charge of energy: it is capricious and ready at any moment to explode spectacularly. It is a beast of burden in one sense only. If man is a 'fallen god who remembers . . . ', the

---

1 This is my own rendering of Bataille's French. The *International Standard Version* of the Bible has the following translation: Do you instill the horse with strength? Do you clothe its neck with a mane? / Can you make him leap like the locust, and make the splendor of his snorting terrifying? (Job 39:19–20). [Trans.]

most ponderous horse has something of an unleashing of energies about it. You may calculate its working power and employ it: warlike impetuosity, the charge, and the sudden, total, unstoppable expenditure of energy are bound to it nonetheless—if not specifically to an individual horse, then at least to the species it represents. The horse doubtless succumbs beneath the weight of human labours, but in the subdued world of calculation and dejection it maintains the principle of being, which is nothing if it is not uncontrolled.

This image of being, envisaged as a flashing movement of force, not as a static screen, is perhaps paradoxical. It is paradoxical too to state that, if not the clear and distinct consciousness of objects, then the acute awareness of what is—of the game that beings play with the world—is linked to possibilities of unleashment. Nonetheless, these shocking truths are the foundation of the deep sense of the friendship between man and beast. Reserve, restraint and, ultimately, the escape into some futile private activity are failings that give human beings that shifty look, that feebleness of hands and teeth that announce a generalized abdication. The pacts struck between horse and man at least kept life in the grip of tensed explosive forces. Horse riding does not provide some virtue that would otherwise be inaccessible. But it is the case that, in becoming one with the animal that has such fearsome forms of release, even if he is not himself obliged to engage in some sudden discharge of energy, and even if he were, deep down, afraid of such a thing, the horseman remains open—endlessly open—to its possibility. We may even say that his horizon is that very openness and perhaps this is what gives cowboys and gauchos, not to mention Cossacks and the Camargue's *gardians*, their pre-eminence over pedestrian shepherds: but doesn't the eminence in this case belong to the horse and not the man?

The human attitude is at best very equivocal: it is always dominated by a concern for control. Calmness of mind, in which objects stand out as on a screen, beyond our grasp as it were, requires us not to give in to frenzy. If we give in, we lose the opportunity to act on things. And we are then no more than animals. But if we act, if in our now clear consciousness we reflect on these series of objects, whose interrelations order the intelligible world, we leave life suspended within ourselves. Then not really living or, at least only half-living, we accumulate the reserves that are useful for life, which is simply the expenditure of those reserves. Thus chlorosis, boredom, futility, lying and even an affected animality are present in the essential human attitude which keeps the human being, as far as is possible, from the possibilities open before him. This is why value, in human terms, always has something of crime about it. It is why remorse—*in both its senses*—is to man what air is to the bird. In these circumstances, morality is never a rule and can, in truth, only be an art: similarly, art can only be a morality, and the most demanding morality, if its aim is to open up some possibility of an unleashing of energies. But art being, in this way, the purest moral exigency is also the most deceptive: the possibility it opens up, it opens up only as 'image' for the 'reflection' of an audience. And there is no point protesting against this deception: if these men in suits and these women in their finery, shimmering with diamonds—avowed accomplices of the laws that stand out against our bouts of release—look on impassively at the performance of a tragedy, they are not the impediment to art but the pre-condition for it: calm spectatorship is nothing less than *clear consciousness* ultimately *reflecting the very being* which, for the sake of being clear, it had excluded. This is the realm of lies, its opposite being a desire for straightforwardness: but man is exactly that realm and to flee from it is yet another form of evasion: the hatred of art is most often the product of fatigue, and art has no worse enemies than crudity and mawkishness. Admittedly, wishing to respond to the exigency he felt, the poet has at least opened himself up to frenzy, but his frenzy, though not feigned, is addressed, from the outset, to unfrenzied minds; it calls, from the outset, for this calm consciousness, its opposite, which would not exist if frenzy had not fled away. Hence, despite everything, the remorse and the comic character of 'Pegasus', who is not the *real* horse and whose unfettered bursts of unleashed energy are directed against nothing. Clearly *Dada* played on the harmony between this remorse and itself, but was *Dada* actually Dada? Or was it just a play acting of Dada? Man's extreme opposite is no more accessible to him than the nudity of animals.

Giraud – Pastoureau – Benda – Du Moulin de Laplante – Govy

Victor Giraud, *La Critique littéraire. Le problème. Les théories. Les méthodes, L'histoire littéraire* (Paris: Aubier [Éditions Montaigne], 1946), in 16°, 208 pp.

Looking back over the experience a long career has brought him, M. Victor Giraud seeks to lay out the principles that governed his activity as a critic for almost a century. To define these principles better, he has tried to situate them historically. It is to this end that he sketches out a history of 'high criticism'—at least in France, and at least of what *he* calls by that name.

It is the genesis of literary works that seems to M. Victor Giraud to be the fundamental object of criticism. 'The essential question to resolve', he tells us, 'is, ultimately, always the same. Given the individual Pierre Corneille and the individual Blaise Pascal, why was the one led to conceive and write *Le Cid* and, the other, *Les Pensées?*' Sainte-Beuve, Taine and Brunetière approached this problem with various different methods. 'Sainte-Beuve was too easily persuaded, by the words and flattery of his young disciples, the Taines, Renans, Scherers and Émile Deschanels, that he was working seriously in his laboratory on the natural history of minds . . . ' In reality, it was only his successors who would strive to lend their analyses an objectivity and methodical, dogmatic tone that matched that formula. Sainte-Beuve, with whom M. Giraud claims kinship, was more spontaneous, instinctively following an 'inner principle' which he became aware of only late in life. By contrast, it was entirely systematically that Taine, a Hegelian, sought to explain works by *race, milieu* and *moment*. His work undoubtedly came out of Sainte-Beuve's, but he was, for all that, of a more philosophical than critical cast of mind. Brunetière, more 'scientific', compared literary genres to the 'species' of natural history that are born, evolve and decline. Faguet was more dilettantish and Lanson regarded literary history as a component of the history of civilization. For his part, M. Victor Giraud sees the examination of deep moral crises as the key to an explanation of genius.

All this is honest, clearly expressed and, as we can see, very limited. By way of example, the author provides us with a fair number of analyses of crises affecting well-known writers, from Calvin to Chateaubriand, and from Lammenais to Taine and Brunetière themselves.

There is, it seems to me, in the modesty of his remarks a sort of unconscious temerity that deserves to be brought out. Criticism is nothing (a mere exercise in literary history or a messy dialogue with the author) if it is not the expression of a philosophy (one ought even to say, more generally, of a religion or system of life). To wish, out of modesty, to regard it as a limited field of the mind's activity leads to reducing literary works to dimensions which their nature undoubtedly exceeds. And if it is true that a philosophy would remedy this, it would do so only on condition that it appeared from the outset as contesting the possibilities of criticism. One may possibly regard such a precondition as a merely temperamental matter, quite alien to the reality of criticism, but that is not the case at all. *In fact*, the formula I present corresponds to the method of Maurice Blanchot. Without this fundamental contestation, one might believe one is speaking of poetry (poetry in literature is the essential, it is *what touches* the reader), but in fact one is turning away from it.

But we are far from that academic tradition of which M. Giraud has today published an excellent overview. Far also from the properly literary tradition.

On this basis, the play of language, understood in the sense of an opening on to the whole of the possible, is *associated* by criticism with the effort of discursive thought. To put it in exact terms, criticism describes the limits of that effort (which is its own), positions itself on those limits and defines itself as the extreme possibility of philosophy. (In a sense, this method corresponds rigorously to concerns formulated by Surrealism.)

HENRI PASTOUREAU, *La Blessure de l'homme* [Man's wound] (Paris: Robert Laffont, 1946), in 16°, 179 pp.

A young Surrealist writer, held prisoner of war in Germany, could form no better intention than to depict 'the irremediable wretchedness of the human condition'.

With that aim in mind, the right approach seemed to be one of self-effacement. He confined himself to letting Pascal and Baudelaire speak, wishing 'neither to set them against each other, nor even to comment on their words'. He sets out their arguments, quotes them and, ultimately, remains silent. We know nothing of his thoughts, except for the little he tells us of them in a two-page 'foreword'. There he subscribes to a conception that excludes 'any perfectibility of man or the world'. As he sees it, 'Our sins do not imply any remission. Our misfortunes do not imply any pity. Our woundedness does not imply any healing. Our captivity does not imply any escape. Our revolt does not imply any revolution.'

This would seem to turn its back on the principles of Surrealism. Nevertheless, in the publisher's blurb, the author has allowed the following sentence to stand: 'At the end of this book, a question is raised, which Henri Pastoureau refrains from answering. But the answer will radiate out tomorrow around that point at which contrary solutions are no longer perceived as contradictory!' This is an allusion to the key passage in the *Second Manifesto*, in which André Breton declares:

> There is every reason to believe that there exists a certain point in the mind from which life and death, the real and the imaginary, the past and the future, the communicable and the incommunicable, the high and the low, are not perceived as contradictions. One would search in vain for any other motive for Surrealist activity than the hope of determining this point.[1]

Might we not be more precise and say: *The determination of this point requires that I grasp as an inescapable truth these words: 'our woundedness implies no healing' (I am effectively, from this very moment, dying . . .); and that, grasping it, I take from it just as much pleasure as impatience. In other words, how, if I knew there was no healing to my woundedness, would I*

---

1 This is my translation. A version of this passage can also be found in André Breton, 'What is Surrealism?' in Franklin Rosemont (ed.), *What is Surrealism? Selected Writings* (New York: Monad, 1978), p. 129. [Trans.]

perceive the truth that [René] Char's phrase so sternly expresses: 'If we dwell in a lightning flash, it is the heart of the eternal'?

That principle being stated, what engages me most in Pastoureau's understated work, is that this *extremist* Surrealism, breaking with a tradition of the movement, does not hesitate to cite in its cause the experience of a religious believer (Breton himself did pay attention at times to Christians— such as Raymond Lulle—though for some reason external to Christianity). It is, in fact, dangerous, from the standpoint of Surrealism, to view experience exclusively the way that writers and poets have done—and to neglect the extreme rigour and rages of those who attempted to live out the human adventure to the end in Christian fashion. On the one hand, the unfettered violence of poets is the only response to present excitation, but missing is a resolve that would exhaust the whole of the possible. As it seems to me, the foremost enemy of Christianity Nietzsche had it better when he wrote: 'We wish to be the heirs to Christian meditation and penetration . . . surpassing the whole of Christianity by means of a *hyperchristianity*, and not merely contenting ourselves with throwing it off.'[2] I remember Breton many years ago reading me a letter from Dali—a man whose innate buffoonery gave him considerable license—that began with more or less these words: 'It is time we Surrealists thought about becoming parish priests . . . ' And it sometimes seems to me that poets would be the better for being, if not priests, then theologians or, better, *a-theologians*, habitués of an illusionist abyss. It is odd that human beings give so little thought to producing a compendium of their remotest *knowledge* (or do it so badly). And, to be sure, some stray impulses in this direction haven't produced very encouraging results, but it comes as no surprise to see a man who does not resile from the Surrealist tradition eventually—and perhaps seriously—exclaim: 'Today, after the experience of the last twenty years, it would take a Radical-Socialist[3] stupidity to refuse to make room for a Pascal or a Rimbaud—and, despite everything, for Kierkegaard, Baudelaire, Nietzsche, Dostoyevsky or Chestov . . . ' (Jean Maquet, in *Troisième convoi*, no. 1).

---

2 This is a posthumous fragment from Nietzsche, dated 1885–86. [Trans.]

3 The French 'Radical-Socialists' were a Centrist party, led during the Third Republic by such prominent political figures as Édouard Herriot and Édouard Daladier. By 1945, when Maquet was writing, the party had been largely discredited for its granting of emergency powers to Pétain, not to mention its repeal of the legislation that introduced the 40-hour working week. [Trans.]

JULIEN BENDA, *Exercice d'un enterré vif* (*juin 1940 – août 1944*) [Exercise of a man buried alive (June 1940 – August 1944)] (Paris: Gallimard, 1946), in 16°, 179 pp.

'Since 1913', writes Jean Wahl, 'this has been a test I have always applied: whoever regards Benda as a philosopher or a thinker, is not a philosopher or a thinker . . . ' *Exercice d'un enterré vif* maintains what might even be called a naïve—certainly, a resolute—distance from the principle of philosophical reflection. 'Where the problems that seem to me essentially insoluble are concerned,' M. Benda tells us, 'I label them "mysterious" and have nothing more to do with them.' But, despite not being philosophical, the thinking pursued in *Exercice* is at least very captivating. First of all, one has to give the author his due: at the age of 73 and forced to flee racist persecution, he has, in the lonely setting of a small town, written a book underpinned by an unfailing liveliness of spirit. No sign of depression here . . . M. Benda runs a rule over himself and attentively studies 'the nature of his mind'. He reveals its limits honestly. Those limits are rigid: the mind depicted for us is committed to the intelligible and regards the sensible with suspicion. No one is less religious than this 'clerk'.[4] His only interest is in ideas, from which he demands clarity and precision. I shall fulfil M. Benda's innermost desire here by saying that, when it comes to the ideas that he likes, they are '*idées fixes*'. In *Exercice*, he gives his 'metaphysics' a name: 'fixism'. His writings are brimming with a taste for equations, the desire to substitute for the sensible world an immutable series of rational operations of equivalence. His love of justice is itself subordinated to this fundamental inclination: he hates any relation 'that does not include equality between its terms, for example between the quantity of energy supplied to a system and that yielded by its transformation, or between the worker's labour and the wage he is paid for it' (p. 116). He artlessly admits that 'he does not much care' about the fate of human beings: 'I shall have concerned myself with humanity to the extent that it offends against my metaphysics or does not,'

---

4 The allusion is to Benda's best-known work *La Trahison des clercs*, which was translated into (US) English by Richard Aldington as *The Treason of the Intellectuals* and published in Britain as *The Great Betrayal*. Despite this, the phrase 'the treason of the clerks' is widely used and I have assumed it to be widely understood in this special sense. [Trans.]

he says, 'and very little in order to make it happy' (p. 114). He openly states that he has no sympathy for progress, which puts an end to the principle of equality. In its extreme form, progress culminates, 'in flashes', in 'the hatred of all that exists' (p. 117). As a matter of fact, he remarks, 'all existence is bound up with the idea of a thing that was granted being, among an infinity of others that were not but had just as much of a right to it. That is to say, there is ultimately no true justice except in nothingness' (p. 117). M. Benda isn't, in fact, in any way a monster, but, like most human beings, having noticed that thinking which did not in some way limit itself led the mind nowhere and left it very unsettled, he set limits on himself. But he became, in this operation, a less comical individual than most, insofar as, though mutilating himself, he did so straightforwardly. He is not a devious person and says everything quite artlessly. This is indefensible and he flounders around in the indefensible, unabashed and humourless. And so we are able to get a grasp—and this is quite captivating—of an essential mental failing which others conceal or correct.

One of the most attractive aspects of his effrontery here shows up in a curious passage of praise for animals. He admits to feeling at one with a poem in which Whitman says of animals: 'Not one is dissatisfied . . . Not one is . . . unhappy over the whole earth.'[5] We should, nevertheless, add: 'Not one has an *idée fixe*'. Apart from this tiny flaw, we might see M. Julien Benda as man raised to the satisfied perfection of the beasts.

But no. We are, on reflection, speaking too soon.

There is another aspect by which M. Benda's self-satisfaction is far removed from animal quietude. The fact is that this contentment derives from *contempt* for his fellow human beings. And it is difficult to forget that that word recurs in his writings at every turn. Does he not even go so far as to regard Pascal or Nietzsche (p. 131) as, in some way, worthy of his scorn?

M. Benda thinks our world is a world of intellectual decay. He isn't necessarily wrong. But we have to marvel at the fact that, in this decline of reason, its pure principle should be represented by so unreasonable a man.

---

5 The translation Benda is working with here renders these lines into French as 'Pas un seul n'est mécontent, . . . pas un seul n'étale son infortune sur toute la surface de la terre.' [Trans.]

PIERRE DU MOULIN DE LAPLANTE, *Histoire générale synchronique. I. Des origines à l'Hégire* [General synchronic history I: From the origins to the Hegira], La Suite des temps, VOL. 15 (Paris: Gallimard, 1946), in 8°, 325 pp.

For a long time, societies lived without leaving deliberate traces of their activity. Then a concern arose to entrust to stone, to memories and, finally, to books, the events that deserved to be known to those who came after. For centuries documents of all kinds accumulated, which modern scholarship set about working up. Humanity is still feverishly discovering history: working with rare historical accounts, it has been possible, through rigorous methods, to reconstruct the past, though it must be said that this cannot go on forever. Historical research is still possible, but it will not greatly expand its scope. It is the gazes of present-day man which, redirected towards the past, have penetrated its distant regions: those who come after us will be able to rectify, deepen, and even in some cases see a little further. But in the same way as America was discovered definitively in the sixteenth century, a sophisticated knowledge of the past will remain something our age has achieved.

This enhancement of our knowledge is, in fact, so recent that the history taught thirty years ago gave a view of the human past that was appreciably different from that of current scholarship. In the past, it was the most accessible facts that received the attention. It was uncommon in those days to go beyond the classical fields. The history of China or of India tempted a small number of minds, but these were objects of study well separated off from the mainstream. Generally speaking, no one as yet aspired to form a single overall view of the network of interdependent movements that stamped its order on global civilization.

Now, recent research has produced results of appreciable significance in many intermediate fields. In particular, the extension of Hellenic influence through Alexander's conquests is better known than it once was. We know that Buddhism spread the forms of Greek art at least as far as China. The little we have learnt of hybrid regions, such as that of the Kushans, who at the dawn of the Christian era founded a semi-barbarian empire in the north of India, where coins were stamped with the figures of

Buddha (with the legend, in Greek characters, *Boddo*), Shiva and the Greek gods, shows tangibly how, in every age, there could be ties uniting all huiman beings to each other. 'A gong cannot be struck at one end of the world,' writes M. Du Moulin de Laplante, 'without making itself heard at the other.' And without any doubt, after the partial—temporally extensive but spatially limited—visions of traditional history, the elaboration of a synchronic history of the world, of a vision of the interrelatedness of peoples, has become the necessary complement to our knowledge of the past.

The work whose first volume M. Du Moulin de Laplante has published today (which runs from the origins to the Hegira) has attempted to meet this need. It is, in fact, a good, handy summary of the whole of current historical knowledge (some of it questionable, but worthy for all that of being noted). The emphasis is on the interrelatedness of peoples and, of course, what we know of that is not very extensive, but the author has constantly taken care to determine the significance of the facts from the standpoint of world development as a whole. This is not sufficient to eliminate a certain equivocal character from the history, dealing, as it does, with both the *explanation* and the bare *enumeration* of facts. But that history is placed on its proper terrain: it describes the development of the human species (not of a people or a limited group of peoples), the paths and direction of civilization in general (and not of *a* civilization).

We cannot criticize the author for not having derived from his chosen approach more than is *prima facie* possible. As it happens, to go further would exceed the mere methodical elaboration of the facts. We feel compelled to show, however, that this approach, of itself, commits us to going further. M. du Moulin de Laplante is particularly eager to stress interrelations properly so-called. (He is even concerned predominantly with showing the decisive value of the spread of Hellenism: the cover of his book is illustrated with a Greek-style head of the Buddha and the content reflects the intention to which that image points). Nonetheless, we may justifiably take the view that correspondences perceptible between independent fields are just as interesting as the simple spread of an idea or a myth, a technique or a form. M. Du Moulin de Laplante is constantly pointing out these latter.

But one cannot deny the importance, among other things, of an evolution-ary parallelism between the Roman Empire and China. The oldest and most striking of these correspondences is the emergence, at more or less the same time, of minds that were to have a centuries-long influence on the evolution of humanity: the prophets of Israel, Socrates, Zoroaster, Buddha, Lao-Tze and Confucius. We may justifiably suppose that these profound examin-ations of human nature are linked, in different places, to the same sort of impoverishment and to the extremely cruel living conditions of a class of the population (to the birth of a class that is both free and wretched). Doesn't the spread, also at one and the same time, of Buddhism through the Chinese empire and Christianity through the Roman, and the relatively similar reaction of the emperors in both cases correspond to inevitable phases and necessities of political development that are themselves necess-ary? But these questions are a clear indication that, though scholarship has lifted the mass of accessible facts out of the darkness of the past, it is far from having extracted from them the knowledge of the sociological laws, without which that mass would tell us nothing. Now, it may be the case that this second task exceeds our capacities; at all events, we cannot criticize the author for not having done what did not form part of his initial intention, the plan he followed confining itself to stressing the need for—and the absence of—such a thing.

We shall, however, note one failing of the *Histoire générale synchronique*. In principle, the author confines his interest to strictly historical facts: the birth, development and decline of powers and their rivalries. Though he briefly describes the external markers of civilization—commerce, arts and sciences—he is niggardly with details on the organization of work—modes of production—and on technical development (ultimately, only naval build-ing holds his attention). This is a regrettable lacuna in an admittedly well-structured brief history of the world, which, precisely by dint of its principles, will add numerous essential facts to the fund of knowledge of the majority of its readers.

GEORGES GOVY, *Sang russe* [Russian blood], Collections 'Esprit': La condition humaine (Paris: Éditions du Seuil, 1946), in 16°, 238 pp.

Recounting the lives of individuals caught up in the storm, the author depicts the last phase of the revolutionary war in Russia (the moment when the defeated Wrangel army had to withdraw from Crimea). The book consists of short stories plainly told, conveying, tensely and comprehensively, a sense of an inhuman necessity that both chills and stiffens like a cold wind; the bedrock—the basis of the reality—is laid bare; and one must look without pity, without political passion—and without allowing the later, known outcome of events, to suppress the immediate tangible significance of the killings—on executions, death and helpless anguish. To express, with the requisite simplicity what has so often been the course of human life throughout the ages calls for a cruel sureness of touch, which Georges Govy clearly possesses. But the mixture of history and fiction is not without its dangers. Ordinarily, for the novelist, fiction is the way of attaining and expanding *the possible*. He may also disregard the virtue of invention and use it merely as a stopgap solution, the better to grasp—and mark the bounds of—*the real*. But at that point, with the author wishing to duplicate the work of the historian, the freedom of fiction is a sort of impediment to him. This is because it gives rise to a doubt: if Georges Govy attributes what is quite commonly known as 'the Slavic soul' to the officers of the White army, how are we to know whether he is reflecting the reality of the event or yielding to literary tradition? It must, nonetheless, be said that the value of *Sang russe* lies in the sense of photographic truth which the author's toughness of mind and talent most often impress upon us.

On the Relationship between the Divine and Evil

SIMONE PÈTREMENT, *Le Dualisme dans l'histoire de la philosophie et des religions* [Dualism in the history of philosophy and religion], La Montagne Sainte-Geneviève (Paris: Gallimard, 1946), in 16°, 132 pp.

At a deep level, morality continues to be beset by uncertainty and yet we cannot deny the importance of a decisive move that pits Good against Evil and faces human beings with a choice between the two. We may go further and define a possible state that lies 'beyond Good and Evil', yet we cannot for a moment forget that humanity still marks out the dividing line for us. Even the will to pass beyond is a continuation, if not of the desire to find the Good, then at least of a concern for moral truth, which is, within us, an unassuaged passion *par excellence*. In every life there is something constantly at stake which is not life (the life that death threatens and pain lays low), and which isn't happiness either, but the possession of a grace, without which neither life nor happiness *are of any worth*. It is in this way that human thinking is devoted, impersonally, to seeking out the true and that pursuit becomes, at one point, if not solemn, then at least more passionate: if it is about deciding—above and beyond what *is*—what man *wishes* to be.

Human beings in the world are faced with a puzzle to solve, and if other concerns seem base by comparison, that is because the quest is not limited to the past, but might be said to relate mainly to the future. For we are not simply something *given* (consequently, the world itself is not something given) and the desire to solve the puzzle is not so much a desire to *know* as a desire to *do*: our actions or our ways of being—the ways by which make the possible available to us—may even be said to be the least deranged answers to the questioning that gnaws away at us. (And if it is the case that a natural fatigue drives humanity towards escape and humanity's commonest response is to forget, there is no forgetting or escape more frivolous than a quest that distances us from all action—the passionless, desireless, unhurried quest of science.) In other words, morality, which at one and the same time illuminates the origin and the end—which decides, as metaphysics or science do not—is the only approach that answers directly, that meets head-on the silence in which we shall die. But would morality in these conditions be moral if it did not open up within itself, without limitations, all the possibilities of the quest?

Indeed, morality, the only out-and-out way of questioning, cannot be separated from the determined will to know what *is* when the world *is* and gives birth to us. But it cannot be separated, either, from a doubt about the value of acts: it is the questioning of the possible, not the acceptance of rules that would have existed even if nothing had ever been questioned. Even if we are simply accepting rules, the value of an act still derives from the alternative, but questioning about it cannot be limited in any way. I cannot accomplish any act that assumes value for me without having asked myself the *question* of value in respect of it, and the question of what that value is grounded in. Morality is, in its essence, a questioning about morality; and the decisive move in human life is constantly to use all available sources of enlightenment to seek out the origin of the opposition between Good and Evil.

This is what makes Simone Pètrement's[1] little book on the history of dualism worth reading, a book which, by the firmness of its intent and the tautness of its approach, goes beyond the bounds of scholarly research. What is striking in these few pages is the rightness of tone which, with an unyielding simplicity, matches up to the seriousness and 'divine' nature of the subject. If thought situates its limited objects in relation to others which it cannot limit, then an awareness of what lies 'beyond' the graspable content of its statements is unflaggingly demanded. But the constancy of that awareness itself involves calm, patience and sureness of touch. These are the rare virtues that have enabled Simone Pètrement to reduce the various forms of religious and philosophical dualism to the decisive moment in which thought posits the transcendence of the divine. There is, in effect, an instant at which a leap is made, when the mind, pushing beyond the limits of what

---

1 I have retained the spelling of the original article, though it would seem that Pétrement, with an acute accent, is, in fact, the correct form. [Trans.]

is given to the senses, accedes to the knowledge of a 'separate truth' that is no longer subject to the errors of appearance, and is divine and transcendent. Dualism 'at its highest level' is the expression of this instant: it is at that point the 'description of strange transitions, of total transformations, of sudden illuminations, of flights so profound that they may be termed ecstasies'.

What the author is writing of with such ardent commitment is Platonic dualism, which she is not wrong to locate at the origin of philosophy and morality (of philosophy which is necessarily morality, of morality which is necessarily philosophy). It is the separation of the sensible world and the intelligible sphere that founds Christianity and Western thought. That separation is not in itself the positing of Good and Evil: the world of sense perception, which is objectively matter and subjectively ignorance, is not the *principle* of evil. What Simone Pètrement formulates with regard to the Manichaeans is also true of Plato, for whom Good and Evil 'are more the outcome of the order or disorder that reigns between the two principles than produced specifically by the one or the other' (p. 104). For 'evil is not the fact that there are passions, but that those passions enslave reason and make it work for them. Evil is when reason thinks according to the passions and not on its own terms, and good is the deliverance of reason, of enlightenment, the re-establishment of an order in which the knowing dominates the unknowing' (p. 105).

This clear posing of an *external* dualism (in which one of the two principles lies outside the world) against an *internal* dualism (in which the two principles, good and evil, are both in the world) enables Simone Pètrement to reduce the former to the latter. This is because, if one:

begins by positing the dualism of Good and Evil, it is impossible to understand why this dualism is always associated with that of transcendence, of mind and matter, of thought and ignorance. On the other hand, if one begins with the notion of transcendence, it is easy to deduce from it the dualism of opposites and of the principles of good and evil. The transcendent signifies the *distinct*, the *separate*. There are, then, two orders, and, following on the heels of that, two substances within us, for we are linked to these two orders and the more distinct they are, the more what is within us that corresponds to the one or the other must be distinct. And, consequently, there are two principles within the sensible world, for we are in the sensible world. The dualism of the invisible and the visible, of the true and sensible, of the divine and the human, of the eternal and the temporal, of the other world and this world, leads to the dualism of soul and body, of mind and matter: and this latter to bringing into the world a principle of knowledge and a principle of ignorance, which may be termed Light and Darkness. It is easy to understand how, after explaining Evil by the mixing and jumbling of these two principles and Good by order, one can gradually slide from this theory to the simpler one that sees Good as the product of light alone and Evil as the product of darkness. (pp. 105–6)

In this way, we can see possible 'stages' of dualism, moving towards a more easily graspable form, but deriving in the beginning from the positing of a transcendence:

The Mazdeans' *world of the mind*, the Albigensians' *invisible world*, the Platonists' *realm of Ideas*, the idea of the *perfect* that derives from the perfect (that is to say, that is not explained by anything else) in Descartes, the *noumenon*, the world of *freedom*, the *fact* of practical reason (named fact in this way because it is not explained by anything else) in Kant, *grace*, that is to say inexplicable deliverance for the Augustinians [. . .] (p. 109)

But the positing of a 'transcendental dualism' not only contains the possibility of a more accessible morality: 'It is when dualism has become the clear notion of two principles, of the same nature even though opposed, each acting within a single whole, that the opposition is closest to being *overcome*. For opposites are correlative and cannot be conceived the one without the other' (pp. 109–10). Thus Plato, having himself in his late thinking posited two principles, this second Platonic dualism (the one that Aristotle ascribed to him, that Aristotle described) 'made Aristotle necessary'. That which actually constitutes the 'original dualism', which is 'rupture, absence of connection, the incomprehensibility and impossibility of passage between two spheres' (p. 111) being, by its essence, perturbation, allows the mind no possible rest: doctrine either emerges out of a sudden awakening or declines. Derived dualism (the dualism internal to the world of principles) facilitates a proliferation of crude myths and superstitions or, on another level, summons a reduction to the unity of monism. The natural movement of a thought that is no longer in a state of inspired awakening leads it on each occasion to follow the slope that runs from the original Platonism to Aristotelianism. Spinoza and Leibniz after Descartes; Fichte, Schelling and Hegel after Kant; like Aristotle after Plato all establish a correlation between opposing principles, reject the scandalousness of an absolute separation, the subjective, strained, sceptical position of dualist philosophy, mainly oriented, as it is, towards total conversion, reversal and salvation. If this were how it is, there would be no 'essential difference between the various religions (the great religions) nor between the various philosophical schools': the difference would be 'within these religions and these schools, between the successive stages of an evolution that is always, in broad outline, the same.' The difference would be 'between an eternal Platonism and an eternal Aristotelianism', so that there would be 'barely any progress (or progress only in the detail of knowledge and technique, but not in general or fundamental conceptions)'; there would be, 'rather, recognitions, made necessary by this continual fall from the paradoxical living Platonism, "improbable but true", into a doctrine that is apparently more reasonable but close to slumber' (pp. 120–21).

The circumspection—the timidity, I shall call it—of this little book is deceptive: it conceals a rare tough-mindedness (and perhaps a foundation of timidity, silence and reserve may even be said to be the precondition for tough-mindedness). Simone Pètrement's thought is not a system—in that respect it is very faithfully, and firmly, Platonic—but it meets the first requirement of thought which is nothing if it is not, first, consciousness of its errant, uncertain and disappointing nature (a consciousness that follows from the abyss that the history of philosophy opens up for the philosopher); if it is not an awakening, in the strong sense, to the whole possibility of thinking, which remains accessible in all directions. It seems to me also that the point upon which attention fully *awakens* here is the one that merits this excessive tension, which baulks at any possibility of reduction. But would awakening *be* awakening if those awakened found themselves at some point *satisfied* with what they discovered? If they did not push yet further, and unconditionally, the *questioning* in which that awakening consists? I believe it is necessary here to open our eyes wider.

I simply wish to give a rapid glimpse now of the conceivable perspectives that lie beyond the position defined by Simone Pètrement, which is essentially that of the transcendence of the divine. To that end I shall draw, as she herself did, on a detour through historical analysis (though the meaning of the forms we are considering is given *to us from within*): this method has the advantage of being clear, but, since I wish to be brief, I have to say that I shall not, *at each stage*, point out, as Simone Pètrement does, the need for *awakening*, without which the following analysis would be a dead letter. I shall even put matters in a quite rough and ready way.

From an external standpoint, I shall demonstrate the weakness of this little book on dualism by showing that, while being historical, it only partly considers the subject historically. The author deals cursorily with the religions that have no morality, the so-called 'primitive' religions. And that means neglecting, no doubt rightly, elements of dualism (such as the Greeks' chthonian/Olympian pairing and the *yin* and *yang* of the Chinese) which appear in them and whose meaning is wholly unrelated to the opposition between the transcendent and the this-worldly. But is it the same with a more general dualism that no religion seems to escape, in which the *profane* stands opposed to the *sacred*? That may be doubted. Pètrement writes of the 'transcendence of the divine', but the *divine* is the same thing as the *sacred*. I can see immediately what perhaps stayed her hand here: the *sacred* of simple forms of worship cannot be related in any way to transcendence; it has nothing to do with the intelligible sphere. When applied to historical forms, 'awakened attention' runs up here against this fundamental paradox: *if the divine is considered independently of its intellectual forms, it is not transcendent but sensible and, in the most undeniable way, immanent; transcendence by contrast (the intelligible sphere) is given in the profane world; in its classical form, which Pètrement's essay brings out clearly, religious dualism is therefore the inversion of its primitive form.*

The *sacred* is indeed, as Rudolf Otto has it, from the outset *wholly other* (which made possible a later identification with the transcendence of the supra-sensible). But it is essentially *communion, communication* of unfettered, dangerous, *contagious* forces from which the world of life based in useful, reasonable operations has to be protected. It is insofar as we are normally steeped in this world of operations that a sacred element is something *wholly other* for us. So true is this that *life* itself is *sacred* insofar as it is irreducible to the *things* of the *profane* world. Not life reduced to effective activity, enslaved to results, but the play of life and its unleashing in the very moment, having meaning only in respect to itself—thus no longer having meaning, at the height of *awakening*.

The *profane*, by contrast, is the world of *reason*, of *identity*, of *things*, of *duration*, of calculation. Each *thing* in that world receives meaning from its lasting relation to another: such is the *intelligible* world, in which *sensible* elements are reduced to operational signs and have value only with regard to subsequent possibilities.

These categories are so clear and well defined that it is difficult to escape them: any objection is attributable to the traditional confusions, derived from the reversal that made the divine (the sacred) the transcendent and the profane the immanent. Nor will we have any great objection to a simplified representation that pinpoints work (the use of tools) as the decisive step that turned the animal into a human being. The human situation is entirely given in the operation that ranges the calculation of future effects against immediate release. But, in these conditions, release (*present* life) remained at one and the same time a constant danger and an ultimate end—which is what the *sacred* is.

The reversal itself is pre-given in this initial position. As a creative determination asserted itself, the profane side of man tended to win out, if not by the value it assumed, then by the place it occupied. Multiple possibilities arose out of the fact that the divine transcended a profane to which, insofar as human beings treated themselves as things, they became immanent. At that moment, primitive dualism ceased, if we may put it this way, to be simple: it broke down and was recomposed: *a* broke down into *a'* and *a"*; *b* into *b'* and *b"* and a complex opposition ranged *a'b'* against *a"b"*. This schema seems crude. Yet the *sacred* was divided, nonetheless, into a transcendent *sacred*, heavenly and pure, and a diabolical *sacred*, earthly and impure; in the same movement, the profane world divided into *idea* (into *reason*) and *matter*; the rational idea became strongly bound to the heavenly transcendence of the sacred, and diabolical impurity to matter.

The division of the sacred world into two opposing parts (probably the oldest division, though no matter) has not been known long. It appears in *The Religion of the Semites* by Robertson Smith[2] and Durkheim formulated it clearly: [T]he whole religious life gravitates about two contrary poles between which there is the same opposition as between the pure and the impure, the holy and the sacrilegious, the divine and the diabolic.[3] And, further on, he adds: 'The pure and the impure are not two separate classes, but two varieties of the same class, which includes all sacred things.[4] Durkheim made little of this internal duality of the sacred. It is not a part of his theory: he confined himself to taking up Smith's findings and formulating them elegantly. Nothing has come along since to invalidate these principles, which resolve many difficulties. The importance of this position in the debate on the dualism of transcendence and the world is well underlined by a young disciple of Durkheim's, who died before he could advance further with a study that has remained famous for other reasons, in which he writes also that there is an 'affinity of nature and almost an equivalence between the profane and the impure'.[5] This is true insofar as the slide from the impure *sacred* to the profane (towards matter) cannot be avoided, but that truth is the expression of a 'stage' *beyond* primitive dualism: in their succession, the historical data—whether they precede or follow intimate experience—do not accord it the fundamental value. By degrees, Simone Pètrement's book reaches back, all in all, from Aristotelian monism, which is already soporific, to Platonic dualism, which has the sense of awakening about it. But can we not go back beyond that? It may be that full awakening obliges us to aim further than divine transcendence: we

---

2 W. Robertson Smith, *Lectures on the Religion of the Semites. First Series: The Fundamental Institutions* (Edinburgh: Black, 1889).

3 Émile Durkheim, *The Elementary Forms of the Religious Life* (Joseph Ward Swain trans.) (Mineola, NY: Dover Publishers, 2008), p. 410; translation modified.

4 Durkheim, *The Elementary Forms*, p. 411.

5 Robert Herz, 'La Prééminence de la main droite. Étude sur la polarité religieuse', *Revue philosophique* 1 (1909): 559.

would then get back to the authentic vision in which, awakened at last to fever pitch, we would know, instead of the idea, which is meaning, the instant that snatches away meaning. But at that point, precisely, thought runs up against its sternest test.

If awakening takes us back to the point where the collapse began, if we already regard ideas as a lesser form of consciousness, *since full awakening would be consciousness of the instant*, it is animality, the precursor to unhappy tool-based life, that would be the perfect opposite of sleep!

We cannot deny an inclination towards sleep, but it is far from certain that, in wanting to climb back up the path we have come down in the guise of an awakening, we are doing anything other than falling further asleep. Admittedly, awakening consists essentially in the desire to be awake. But if it takes us backwards—and if it is strained—we soon know that it calls for our passing beyond it. Awakening cannot consign us endlessly to the moment before we fell asleep: it opens our eyes on to a no man's land 'in front of' us. Nothing is worked out, all is bare and stark, and we are driven onward. At that point Plato is no more of a guide than a wolf. We are, admittedly, no longer beasts: we are still moved by the charm of the dialogues, but we find only a compromise in them and, if that charm awakens us to an infinite degree, it does so only because we find no assurance there, but rather a cause for humiliation. It is beyond Platonic morality that a heightened exigency carries us today. That exigency can, no doubt, be formulated and, in its turn, it overturns an established order. What Plato regarded as evil, as we saw, was the subordination of reason to the unleashing [*déchaînement*] of the passions. But in reason (a necessary obstacle to release [*déchaînement*], without which the instant would be immediate and animalistic within us, instead of being, in a human way, elusive ecstasy) we see something other than a sovereign principle. We see, by contrast, in the truth of the instant—in a gleam that dazzles without enlightening—the inaccessible end-goal that gave moral questing the power to *awaken* the whole being. For us, reason is the most well established of things, but when reduced to the operations that lay the object before us— and, after it, the subject—in the succession of time, it lacks the lustre in which we see the end-goal of the moral exigency. And it may be that no one has ever been more faithful to reason than we have, but that is precisely because it has ceased to seem divine to us. Thus, we accept the principles of reason as a rule of action, but no longer accept that reason should *subordinate the passions to itself*; it is even in the enslavement of the passions to reason—when reason unleashes blind passions to serve its ends—that we see evil,[6] which begins if what is irreducible within us is finally suppressed. Plato could hold passion under the sway of intelligence insofar as it was reason, not passion, that seemed divine in his eyes. For us, it is passion that is divine, matter that is rational. And if it is true, as I believe, that the slippage in which nascent reason merged with the elusive horror of the sacred was the crucial moment of awakening for human beings, uniting all that was possible in a single burst, the harsher truth to which we are awakening today calls for no less a tension. That truth responds with a perfect return to the Platonic reversal. And it is putting an end to the religious era opened up, in various regions at the same time, by the paradoxical positing of a supra-sensible sphere to which the believers devoted their lives and by the condemnation of the sensible world. These positions, which were the basis of Mazdeism, Gnosticism, Christianity, Buddhism and Jainism, seem to have been linked to a single form of social evolution in various different countries.[7] It is probable that the rapid transformation of the world itself requires another morality today. Of itself, the development of industry submits the world to the rule of an economic rationalism hostile to any religious sovereignty and, in fact, alien to any sovereign principle. But by the same token precisely, *sacred* value breaks free of moral justification and grants itself the pure, unfettered liberty and ruinous innocence of poetry.

---

6 I am not laying down the principles of a personal morality here: I wish to express the values demanded by the current conditions of life—values which, to all intents and purposes, are already recognized. This is why I write 'we', my aim being merely to anticipate. And who cannot see that today *evil* is given in a fundamental way in the bestiality subserving *raison d'État*: without this character, Buchenwald would not be the decisive, undisputed, irreducible mark of *evil*.

7 Scholars as cautious as [Marcel] Mauss and [Antoine] Meillet have noted the relations between this quasi-universal birth of the moral religions and the mode of distribution of wealth (the position of Christianity is given, on the one hand, in Hebrew prophecy and, on the other, in Platonism).

Pierre Gordon

Pierre Gordon, *L'initiation sexuelle et l'évolution religieuse* [Sexual initiation and religious evolution], Bibliothèque de philosophie contemporaine: Psychologie et sociologie (Maurice Pradines series ed.) (Paris: Presses universitaires de France, 1946), in 8°, 274 pp.

M. Pierre Gordon's ambition exceeds what is simply stated in the title. The 'sexual initiation' the book discusses is not, as the author sees it, one rite among others, evolving with religious forms as a whole. It is a fundamental institution, of which a large number of well-known practices are secondary, derived and often warped forms, such as human sacrifice, sacred prostitution, circumcision, *ludi funebres* (funeral games) etc. Its underlying principle is the initiatory deflowering of a young virgin by a sacralised figure. For M. Gordon, the rite had, at some indeterminate period, such a value

> this ceremony seemed so honourable, so transformative, so glorious, so divinizing, so crucial, that it was ultimately shameful not to perform it, just as, in our rural areas a few decades ago, it would have been shameful for a young girl not to take her First Communion or marry in church. An essential halo of virtue would always have been missing. She would not have been a whole woman, but a brutish creature. (pp. 163–64)

Legends of dragons and werewolves are related to this custom, as the initiators, formed into confraternities, often wore animal masks. The same is clearly true of the *jus primae noctis* which survived in France into the Middle Ages.

It is from this rite that M. Gordon explains social forms such as *Amazonism* (in which a community of women lives in symbiosis with a neighbouring community of men), exogamy and the incest taboo (associated with the need to find from outside the sacred force required for defloration, a certain endogamy becoming possible within groups holding sacred charges to an excessive degree), together with a certain number of biblical legends and myths of Antiquity.

All in all, these interpretations are no less plausible than many others: taken together, they may be seen as an apparently fertile hypothesis, based on facts that are most often neglected. However, their author, steeped in 'traditional' and 'initiatory' ideas, states them as certainties. Instead of a hypothesis, we are presented with a doctrine littered with mystical assumptions about the Paleolithic and Neolithic religions (without blenching, M. Gordon writes, in just the same way as he does of the most solidly attested historical institutions, of a certain '*Grande Église néolithique*' [Great Neolithic Church] . . .). It is curious, moreover, that an explanation that might be thought *demeaning* in nature should be linked to the purest idealism. In these sexual practices that take religious form, M. Gordon sees only the quest for a *sacredness*, to which he himself subscribes and which, beneath an appearance we find disconcerting, is *transcendent*. He employs this epithet frequently, applying it even to the word *mana*. But this is ambiguous. It often seems that he is speaking of the transcendence of the intelligible, as opposed to the sensible world. 'Human history', we read (p. 135), is always grounded in ideas, for man by his nature cannot live at the level of sense perceptions; his dwelling place, whether he is aware of it or not, is in the bosom of thought', but, as the end of the sentence informs us, that 'bosom of thought' is identified with 'the universe of eternal energy'. This 'transcendent sacredness' is 'radiant matter' (p. 145). It is surprising to see a work dedicated to the memory of Émile Durkheim when it is so far removed from *the rules of sociological method*.

What Is Sex?

ÉTIENNE WOLFF, *Les Changements de sexe* [Changes of sex], L'Avenir de la Science, VOL. 23 (Jean Rostand series ed.) (Paris: Gallimard, 1946), in 8°, 307 pp., illustrations, plates.

From Immediate Sense Data to Scientific Data

We are habituated, from childhood, to recognize the sex of our fellow human beings by their clothing, but that habit can only precede a more intimate experience. Essentially, the knowledge of distinct sexes seems given to human beings in the same way as the more general knowledge we have of other people. We do not know *others*, our fellow human beings, from a lengthy process or by observing and reflecting, discovering by stages that, since they are our fellows in appearance, they must also be so on the inside; we know them at a stroke, from childhood, by an intimate revelation which cannot be separated from the fact of contact. Communication between like individuals—the sense one has of the presence of the other, inasmuch as the other is, at bottom, the same as oneself—is as much a foundation of consciousness as sensation. Particular sensations (visual, tactile etc.) bind themselves to this immediate sense of presence and become the mark of it, but they cannot create it in the child by deduction (as Pierre Janet demonstrated). And we shall never account for it by reason. Now, the senses we have of our own and the opposite sex are apparently only two aspects of the obscure sense of the presence of others. This general feeling is not, in effect, always exactly the same and we cannot reduce all modifications of it to the judgements we base on the analysable data—external signs or experience of characteristics. Like feelings of femininity or masculinity, feelings of sympathy and antipathy are such that we cannot account for them by way of reason: the possibilities of difference, in this regard, are as numerous as they are elusive. It is, however, true that it is difficult, in each case, to pass from the feeling itself to an exact notion of how it differs from a judgement. We always find reasons to explain our likings or our hatreds, and the sense of feminine (or masculine) presence is always associated with some intelligible sign of the feminine (or masculine) sex. It is even apparently the case that, where sex is concerned, our parents teach us to distinguish its external marks (in terms of clothing) before we have the intimate sense of difference. But the 'sense of presence', distinct from the act of judgement, is discernible in that an elusive element remains of which we can speak only in vague terms and which we can never pin down. We try to analyse femininity and masculinity and say that the one is active and the other passive, the one gentle and the other tough, the one evasive and the other aggressive, but these ideas correspond to the experience we have of the effects—in fact, random—of the one or other gender. Admittedly, a sense of feminine presence is always accompanied by intelligible signs and the experimental notion of the characteristics specific to that sex, but it is at bottom a highly distinct, immediate, sensory element known to us all, relating to the modality of a constant communication between individuals of the same species (analogous, no doubt, to that sensory communication between cells of a single individual that underlies consciousness).

And indeed that sense is also distinct from the genetic reactions that it brings about: the male homosexual, hostile to the possibility of contact with the opposite sex, feels it as much as the normal man. Moreover, the signs and notions with which it is commonly linked produce it by association: a photograph, a picture, and at times a costume suffice. And, quite clearly, one could not rely on this sense when it comes to objective knowledge. The mere sense of presence carries no weight in itself. At the level of clear and distinct knowledge, a 'sense', even an essential sense, contributes only a qualitative accent to the data of observation: it is about value, and not use-value, but sensory value: a value of presence or of femininity. Yet sensory value can never be apprehended; 'discourse' (the analytical statements of science) cannot communicate it.

At the very best, we can strive to determine an *objective constant* that corresponds to the sense or feeling. If, when dealing with our fellow human being, we have a sense of presence—in other words, an impression of identity (the presence, which I am, extended into the other, identical in the other)—we can see this as the normal response to the appearance on the scene of other individuals, whose nature is determined objectively by biology. Thus, where human beings are concerned, we can add constantly to the data of objective knowledge—of which science is the elaborated form—the qualitative accent of an identity with our intimate existence. But even if that accent always accompanies the object (the individual of the human species), it cannot be mistaken for it. For if we erroneously take it for the object—if we situate intimate existence at the level of the object, we reduce that existence itself to the state of object. Subordinating that existence to the laws of the order of objects, we substantialize it and speak of a *soul*—something of which objective science necessarily knows nothing. Similarly, science knows nothing of the notion, drawn from intimate experience, of an objective feminine nature, differing in its essence from the masculine.

Scientific Data

In fact, science rigorously eliminates what we have to call the 'fundamental givens' of life, which go to the boundless depths of our being, the most important of which are the sense of the presence of others and the sense of sex. All in all, it destroys the construction based on the sense of presence, it breaks up individual intimate existence into shifting objective representations in which it is denied any solid substratum. It removes reality and substantiality from the intimate, apparently immutable notion of sex. It shows that a tumour in the adrenal glands can give a pretty—and, up to that point, very feminine—woman a beard, atrophy her mammary glands and modify (if not invert) her sexual organs. Among certain animals, science even observes complete sex changes and describes a range of inter-mediate states between the two sexes. Moreover, sexual reproduction loses the simple character commonly attributed to it. As a general rule, one sees differentiated gametes, male and female, but in some species of a primitive nature the gametes differ only in their behaviour at the point of fertilization; among the Protozoans of the Foraminifera group, even this latter difference disappears: 'the sexual phenomenon still exists, but there is no sex' (Wolff, p. 27). And the biology of the animal kingdom, having to base the elementary separation of male and female individuals on a definition, cannot rely on the sexual function to do so. That function is not decisive. It is a primary sexual characteristic, distinct from the secondary ones (which relate to behaviour, outward appearance and the voice and appear at some late stage—mainly at puberty), in that it is marked from birth by the constitution of a differentiated organ, but the primary characteristic determines only the genital sex (the production of spermatozoa or ova). The fact is, however, that a male and a female organism differ from each other in a deeper way. The determination of genital sex does not begin to appear, in chickens, until after the seventh day, and in human embryos until after the seventh week, of development. The embryonic male in no way differs from the female up until that point. Both possess the same rudimentary sex organs, which can take either a male or a female course of development. In its rudimentary state, the testicle is in no way different from the ovary, or the penis from the clitoris. To the point where, in the laboratory, an appropriate injection can determine the *genital sex* of the embryo. But the *genetic sex* cannot be changed, being given once and for all at fertilization. There is, in fact, a fundamental difference in the structure of male and female cell nuclei. We know that the union of the gametes, each of which possesses half of the elements required for the formation of a nucleus, produces a single cell (the egg) which will form the complex organism by dividing itself by degrees into a multitude of cells. Now, in most species (except for birds and butterflies/moths, which show the opposite disposition), the ova, which are all alike, can determine nothing, but some of the differentiated spermatozoa determine the male sex and others the female. An element (*a chromosome*) of the half-nucleus of the spermatozoon introduces a variable. In most cases, that element is sometimes homologous with the corresponding element of the ovum, in which case the mother-cell is female (and, in its wake, all the cells of the organism, which are homologous with the mother-cell), and sometimes different from it, in which case it is male (but in the human species, the element is at times homologous and at times absent, the absence of the homologous chromosome having the same effects as the presence of a different chromosome). This primordial determination constitutes the genetic sex, which is of decisive importance. As a general rule, the genetic sex determines the genital sex and if, from natural causes or following an intervention, the genital sex changes, the genetic sex remains, ready to return the genital sex to its original state. The injection of female hormones can determine the development of female organs in the embryo, but in most cases, if the treatment is not sustained, a genetically male organism changes sex again and we see a return to organs of a male form: the gametes produced are spermatozoa.

From 1935 to 1938, Étienne Wolff and Ginglinger carried out experiments at the laboratory of the Faculty of Medicine in Strasbourg and their stunning results have enabled us to provide a detailed account of the operation of the main factors in the formation of sex. We know that the genital glands secrete *hormones* that differ according to sex. It is male or female hormones that determine the formation of secondary characteristics, such as the breaking of the male voice or the development of breasts. These hormones are more or less the same in the different vertebrates and, from 1928 to 1935 biochemists determined the formulae of these ternary compounds (oxygen, hydrogen and carbon) and succeeded in extracting them industrially in the pure state. Wolff and Ginglinger, making a circular opening in the shells of hens' eggs that had been incubated for a few days (two to four days), placed a few drops of hormonal solution—some male and some female—on a membrane belonging to as yet undifferentiated embryos. Having affixed a thin strip of glass over the opening, they were able to observe the development of the embryo. When a female hormone was introduced in this way into the growth of an embryo of male genetic sex, the genital organs, initially undifferentiated, followed a more or less distinctly female line of development, depending on the quantity of hormone injected. In the best cases, the incubated chick bore a barely hybrid character, in which the female element dominated so clearly that it was difficult to distinguish manufactured females from natural ones. But if it so happened that one of these laboratory creatures survived, it returned, after hatching, to its genetic sex. The only things that remained were the female genital tracts formed during incubation: the genital glands, having become ovaries in the phase that followed the undifferentiated state, developed, the ovarian cortex regressed, and the testicular medullary tissue resumed its development. With a slight delay, the animal took on the normal appearance of a cockerel (comb, plumage and spurs), sang and behaved sexually like a cockerel, and its testicles could produce mature spermatozoa. Effects of the same kind, both less distinct and more consequential, were observed in the case of embryos of female genetic sex: the gonads were not altered, but the embryo acquired a male genital tract; thus, an eight-month-old hen which, in the embryonic state, had received injections of male hormone, was unable, with its blocked oviduct, to lay eggs and these accumulated in the general cavity of the body. In fact, the whole range of results obtained during incubation may just possibly be maintained after hatching. Repeated injections of female hormone into a young male develop the oviduct and even the left ovary, which produces the ova: its genital sex is therefore genuinely changed. But in that case the ovary is small in size, the ova are fewer than in a female specimen of the same age and the animal is incapable of laying. Étienne Wolff cannot hide 'the mild disappointment this remarkable result brought him, amid the enthusiasm of the research he conducted between 1935 and 1938' (p. 186). The general results of the experiments are, nonetheless, clear: on the one hand, it is evident that the factorial element of genetic sex operates through a median term, namely a secretion from the interstitial tissues of the genital glands;[1] on the other hand, a fundamental male or female nature is provided by the factorial element of genetic sex. In these conditions, the effects of a factorial element that is given once and for all can be modified, but the modifications are fragile: the real sex is the genetic sex. As a consequence, Étienne Wolff continues to refer to these laboratory animals that have ovaries and ova as males.

Considered in practical terms, these possibilities of changing the genital sex are still far from meeting the desires of those who would like to ordain what sex their children will be. The scientists' preoccupations were not by any means unrelated to such wishes. Writing of the feverish activity, enthusiasm and impatience of the biologists engaged on this kind of work in the pre-war period, Étienne Wolff admits that a particular hope underlay it all:

---

1 It is not, in fact, the germ cells of the gonads, but the cells of the tissues surrounding the testicular tubes or the ovarian follicles that secrete sexual hormones.

'Could one,' he tells us, 'change the sex of a foetus, choose to have a child of a particular sex? These are the remote aspects of the problem to which this research is responding.' It was with greater eagerness for results that operations were carried out on mammals, but the mice and opossums treated did not respond well to these expectations: it is more difficult in mammals than in birds to reach the embryo in time. Hormone injections modified the genital tract, but the scientists were not able to reverse the differentiation of the gonads. And, naturally, nothing could be attempted on humans. Even supposing that one might effect the decisive inversion one day, there would be a risk of producing a monster. And how would it be with the life of a viable creature obtained in that way: imagine a man having to undergo continual treatment to remain male, and threatened, if he broke off that treatment, with losing his testicles (pp. 202–3).

This is not to say, at least without reservations, that different methods will not achieve other outcomes. But if we go back to the theoretical level, we may observe that the science defining sexuality is nonetheless inclined, as of now, to grant a fundamental value to an element that is wholly external to the sexual function. There may, perhaps, be insufficient justification for doing so. The fact that chromosome constitution—genetic sex—prevails over *de facto* sex does not mean that sex is, in its essence, that constitution. This alleged genetic *sex* is, ultimately, an external decision *governing* the fact of sex, but differing from that fact itself. In organisms where the determining pair of chromosomes corresponds to the principle of the male sex, there is agreement that one normally observes the male sex. But it has to be said that one sometimes finds the female sex too. Is it reasonable then to assert that that female sex is male? (and to say, as Étienne Wolff does, that we have here an intersex male?) The male in question is perhaps only a potential female but, for the moment, it is a female. Agreed, general conditions and the predictable operation of factors will prevent this from being the lasting character of the organism: nevertheless, for the moment, *so far as sex is concerned*, nothing in that female is male.

Moreover, this genetic 'sex' doesn't always have the last word. Étienne Wolff cites a 25-year-old human subject, presenting the characteristics externally of both sexes (the general conformation of the body and the sex organ are masculine, but the scrotum contains only one testicle, and the chest is feminine, the skin soft and face beardless). This individual had suffered for several years from period pains, which justified an abdominal operation. At that point developed elements of female sex organs were discovered—an ovary in a *functional* state. After the removal of that ovary, the subject changed rapidly: a few days later, the breasts were withered, the face covered in downy hair and the voice deeper. Étienne Wolff admits, however, that the subject was 'probably of female genetic sex'.

It is clear that the factorial element itself, differentiated at fertilization, may, from the outset, involve anomalies (p. 233). But how, in that case, can we refer to a factor that does not distinctly govern functional difference as sex: this creator of uncertain effects has about it an ambiguity that is never present in the function. An individual may have a double function (outside of the case of hermaphroditic species—the simultaneous hermaphroditism of the snail and the successive hermaphroditism of the eel, with its differently sexed phases—this is very rare). The organs themselves, in their development, pass through indistinct states; they may indeed pass from a distinctly male to a distinctly female structure (or vice versa); only the production of a spermatozoon is something quite clearly different from the production of an ovum.

There are, indeed, quite a large number of cases in which 'genetic sex' does not decide matters. As early as 1921, because they retain a rudimentary, non-functional ovary, akin to but distinct from a testicle, male toads of the genus *Bufo* were being changed into *fertile* females by the removal of their testicles. Larvae were obtained which were raised to metamorphosis, resulting from what Étienne Wolff calls the 'crossing of two males' (p. 232). More recently (1940–44), Gallien obtained a stable sex change in a frog, *Rana temporaria*, which was given a hormone injection at the larval stage.

The case of the green spoonworm (a marine worm that lives among Mediterranean coastal rocks) is the most striking (pp. 212–20). The female of that strange animal is more than a hundred times larger than the male. It is made up of a globular body about the size of a plum and a narrow proboscis that ends in two pointed lobes which open like the petals of a flower. It is 20–30 cm long. The male, for its part, measures 1–2 mm.: it is a small, oval, ciliate organism, living parasitically upon the female, first in the mouth, then in the intestine and ending up in its lover's womb. This animalcule does not use its mouth to eat (it feeds itself by tegumentary osmosis) but to emit the product of its seminal vesicle. A Swiss zoologist, Baltzer, spent many years (1914–40) studying the mechanism of the sexual differentiation of this worm. 'If the newly hatched ciliate larvae lead an independent life in sea water, they almost unfailingly become females. If they attach themselves, after hatching, to the proboscis of the female, most of them become males.' This runs entirely contrary to the determination of genital sex by genetic sex, which, according to the law of probability, would see each group having an equal number of males and females. And indeed the masculinizing effect of the secretions from the proboscis has been demonstrated by Baltzer, who obtained 'different degrees of intersexuality, closer to or further from the male type, depending on the length of contact with the proboscis.' According to Wolff, 'we may accept that the determination of sex is acquired at the moment of fertilization . . . , but the *genetic constitution*[2] that ensues has only a weak and labile action on sex differentiation'.

One other form of the determination of sex outside of the effect of the 'genetic sex' is worthy of attention. It is particular to an annelid, *Ophyotrocha puerilis*, which presents successive hermaphroditism (p. 66).

> While always male in the young state, it becomes female when it acquires more than 15–20 segments. But if the animal is prevented, by repeatedly cutting off the posterior segments, from having more than 15 of them, it remains indefinitely male . . . *If two adult females are isolated, one of them, generally the younger—'the less female'—turns into a male on contact with its partner.*[3]

---

2 My emphasis. [G. B.]
3 My emphasis. [G. B.]

Sex Is Simply a Characteristic,
Analogous to the Solid or Liquid State of a Body

This set of facts shows rather clearly that the rigorous division of individuals into males and females, even though it applies in the immense majority of cases, is based only on random factors. Only functions are clearly differentiated. Asexual gametes are exceptional and the undifferentiated state of origins changes nothing about the clear-cut nature of an opposition that is observed generally. That opposition is definable and, from one end of the living world to the other, it is easy to distinguish the production of male gametes from the production of female: there is no debate about whether a particular *functioning* gonad which was viewed as male is not actually female. By contrast, the association of a function that is the production of gametes of one of the two genders with a given individual is random. There *is* discussion, no doubt wrongly, about whether a particular individual, whose sexual function is currently female, is not ultimately a male. In reality, discussion does take place, for want of being able to say anything that is well founded. The individual producing ova is female: the female characteristic may be stable or unstable within that individual; the individual may have a 'genetic constitution' that is liable to develop within it the male characteristic (meaning the primary characteristic, which conditions the production of male gametes), which renders that female characteristic entirely precarious. It is awkward to call that individual female, insofar as science is based on attributions of stable characteristics. But science takes into account the *change* of characteristics just as much as it does their *state*. And if the awkwardness continues where the sexes are concerned, that is because the notion of sex as a fundamental attribute of the individual is anchored in us by intimate reactions, which an ingrained popular experience seems to confirm. In reality, if we speak—if a scientist, Étienne Wolff—speaks of authentic males and females, we—and he—are merely substantializing those reactions. We should make no mistake about it: in speaking of 'authentic males', the author of *Changements de sexe* is substantializing his vocabulary, but this is superficial: the necessary changeability of his notions is stayed only for a brief moment by it. If he clings on rather long to the notion of genetic sex, which rescues the popular representation by displacing it, he is ready, as soon as it is necessary (as we have seen) to substitute the—more prudent—expression of genetic 'constitution'. At no point, in a long and remarkable book is the infinitely complex aspect of the facts simplified to conform to conceptually ordained limits. The foregoing argument might even pass for pointlessly finicky if we had not been concerned to show that the results of the recent biological research, carried out or reported by Étienne Wolff, render worthless static representations, founded—and poorly founded—on intimate experience. This in no way runs counter to a book whose keynote is *change*. Intimate experience itself has full value only when it is extricated from the intellectual errors it has permitted. It reveals, in fact, nothing substantial: the sense of another's sex is simply one modality of the intimate communication between fellow creatures; it seems that this knowledge of our fellows is all the more intimate for the fact that it is within the confines of the greatest similarity that dissimilarity is at its deepest. But what science teaches us about that dissimilarity clearly casts no light on the subjective knowledge we have of it. If we focused on the perceptible difference present in the external cause of the determination of sex—the difference between the two kinds of genital hormone—we would see that it is the most insignificant imaginable: their chemical formulae are closely akin to each other. According to Wolff, 'some as yet fragmentary research tends to show that oxidations are more intense in the cells treated with male hormones than in those treated with female hormones' (p. 296). This answers in an entirely external way the sense that man has of femininity (or woman of virility). It is the same with the sexual function, with the production of gametes, some of them changeable, others remaining more or less in a waiting state. The sense of femininity, of virility is merely a very acute modality of the sense of presence. It is, for the opposite sex, a mixed—even an exasperated—sense of identity and otherness, of the known and the unknown, and thereby, at one and the same time, consciousness of totality (by complementarity) and frustration. It is right to separate the analysis of objects—science—from these products of feeling which, in the confusion, incline the mind to idealism. As for the entities which, in that confusion, are underpinned by experience and feeling, we have at the extreme the masculinity of God (counterbalanced by the femininity of the Virgin). Science is, in all necessity, as far removed as can be from these notions. But it is still only half-way from them if it is not stated clearly, of sex in general, that it is not an essence but a state. No doubt the female state of a being is less labile than the liquid state of a body, but that is just a difference of degree. This woman whom I find attractive is no less human than water is ice. Beings, admittedly, are barely imaginable without sex—and the absolute being is, by general consent, viewed as male. But science makes this overall finding: it removes from the beings claimed as such the possibility of serving as the basis for the idea of being. It dissolves into interactions what primary experience represented as substances. The only image of things that it countenances is that of continuous communication, in which beings and sexes disappear (for example, love, if we give that name to the conjunction of living beings, is the primary fact—not *man* or *woman*). Ordinarily, we object to these kinds of representations based on the facts of science, calling them scientistic. Nevertheless, the problem of being is dissolved in these shifts.

A New American Novelist

FREDERIC PROKOSCH, *Les Asiatiques* [The Asiatics] (Max Morise trans.) (Paris: Gallimard, 1946), in 8°, 300 pp.

His face, eyes closed, shone serenely in the lamplight.
Beautiful it was, the deep ridges, the brooding lines,
the lines of exhaustion, of bewilderment, of dreamy
anger, of a fulfilled heterosexuality—beautiful and
venerable they made his face. 'We stole sacred
objects and gold, we burned barns, we killed cattle, we ravaged the
fields.'
'What else?'
'We played the spy, we frightened the children, we
brought dissension into happy families.'
'What else?'
'We corrupted the young, we disillusioned the aged,
we made love seem a shocking and shameful disease.'
'What else?'
'We betrayed each other.'
All of us sat back and closed our eyes. More garlic was
brought, the glasses were refilled with vodka.[1]

We often forget that literature is revelry [*fête*]. The ambiguity of the word, its contradictory meanings, encourage and ultimately even justify our negligence. Revelry? Drunkenness without any doubt, joy and glory in living, but at the same time death, anguish and excess. It is, in fact, quite

---

1 Frederic Prokosch, *The Asiatics* (London and Paris: The Albatross Modern Continental Library, 1947), p. 80.

difficult to relate the notion we have of literature to revelry. I would have liked to have avoided the ambiguity to which the revelry image brings me back. And if I say *literature is the use of words that fills us with wonder*, I suddenly give up on defining it: I have my glass in hand, I have lost the right to *speak* about it.

Without a doubt, instead of enchanting—and amazing oneself as one amazes others—to *speak* of the enchantment of a book is tiresome. In strict terms, *speaking* of enchantment does not enchant. I may compare a book to heady wine but I have not, for all that, taken a drink, nor even poured one out. In speaking of *The Asiatics,* I nonetheless feel a kind of sly amusement: at a practical joke in prospect, designed to enchant its victim . . . I even feel a little in league with the author.

At all events, I can only substitute for the book itself a brief glimpse of it that will disappoint (the book too may not exactly meet the expectations I have raised, though that is another matter). The author was born, we learn, in Wisconsin in 1909 of Austrian parents. He was a professor, teaching English in American universities. *The Asiatics* was published in 1935. It was his first book and already his compatriots rank him among the great writers. Nonetheless *The Asiatics* will disconcert those who love American novels. It is the story of a journey through Asia of a penniless bachelor travelling light, living and wandering where chance takes him. He runs across adorable, perverse girls, both native and foreign, obscure adventurers, old ladies, bandits, rajahs, thieves and an endless gaggle of characters happy and unhappy, rich and poverty stricken, friendly and cruel, succeeding each other without rhyme or reason, driven by necessity, brought together in an intoxicating swirl of anxiety, desire and laughter. To the point where only in one sense is the subject of the book travel: the traveller is, rather, the screen on which an orgy of confused scenes play out in which *humanity* reveals itself.

In another sense, the constant penury and stupefying strokes of luck that govern this long journey succeed in detaching a vision, like a dream of unravelling clouds, from a rational system in which calculations of money, work and bread prevail. Asia itself, on account of its immense size and irrepressible disorder, plays its part in positioning this childlike revelry outside of time, a feast of humanity overflowing in all directions the limits it set for itself, drunk with mischievousness and oblivion (isn't revelry this complete letting-go, this gay abandonment to the limitless world of fear?). It is odd that happiness should alone have the virtue of opening up such a distant possibility: the happiness that destitution (play, uncertainty) and absence of care can afford. And indeed the book closes on an apparently unmotivated statement: '[T]here was no denying it, I was feeling very happy'. Happy as it is possible to be for someone who is ignorant of nothing, who has nothing between him and the abyss possibility opens up beneath his feet.

How, without this light-hearted happiness would we know sympathy? We sink so easily into pity, which is often the pretext for hatred. By so doing, we cease to be subject to the play of the world: it is no longer this place of enchantment and terror, but a field of activity dominated by judgement, discourse, accounting. And the immense, elusive, salacious face of humanity, all too shameful to mention, escapes us. It is, admittedly, foolish-ness, to give in, like the irrational drinker, to the impulse of sympathy: that impulse which undoes, disarms and bewitches us, and which, like life, leaves us at the end only with death. But we live astride a base of laws; we are moral; within us, pity constantly ordains the salutary activity of the judge. And for sympathy we have only the time-outside-time of revelry: as a general rule, we live in an atmosphere of unhappiness—assisted in that by the police and prisons.

It is one of the shared features of literature and revelry that they both permit the suspension of laws, the overturning of moral rules. The folk tale, which fills us with wonder, partakes very faithfully of revelry, insofar as the teller abandons himself to fellow-feeling. And we have to say of Frederic Prokosch's abandonment that it exceeds the normal measure: for it is com-mon to *show understanding*, to reach down to depths where the vilest acts are explicable, but the author of *The Asiatics* stands at the opposite pole: he does not condemn, does not understand and never ever questions. If the narrator's best friend brazenly robs him, stealing his last penny, he is aghast for a moment (not at the consequences, but at the fact of the theft), yet the two carry on drinking together: they do not have the matter out with each other. And nor shall we know the reason why the beautiful Ursule suddenly killed her first lover (he dies poisoned at a picnic, falling asleep as he speaks, while Ursule, followed by the 'best friend' is 'off . . . for a little walk').[2] 'Anything goes' and the characters in the drama do not weigh it down with their motives. No one has to justify themselves in the author's mind: everyone simply enjoys a freedom that belongs to the wide world, to the countless human beings whose presence in the night brings tears to the narrator's eyes. But this leaves no scope for indifference—and it would even, in a sense, be wrong to speak of humour: the book is the realm of measureless sympathy.

2 Prokosch, *The Asiatics*, p. 261.

Sartre

JEAN-PAUL SARTRE, *Réflexions sur la question juive* [translated into English as *Anti-Semite and Jew*] (Paris: Paul Morhien, 1947), in 16°, 199 pp.

Written in October 1944, this study of the respective characters of the Jew and the anti-Semite is the direct consequence of one of the darkest acts to be laid at the door of humanity. There is, generally, in the fact of being a human being an oppressive, loathsome element that has to be overcome. But that oppressiveness and loathsomeness have never been so heavy to bear as they have since Auschwitz. Like you and I, those answerable for Auschwitz had human nostrils and mouths, human voices and reason. They could marry and have children. Like the Pyramids or the Acropolis, Auschwitz is the work—is the mark—of man. Humanity's image is henceforth inseparable from a gas chamber . . .

If we are to rise above the horror of this, we cannot just offload the guilt on to an execrated category of human beings. To do that is to reproduce anti-Semitic cowardice and the fraudulence of scapegoating. We have to go further and think seriously about the Jewish question.

Humanity's good fortune has depended, perhaps, on the power to dominate initial reactions that are both cowardly and destructive, anti-Semitism being the vilest of these. (We should recall here that the places where it has raged have consistently met with disaster: Spain's decline followed the departure of the Jews; the class responsible for Russia's pogroms is now destroyed; and if anti-Semitism were not protected, in advance, from being viewed clearly and honestly, then the German, faced with the catastrophe he perpetrated, would have had no way out but suicide.) This is why the unvarnished portrait Sartre has painted of the anti-Semite can serve as a necessary lesson. What, according to Sartre, distinguishes the anti-Semite is that he belongs to the past, yet, like some creature of stone, remains in being in the present. He can do so as long as he resolves to be 'impervious to reason and to experience'.[1] He brings nothing to society except the obtuse psychology of crowds. Being incapable of constructing anything and ignorant of the mechanisms of a modern society, he injects into it the derangement of an entirely primitive passion. The Jew is, in his eyes, as cursed, sacred and untouchable as the pariah is for the Hindu. That way, he can look upon himself as noble (which he isn't), finding in exercises in loathing those moral prerogatives that entitle one to property ownership. The anti-Semite is generally petty-bourgeois and does not possess land, but through anti-Semitism he grabs for himself the vital, irrational values that are the prerogative of the rural landowner. As he sees it, good and evil are given once and for all at birth. The good that is in him is as imperishable as the evil that is in a Jew. And the anti-Semite, who is not in any way afraid of the Jew but fears everything that challenges a static conception of things, is *always* afraid. That is why, like the humiliated coward who beats his horse, he has to terrify the defenceless.

Sartre, somewhat paradoxically, criticizes the democrat and the Jew himself, who most often hold to a rational, undifferentiated conception of human beings. He terms inauthentic the Jew who, for want of access to the Christians' vital values, which are both situation bound and *particular*, ranges the universal of reason against them. Thus, as he sees it, not only Bergson (reduced to a 're-branded rationalism'[2]) and Husserl, but also Spinoza are inauthentic. I think the vocabulary here lends an excessive rigidity to things. It is true that the universalism of Jewish thought has an evasion at its origin: the desire to deny a particularity that saw every Jew excluded from vital communities. But that denial is also the indirect expression of a 'situation', the transcendence of which it represents. That way, Jewish thought coincides with revolutionary thought (isn't Spinoza the first democratic thinker?). We may discuss the foundations of this (particularity is denied only verbally), but hasn't rationalism become, in its turn, the particularity that ranges the Jew against the rest of the world? Hasn't anti-Semitism's critique become primarily the critique of rationalism? And

---

1 Jean-Paul Sartre, *Anti-Semite and Jew* (George J. Becker trans.) (New York: Schocken Books, 1965), p. 19.
2 Sartre, *Anti-Semite and Jew*, p. 116.

the Jewish world, by denying that it represents a particular world, certainly contributed to the birth of an authentic universal world, with anti-Semitism's struggle against it lending that world the authenticity of an existence 'in situation'. The Jew stood aside here, keeping this world non-Jewish in character, but was he thereby relinquishing authenticity? I do not say that Sartre's critique is without value (there is a form of evasion at the base of the universal), but there is an epic of reason and the Jews have written some authentic pages of that epic. And doesn't Jewish authenticity consist precisely in the fact that, in the suffering of their flesh at Auschwitz, it was reason that was suffering.

A Morality Based on Misfortune: *The Plague*

ALBERT CAMUS, *La Peste* [translated into English as *The Plague*] (Paris: Gallimard, 1947), in 16º, 339 pp.

——. *'Le Malentendu'* [translated into English as *The Misunderstanding*] *suivi de 'Caligula'* (Paris: Gallimard, 1947), in 16º, 215 pp.

——. 'Remarque sur la révolte' [Remark on revolt] in *L'Existence*, La Métaphysique, VOL. 1 (Jean Grenier series ed.) (Paris: Gallimard, 1945), in 8º, pp. 9–23.

——. 'Ni victimes, ni bourreaux' [Neither victims nor executioners], *Combat*, 19–30 November 1946.

It would be paradoxical, as a rule, to compare Albert Camus with Sade. The author of *The Plague* is keen to be useful: he is the natural-born enemy of death and pain; if he could have his way, apparently no one would die or suffer. Reading *The Plague*, one would rank him among the 'fine souls'. I do not think that counts for nothing. The fine souls of our day have a soft spot for monsters, but, for all that, they are not monstrous. It could be (though one should never judge *in advance*) that Camus is currently mistaken about himself (and that he is deceiving us involuntarily).

It is possible that he is caught in a trap of his own making. A sadness in him necessarily implies humour, but that sadness already seems affected. I shall try to show that the initial thrust of his thinking nevertheless places him alongside Sade, that one can only see the import of his moral attitude by comparing it with Sade's.

The Plague is the story of a long struggle fought against death, in conditions of almost total impotence, by Dr Rieux and Jean Tarrou. Tarrou, who himself dies at the end of the epidemic, who expresses some of the author's ideas, confides to Rieux, before dying, the feeling that drove him from the beginning: he cannot accept the fact of the death penalty. His whole life's struggle had only one meaning: to create a society that would have no place for the death sentence. The death penalty, applied in an absurd way, was already the theme of *L'Étranger* [translated into English as *The Outsider*]. We know now, in addition, that the hatred of *legitimated* murder governs the author's politics: that hatred is the basis of a programme laid out in this series of articles entitled *Ni victimes ni bourreaux* [Neither victims nor executioners], which appeared last year in *Combat*. 'People like me', he says (20 November 1946), 'would like a world, not where no one is killed any more (we are not so mad as to call for that!), but where murder is not legitimated'. And he calls first (29 September 1946) for 'a code of international justice that would have as its first precept the general abolition of the death penalty.'

Sade was moved by this same concern, writing (in *La Philosophie dans le boudoir*), that 'these supreme principles [the reference is to the diversity of characters] make it necessary to promulgate mild laws and, *above all*, to wipe out forever the atrocity of capital punishment . . . because, unfeeling in and of itself, the *law* cannot be accessible to the human passions that *legitimize* the cruel act of murder.'[1]

Thus the two 'moralists' share a horror of murder carried out legally. Of the two, Sade alone indicates the deep reason for this, which is that, 'Nature gives man the impulses that can make him excuse such a misdeed; while the law, on the contrary, forever opposing and not receiving anything from nature, cannot be authorized to perform the same excesses: Since the law does not have the same motives, it cannot possibly have the same rights',[2] But the sentiment that inspires Sade is implicit in the words of Tarrou (*La Peste*, p. 276): 'that dirty occasion in which dirty, plague-ridden mouths told a man in chains that he was to die and arranged everything so that he would, indeed, die . . . ' Camus does not hate the murderer but the judge: Tarrou is the son of a Deputy Director of Public Prosecutions, and, between this father who 'calls for a man's head' and the indicted criminal,

---

1 Marquis de Sade, *Philosophy in the Boudoir, or, The Immoral Mentors* (Joachim Neugroschel trans.) (New York: Penguin, 2006), p. 119; my emphasis. [G. B.]
2 de Sade, *Philosophy in the Boudoir*, p. 119.

he has made his choice. The difference between the two begins with a generalized detestation of murder that drives Camus. Sade simply contents himself with showing that death sentences do not reduce the number of murders: '[t]here is no worse calculation than to put a man to death for having killed another, since the outcome of this procedure is that, instead of there being one man less, suddenly there are two . . . ' But Sade does this, so that, a little later on, he can defend the crime of passion, the murder carried out under the influence of uncontrollable desire. There is a difficulty in the fact that, for Camus, the murder that is not simply a judicial matter is the kind legitimated by war, with which Sade did not concern himself (a special concern with military murder is a thing of recent date).

In truth, if we were to confine ourselves to *The Plague*, the decision to elucidate Camus's morality by way of Sade's would be difficult to sustain. In fighting the death penalty, Tarrou is seeking to fight murder. But *The Plague* is doubtless, if not the least perfect, then the dullest of the books of Camus, whose finest work is surely *Le Malentendu* (though the richest in meaning is *Caligula*). In *The Outsider, murder* is merely a furtive element, an unfortunate chance event. But in *Le Malentendu* it is the *terrible passion*, in *Caligula* the *active principle*, before which reason does not yield but bends.

It is strange that Albert Camus should have expressed himself coolly and in a realistic, prosaic manner in his novels, whereas in his plays his language is lyrical and high flown. *Caligula* is certainly a tragedy, taking its subject from Roman history. But *Le Malentendu*, though it is based on a minor news item and its characters are humble contemporary Czechs, is itself no less of a tragedy than *Caligula*—even in the noble sense of the word. The innkeeper's daughter not only has the excessive passion of tragic heroes, but their taut language, their sky-high lyricism. I remember that as the curtain went up, for no explicable reason a *sacred horror* radiated out from the stage, chilling the blood. Clearly it was not produced by the text, but the whole text called for it. We know that *The Misunderstanding* was initially unsuccessful (unlike *The Plague*, which was received a little hastily as a great book). *The Misunderstanding* was disconcerting: some evident clumsiness accentuated the improbability of the plot. It was hard to understand why the son, happy to return as a rich man to the home he had fled twenty years earlier, should delay in making himself known, leading to the irretrievable 'misunderstanding' of the title: his mother and sister killed the man for his money, seeing him merely as a chance visitor to the inn. Few spectators were receptive, then, to the play's disconcerting language. How could one not be astonished to hear a criminal telling her victim's wife:

> By now my mother's lying with her son, pressed to the sluice-gate, and the current is beginning to gnaw their faces, and buffeting them against the rotten piles. Soon their bodies will be drawn up and buried together in the same earth. But I cannot see what there is even in this to set me screaming with pain. I have a very different idea of the human heart, and, to be frank, your tears revolt me.[3]

Or, further on: 'Stop! I told you not to touch me. At the mere thought that a human hand could lay its warmth on me before I die; at the mere thought that anything at all resembling the foul love of men is dogging me still, I feel the blood pulsing in my temples in a fury of disgust.'[4] Above all, what was difficult to accept willingly was that a tragedy, which necessarily arises out of exasperated passions, should rest on the inhuman passion for killing. The author himself ought to draw a veil over such grave evil. He justifies Martha's crime; she did not know that she was killing because she had succumbed to cold, vicious, calculating, murderous rage: for her, all that horror had a purpose; she wanted to be *free*. What stiffened her resolve was that she could not bear her condition, that she was disgusted by her existence within the stagnant confines of a small town. But we cannot know, in this case, what is truly liberating: the stolen money, without which she could not flee a place which was, as she saw it, a prison, or the actual act of murder, by which she was escaping, morally, the rules that were the walls of that prison? Of course, the vice of murder was more perfectly represented in a veiled form. But it was no less difficult to accept: how are we to follow an author into such a foul region of the soul? And such a closed region? At that point, we were reaching the extreme limit of tragedy—when the tragic hero, transgressing

---

3 Albert Camus, *Caligula and Three Other Plays* (New York: Vintage Books, 1958), pp. 129–30.

4 Camus, *Caligula*, p. 131.

the law, does so precisely because it is the law. This is because freedom is found only in crime (Christians would say: in sin). And if, in their ignorance, the sister killed her brother and the mother her son, the transgression took on the sacred character of excess, of unbounded horror. When the truth was revealed to the criminals—at the point the daughter opened the victim's passport and read it—it was only the mother who could not bear it (going off to do away with herself in those very waters in which she had blindly drowned her son): the daughter—even though at the end, through her mother's being overwhelmed with grief, she in turn succumbed—at least did so without flinching, so that her voluntary death was a fulfilment of the excessiveness of her act, which she did not disavow. She had lived a life totally devoted to her murders—to her vice; her death was one step further, the most terrible step, on the path to a freedom that tears up the law. Dying, she fully revealed the meaning of her crimes: 'My calamity', groaned the woman whose lover she had just killed, 'was . . . too big for me'.[5] The murderess then replied: '*But still not big enough; it has left you eyes to weep with. And I see that something remains for me to do before leaving you for ever. I have yet to drive you to despair*.'[6] In these few words, which have all the loftiness of tragedy, the pure desire to kill, stretching the limits of the possible, found—whatever the moral judgement of the author—truly unfettered expression.

By contrast with the condensed—churchy, vice laden—atmosphere of *The Misunderstanding*, *Caligula*, written five years earlier, involves an entirely external form of disorder. There is some superficial staginess in *Caligula*, a resorting to over-elaborate techniques. And this first effort, though often admirable, is mainly interesting for its failing, which is its desire to demonstrate. If we have to judge the power and authenticity of its urgent message to the world, *The Misunderstanding* alone has this oppressive power of silence by which one recognizes an author's abandonment to some impulse that had him in its grip. But if we are looking for the moral intention, it is presented in plain language in a work expressly constructed to show it.

---

5 Camus, *Caligula*, p. 131.
6 Camus, *Caligula*, p. 131.

Not unlike some *grand seigneur* in Sade's *Juliette*, Caligula is committed in a systematic, conscious way to the pleasure of flouting the laws: he is all-powerful and, rebelling against the limit within which life is normally lived, he wishes at least to show the world what a free man in all his fullness looks like: that is why, as the fancy takes him, he begins to kill some of those around him. He kills and humiliates; he scoffs at his victims: he embodies the sovereign unleashing of passions made possible by absolute power.

And so *Caligula* gives murderous desire a clearer, more general, more insistent—if not a purer—expression than *The Misunderstanding*. Clearer, above all, in the sense that the author situates that expression in relation to himself: for Camus is not absent from this play, in which he speaks his feelings through the voice of Cherea (one of the emperor's companions); asked why he does not like him, Cherea says: 'I understand you far too well. One cannot like that aspect of oneself which one tries to keep concealed'.[7] The author's sympathy for the hero, combined with horror, lends the play its pathos. For he cannot despise the monster; he despises his victims more. He cannot ignore within himself the pent-up instincts which Caligula's power unleashes. And he condemns such an unleashing; at least he makes of it—implicitly—a principle of poetry. Camus who is usually uninterested in poetry speaks of it in *Caligula* in strange terms. In a discussion on the opportuneness and possibility of a conspiracy, Cherea defines the ruler's madness as 'that inhuman lyricism beside which my life means no more than a speck of dust'.[8] When Caligula's mistress asks him shortly afterwards what that discussion had been about (it had become animated), Cherea replies: 'Our quarrel arose from a discussion whether poetry should be bloodthirsty or not'. The same man, a little further on, suggests that a work written by Caligula is apparently about 'the murderous power of poetry'.[9] This parallel between poetry and dangerous releases of passion may simply have been playful on the author's part. There is, nonetheless, a basis to it. Not that poetry is usually motiveless, unlike Caligula's whims. But it has, if it is poetry, some property that lends it a terrible aspect, a *sacred* character.

---

7 Camus, *Caligula*, pp. 50–51; translation modified.
8 Camus, *Caligula*, p. 22; translation modified.
9 Camus, *Caligula*, p. 28.

That obscure word points us to dangerous, contagious bursts of passion. The sacred is always in one respect similar to the plague, to which Caligula himself compares his whims. It is a *murderous power* par excellence and sacrifice, which is its effect, is most often a murder. Conversely, it would be hard to define the sacred better than through the character of Caligula (as it would be to define the profane better than through Cherea). This is unsurprising if we remember that the play is tragic, that all tragedy flows from sacred forces wreaking havoc, from a wild unleashing of passions.

Obviously, nothing can prevent Caligula having the advantage over Cherea. The former terrifies and suffocates; he has the seductiveness of indecency. The latter reassures and bores us. To put it another way, we cannot imagine an actor preferring the role of Cherea, barring some other reason to do so. 'I want to know where I stand,' says Cherea, 'and to stand secure'.[10] For, in Cherea's eyes the possible counts, just as the impossible counts for Caligula. The possible, happiness . . . 'There is no valid life', writes the author ('Ni victimes ni bourreaux' in *Combat*, 19 November 1946), 'without projection into the future'. Cherea's viewpoint is beyond debate: we live in pursuit of the possible.

This language is not refutable: 'I want to live,' he says,

> and to be happy. I believe that one cannot do either by taking the absurd to its fullest extreme. I am like everyone. To feel liberated from them, I sometimes wish for the death of those I love, I covet women whom the laws of family or friendship forbid me to covet. To be logical, I should at that point kill or possess. But I take the view that these passing notions are of no importance. If everyone went so far as to carry them out, we could neither live nor be happy. Once again, that is what matters to me.

Concern for what is possible lends the future primacy for us over the present: the present is a luxury, it is useless ('these notions are of no importance'); it is the unleashing of what a concern with the future shackles; it is excess, the impossible, passion. If we give in to the primacy of the present,

---

10 Camus, *Caligula*, p. 51. This is quite a free translation. More literally, Cherea says: 'I have a taste—and a need—for security.' [Trans.]

we have for an instant the power of Caligula, who himself only fully possesses that power on condition that he kill the concern for the future within himself. This opposition between Caligula and Cherea, passion and reason, the impossible and the possible, the prodigal primacy of the present and the parsimonious primacy of the future, is of the same nature as the opposition between the sacred and the profane. We often make the mistake of confusing the sacred with the good, the sacred with value. Of the sacred, we know only its limited form, that form which, with the aid of religious rites, is rendered harmless. We believe that those rites, which invoke sacredness, are intended to put us in its power: actually, they have the opposite intention of allowing us to escape it. Those rites exile it, banish it, bind it: for whoever celebrates them, it is an object of horror, not of love. It is only if the sacred is bound, not subjugated but exiled, firmly locked away, that *possible*, profane life begins: this possible life needs the sacred, but it has a greater need to be free of it, to *confine* it. And life has need of it only to the extent that it has first confined it, rendered it inoffensive: life calls for a release with limits set to it that are immovable from the outset, an unleashing that is only unleashed *up to that point*—and which, in a sense, is not unleashed at all, since it is compliant. There is no possible life without passion, but with passion all life would be impossible if the possible were not firmly *separated* from it in advance. What in these conditions we mistake for the sacred is perhaps its image, but in the restrictive sense of the word: the image of lightning is not lightning and the image of Caligula is not Caligula but theatre. Religion works by changes of this kind: religion does what the theatre does, but the theatre which, for its origins, requires a flesh-and-blood Caligula, also requires the real Cherea, the man who once put an end to the plague. With the limit set, we can allow the fire to burn before us—the possibility of the impossible! But, in the play acting, the inevitable reversal is already built in. The unleashing of passion, which the sham nature of the stage limits—it can be altered at will, since it is imaginary—is distorted to such a degree that the image itself is no longer limited merely by the fact of its unreal character but by the nature of the object represented: from Dionysus to 'the Good Lord' there is only an imperceptible decline, but a 'Good Lord' is much better than Dionysus at satisfying the thirst for security.

I have lingered over these problems not just because they are crucial, but on account of a general theory of Camus's, who places them at the source of morality. In 'Remarque sur la révolte' [Remark on revolt] (the only published part of an essay), Camus bases morality on revolt. I have no objection to that, but without a clear decision as to what form of revolt is being referred to, this argument leaves the main point unclear. The essentials of revolt, as seen from Camus's moral standpoint, lie in the fact that the heroes of his tragedies, Caligula and Martha, are rebels, and even that they give a complete, extreme and, from one angle, decisive expression to revolt. Of course that expression 'is not the right one', but without it—without the impossible that is linked to it—we cannot look at this impulse which is indeed, as Camus says, the origin of value. In this sense, Sade too expresses the extreme of revolt; and revolt in Sade, scarcely less than in Caligula, is utter indifference to the possible. But it was not without good reason that, at the beginning of this piece, I introduced the principle which he pits against the death penalty, which states that passion alone can legitimize the act of revolt that is murder. The fact is that the gap between revolution and revolt is precisely the same as between reason and passion. Revolt is always the contestation of a legal power and of the legitimacy of the laws. It is the product of passion, rejecting the governance of reason. Revolution, on the other hand, wishes for laws that will at last be legitimate, and for the state it founds to be grounded in reason.

Doubtless the notion laid out in 'Remarque sur la révolte' steers a middle course—aims to steer a middle course—between these fundamental opposites. It might be said that that notion only differs, essentially, from a principle of revolution by a general contesting, in advance, of the *absolute*: 'the value contained in the affirmation of revolt is never given once and for all . . . it has to be constantly sustained' ('Remarque', p. 21). There is no rest to be found in revolt. But if that is how it is, it is because revolt is passion. It is because it expresses an irreducibility of human beings to laws and limits—whatever those laws and limits—it is because the man who is obliged to shackle the passion within him cannot prevent that passion being greater than the force shackling it. The value affirmed by revolt is always insubordination, passion that is not subordinated or fettered. Can it really be said to be by chance that Camus's attention was drawn first to the ghosts of Caligula and Martha?

There is revolt, for Camus, from the very moment individuals exceed themselves and, rebelling, see in their act of rebellion that a part of themselves which cannot be reduced by oppression is, at least, reducible to humanity in general. 'There is simply,' says Camus, 'an identification of destinies and a taking of sides. The individual is not, in himself alone, that value he wishes to defend. It is in revolt that the human being passes beyond himself into others and, from that point of view, human solidarity is metaphysical'. Admittedly, philosophy today stresses a problem that is apparently insoluble: how is one to break out of oneself, to get outside the solitude to which individual life confines the human being? But what if we were never inside in the first place? What if existence, *physically* (independently, at least, of scientific thought), existed only outside of itself. What if the knowledge of others, like that common sense which is the commonest thing, were not the product of thought but the precondition for it? The advantage of an idea of revolt *as metaphysical experience of solidarity* is that it is a rejection of Caligula and Martha, for whom there is no solidarity (this is not entirely true: there is, at bottom, a complicity in crime and Martha is complicit with her mother; Camus even prefers the more urgent and sweeter idea of complicity to the idea of solidarity: does he not say of his morality that it is 'the morality of accomplices' ('Remarque', p. 12)?) The fact is that, though it is not generally necessary for individuals to move outside themselves—they are already outside—it is necessary for Camus to move outside of the solitude in which Caligula (or Martha) is confined: hence the—initially, timid—shift of 'La Remarque sur la révolte' and the more recent—marked—shift of *The Plague*.

Camus sets out from the impossible, criticizing it for not being *the possible*. Would revolt be revolt if it were not, first, contempt for the *possible*? But revolt would in no way be different from sacrifice, and rebellion would have no other issue than the death of the rebel, if it did not compromise with the *possible* (Sade himself compromised, spending part of his life out of prison). This amounts to saying that it is necessary with the sacred, which is an unleashing of passions, to give it both scope and limits. But it is easy to get that operation wrong. The best means to win a woman is not to be so anxious in one's desire for her, and to pursue something feverishly is sometimes to lose it.

The trouble is that, in searching feverishly for a morality that escapes the decline of morality—something we are led, or even obliged, to do today—we put ourselves in a decidedly unfavourable position. On the one hand, our search has to be both relentless and carefree, while, on the other hand, the slightest inattention can lead us astray. Camus is right to look to revolt as the foundation of a morality that escapes the obvious servility of conventions. But it is immediately apparent to him that part of humanity remains a stranger to revolt. So can revolt be said, then, to have the universal character required to serve as a foundation? He has, in fact, to press on regardless and say (the world that ignores revolt being, in his eyes, the world of the sacred):

> The rebel is the man expelled from the sacred and intent on calling for a human order in which all the answers are human.[11] From that moment on, every question, every word is an act of rebellion, while in the sacred world, every word is an action of grace. On this basis, it would be possible to demonstrate that only two possible worlds can exist for the human mind, the sacred world (or, to speak in Christian terms, the world of Grace) or the world of revolt. The disappearance of the one is equivalent to the appearance of the other [...] ('Remarque', pp. 14–15)

In principle, this is true, but because he does not find the fundamental theme of revolt within the confines of the sacred world, Camus strangely restricts the scope of his attitude. Let us freely admit that the opposition between the two is undeniable. But can the negation that governs it—'in the sacred world,' says Camus, 'the problem of revolt is not found (p. 14)'— really be said to deprive the position of universal value? No, in the sacred world one finds *only* the problem of revolt. And the problem framed in this way is not just *the essential problem of revolt*, but *Camus's essential problem*, since, as we have seen, it is Caligula's. The limiting of the sacred to within

---

11 As we can see here, Camus identifies the sacred with divine transcendence.

the order of religion is indeed a formula for submission, but done in response to the necessity of revolt to which concession has already been made. Revolt in the accepted sense is necessarily hatred of the sacred, for at that moment the sacred is no longer anything more than the order that it, the sacred, founds, which is its negation. What always differentiates revolt from a revolutionary enterprise based on reason is that it attributes ultimate value to pride—that is to say, to insubordination. All life for revolt is sovereign, rebellious, not just the impossible objects that the priests keep apart from profane or servile activity.

Even if I open my eyes to the truth of revolt, seeing at the same time the possible and the impossible, constriction and openness, I would have to admit that the position doesn't seem very tenable. At least I shall be tempted to hold on to—not to yield—the essential thing: *the irreducible part within me that is passion*. I shall have gauged its danger, but I shall have spoken out against an even greater danger, which is to give up on that passion out of a concern to live (or, beyond my own case, to hold in reserve what is possible, the tolerable survival of human beings). But the position is so difficult that a mistake here is not permissible: at the slightest release of tension, one slips from 'Remarque sur la révolte' to *The Plague*. The concern with misfortune, death and suffering was already substantial in *Caligula*; it already reintroduced the themes of vulgar morality. At least the 'plague' was clothed in bright colours at that point: it was chilling, but it was human and affecting. In the book that goes by that name, it is no longer anything but serious, natural calamity, an inhuman epidemic, and the surge of rebellion against it is, in the end, acceptance of the law of misfortune: there is death, we learn, which cannot be tolerated; all we can do is fight against it and we shall, of course, do so in vain. It will be an 'endless defeat'.[12] Even a victory would have less meaning than this defeat which, for the one who struggles to the point of excess, holds *sainthood* in store (I don't know what this word refers to. Contact with death or horror? Or an awareness of immeasurable struggle and inner peace? Or both? No doubt both). But what are we to say about this position? It seems from the outside that the author has lost his footing and, wishing to rescue a semblance of coherence, has

---

12 Albert Camus, *The Plague* (Robin Buss trans.) (London: Penguin Classics, 2020), p. 98.

conjured up these bloodless assertions out of weariness. How far removed all this is from a morality based on revolt; the morality preached in these severe, sober, often dense pages is something we know: it is the morality of the ages; it is, niggardly and lifelessly, a morality based on misfortune. Value isn't the value that is founded on insubordination and revolt: it is 'health', the fact of avoiding death without suffering. What counts is, negatively, not to die, not to suffer: 'Have you ever heard a woman cry out "Never!" at the moment of death?' (p. 98). The source of these teachings is given by the author in one word: 'misery [*la misère*]' (p. 99).[13] A hopeless weariness dominates the picture here: 'The only thing I'm interested in,' admits Tarrou, 'is to find inner peace' (p. 23). And, in a moment of relaxation, he just barely takes the trouble to add: 'Of course a man should fight for the victims. But if he ceases to love anything else, then what is the point in fighting?' (p. 197). He then suggests to his friend that they go and bathe in the sea. In order to find, like Tarrou, 'inner peace', must we learn to love nothing more desirable than a swim?

Camus's example shows how one may start out from a revolt-based morality and slide back quickly into a depressed one.

This is because a morality founded upon passion, upon an irreducible part of ourselves, is often accompanied by bad conscience: how are we to avoid feeling guilty, certain as we are that we are concealing the face of Caligula within ourselves? No one is in any doubt, the power associated with the unleashing of passion is a fearsome danger for *possible life*. What is ordinarily missed is that the evil is not then the product of passion but of power. Even in Caligula one could not say that the evil was profound, since his capricious acts rapidly destroy his power—and he knows it. Evil is what is done by the SS in the concentration camps; it is what acquires power by killing and, by killing, increases the power of the regime it serves. One cannot even say exactly that evil lies in power (otherwise there would be evil in tigers): evil lies in the fact that passion has grown servile, has placed itself in the service of a legal power that can only exert itself coldly. Pure

---

13 Translation modified: Buss translates *misère* throughout as suffering, which rather obscures the connection with *malheur* in the context of Bataille's remarks. The *Grand Robert* dictionary defines *misère* in its more literary sense, as '*malheur extrême*'. [Trans.]

passion is naturally in revolt and never wants legal power: generally, it does not even have power as its end but ruin, excessive expenditure rapidly destroying power.

It is for this reason that one cannot overstate the importance of Sade's paradox when he says that the state cannot kill (for the *law* which founds it is cold and has nothing to do with passion). The state, the law represent the rule of reason, but there is no rule of reason if the state allows passionate impulses to exert themselves within it and kills. Now, it is precisely the fear of misfortune that reintroduces into the state the passion required for murder. The concern with misfortune is generative of a whole hate-filled morality, which gives the prosecutor and the judge a good conscience. It is, most importantly, the origin of legal terrors which unleash these shameful, cowardly, subservient passions, and which are to passion what treason is to battle. It is, ultimately, all about knowing if we want a world entirely cowed and enslaved: if we have any other interest than the negative one of escaping misfortune, there will be nothing left in us that is not *subordinate*, since our goal will be negative (the *cautious* desire to be happy is itself only the desire not to be unhappy). Then man's only passion would be reduced to suppressed hatred, which does not assert itself openly, but does its—dirty—work in the shadows. Do we have to say that the inversion of negative passions, of the passionate desire to kill and humiliate others, can come as no surprise? Those passions cannot be openly proclaimed—the murderess of *The Misunderstanding* and Caligula are terrifying exceptions—those passions from the outset prompt a sense of shame at oneself and dissimulation and hence some form of degrading servility and the very opposite of a passionate attitude: the S.S. puffed themselves up with contempt and *legitimated* their crimes because they saw their victims as the cause of public misfortune. There is an inevitable link between the deniers, eager to enjoy the misfortune of others, and worlds in which the fear of unhappiness dominates. The virtue of passion stands at the opposite end of the scale from these depressive possibilities: it simply takes on a *gamble*, by which the concern with misfortune is removed, since, in gambling, I am preferring risk.

I shall, lastly, argue that value, being passion (divine intoxication and enthusiasm), can only reside in the *purity* of the passion. That word is not the product here of a vulgar idealism, but refers to insubordination (the refusal to fall in with some operation of constraint). It is for this reason that, in spite of deceptive appearances (or deliberate ambiguities), the demand for morality has so much to gain from engaging with Sade. And for the same reason, I cannot believe that, in spite of *The Plague*, Camus would himself be averse to an ethic involving desire and not fear. It is true that he gives the word a negative sense (a sense of misfortune suffered), but this surprising term *sainthood*—left suspended and unintelligible here—to which value he ultimately pledges the book, still betrays a nostalgia for passion and for pure burning desire.

Letter to Merleau-Ponty

Paris, 24 June 1947

My dear Merleau-Ponty,

You offered to let me reply in *Les Temps Modernes* to misguided accusations that have been made against Nietzsche. I was pleased to accept, but I am compelled today to present you with the reasons that will prevent me from following through with this project.

The last issue of *Les Temps Modernes* takes on Surrealism. Surrealism itself is attacked and the fact that these attacks come from Sartre changes nothing: they seem to me no less misguided than those aimed at Nietzsche.

I wish to make my feelings known on this matter in this letter.

We would, I imagine, concur in the belief that action—revolutionary action—has the right and the obligation to contest values which, though reconcilable with it, are nonetheless associated with inaction, or at least with some temporary suspension of action. Those values are generally ones that make the world a place of beauty, luxury being the most fragile aspect of this. And for each of us they raise the same dilemma in our everyday lives: we have constantly to neglect, or deny, interests that temporarily deflect us from activity. But, above and beyond inevitably contesting them in the name of action, it is, of course, necessary to maintain the principle that interests associated with leisure are our principal concern (that they remain valid) even at the point when we neglect them in order to act. Such are, in particular, insofar as they point to the intense possibilities for felt emotion—poetry, passion—the interests that surrealism represents: they are not contrary to action (they might even be said to be the end-goal of action), but they have to be suspended for us to act.

The fact that men of action are inclined to consider rather summarily—and with some irritation—these interests, in respect of which they act but which thwart them in their action, clearly brings a danger. It is, then, a pity, as I see it, that a writer who does not act and who confines himself to thinking (Sartre *speaks* of acting, but is that enough? Is it not, even, the worst of things?) should exacerbate the inevitable misunderstanding that brings *those who act* into opposition with their ultimate interest. This consideration is in no sense theoretical. The opposition is, in the end, all the more difficult to resolve for that fact that Surrealism is precisely the movement which *strips bare* the 'ultimate interest', frees it from compromise, in fact resolutely shows it up as caprice itself and, to be absolutely honest, lends it a trivial, indefensible appearance.

Because he has paid no attention to this overall meaning of Surrealism, Jean-Paul Sartre has produced a hasty analysis of it that does no credit to his methods of working. There is much facile talk of the dishonesty of his master Heidegger. However that may be, I cannot imagine Heidegger penning such cursory judgements dictated by superficial contempt; were philosophy to intrude into these problems, it would open eyes to a painful degree. But nothing in the present case goes beyond vain polemic, self-satisfaction and glibness. (Just take a look, finally, at the sparkling babble that opens the discussion: did Breton, who has done everything within his power to wrest literature away from mere *Sprecherei*, deserve this shabby farrago?)

The clear-sightedness of certain views changes nothing: it merely puts a sheen on argumentation from which only one truth emerges: that the author is in a confused tangle. Pertinent arguments deployed without getting to the essentials have their place in politics: they are misplaced coming from Sartre. What would you think of me if I based my remarks here on the fact that, of the bourgeoisie's literary parasites he is the fattest I have known? I speak of this only to show the pointlessness of such narrow-minded comments.

I shall, in fact, revisit my reasons at a later date, but I had to convey the crucial point to you today.

I naturally hope that you find nothing in this to detract from the esteem and fellow feeling I have for you.

Is Lasting Peace Inevitable?

LUCIEN MORICE, *Vers l'empire du monde*, Liberté de l'Esprit (Raymond Aron series ed.) (Paris: Calmann-Lévy, 1947), in 16°, 215 pp.

It was M. Lucien Morice's intention in this little book to show that history had laws, that events necessarily succeeded each other in a particular order and that, from them, one could deduce that lasting peace in the world would come soon. And naturally one could not say that M. Morice is entirely convincing. Yet nor can one deny the merits of an essay that eschews oratory, is clearly written and argued and based on solid, if not comprehensive, research.

*

I shall stress first the particular merits of this book, the most important of which is undoubtedly that it is firmly opposed to nationalism. No one actually doubts that it is necessary and praiseworthy to work for the prosperity and safety of one's country, but everyone knows now that that is only a secondary problem. The essential problem in our day is no longer to form nations but to destroy them, and anyone who doesn't commit themselves resolutely to that task takes on a responsibility incompatible with good sense. It is clear that a national border today is no longer a protective rampart to be defended (the rampart no longer protects anything, there is no longer any possibility of defending it), but a difficulty to resolve. It would be as regrettable now to ground politics on indefensible entities as it was not so long ago to base strategy on fortified lines. The reality of a nation was military, it was *a militarily isolated bloc*. A nation existed politically only if it was an autonomous military reality. It only remains for us to draw the consequences from these facts and base our politics on firm principles: namely, that only an empire can still have a political existence and, moreover, that the universal state is the only real frame of reference for action from now on (at least insofar as action is to have a rational goal). M. Morice cannot be praised enough for striking out resolutely on this path.

Another merit of this book, as I see it, is that it stands out against the argument commonly advanced on the Allied side during the war that any project to conquer the whole of Europe *necessarily* fails in the face of a coalition. M. Morice is perhaps wrong to think that if Europe in 1940 had still been an isolated system, the logic of history dictated the victory of Hitler and the formation of a European empire. These sorts of ideas make only dubious sense: in isolation, Europe would have had to deal differently with its demographic growth, so that it would have been very different in 1940 from the place it has become solely through emigration and the formation of America. But it is true that it was only the need to fight at the global level that doomed Hitler's *coup de force* and it was, at least, strange to base an argument—as was done—on a law of history derived from the failure of Napoleon!

*

The strangest thing in this regard is that, in thinking that informs the most important judgements (on matters of life and death), people frequently start out from supposed historical laws and yet protest against any attempt to establish such laws with any rigour. And on this point again, we should be grateful to M. Morice for going ahead and taking no notice of this widespread preconceived notion.

It may, in fact, be difficult to discover laws in highly irregular series of events and there is, arguably, a simple reason for this difficulty: namely, that the field of history is unlike those in which science establishes laws, in that it sets before us facts which are always different from one another, rather than those repetitions that enable us to say: each time this occurs, then that will happen . . . But this last objection is not as weighty as it seems. History no doubt marks out the ideal terrain of the dialectic, which embraces the notion of unprecedented changes, a thing that science cannot do. But there are—or have been—real changes and, at the same time, constants in all fields. M. Morice accepts that where a grouping of civilized peoples exists— circumscribed by seas, deserts or mountains that cannot easily be crossed (what he terms a *cohesion*), it tends naturally towards political unification.

He bases himself, naturally, on the examples of the Chinese and Roman empires which, isolated from each other, provided evidence of that law at the same time and along similar lines. But he shows that the same law has operated in other cases. It is, as he sees it, the effect on each occasion of the same cause, a cause present in the character of human beings. Why not, indeed, recognize that, in the last analysis, the tide of history may well be moving in a direction conducive to the general interest? That interest requires that, in place of *diplomatic peace*—a mere balance of forces, a suspension of hostilities between two wars—there should be *organic peace*, which is the only true kind, because it alone is founded on political unity. These terms, proposed by M. Morice, are sound and meet the need for a fundamental distinction: *diplomatic peace*—the only kind our civilization has known—is, all in all, the breathing space required for war to resume: *diplomatic peace is the state of permanent warfare.* Anyone with any sense sees war as inevitable so long as armed force belongs sovereignly to distinct nations. Yet it is in no way inevitable that, when viewed in the light of a definite interest, peoples will *always* prefer their nation to peace. The opposite is actually self-evident: only in appearance has national sentiment been exacerbated in our day: it is, in fact, only so intense as a result of a dissociation. The dread of war may just possibly have decreased (whatever is said of it), but the weariness is immense and weariness in this case is more salutary than dread.

And it seems to me quite natural to concur—in principle—with M. Morice's judgement that, from this point on, the establishment of a lasting peace is inevitable.

*

Nevertheless, some serious reservations are required. The first is a general one and concerns the nature of history: history is not a field of unlimited possibility, but of possibilities whose limits we cannot know. This is not the most serious reservation.[1]

---

1 If we cannot see everything and even if what is essential is hidden from us, that in no way means that perspectives are strictly limited to the past and the present. The fact that the future is what we cannot possess does not mean that we cannot *orient* ourselves towards it.

It is inadmissible to assert as M. Morice does, on the pretext that it is historical law, that organic unity, once established, will break down later—after an unspecified period of time. The conditions in which the ancient empires were established are not wholly different from current conditions (the general interest is continually winning out and revealing its pre-eminence over the private interests of nations). But we know literally nothing of the conditions in which a breakdown of a universal order would be inevitable (I do not say that it is sure to be maintained in perpetuity, but simply that we know nothing about it).

However, the most serious weakness of M. Morice's book lies in his extreme indifference to the economic question. As soon as his aim was expressly to identify a general law of history, he no doubt had little need to linger over those current conditions that differ profoundly from the historical conditions in which the ancient empires became necessary. But M. Morice does not confine himself simply to establishing that law, he draws consequences from it. He has attempted not just to show one of the inevitabilities of history working itself out, but to say generally what the current world holds in store. This is something it is impossible to do on the basis of isolated factors operating within the specific necessity of a given law. History (that is to say, humanity) cannot be exhaustively explained by a single kind of determination, even if it were determination by the universal state: that is still merely the empty shell, the framework in which disastrous contradictions might be resolved. The movement of history is, *primarily*, the resolution of those contradictions. No doubt M. Morice is far removed from those thinkers who wish stubbornly to encase the play of historical forces in formal frameworks that neutralize them. But, for want of taking those interplays of forces fully into consideration, he is indulging in hollow speculation when he indicates the conditions in which the importance of nations might be curtailed. To listen to him, a federation would do the job . . . But there is nothing surprising in this: an analysis that sidestepped the nub of the matter was fated to have no other outcome than an empty formula.

*

On the crux of this book, I shall confine myself to a small number of positive comments.

1) We have to take into account the evolution of nationalism and what nationalism is *now*. It may be said that fascism, as the fulfilment of nationalism, has struck it a death blow. It has forced the nationalists of all countries to fight against it, to fight against nationalism incarnate, or to sink into the kind of betrayal that was most contrary to their guiding principle. Nationalism is the deadest thing in the world today: it is virulent only if it is camouflaging some other force or camouflaging itself. It is necessary, then, to take account largely of oppositions that have another sense than the national and to regard as accidental the national forms of a potential conflict.

2) The fact that classes, ranged in opposition against one another, can no longer come into violent confrontation—on account of technical developments in weaponry—except in the form of conflicts between nations, forces us to envisage new nonviolent methods, if we wish to resolve the flagrant contradictions of the economy without losing our senses.

3) Recent conflicts have shown that unification by conquest no longer has any sense. I wrote above that human beings will undoubtedly prefer peace, in the end, to their nations, but they have proved rather convincingly that they will always prefer war to servitude (even were one to show them it was just a difficult stage to be gone through—after which Gaul becomes Roman Gaul). Britain today is leaving India: this is the decisive mark of a limit to the power of arms.

Moreover, there is a very deep difference between past and current conditions to be seen in the way the *racism* of the conquerors has made it impossible for Europeans to effect the assimilation of the natives in their colonies. That fact has extraordinary consequences. On the one hand, there is no colony in a stable state and, on the other, in Europe foreign domination has become infinitely more ignominious than it was in the past, as something that can only be suffered by inferior races.

Conditions were generally such that, even before it began, an attempt at the military unification of the world must have been to some extent inhibited. Hitler's failure has confirmed that state of affairs.

4) The current empires vying to govern the world are, therefore, both very unlike imperialist operations in the Roman style. Their capacity to rule over other peoples is in no way based on military capabilities, but on the power both have, each in its own way, to resolve current economic problems, which are global ones. Obviously, if one of these powers comes to govern the world, we may suppose it will be because it has defeated the other militarily. But the world domination established in that way will not be the product of conquest: it will simply be the result of a triumph—even if it were a military triumph—of one of the ways of regulating industrial life. That is why we may ask right now whether the struggle might not be fought out *first* at the level of economic solutions. If, instead of preparing for war, the United States were to envisage a radical battle on that terrain, humanity would quickly reveal one of the most remarkable changes that recent history has accomplished—a change that shifts the power to settle all matters away from military solutions.

Joseph Conrad

The business of literature today is a quest for ultimate realities, for a sacred truth, which may, at a pinch, be comic but which ordinary (discursive) language cannot express. Some will have none of this, but their considerable efforts are in vain: from the moment literature stopped being the poor relation—or the servant—to religion, it inherited religion's power and its charge. But, insofar as this is the case, insofar as literature is, consequently, the object of ultimate concerns, attention to Conrad seems misplaced.

If we think of what captivates us in the literature of our country, from Laclos through Rimbaud to Proust, there is in Conrad's work a ponderousness, arising as it seems to me from a cleaving to the dense reality of this world. There is, in truth, no transparency in this 'mirror of the sea', the writer's resignation expressly imparting to it the sadness of a wall. This is because transparency, no doubt, is the product of revolt; a perverse [*vicieux*] refusal to accept the condition imposed upon man in his times perhaps underlies all tension. But clearly Conrad rejected perversity [*le vice*] and extolled service to society.

This *perverse* refusal (perverse in that it separates from common humanity, though it is the *perverse* world that is sacred and common humanity, profane) is indeed so important that modern American novels, despite their realism, are also read and loved by those who regard literature in the way I have outlined: it is enough not that they aim to reform, but that they cynically describe an unbridled world that is not reducible to rule-governed society. *Sanctuary* and *Tobacco Road* matter to us because they mark out a world radically *outside* this one: this agreed, avowable, judge-like world. By contrast, Conrad's novels remove us from that world only by way of a questionable exoticism. Stories of far-off islands may charm dreamy young girls, but they are nothing more than escapism, a literature that helps us, through sham and pretence, to flee that violence which *forbidden* literary questing takes as its subject. Conrad himself went so far as to remove even the benefit of the doubt on this question. If he judges society severely, he does so on the basis of the principles he has received from it; there is no revolt. More even than the established order, he disdains thought, which is the contesting of that order. In his eyes, only action provides us with justification, but action, as he sees it, simply stands in the service of order—it is a dangerous struggle, but not a subversive one, against natural obstacles (and not against a limit laid down by some established order that would seek to shackle us tightly).

In this sense, Conrad may even be regarded as a type: no one perhaps has better, or more humanly, embodied the bourgeoisie at its zenith, dreaming of escaping its revolutionary origins, not to mention its mania for exploitation. In actual fact, he was not precisely of bourgeois origin. He belonged to a social class shorn of any real significance, a class consigned by history to something of an absurd position, a class that had nothing and was confined to making noble but hollow claims. He was the son, orphaned at an early age, of a Polish nobleman called Apollo Korzeniowski, who gave his life in the cause of his country's dangerous—even senseless—revolts against the Czar (Apollo Korzeniowski seems to have died a victim of the repressive measures he suffered). Oddly, the young Conrad decided to become a sailor: he left Poland and signed up with Western ship owners, first French, then English (hence the adventures he related in his books, which began with *The Arrow of Gold*, set in Marseille). And it may be said of him that once he entered the bourgeois sphere, he constantly imagined it resembling the feudal life that lay beyond reach: a life unchanging, based on struggle and loyalty. He found two elements of modern life odious, both of them associated with the rational construction of history: the French Revolution and the idea of Progress. He was, nonetheless, *liberal*, though that is another matter: as he saw it, the bourgeoisie simply had to throw off its disastrous association with the concern to change the world. If the bourgeois order had become forever fixed (if, in particular, it had not substituted vulgar steamships for—elegant and virtuous—sailing vessels . . .), Conrad would have had a silent place in it (outside of talk of citizens' rights or Progress). Conrad was not naïve: he admired and praised nothing except *renunciation*, and he renounced things only in favour of a world in his image, a renunciation which, through silence, would, in forms corresponding to such a perfect consumation, be the negation of revolutionary hope. During the first war, he was ardently democratic and anti-German and he died in 1924, reacting with nothing but total incomprehension to the world then being born (in the USSR).

But this—wilfully—limited character of Conrad goes, in a sense, beyond the mere nostalgia for lost possibilities. His abhorrence of revolt has, perhaps, a specific source. Conrad does not seem to have been faithful to his rebel father's ideal. Not that he ever stopped expressing his attachment to his country. But the cause of Poland no doubt had only a small place in his heart. We may even be right in thinking that it was precisely the downright imprudent, Romantic character of Polish agitation that repelled him. In the play of imagination and discourse—and in thought generally—he seems to have hated a deep inappositeness [*inadéquation*] and, on the other hand, to have seen in action—and to have esteemed highly—a form of irrefutable appositeness. I do not know whether Georges Jean-Aubry is right to see this lack of concern for Polish rebellion as the origin of the anguish (the sense of guilt) that inspired *Lord Jim*, which is, in a sense, the pinnacle of his *oeuvre*. Perhaps it is not so simple: multiple elements seem to find resolution in Conrad. An unspoken sense of impossibility, in which mingled despair and wonder are at once exacerbated and appeased. There is no salvation for him: the renunciation in which this ineffable state originates is, fundamentally, renunciation of salvation. It is even a form of remorse too, since at one point the expectation of someone harbouring hope was dashed . . . someone who was hoping in vain, but still hoping. A faithful adherence to the most limited of possibilities—of professional activity and productivity (the basis of Conrad's conformism)—cannot put us off the scent for very long: it is not about accepting the world and the way it strangely persists, but suffering these things—being resigned to them. Naturally, this renunciation stands opposed to revolt: it is, to say the least, the complete opposite to it; the opposite of the rebel's discontent is not the crude egoism of the contented, but final renunciation in the certainty of incurable discontent. Conrad no doubt personified the bourgeoisie seeking to evade its destiny—his work is escapist literature—but that is not the only aspect of it: if he shied away from the *particular* necessity of the world of which he was a part, he did so for a *universal* necessity, such that, at bottom, no possibility of escape remained.

In fact the shams and pretences Conrad employed had a dual purpose. Without a doubt, for the consumption of superficial readers, he built up an ultimately limited world that was attractively picturesque. But this can be interpreted in two ways. He was opening up a possibility for harmless escape, and that is the most conspicuous aspect. But in the long run you cannot help noticing that the more attractive he makes this, the more he disappoints: this exotic, empty side of things, which hadn't perhaps been intentionally impoverished in the first instance and which is presented with debatable but consummate art, only apparently offers an *opening* for escape. And, if it is true that, without revolt, there is only a flimsy kind of escape and, at a deep level, there remains an acceptance of the status quo, the author actually wanted the opposite of what we initially ascribe to him: if he represented escape, he did so to arouse the desire for it, but only to reveal a little further on, like some secretly monstrous truth, that it was impossible; to close down discreetly at the end what we had prematurely imagined he was opening up. The feeling that dominated Conrad was the sense of the *impossible*: this is the ultimate meaning of his work; it is how, despite its ponderousness, it captivates the reader.

This ambiguity accounts for the divided reactions one often sees to Conrad's works. Many people, inspired by undeniable feelings of revolt, read him but do not talk about him, reserving their real concern for other subjects. They avoid mingling his voice with those whose violence or underlying character fascinate them: Conrad occupies a special place for them, only half-admitted. But though small, that place is, in some obscure way, deep in their heart. This is because even a facile side of his books— and that side in particular—conveys an immense love of human beings, a wonderful capacity for enchantment, though nothing escapes the constraint limiting the enchantment to that suspended sense that goes by the name of the 'impossible'. It is not mere despair, which is simply the unhappy side of hope: it is the awareness linked to the intensity of the instant, knowing the instant irrecoverable, and knowing too, if it is perfect, that the desire for something enduring annihilates it. This sentiment which finds expression, to all appearances, in the mode of disenchantment is, in a sense, the most contrary to revolt, which is, in theory, driven by hope for reform: it may even be said to find its intensity only on the contrary path to renunciation. But at one point rebellion and resignation coincide, and Conrad's undeniable opacity would seem to come from his not seeing this (conversely, the thoughtlessness of revolt rather quickly clouds the presence of the instant). We are faced here with the ineffable and, one way or another, something is always beyond our grasp. This is exhausting and no doubt militates in favour of impatience: how, then, to reject the violence of revolt? But impatience and violence both deceive us and open up the most pointless escape routes. *Wisdom* responds unspectacularly, but its modesty deserves our attention. And these principles of Conrad's art, which I now quote in conclusion, also have a far-reaching significance, extending beyond their apparently platitudinous nature. He writes:[1]

> To arrest, for the space of a breath, the hands busy about the work of the earth, and compel men entranced by the sight of distant goals to glance for a moment at the surrounding vision of form and colour, of sunshine and shadows; to make them pause for a look, for a sigh, for a smile—such is the aim, difficult and evanescent, and reserved only for a very few to achieve. But sometimes, by the deserving and the fortunate, even that task is accomplished. And when it is accomplished—behold!—all the truth of life is there: a moment of vision, a sigh, a smile—and the return to an eternal rest.

And further on:[2]

> To snatch in a moment of courage, from the remorseless rush of time, a passing phase of life, is only the beginning of the task. The task approached in tenderness and faith is to hold up unquestioningly, without choice and without fear, the rescued fragment before all eyes in the light of a sincere mood. It is to show its

---

1 Georges Jean-Aubry, Preface to *The Nigger of the 'Narcissus'* in *Sagesse de Conrad* (Georges Jean-Aubry ed.) (Paris: Gallimard, 1947), p. 41.
2 Jean-Aubry, Preface to *The Nigger of the 'Narcissus'*, p. 47.

vibration, its colour, its form; and through its movement, its form, and its colour, reveal the substance of its truth—disclose its inspiring secret: the stress and passion within the core of each convincing moment. In a single-minded attempt of that kind, if one be deserving and fortunate, one may perchance attain to such clearness of sincerity that at last the presented vision of regret or pity, of terror or mirth, shall awaken in the hearts of the beholders that feeling of unavoidable solidarity; of the solidarity in mysterious origin, in toil, in joy, in hope, in uncertain fate, which binds men to each other and all mankind to the visible world.

Is it any surprise that, from such a starting point, Conrad's stories are so often arranged in a dream-like fashion and what remains of them in the end is merely something elusive? (I am thinking of *Heart of Darkness*, of the end of *Victory*, and of those feminine figures whom a wearying fatefulness lifts out of the world of passing time).

Recent Publications on Joseph Conrad

GEORGES JEAN-AUBRY, *Vie de Conrad* [Life of Conrad], Leurs Figures, VOL. 3 (Paris: Gallimard, 1947), in 8°, 304 pp.

This biography is the fruit of twenty years of meticulous work. It is not, like so many other 'lives', the hurried exploitation of already established facts, but a solid and substantial piece of work.

JOSEPH CONRAD, *Sagesse de Conrad* [Conrad's wisdom] (Georges Jean-Aubry ed.) (Paris: Gallimard, 1947), in 16°, 143 pp.

'Over a long period of time spent following the works of Joseph Conrad,' G. Jean-Aubry 'has taken note of most of the remarks of a general order with which his writings are studded'. This little book conveys the essentials of the novelist's thinking in condensed form: it is in no way disappointing and the title *wisdom*, in the ordinary sense of the word, is entirely appropriate.

Preface to the Gaston-Louis Roux Exhibition

Disrupting the order of things on the canvas; taking a full world and opening a rectangular hole in it through which—from another end and, as it were, the wrong way round—we see the other, previously unseen face of the sun. We are so familiar with how this works that we most often perceive only the skill of the painter and his individual difference—things it is possible to speak about. But if we accept that the challenge of painting is as I say it is, and that we shall, in the end, look, beneath its skirts, at the splendour of the skies, perhaps we have less to say and are reduced to a furtive silence. It is one thing to appreciate skill, art and powers of execution in a painter (without them, the trick fails). It is another to look to the artist for a sense of emptiness, boredom and disappointment. Disappointment is, in fact, the mark of the splendours that were revealed to him but remain elusive. So a painter must have some tricks up his sleeve, and at the same time be the victim of his own trickery.

I shall now describe what is going on here more precisely. On the one hand, the immediate splendour of the day; imagine marshes, ponds, the sea, the sky and light—a disappointing, inhuman, intoxicating immensity, insofar as it is, from the outset, concealed from us (what await us are a car, a table, objects ordered and disordered). And on the other hand—and the other way around—an equal beauty, but no less hidden, fashioned from the impossibility of a world in which objects are both neatly ordered and disarranged: a play of light in which those objects themselves vanish into air and cock a snook at us, but this reverse side of the day, sick as it is, is human: it is the human light or immensity that a painter sees and presents to us through the window of the painting.

In the end there remains scant difference between the pure immensity of the sun's face and that of its other side, where we lose our bearings. But if it is true that both ultimately elude us, we would enjoy our dealings with both the less if we had not, within objects, opened up the window of painting.

I say this about the Roux exhibition for having glimpsed it—very painfully—while watching him paint. Imagine an angry, worried man standing alone, gnawing away at himself with a permanent sense of frustration, striving to open a window onto the world: knowing nothing and being driven back short of his goal, groaning. A sadder, more painfully childish passion I have never seen: and the sadness, pain and childishness, because they had rejected prudence, turned into mischievousness, into farce, into a comical cock's crow at dawn! The authenticity of the operation, of the piercing of the opening on to the world, could hardly be greater. And only the blind would not see that Roux's window authentically strips bare the back side of the world.

From Existentialism to the Primacy of the Economy

EMMANUEL LEVINAS, *De l'existence à l'existant*, Exercice de la pensée (Georges Blin series ed.) (Paris: Fontaine, 1947), in 16º, 176 pp.[1]

JEAN WAHL, *Petite histoire de 'l'existentialisme', suivi de Kafka et Kierkegaard. Commentaires* (Paris: Éditions Club Maintenant, 1947), in 16º, 132 pp.[2]

GUIDO DE RUGGIERO, *Existentialism* (E. M. Cocks trans.) (Rayner Heppenstall ed. and intro.) (London: Secker and Warburg, 1946), in 8º, 52 pp.

JULIEN BENDA, *Tradition de l'existentialisme, ou les Philosophies de la vie* (Paris: Grasset, 1947), in 16º, 125 pp.

No one today denies existentialism a *de facto* dominant place in the philosophical sphere. This generally little-known doctrine is enjoying an exceptional vogue: but that place is not down to vulgar curiosity: it would seem there is nothing in current philosophy to counter the works produced by a school that claims to be renewing the notion we have of existence.[3]

This superior position naturally irritates various groups. It irritates the Marxists, who see it as the expression of a decadent class. It irritates Idealism's survivors whose positions it directly targets.

---

1 Translated as *Existence and Existents* by Alphonso Lingis (The Hague: Martinus Nijhoff, 1978).

2 Translated as *A Short History of Existentialism* by Forrest Williams and Stanley Marron (New York: Philosophical Library, 1949).

3 There are several changes in this first paragraph: 'This generally little known doctrine has *for some time* enjoyed an exceptional vogue; but that place is not the effect of this *superficial vogue*: it would seem there is nothing in current philosophy to counter the works produced by a school that claims to be reviewing the notion we have of *ourselves and the world*.' (This latter expression is replaced by: *of existence*). [Eds]

The way existentialism is opposed to Marxism is, however, very different from the way both those philosophies are opposed to idealism.

First, the minor position of contemporary Marxism is deceptive. Admittedly, recent works representative of that philosophy lack the appeal of novelty; in a word, insofar as we are familiar with them, they lack the range and general scope of the great existentialist works. But among Marxists philosophy is not the main concern: Marxism acts. And, though it may not occupy as much of a place *in the philosophical sphere* as existentialism, it is infinitely more *influential*.

Furthermore, the Marxist position is not the exact opposite of existentialism. The primacy of life over thought is common to the two doctrines. Karl Löwith[4] has shown that both opposed the idealism of Hegel; he has identified common features between Kierkegaard, Marx and Nietzsche. (But obviously, of the three, Marx is the least distant from Hegel and, in any event, the primacy of life is more real among the Marxists. The existentialists are not particularly faithful to their starting point: they philosophize and the Marxists live. For the latter, as it was for Marx, the point is no longer to understand the world but to change it).

Curiously, Julien Benda himself associates existentialism in one respect with Marxism (which he, in fact, omits to name). This pure idealist, who is relatively indifferent to the fate of human beings and who, in brief sallies, gives in to a 'hatred of all that exists', attributes modern philosophy to *the crowd*.

> Attachment to thought in its opposition to life is something one finds in exceptional men, who are few in number, generally solitary and rather lofty: let's say that one finds it in an aristocracy. It follows that we may say that, with the revolution of the nineteenth century, *philosophy, which was up to that point aristocratic, became a thing of the people.* Once again, the Word was made flesh. (*Tradition de l'existentialisme,* p. 24; Benda's emphasis)

---

4 Karl Loewith [Löwith], 'L'achèvement de la philosophie classique par Hegel et sa dissolution chez Marx et Kierkegaard', *Recherches philosophiques* 4 (1934–35).

In his view, 'Bergsonism, Nietzscheanism and existentialism are *popular philosophies*.' There is not a lot of sense to this, but, as regards Bergsonism, we may let that pass: this is about subversion, the primary object of Julien Benda's hatred. Subversion does, in fact, chime with a proud, animal dimension of the people; the primacy of life is subversive—it contests the *law*—and the crowd is as opposed as can be to the primacy of thought (at least to the primacy of the stability on which it is founded).

It is obviously bizarre (though unimportant) that, holding this opinion of nineteenth century philosophy, and seeing it oriented towards life, as it was in its active dimension, Julien Benda should make no reference to Marxism. But at least his unorthodox view helps us to grasp the irresistible philosophical thrust that continues into our own thinking, which is the refusal to present thought itself as the end-goal of thought. Do we have to say that, in resisting it as he does—by an arrogant vapidity—Benda is actually serving a cause he attacks?

The old—pre-Hegelian—idealism is, without a doubt, the form of philosophy that is most alien to our barbarous, impatient minds. We can feel no affection for its hypocrisy. At the same time, in Marxism and existentialism, a disrespectful bluntness and a 'resolute decisiveness' put us at odds with eternal ideas. This isn't always attractive: a flabby need for anguished emotion, a sentimental bad taste underlie the fashion for existentialism. 'Existentialism', to use the Italian idealist Guido de Ruggiero's expression, 'places us in existence as if in a detective novel' (*Existentialism*, p. 19). But the idealist anger isn't inspired by this ponderous frivolity. It is directed at the relative nihilism and the ease with which 'the murky depths of life' are penetrated.[5]

---

5 However, between the Roman professor's book and Julien Benda's, the similarities are confined to the subject and the authors' idealist standpoint. Visibly, Julien Benda has only the vaguest idea of the philosophy he writes about. He limits himself to the facile charge that 'it's as old as the hills!' Guido de Ruggiero gives a brief but fulsome and clear account of so-called existentialist philosophy—as represented by Kierkegaard, Heidegger, Jaspers and Gabriel Marcel. And one can understand why the British translated this little book as an introduction to a doctrine about which hardly anything is known in their country: the author's hostility is, in fact, directed more at their readers than at the philosophers whose thinking he is summarizing. The preface by Rayner

The moment came, in the nineteenth century, when human intelligence, raised to its most acute, ceased to regard itself as the centre and fulfilment of the world. A sense of infinite dignity gave way to feelings of distress and abandonment. Irony undermined dignity; hunger and passion rendered it detestable. If *I know* that I am hungry and that, beyond a hunger that might be appeased, an unlimited desire will torment me, then the contentment of knowledge turns into its opposite. The primacy of life over thought takes these two forms: Marx asserts the primacy of needs, while present in Kierkegaard's position is the primacy of a desire that extends beyond the satisfaction of need. I shall speak first of the primacy of desire (having to show, in fact, that it, like the primacy of need, is reducible to economic facts).

For philosophers in general and for Hegel, knowledge was a pursuit of the object: this also implied an adequation of the subject (the human being, the philosopher) to the object (that which is, the world, God, or the absolute Idea). That object was an immutable, eternal essence and a 'universal truth valid for all time': the—random—subject and his/her needs and desires were necessarily subject to that truth, crushed by it. Hegel, admittedly, posited the object as a totality of which each subject was a part: each individual, each thought was a moment in the universal becoming, in the system of the world. But the subject knew that he/she was in the end reduced to being a

---

Heppenstall shows up very clearly the extent to which 'the existentialist adventure', by which I mean the sudden development of the French school and the hullabaloo around it, is unintelligible from outside. Its author, who was writing in November 1945, draws his information mainly from an article by Madame Claude-Edmonde Magny. For my own part, I am sorry to see myself listed among the French existentialists. As I see it, the whole affair is unfortunate, a generalized confusion sustained by journalistic frenzy. Moreover, Heppenstall seems to suspect as much, his preface being not at all reassuring. It says, more or less: 'Kierkegaard, of course (he became known in Britain even later than in France). Then come this person and that, though we can't make much sense of them . . . ' What Mme Magny says about the books of Sartre, Camus, Blanchot or my own (so only one existentialist out of four) seems rather distressing to him: this is not what he was expecting from France after the silence of the Occupation. And he is happy to quote Benedetto Croce's judgement to the effect that the philosophy of existence 'clutters the world of the mind', that it is 'over-excited, poisoned and perverse—a sort of swelling of the groin.'

mere 'paragraph' in the whole—in the system. They could only bury themselves, destroy themselves in the knowledge of a totality of Becoming, of a *completed Becoming*, an *immutable Becoming*. Only on one condition could they *be*: namely, on condition of knowing that 'they' *were not*, except as a subordinate part of an immense, necessary ensemble, as a 'useful component', and that, if they believed themselves to be autonomous, they were committing an error. Hegel's desire thus resolves itself into a knowledge that is absolute, which is an elimination of the—relative—subject who knows. In these conditions, *one no longer exists*; first of all, history is assumed to be at an end and the life of the individual subject must be so too. Never, on reflection, has anything been conceived that is deader: multifarious life was the enormous game and the enormous error that the fulfilment of that death necessitated. Towards the end of his life, Hegel gave up on the problem: he repeated his lecture courses and played cards.

In protest against an inhuman philosophy, Kierkegaard raised the cry of a stifled existence. Against the contentment of the eternal idea, he pitted the intensity of individual feeling and this randomness of the possible, which may be or may not, leaving us in a state of anxious suspense. He was, for his part, an *existent*: even if existence, as he believed, was sin, he wanted it, in himself, to be intensified, taut and suspenseful. The God before whom he existed was not immutable truth but that unknowable and unjustifiable existent beyond the reach of reason that is the God of Abraham.

On this basis, there cannot properly speaking be any philosophy but rather the cry I have referred to: it is the expression of an existence, a subjectivity. That expression may be the act of one versed in the problems of philosophy, but, for all that, it will not constitute a system. Hence Jean Wahl, who takes the view that 'one cannot define the term existentialism satisfactorily' (*Petite histoire de l'existentialisme*, p. 12), compares Kierkegaard to Rimbaud, if not indeed Van Gogh. And what is expressed by Rimbaud— what he experienced—would be on the same footing in terms of its interest as the works of Kierkegaard. An emotionally sensitive existence, forcefully expressed, would substitute for the stating of philosophical truth. The role of a philosopher would be limited to showing how philosophy resolves into statements about existence itself. Jean Wahl has spoken of poet-philosophers:

if I understand him right, this would mean people who are philosophers by their origins but are so in order to liquidate a heritage: they would constantly be resolving the sustained effort of philosophical research into sustained poetic outpourings.[6] All in all, it is very natural, from Kierkegaard onward, to return to the attitude of a religion, which sees myths and rites as being of more interest than philosophical—or, indeed, dogmatic—knowledge (we should even, in this connection, assimilate ancient myths to these privileged experiences which take precedence over thought).

I have described here only a first move by which existentialism detached itself, in Kierkegaard's mind, from classical philosophy. Though to apply the term 'existentialism' to Kierkegaard is an extraneous addition. Jean Wahl himself does not claim the term for his own thinking, which is happy to pit Kierkegaard against modern existentialism.

Compared with Kierkegaard's position, modern existentialism is a com-promise. That philosophy and philosophy in general do, indeed, stand opposed to one another. The latter is, in principle, the pursuit of a changeless essence. And existentialism asserts (this is its textbook definition) that exist-ence *precedes* essence. It nonetheless seeks out in some way the essence which the existence precedes. This isn't entirely clear, but Heidegger, Jaspers or Sartre speak of *existents*, of human beings *in general*. This slippage is accompanied by a hypertrophy of the intellectual approach. It is still all about *experiencing* existence, about living *first* and knowing *afterwards* (otherwise, existence could not precede essence), but there is everywhere an excess of knowledge and professorial attitudes (particularly in Sartre). And it is no longer the subjective life of the individual that raises the ques-tions but the very demands of thought. No doubt it is for this reason that Jaspers—Jean Wahl quotes him to that effect—said that existentialism was the death of the philosophy of existence. One may, at a pinch, argue (as Emmanuel Levinas does) that it was professorial existentialism that brought

---

6 At this point, Bataille removed the following note: 'There are the greatest differences within the existentialist world. The systems of current existentialism run totally contrary to this position. A literature *illustrating* a system moves further away from it. Kierkegaard's position was romantic; that of Heidegger, who calls Hölderlin to witness, is so still, but Sartre has broken decisively with them: he is a foreigner to poetry.' [Eds]

Kierkegaard to light and gave him his precise place in the history of philosophy. If that is the case, then the existentialism of our day is comparable to the sacrificer of ancient times who revealed the truth of victims by killing them.

The repudiation here is surprising—as though an excess of intellectual power gave rise to moral impotence. The language of this philosophy is cumbersome and laboured. There is, it seems to me, a hesitation at its base. Existentialist thought is always elusive, but never in itself achieves the annihilation of thought. The way a child beset by urgent need dances on the spot and can't make up its mind, it is a form of thought that evades but does not die, sick as it is with a morose virtuosity. All its elements sway one way and then another: Heidegger's nothingness becomes being . . . I am astonished that, at this point in its development, it should take *several* minds to produce the cacophony of divergent possibilities: discoursing on time and being, surely *one single mind* could find ten kinds of nonsense to spout about them. If we cannot get to 'a universal truth valid for all time', then, in terms of positive philosophy, we are merely joking. A truth valid for only one time is merely a convenience; in this case, it is merely a reference to action, or represents just a moment of the eternal truth it is referring to, or is simply a painful[7] contemplation of the void.[8]

If one is willing to see them for what they are, these brilliant developments of contemporary philosophy are confused. Heidegger has to be admired for the way he has managed to synthesize traditional religious

---

7 Variant: the published text used to term *affreusement*, suggesting a horrified contemplation of the void. Bataille substituted the word *douloureusement*, then replaced this with *péniblement*, which he first crossed out but eventually retained. [Eds]

8 Hegel construes the successive truths of different ages (the history of philosophy) as the necessary moments of the absolute Idea. Kierkegaard, drawing upon an unintelligible revelation, asserted the rights of the subject against an objective positing of necessary truth. Marx was focused on action. Nietzsche spoke in the darkness of an absolute non-knowledge, announced the absence of revelation and truth, the absence of God. Heidegger comes to a position akin to Nietzsche's. On the face of it, Sartre might be said to limit himself to speaking the truth of his times. I struggle to believe this: how could a *philosopher*, in such a situation, carry on regardless, without subjecting such a limit to fundamental reflection?

experience and an academic philosophy associated with atheism; what he teaches comes out of the most meaningful investigation yet made into the spheres of the profane and the sacred, the discursive and the mythic, the prosaic and the poetic.[9] But if we put the emphasis on the sacred, on what Heidegger calls more generally the *authentic*—were we to wish in that way to avoid a value judgement—then the door is thrown open (as it commonly has been throughout history) to any *viable* folly (and the margin for error is great): there is only one remedy: to regard the *authentic* and the *viable* as strictly opposed to each other, and to regard as authentic life only an intense consumption[10] that is bereft of meaning and strictly useless (passion cannot

---

9 A sentence is struck out at this point: 'Accusations are made against him at the political level and this is perhaps a little overdone: from what is regarded as vile to pardonable error, there are simply differences of degree.' [Eds]

10 '*Une consumation intense*'. It seems quite evident here that Bataille is using the noun *consumation* in what the Centre National de Ressources Textuelles et Lexicales and all the standard French dictionaries describe as its 'rare, literary' sense as the noun of action of *consumer*, to convey the meaning of 'consuming something, destroying something, (as) by fire, progressively and completely'. This was an archaism in Bataille's day and the equally rare word 'consumation' seems to offer an almost exact English equivalent, being defined in the *Oxford English Dictionary* as 'the action of consuming, destruction'. As with French *consumation*, the only examples cited before Bataille's time are from the early modern period (the most recent citations in the OED going back to the early 17th century). The sense of 'the using up of material, the use of anything *as food, or for the support of any process*' (my emphasis), which is perhaps the dominant meaning of 'consumption' in contemporary usage (and in 'consumer society'), does not appear to attach to 'consumation'.

Some previous translators have rendered Bataille's *consumation* into English as 'consumption' or 'consummation'. This appears to me to miss the centrally important economic distinction he makes between the consumption that goes into the production of other material objects (e.g. the consumption of steel by the car industry) or into the reproduction of life and labour-power (e.g. food or clothing) and the 'destructive' consumption that anthropologists identify in potlatch and Bataille finds in other, parallel instances in modern life, particularly those associated with *la fête*—revelry, feasting or partying.

There is an interesting discussion of the tendency to confuse the English words 'consumation' and 'consummation' at a scholarly level in Hunter Kellenberger, '"Consummation" or "Consumation" in Shakespeare?', *Modern Philology* 65(3) (February 1968): 228–30, which further helps to clarify the issue. [Trans.]

be subordinated to practical ends—there is no non-servile, sovereign life other than in the rejection of being in charge, of enslaving legally: this is Sade's attitude). On this point, the poverty of this philosophy seems to me to derive from its origin: Kierkegaard's authenticity was inapplicable to the world, it was such an intense consumation of life that it left the development of knowledge in the background. It is difficult to see in Heidegger anything that corresponds to Kierkegaard's passion, a passion roared out in virtual madness: the authentic in Heidegger is consciousness of the authentic, or nostalgia for rare authentic moments, followed by a life of professorial studies, a life devoted to the *knowledge* of the authentic. That life does not seem to be *dominated* by an unjustifiable passion.[11] What seems to have dominated Heidegger is no doubt the intellectual desire to reveal being (being, not existence) through discourse (through philosophical language).[12] Jean Wahl rightly says that the 'existentialist's knowledge and even his existence' are likely to be troubled [*troublées*] (I shall go further and say *confused* [troubles]). He goes on: 'isn't the existentialist in danger of destroying that very existence he wishes above all to preserve? The question is whether existence is not something that should be reserved for solitary meditation' (op. cit., p. 61). But there is no need for Christ or myth here, the silence of discourse that Wahl points to has no limit other than the cry of a useless passion, and cannot fail, if it avoids the return of the phrases that bind us to other human beings (that deprive us of solitude), to

---

11 Greatly amended paragraph: in the text published by *Critique*, passion and *déchaînement* are both included here ('la passion et le déchaînement ne peuvent être subordonnés aux fins pratiques'): the words 'the attitude of Sade' replace 'the morality of Sade'. The words 'to derive from its origin' replace 'to be a response to its essence'; and part of a sentence is left out: 'That life does not seem to be *dominated* by a terrible passion: consequently, it comes as no surprise that there is a slippage, not a necessary but a possible one, from the authentic to Hitlerism (or *of agreement with Hitlerism*). [Eds]

12 A note has been removed at this point: 'Heidegger's hostility to the word existentialism is well-known: though he responds to Kierkegaard's initial move with a concern for the authentic, he distances himself from it in his questing after being. He does not even accept, as Jaspers does, the name 'philosophy of existence': he calls himself a 'philosopher of being'. [Eds]

consume life to the very brink of death.[13] There is no bombast in this: the experience of emptiness, of solitude, of the presence of the world within oneself and without, as the presence of an unintelligible violence, is not less but more pathos-laden than the religious person's experience before the cross. To devote oneself as a matter of principle to this silence and at the same time to philosophize, to speak, is never a straightforward thing to do: the sort of slippage indispensable to the exercise then becomes the very movement of thought.[14]

I come back to the position of Hegel, as given at the beginning of the movement.

It is strange today to glimpse something Kierkegaard could not have known: that Hegel, like Kierkegaard, when faced with the absolute idea, experienced a rejection of subjectivity. One might, in theory, assume that Hegel's rejection was the product of a conceptual opposition, but the contrary is true. We do not have this fact from a philosophical text but from a letter to a friend, to whom he confides that for two years he thought he was going mad. The reason was the need he felt to relinquish the individual within himself (representing to himself the need no longer to be the par- ticular being, the individual that he was, but rather the universal Idea, the need to fall, so to speak, into divine inanity—in a word, to be *God*, but hav- ing to, *wishing* to, die—he felt he was going mad). And this lasted not for a night or two days, but for two years. In a sense, Hegel's cursory sentence even has a force that Kierkegaard's long cry did not possess. It is no less

---

13 Jean Wahl's vocabulary seems unfortunate: 'meditation' is a weak word and 'pre- serving' existence or being afraid of 'destroying' it might, at a pinch, be understood in the opposite sense than intended (one has to 'lose' one's life to 'find it'; and not to 'pre- serve' it but to 'consume it' if one is not to be cheated out of it.

14 The following passage was removed at this point: 'And if one remembers that all this enormous effort is, from the outset, devoted to the discordance between different philosophies, which can only aspire to a truth relative to the absence of truth, then such a great labour gives off a whiff of the suspicious and the shady that leaves the head reel- ing, as much as it also thrills with a prodigious wealth of viewpoints.

Considering the degree of wavering exerted here, the incessant vacillation and shifting of thought, it is necessary to come back to Hegel's position, given at the begin- ning of any movement.' [Eds]

given in existence—which always exceeds its limits—than that cry. But Hegel stands opposed to Kierkegaard in that the demand for the universal does not come to him from the outside. It is all about a need—*and this is more serious*—that is at once impersonal and internal, but immanent to the spirit it imposes, rigorously articulated, offering no way out. Kierkegaard was free to argue, or subtly to sidestep the arguments of others (to misunderstand them). Hegel could only obey his own reason—or lose it.

Reading *The Phenomenology of Spirit*, or viewing the portrait of the aged Hegel, one cannot fail to be struck by a chilling impression of fulfilment, in which all possibilities come together. That phenomenology isn't an intellectual construct but the emergence and elimination of subjectivity in the world; it is the immense succession of woes, efforts, labours, errors, downfalls and revolts that take that subjectivity, in an exhausting epic, from the particularity of subject to the universality of object, to the consciousness of self as consciousness of a universal; it is the real history of the human species, reduced to the changes that have built, in struggle, the necessary edifice of Spirit, which in the end embraces totality through knowledge. That movement, going forward in a world of ruins, of death and the gnashing of teeth, cannot be reduced to tragedy: 'but that man is ceaselessly, of himself, moved to match up to death is its origin and its force. The spirit that retains within itself like a moving mirror' this unfolding of the history of subjectivity through wars and oppression, anxiety and tribulations can be salved: but salving it is, nonetheless, an endeavour on the scale of the immensity unleashed. The harsh truth of the *Phenomenology* is that spirit or mind is the same thing as history; that its straining and repose boil down to distant effects of the ruthless struggle that has taken place on the Earth. And what is at issue in this stormy birth, the rhythm of which is given in the—unequivocally real—velocity of an arrow piercing the body,[15] is, at the same time as the positing of the individual (whom death individualizes by the anxiety he feels because of it, because no one can die in his stead), the reduction to the universal of the individual, whom anxiety rivets to his particularity; but this salving reduction is in no sense the product of a slowly acquired wisdom: it is a scandalous, suffocating destruction, *even though it is accounted for, and demanded by, reason*. And the ravaged sense of calm

---

15 Variant: the heart. [Eds]

that shows on the features of the aged Hegel, who appears both overpowering and reassuring, is not in any way the *forgetting* of the impossibility from which it issued, but rather the image of that impossibility: an image of death and fulfilment.

And if we look, by contrast, at the maintenance of subjectivity and of the individual in the *cry*, what is striking is that there is no rescuing of subjectivity there either: it is simply foreign to that which is destroying it (what is destroying it appears to it as something transcendent). But the experience of deep subjectivity is always subject to one condition: that it destroy the one who has that experience. Jean Wahl's choice of Rimbaud and Van Gogh is significant; these are spirits so taut that they do not survive. Kierkegaard himself quickly burned himself up. But those who, on condition that they disappear, express existence intensely are not destroyed by a necessity of which they are *conscious*. They themselves do not achieve any universality: only commentaries and the effect of their works—and their lives—on others make something universal out of their particularity. But one illusion is maintained: in the value attributed to the work, it is not evident that the intensity of the feelings, which lends the work its attraction, also—by the destruction of its author, which it heralds—grounds a universal; *A Season in Hell* and Rimbaud's silence are seen as two separate things: it is not easy to perceive or clearly discern the silence that is already there in the cry or the cry that is still present in the silence. To come back to my analysis of Kierkegaard, he was not aware, as he died (though death here matters little; this is about failure, dissatisfaction, and woe) that he might at a pinch, a hundred years later, afford his reader the fulfilled satisfaction of Hegel (though connected—and immanent—to its opposite): nevertheless, readers in general would not see this clearly and would emphasize the 'cry' element (the individual's protest), not the silence, at the same time as a sense of calm desolation would already be descending. There are opposing possibilities that meet and are bound together. Tragedy occurs at a point adjacent to the moment when the actors and the crowd will have left the theatre. Memory lingers when it is time to grasp this ungraspable fact, one that Kierkegaard himself grasps the day he sets down in his *Notebooks*: 'My head is as empty as a theatre where a play has just been performed.'

What deceives us is that individuality has, in human terms, become the condition of the universal. Only rich individuality, calling intensely on subjectivity to be what it is not—that is to say: universal—accedes to true universality, and this is not the inner being-ness to which Kierkegaard opens himself—Kierkegaard, who 'maintains by destroying' and 'overcomes' (Hegel used the single German word *aufheben*) subjectivity. But Kierkegaard could not see that the intensity of his rejection was *in no sense* removed from Hegelian fulfilment; that his very *blindness* and his rejection were the precondition for fulfilment. It has been said that Kierkegaard could not be understood without Heidegger: that is questionable. But Hegel probably cannot be fully understood without Kierkegaard, just as, for a long time, he could not without Heidegger. One cannot, in effect, overstate—one cannot, in particular, avoid giving a pathos-laden meaning to—this need within us to push individuality to the extremes of tension, but only in order to destroy it. Propositions like 'we are nothing without subjectivity' or 'subjectivity is nothing if it is not a universal' force themselves on us in their contradictory obviousness. But these propositions themselves are nothing if we have not seen in this contradiction precisely what is at issue in human life, and more precisely, in a fundamental way, in heart-rending experience. Philosophy is obviously no stranger to the question, it is *its* question, and existentialism has precisely this meaning: that it posed this question, as I have said, by way of an error without which it would have been poorly posed: the question is, in fact, never better posed than through an excessive assertion of the sentiment that inclines us to avoid it.[16]

---

16 How are we to situate or define *existentialism* other than in this way? But the word is decidedly awkward. It is convenient—and has even become unavoidable—to use it to refer to a given movement in the history of philosophy, running from Kierkegaard to Sartre. But it can have a *living* meaning only on condition that one regard Sartre as a toned-down variant, a rather distant offshoot of the movement (I am, in a sense, so little an *existentialist* that I detest writing the word *existential*: is it not out of place to use a pretentious word to refer to what we mean here? This is the impasse that confronts modern existentialism). And, among the existentialists, Sartre is precisely the only one to have taken ownership of the word, to have given it resonance and notoriety! And this is in the nature of things. Being what it is, existentialism cannot but be reluctant to put itself forward under a determinate name (see *A Short History*, p. 33). To name itself, it first had to be dead.

Of course, regardless of this emotive posing of the problem, the question of the universal and the particular is the central problem of philosophy, where it has taken on numerous forms. For Emmanuel Levinas, what Heidegger's philosophy brings that is new 'consists in distinguishing between *Being* and *beings,* and in transporting relation, movement, efficacy, which hitherto resided in the existent, into Being.[17]

Whatever the importance of the problem in Heidegger and the way it is posed,[18] Levinas, who was his student but has moved away from him appreciably, has made this the subject of a little book published as *De l'existence à l'existant* [translated as *Existence and Existents*]. The existence/existents opposition is no different from the Being/beings opposition. Existence is impersonal, it is universal. The existent is the individual. It is the noun of which existence is the verb: existence for Levinas is a 'pure verb' that is hypostasized when it becomes a noun.

What Levinas is looking at takes us a long way from the perspectives I have outlined: he is interested in the *de facto* connection between the universal and the particular, as if that were given once and for all in a static relation between existence and the existent. He does not study the reversals and wrenches that arise from that relation. He is concerned with the possibility of hypostasis irrespective of its history. The difficulty of the task is palpable: the animal is itself an existent in existence and modern man is separated from it by the successive appearance of very different forms of subjectivity. But a recourse to historical facts is very far removed from the methods of modern existentialism, which is happy to retreat into present subjectivity. Emmanuel Levinas's little book is worthy of attention

---

17 I am quoting the contribution by Levinas to a 'Discussion' published as an appendix to Jean Wahl's *Petite Histoire*, pp. 84–85. See Jean Wahl, *A Short History of Existentialism*, p. 49; translation modified.

18 De Ruggiero (*Existentialism*, p. 49) gives a different interpretation of the position of Jaspers and Heidegger: 'We are told . . . that existence is never a predicate, always a subject.' And he complains of the ease with which 'existence' is confused with 'existents'. But it may be that Levinas's very precisely articulated interpretation shows up what is perhaps an incomplete interpretation on de Ruggiero's part.

nonetheless,[19] and his static analysis enables us the better to see the facts of the drama being played out, which concerns the relation of the thinking individual to the instant—that instant being the universal which is within him, but which the pursuit of the universal—that is to say, thought—is unable to reach.

*

In a sense (if the expression refers to a cohesive grouping, whose main figures are Sartre, Simone de Beauvoir and Merleau-Ponty), Emmanuel Levinas stands outside 'French existentialism'. His philosophy is largely unrelated to that of Sartre. A long period of captivity in Germany, where he was a military prisoner, even prevented him from reading *Being and Nothingness* before finishing his book. But he was one of the first in France to spread the word about the thought of Heidegger, under whom he studied and to whose thinking, though he opposes it, his own is linked. 'If at the beginning,' he asserts, 'our reflections are in large measure inspired by the philosophy of Martin Heidegger . . . , they are also governed by a profound need to leave behind the climate of that philosophy, and by the conviction that we cannot leave it for a philosophy that might be described as pre-Heideggerian' (p. 19; translation modified). On slippery terrain, it is difficult to be precise about the ways in which Levinas is at odds with his teacher. He associates anxiety with being, rather than with nothingness. But is not Heidegger's nothingness ultimately being? There are, nonetheless, some palpable differences of 'climate' between the two ways of thinking,

---

19 The corrections relating to the words *digne d'attention* [worthy of attention] here reflect the general slant of the re-writing of the article: two paragraphs earlier, Bataille crosses out expressions like 'à l'extrême du déchirement' or 'dans le déchirement de cette vie, et ne peut être en cause qu'en déchirant'.

Here, he first writes that 'Emmanuel Levinas's little book is of remarkable interest nonetheless' (the version published in *Critique*), then 'is of the first importance nonetheless', which he amends first to 'is good nonetheless' and finally to 'is worthy of attention'.

The two articles continue the line of thinking begun with 'La notion de dépense' [The Notion of expenditure] (*Œuvres complètes*, VOL. 1, pp. 302–20) which will be further developed in *La Part maudite* [translated as *The Accursed Share*] (*Œuvres complètes*, VOL. 7, pp, 17–259). [Eds]

underscored by a diametrical opposition of terms. Human being for Heidegger is faced with death (*Sein zum Tod*); Levinas (like Sartre) is critical of the conception of 'being-unto-death'. But that opposition is something that is constructed: it is the opposition of 'the fear of being to the fear of nothingness'. 'While anxiety, in Heidegger,' as we read on p. 58, 'brings about "being-unto-death" . . . the horror of the night "with no exits" which "does not answer" is an irremissible existence. "Tomorrow, alas! one will still have to live"—a tomorrow contained in the infinity of today' (p. 63). It is not death that frightens Levinas but 'the impossibility of death' (p. 61). And to express what is oppressing him, he cites the suffocation of Racine's Phèdre, when she bewails that:

> The sky, the whole world's full of my forefathers.
> Where may I hide? Flee to infernal night.
> How? There my father holds the urn of doom . . .

One gleans from Levinas's words an empty and *reasonless* pain, which only the baying of a dog at the moon would not traduce with misplaced unintelligibility: and yet it will also be necessary here to reject the widely shared (superficial) idea that associates death with the expression of the impossible. He writes:

> When the forms of things are dissolved in the night, the darkness of the night, which is neither an object nor the quality of an object, invades like a presence. In the night to which we are riveted, we are dealing with nothing. But this nothing is not that of pure nothing-ness. There is no longer *this* or *that*; there is not 'something'. But this universal absence is in its turn a presence, an absolutely unavoidable presence. It is not the dialectical counterpart of absence, and we do not grasp it by a thought. It is immediately there. There is no discourse. Nothing responds to us but this silence; the voice of the silence is heard and it frightens, like the silence of those infinite spaces Pascal speaks of. (p. 58; translation modified)

I have myself introduced an ambiguity by pitting the impenetrable barking of a dog—despite, or rather, because of its meaninglessness—against thought's intelligent dread (though the dog, apparently, is closer to Levinas's empty feeling). 'What we call the I,' he goes on to say, is itself submerged by the night, invaded, depersonalized, stifled by it. The disappearance of all things and of the I leaves what cannot disappear, the sheer fact of being in which one participates, whether one wants to or not, without having taken the initiative, anonymously. Being remains, like a force field, like a heavy atmosphere belonging to no one, universal, returning at the very heart of the negation that removes it, and in all the degrees of that negation. (p. 58; translation modified)

There is nothing less *human*, so that an animal that is distraught and losing the basic sense of animality is closer to it than when correctly responding to the demands of its condition.

Levinas gives the name *there is*, the *there is*, to this 'impersonal, anonymous, yet inextinguishable "consumation" of being' . . . The *there is*, he argues (p. 57), 'transcends inwardness as well as exteriority; it does not even make it possible to distinguish them'. It is neither subject nor object: to objects and subjects it stands opposed in the same way as *existence* (universal existence, existence in general) stands opposed to *existents* (individual entities, particular things). Or, to put it another way, in the situation of the *there is*, the *existent* is dissolved in *existence*.

Of course, this situation is general, and though the clear and distinct knowledge of external objects and of the inwardness of the self dispels it, that can never eliminate its return. The intelligence itself accedes to it in the end, by an operation through which a system of operations, all linked to precise objects, culminates in a total operation, in which the foregoing ones disintegrate. But only in appearance does ordinary, coherent discourse arrive at this dissolution: it speaks of it but cannot accomplish it, insofar as it always utters a meaningful proposition, the meaning of which is necessarily limited. Even if its coherence were absolute, there would be no isolated sentence that expressed it truly, since it would then have to dissolve itself. With the result that, at its high point, the discourse that no longer seeks to set against the '*there is*' a sentence that speaks about it (and dispels it by the very fact that, once uttered, it limits the utterer to the world of clarity), ceasing to speak about it in order to attain to it, necessarily expresses—by being totally chaotic—an inability to achieve anything but the reverse of its intention. Referring to a number of pages in Maurice Blanchot's *Thomas the Obscure*, Levinas says they are the description of the *there is*. This is not quite exact: Levinas describes the *there is*, but Blanchot utters it, so to speak, as a cry.

> He went down into a sort of cellar where the darkness was total . . . Before, behind and even above him, some very solid brick-work blocked his path; and that wasn't the biggest obstacle, he also had to rely on his will—his will which was fiercely determined to let him sleep there, in total oblivion, in a death-like passivity . . . Thomas's first observation was that he could still use his body, particularly his eyes; it wasn't that he could see something but what he was looking at disdained his gaze without allowing him to avert it. That was, in time, sufficient to bring him into relation with a nocturnal mass in which he bathed and which he vaguely perceived as being himself . . . by dint of believing himself in contact with an intelligence which his gaze or his hand could touch, he was gradually overtaken by a sense of horror that he could not over-come. Soon the night seemed to him gloomier and more terrible than any other night, as if it had in fact issued from a wound of thought that had ceased to think, of thought taken ironically as object by something other than thought. It was night itself. Images that constituted its darkness inundated him and his body, trans-formed into a demoniacal spirit, tried to imagine them. He saw nothing and, far from being distressed, he made his absence of vision the culmination of his sight. Useless for seeing, his eye took on extraordinary proportions; it developed excessively and, reaching out to the horizon, let the night penetrate into its centre to create an iris for itself. Through this void, then, sight and the object of sight mingled together. Not only did this eye that saw nothing apprehend something, it apprehended the cause of its vision. It saw as an object that which prevented it from seeing.[20]

---

20 Maurice Blanchot, *Thomas l'obscur* (Paris: Gallimard, 1941), pp. 13–15. [An English translation of the later, revised, shorter edition of 1950 was made by Robert Lamberton and published by David Lewis, Inc in 1973. The present translation is my own. (Trans.)]

The effect that is usually inhibited by a desire to insert into the sphere of objects of thought what properly belongs only outside it is achieved here by indifference to formal definition. *By way of a formal generalization* (in other words, through *discourse*), Levinas defines what, in Blanchot's *literary* text, is purely the cry of an existence. The principle to which Levinas holds (that of existentialist philosophy) renders his approach incomplete; though he generalizes (though, as a result, he contemplates objectively), he is nonetheless bound to what is individual, intimate, subjective. Conjointly with this, he has had to engage life, which he experiences, in this generalization and to experience it as an item of knowledge, in that very mode in which objects are *known* to us distinctly.[21] In this way, existentialist philosophy changes us into things more deeply than does science, which at least leaves *the intimate sphere* unchanged. If he wishes to, the scientist can, even though it would then be unreasonable, view the world as though the intimate dimension within him had the sense of external phenomena of

---

I quoted the major part of this passage in *Inner Experience* [(Stuart Kendall trans. and intro.) (Albany: State University of New York Press, 2014), p. 103]. In his review of that work [Jean-Paul Sartre, 'A New Mystic' (1943) in *On Bataille and Blanchot* (Chris Turner trans.), The Seagull Sartre Library, VOL. 10 (London: Seagull Books, 2021), pp. 1–61], Sartre bases his criticism on a sentence in that quotation in which he seizes on the 'trick' pulled off by Blanchot and myself: '*It saw as an object that which prevented it from seeing*'. According to Sartre this could be seen as a substantification of non-knowledge, the hypostasis of a pure nothingness. Personally, I say 'I know nothing, absolutely nothing. I cannot know *what is*. Not being able to relate *what is* to the known, I remain lost in the unknown.' *Inner Experience* expresses this situation in its entirety, which is that of Levinas's *there is* and to which Blanchot's offending sentence gives masterful expression. Conversely, Sartre's criticism helps us to grasp Levinas's thinking, which is no different, it seems to me, from Blanchot's and mine. Sartre himself admits that, if I substantify 'non-knowledge', I do so 'with caution, as a movement . . .' ('A New Mystic', pp. 53–54). But, above all, Levinas's position helps to show how Sartre's critique misses its mark. For the latter, the meaning of Blanchot's sentence remains impenetrable and he holds to a proposition that is the perfect negation of poetry: 'Nothing is for me but what I know.'

21 Levinas stresses the positing of existence—in precise terms, of the *there is*—as 'pure verb', by contrast with hypostasis, the object known in its exteriority. Nevertheless, if he speaks about it, the emphasis is put on the intellectual operation and not on an elimination—through ecstasy or poetry—of discursive knowledge.

which it was the effect. But if he limits his life, more or less, just to knowing things externally, if he abandons the intimate sphere, if in practical terms he eliminates it, at least he cannot *alter* it. He cannot incorporate it, as the existentialist does (though hesitatingly and half-heartedly) into the discursive projection of knowledge. For his part, the religious thinker accepted this projection; he altered the intimate sphere himself, insofar as he expressed it through discourse, though not without introducing elements into it that are not reducible to it. The *revealed* and the *sacred* maintained the primacy of life over knowledge: what lay beyond the operations of the intelligence dominated the baseness or humility of discourse from on high. Not by any ritual precautions or poetic liberty does existentialism escape the levelling effect of things known. At best it combines with knowledge a certain hesitation and some slippages. The epithet *existentialist* signifies that a human being is neither a saint nor a poet, that he has tried in vain to wrest knowledge from exteriority, and we are decidedly speaking here of a 'man of knowledge'.

'In vain' here is a criticism. But, overall, it is more of a reserving from criticism.

Levinas deliberately skews the description of the *there is* towards horror and suffocation. The *there is* is what time, the insertion of existence in time, *delivers* him from. To a certain extent, this intimate—individual, painful—character of an experience retains for its expression the value of a cry, but at the same moment the value of a non-sense (if experience does not *generally* have the same sense).

Nevertheless, Levinas introduces the notion of the *there is* by an analysis of the 'materiality' of being. In his eyes, the elimination, in modern painting, of interest in the object, and the emphasis put on the raw sensation of form and colour independently of intellectual interpretation reveal the 'materiality' of objects (a packet of tobacco in a painting no longer has the virtue of evoking the reality in which it is set, of creating by association symbolic values or use-values; it is simply the sensation produced by forms and colours, as free of meaning as are sounds in music). Art, as Levinas sees it, wrests forms from the world (we might say, from the sphere of activity), in which every object takes on a well-defined meaning; it generally has the virtues of 'exoticism'. In other words, if we see things, each one expresses an idea, and it is not its materiality that we see but the thing expressing the idea. Art then—this is what poetry does—destroys its meaning, freezes it and, in its way, reduces it to ultimate silence: what it reveals is its matter, and 'matter is the very fact of the *there is*' (p. 57).

I see nothing to complain of in Levinas's analysis, except that it reaches its object from the outside. Its style is existentialist, no doubt ('the experimentation of modern painting in its protest against realism' is seen as arising from a 'sense of the end of the world'); and this pathos precisely relates the analysis to the author's private feelings, to his horror at being. But the fact of the objectivity of painting means that this relation cannot run in just a single direction. The wresting from the world that is effected in artistic creations cannot be objectively separated from their attractiveness, which is their *raison d'être*. The *there is* determined from outside no longer has the limited meaning that it had when grasped solely from the inside.

Continuing to develop a notion, Levinas is, in fact, led to base it on other objective facts, or facts at least alleged to be such, which he borrows from French sociology. Lévy-Bruhl's 'mystical participation' provides him with the example of an absence of object linked to the absence of a subject.

In Durkheim if the sacred breaks with profane being by the feelings it arouses, these feelings remain those of a subject facing an object . . . The situation is quite different in Lévy-Bruhl. Mystical participation is completely different from the Platonic participation in a genus: in it the identity of the terms is lost . . . The participation of one term in another does not consist in sharing an attribute; *one term is the other*. The *private* existence of each term, mastered by a subject that is, loses this private character and returns to an undifferentiated background; the existence of the one submerges the other, and is thus no longer an existence of the one. We recognize here the *there is*. The impersonality of the sacred in primitive religions, which for Durkheim is the 'still' impersonal God from which will issue one day the God of advanced religions, describes on the contrary a world where nothing prepares for the apparition of a God. The notion of the *there is* leads us, rather than to a God, to the absence of God, the absence of any being. (pp. 60–61)

The move from the view held by Durkheim, for whom the sacred is an object, to that of Lévy-Bruhl, in which participation is apparently based on an objective error on the part of the participant, who sees himself as the same kind of thing as an animal or rain, does not, despite first appearances, move us away from experience founded on observation from the outside. The notion introduced by Levinas, far from assigning participation to an error on the part of the subject, actually helps to establish its objective value. From that standpoint, it is of no consequence whatever that the *there is* should be the simultaneous absence of object and subject. We can know it clearly only from outside, in the constancy of its formal effects, if the knowledge is shared and communicable, as it seeks to be.

The problem introduced by Levinas's short work is exactly that of communicating an *ineffable* experience. The *there is* is apparently the mystics' ineffable: yet the fact is that Levinas has *spoken* of it, though he has only expressed it with relative exactness by way of its formal effects (modern painting, Surrealist art, Lévy-Bruhl's participation).[22] The rest is 'intimate experience', which cannot be communicated as clear knowledge but only in the form of poetry. Knowledge is, so to speak, necessarily something other than effusion, and effusion-knowledge lacks force: it has neither the force of effusion nor that of knowledge. Insofar as it is effusion, it has poetic value (which may be raw material for knowledge); insofar as it is knowledge, it has the value of the formal constants that keep it from being poetry. Poetic effusion or the positing of objective forms each have the power to reach into the intimate sphere, but slippages from the one to the other do not.

The powerlessness of thought is given in the sterility of these slippages: poetry obscures knowledge, knowledge tames poetry, but neither poetic knowledge nor intellectual poetry[23] fully do justice to the human being. Humanity is the demand for an extreme possibility: in both of these fields equally, science and poetry tolerate neither weakness nor compromise. (But poetry is sovereign and can never be enslaved: extreme knowledge, by contrast, requires the recognition of poetry, which is never the means of its autonomous activity, but remains the end-goal of the one who knows—and the end of knowledge insofar as knowledge at its outer limit is the dissolution of knowledge.)

---

22 Levinas is clearly alluding to Surrealism's intentions.

23 This is Lautréamont's '*tache de sang intellectuelle*' [intellectual bloodstain].

In truth, knowledge cannot escape its powerlessness, nor can it dodge its power.

Existentialism sought evasion . . . But already that no longer matters. The only knowledge there is is general and in such knowledge there are only two paths: the Hegelian path of a cohesion of all possible thoughts; the path of *science*, proceeding at particular points to perform precise procedures. And, from the outset, for both of these, a completely successful outcome leads to equivalence with its opposite: there is no knowledge except knowledge as it produces itself, but total (dialectical or scientific) knowledge is also total darkness. Knowledge that has achieved completion is merely the most advanced point of knowledge, but if, beyond this most advanced point, there were no longer the slightest unknown that could in its turn become known, that which was previously unknown being decidedly related to the known, the known itself, as knowledge reaches completion, would be entirely returned to the unknown. There is no overall coherence of the oppositions of thought that does not imply, in advance, this opening on to the impossible. And there is no lucid science that does not sense, based on the state of rudimentary knowledge in which we find ourselves, the *supreme ignorance* of anyone who would extend the operations of science to all elements of the world.

But 'total darkness' and 'supreme ignorance' are not necessarily what they seem. The ignorance into which I fall if I know that, at its extreme, knowledge knows nothing, does not have the same object as common ignorance. I am 'commonly' ignorant of the cause of a particular effect or the effect a particular action will have, or ignorant of the recent death of a particular person: whereas supreme ignorance has as its object *what is*, everything that is, which is not a thing and cannot be called the *there is*. 'Commonly', I am ignorant of the *there is* (in the same way as I am ignorant of a thing) when I know this or that, or when I am ignorant of a cause or an effect. Whereas, in supreme ignorance, I awaken to the *there is* as to the poetry of an empty immensity, opening on to it the door that I imagined led into my own room. By the very fact that it is not *this* which I can relate to *that* as to the genus of which it is an exemplar, the *there is* can exist in me (before me) only in the form of ignorance. Similarly, supreme ignorance necessarily reveals the bareness of what is, reduces it to an unintelligible presence in which all difference is destroyed—to which the name 'there is' is now to be given.

For this reason, I can regard the night of non-knowledge as bringing my deliverance: is it not the fusion of subject and object, of spirit and matter, and are not the necessities of my isolated existence, forced as I am to know through *this* and *that* particular thing, my servitude? But I cannot escape servitude by an indirect route that is knowledge without passion. The passion for knowledge—by this I mean measureless passion—alone has the power to take knowledge to the point where it dissolves itself; while knowledge without passion opens up the infinite possibility of mere verbiage.

The *there is*, for Levinas, is the fact of being, independently of the object perceived and the perceiving subject: it is *existence* or impersonal being in general, as opposed to the *existent*, to isolated being, which is its hypostasis. But the time that belongs to impersonal existence differs from that of individual being. Impersonal existence lacks distinct instants and the possibility of rhythm: in it, all points in time resemble each other, like all points in space in darkest night. 'For the instant to irrupt into being,' writes Levinas, 'for this insomnia that is like the very eternity of being to end, the positing of a subject would be required' (p. 66; translation modified). It is the self that exists in isolation which, as Levinas sees it, takes the instant on board and arrests it, so to speak, in the contraction of an effort in which domination by a personal being asserts itself. The instant can be said to have perceptible existence only insofar as it is grasped in a substantive form of being, in which it is the discerned, isolable property of an isolated subject. But it would then no longer be the atomistic point in time we commonly envisage: it would not be 'a thing on its own,' but rather 'articulated', (p. 18) binding the past to the present in the event.

The instant is truly the philosopher's ink bottle. For Sartre, the instant 'does not exist', while for another philosopher it is 'eternal'. Each chooses a kind of instant the way you choose a dish in a restaurant, depending on how it fits into a system. It is, ludicrously, the case that I can ask the question: might the instant 'not exist' or might it 'be eternal'? I shall never be able to decide other than frivolously. All I can do is order the contradictory ideas in a cohesive way, with a view to the *necessities* of a whole line of argumentation emerging. What I have said up to this point refers to that cohesion (without laying it out); in any case, a notion cannot be envisaged outside of the joint structure of perspectives it opens up in the mind, which is the general possibility of language. But the passion for knowledge is not limited to that path, and the scientific approach, better equipped in this regard, is required to develop this last problem we have broached.

Can the meaning of the present instant be determined by a value assumed in a quantitative system? The economy gives a precise signification to the instant, and it is impossible to set any inner view against that. Economics is precisely the major aspect humanity presents to science and we may say that the economic meaning of the instant has nothing to do with a subject's 'take' on it, over which Levinas lingers; on the contrary, it corresponds to the sense of the *there is*. But without dismissing the idea of a necessary cohesion of contradictory notions, it is not uninteresting to examine the sense of that assertion within the framework of an analysis of the material facts.

Economic science tracks what happens to objects as they are produced and consumed. It takes into account work, human or mechanical, insofar as it forms part of those processes (it then treats as though it were directly or indirectly productive work, work that is not productive but is remunerated as if it were). This isn't always adequate. The production and consumption of objects do not represent the whole of the economic system. And if we have to specify the sense of that system, we must regard as one of its foundations the physiological facts to which it is responding. It then becomes evident that animal activity is at times an acquisition and at times an expenditure of energy. The humblest movements represent such an appreciable expenditure that it is in a stockbreeder's interest to keep a calf lying down: the calf accumulates in the form of fat the energy that it would have expended by moving about. But human activity has developed two distinct and opposing categories of expenditure: the productive (rudimentary among the majority of animals) and the unproductive. The former are the means of making acquisitions (which are not themselves ends, but the means to the latter, to unproductive expenditures). If one looks at the meaning of these operations in time, it is clear that the meaning of a productive expenditure—that is to say, from the economic standpoint, of an acquisition—is given in its relation to the future, but that of an unproductive expenditure is given, by contrast, in the present instant. We may say, conversely, that if economics looks to the future, the only activity that is meaningful to it is productive expenditure (work, or such expenditure as is required for the production of work); an unproductive expenditure is a nonsense or even the *opposite* of sense (unless it becomes an habitual complement to productive activity). We should add, though this is quite another question: if economics looks to the present . . . But actually economics never looks to the present. And indeed this is the reason why economic science is so incomplete. If, however, I look at it in defiance of the economist's approach, then productive activity is the meaningless part and unproductive activity alone has a *value*.

It is only to the superficial observer that an unproductive *value* seems like a simple negation. It is indeed a negation, but of an already given negation. It negates the negation (which has already been made) of the present instant. By contrast, it is the productive value that is essentially negative: it actually denies *what is,* the present, in favour of the future, *which is not.* In fact, unproductive activity in general is always positive. It is obviously a *loss,* but the sense of that word is only really negative if the substance lost is something that the one who has lost it actually misses. That is not the case and cannot be so overall. Living creatures generally have a superabundance of energy: whatever the expenditure called for by necessary work, given an average increase in resources (in productive means), there is an excess of energy to expend in the world. There was a cost to producing it, but we can do nothing about that: a given line of production cannot be limited to the provision of the energy needed to pursue it. Taking the energy committed to that production, it is necessarily—in average conditions—of lesser value than the value produced. One cannot, in fact, organize such a rapid accumulation that it would absorb the totality of the surplus, and, were we to do so, the growth of the plant and machinery would lead in short order to a heightened discrepancy between energy committed and volume of production. Thus the loss that comes about in unproductive expenditures is indeed a loss if one wishes to call it that, but not in the negative sense of the word: here or there it may slow down desirable accumulation, but the energy is lost *to the advantage of the present instant*. And the present instant *is*, whereas the future *is not*.

The word *profit* jars, admittedly, if used in connection with the *present instant*, but that incompatibility reveals precisely what governs the narrowness of economics: the narrowness of the language of knowledge, which is not able, as a general rule, to reckon with the present. In discursive language, the present is the poor relation (or whipping boy): what has meaning only for the present has, in reality, no meaning; what has value only for the present is not useful. An immense State has ascribed to itself the purpose of emancipating human beings once and for all, but that seductive end has led it, in a privileged way, into the clutches of logic: since the present instant has meaning only in a way that runs counter to logic, an entire people is subject to an *actual* heightened servitude, which, as a consequence, does not count, in the name of a *nonexistent* emancipation, which, as a consequence, is the very *meaning* of servitude. And indeed, when it comes to the strenuous effort currently stirring the world, who could set the perfect impotence of the instant against it? I shall confine myself to showing that unproductive expenditure, drawing its meaning from the current instant, is seldom, as we imagine, wastage: as a general rule, *it has the positive value of art*. Living creatures are so constructed that, as they expend themselves, their excess of energy radiates out: the effect of this is the brilliance that attracts us, above and beyond the needs that are satisfied. Art is precisely this positive squandering of energy: it is an economic fact and the economy gives it a—theoretically measurable—value as soon as it accepts the sense of the present.

For Levinas, in fact, art is one of the paths of the *there is*. Art 'wrests objects from the world', but it does so precisely because, in the world, an object has meaning only in the future, and the meaning of art lies in the present moment. This object (the sheet of paper) has the quality of an *object* insofar as I envisage its existence beyond this present moment with an eye to the possibilities inherent in it (the use that will be made of it). If I confine my interest to the present instant, it slides into the unintelligible materiality of what is (something which, as Levinas sees it, art reveals); it dissolves into an awakening to indistinct immensity. In that obscurity, I am myself dissolved (I discern myself insofar as the possibility of my perduring in time extends into the future). The poetry that deprives isolated beings of their position as subject or object[24] is an intense consumation of life in the present. This may not immediately be perceptible: if I write a poem quickly, I may, if I wish, work again right away, but the writing of a fiery poem brings a state of disorder into one's life that is not very productive and is a squandering of available time and resources. The irregularity and complexity of the effects and the difficulty of judging the authenticity of poetry do not entitle economic science to be ignorant here. The fact that a poem lasts and brings in money for its author marks an endless possibility of communicating the consumation (by repetitions of language) and of marking down to the author's account part of the unproductive expenditure the reader is engaged in: the meaning of the consumation is nonetheless given, each time, in the present instant; it is the opposite of work, the meaning of which is confined to the future use of the product.

The fact that unproductive expenditure—poetry, art and, generally, free consumation—tends towards the dissolution of the subject cannot be left out of economics either. The traditional study of the productive economy requires that we view subjects as inscribed in time. The productive economy is, precisely, the domain of the isolated subject: its study involves also the study of the legal conditions regulating the attribution of the values so produced to persons not considered jointly. Conversely, the subject cannot be posited outside of activity, the intended outcome of which is the personal enjoyment of a product. But all unproductive expenditure requires from subjects the temporary abandonment of this move: against normal convention *they deny themselves*, insofar as they are wholly unconcerned about appropriation and they spend with no hope of profit. To take up Levinas's terminology, they behave as *existence* and not as *existent*: no longer are they subjects of the objective world, standing over against the object, which is not themselves and which they appropriate if they can usefully do so. They abandon to others, without receiving anything in return—and even

---

24 'The poetry that upends "existents" in their positing' (p. 82; translation modified).

regardless of any appropriation by others—a part of the wealth at their disposal. This supposes, in the first instance, that they stop, *in the present*, differentiating between themselves and others; it even means, at the extreme point, that they no longer distinguish between the world and their existence. The painter working at her painting no longer makes a distinction between the canvas and herself; her creation is no different from herself, whether or not she intends to paint nature. The fact that pictures are conserved and sold changes nothing here: it does not close off the essential element of painting, which is the communicable movement from the *existent* to *existence*. The importance of the individual characteristics of the author deceives us here: those characteristics are marked, but that is because the elimination of a subject as such actually demands marked individuality. And, on occasion, the authenticity of art, which used to require an ailing subjectivity, has found itself in the end negating it to the point of death.

If we follow this line of thinking, the content of apparently profound ideas, which modern philosophers are introducing, detaches itself from the uneasy subjectivity (which passion did not quickly consume) and enervated style of existentialism. That content expresses itself in scientific data. Such an operation is currently regarded as a mark of vulgarity, but we cannot honestly allow ourselves to linger over judgements that did not have the decisive outcome in view—and which were, furthermore, based on the possibility of a compromise between knowledge and the intimate sphere. When put to the test, the compromise seems contrary to the desires that ordained it: it weakens, at one and the same time, the rigour of knowledge and the passion without which there is no inwardness. If, lastly, it appears that objective analysis in no way limits a field of research, but substitutes clear results for the chancy, hesitant procedures of a philosophy that lacks unity, there is no admissible reason to let preconceived notions stand in the way of my ambitious endeavour. A *general economy* (distinct from the traditional study of economics, which confines itself to the field of production) that no longer ignores bursts of exuberance, occupies a new place in the field of knowledge. It encompasses within its research—alongside labour, the manufacture of products and accumulation—*the unproductive use of wealth* at the end-point of development. It thereby puts an end to the ignorance to which economic theory has consigned the immense unproductive activity of human beings, and to which idealism has consigned the material conditions of life.[25] It does not, however, remove the need for a coherent formulation of language, such that the fullness of its developed possibilities disposes the meaning of each in relation to the others, and reveals the non-meaning—the perfect opacity or, more precisely, the silence—of the whole. (To put it precisely, that formulation of language is the domain of *philosophy*: a *science* ensues from an agreement between minds on method and results, preliminary to agreement on the first principles that ground it; the sciences generally stand out against mythic thinking by dint of continual exchanges with the technologies; sciences possess the truth of the technologies, which the necessities of life are constantly putting to the test.)

There is an appreciable advantage to be had in moving from the vacillating approximations of the philosophers of existence to precise facts objectively afforded by experience. Whether overtly or not, existentialism itself based a great many of its assertions on external observation (overtly in the case of Levinas). But that very method left the door open to individual chance. Levinas defines the fact of being by speaking of the horror he feels at it. Another person might have felt intoxicated, joyful or ecstatic at the same fact. From the standpoint of economics, all that is required is to show the relationship between a feeling experienced and the state of personal resources. This is often possible, if not easy. Asceticism slows down exchanges [*les échanges*[26]] and slowly reduces the amount of energy necessary to keep a subject in being: at the same time, the ascetic limits the use of his resources to a slow, ecstatic consumption, to the exclusion of the hurried expenditures of freewheeling existence. In this way he is able to lose himself, without too much trepidation, in a *happy* fusion, in which he loses the

---

25 This critique cannot be levelled at the idealism of Hegel, whose *Phenomenology of Spirit*, by Marx's own admission, regards *work* as the essence of the human being. The economic interpretation of history, in the precise sense of the class struggle, is already present in Hegel.

26 *Les échanges* is also the French term for trade or trading, which lessens the distance between the perceived individual and social aspects of this economic description. [Trans.]

notion of himself and of the world. At all events, the happiness of asceticism is the formal constant that limits the significance of the anxiety commonly felt in the face of the fact of being. Anxiety itself cannot be considered without taking account of an economic state of affairs: if we suppose an exchange regime on the scale of an individual, anxiety occurs if the possibility of a desirable expenditure puts the continuation of the regime at issue; and indeed it assumes that a compromise is struck. Anxiety is also an expense but generally a less onerous one than if we responded to the desire. But at times it is *the most onerous*: it consumes more deeply than abandonment could have done. By this roundabout route, the anxious individual acquires a fool's boldness. At times he even reaches a more intense degree of consumation by abandoning himself only in a state of anxiety. (The fact of 'freezing' in the face of a possibility is also a formal constant of anxiety, but the possibility in anxiety is always a dangerous expenditure that puts the continuation of a chosen regime in question; at times the expenditure itself does not necessarily seem unproductive, but it is to the extent that it may lead to ruin that it generates anxiety). Of course, an ill-defined anxiety, in which there is no longer a distinct object, always provides the background to any anxiety. But that basis of anxiety can itself only be fully grasped through surface forms. The basis of anxiety is, in effect, the coincidence of an absence of subject with an absence of object, but it is a *possibility*—it is the ultimate possibility, the extreme temptation—which brings into play an unreserved opening-up to the absence of meaning. At this point, it is not the most costly expenditure that is called for, but the most unjustifiable, the expenditure for which there is not the slightest reason: this is out-and-out unproductivity and the radical cancellation of future time. It is in fact, at the same time, rapture, but on condition that, as this possibility presents itself, anxiety conceals it from the mind: otherwise, time-to-come would still be in the picture; otherwise, temptation would have a meaning.[27] This movement *from anxiety to ecstasy* is the culmination of—and key to—a general theory of economy, but it plays no part in a claimed profundity of

---

27 This is the dialectic of the sense of non-sense, which destroys its non-sense. The same aspect can be found in the passage from anxiety to ecstasy, as studied with scholarly acumen by Janet in the mystical experience of a sick patient. See Pierre Janet, *De l'angoisse à l'extase* (Paris: Librairie Félix Alcan, 1928).

thinking. Profound thinking is incomplete thinking: it lacks the quantitative base without which one cannot *follow* anything. There is no difference in nature between elementary considerations on the daily use of wealth and these fundamental insights. But—and this may be surprising—the views of the philosophers of existence are *in no degree* impoverished by light. What I have said ultimately sheds light on the depths of 'mystical theology', but the richness of those depths is not affected by it. It is simply that the pre-suppositions and hypostases (the *mystical* facts) dissipate. *Nothing* remains that is not within the scope of reason, but reason is no longer accounting for the fact of a world within the scope of reason. It is clear, at the extremity of possible ideas, that the furthest extremity is no different from the starting point (this world of elaborate scientific knowledge is no less rich than that of the simplest religions). But, in the meantime, the desire that extends beyond mere need has, like the simple need, expressed itself in economic terms. This substitutes *an incontestable necessity* for the phantoms of religion—or for existential mirages. Economics finds a fullness in these general views; the trivial—and guilty—aspect of the crucial moments has found its justification and gives itself *something like a face*.

A second advantage of this method relates to the place of the particular field of study within the sciences as a whole. A science is generally self-contained: what it contemplates does not, of itself, open up any gap in the fabric of laws and facts it establishes. While the *general* perspective of economy is established from a centre point, which is the subject of knowledge or, more precisely, the subject's *intimate sphere*. In other words, general economy cannot avoid considering the present instant; and all the lines of the perspectives established converge towards that point. For this reason, it could not have constituted itself before the development of a philosophy of inwardness, but it has, from the outset, to put that philosophy in the ground. Beyond a given point, there is only confusion to be had from a method which, on principle, neglects the findings of external observation. The philosophy of existence has posited subjectivity, but it is insofar as that positing necessarily implies the ruin of the posited subject that it is worthy of interest. Moreover, it has had to go part way to this itself. Existence in Levinas's philosophy is already no longer the existence of the subject: it is existence given independently of any subject and any object—though still approached by way of the subject. But the objective path introduces a decisive change: the servitude of the operations of knowledge—the substitution by philosophy of known existence (known by an intellectual procedure) for raw existence—is ended at the very point when *the intimate sphere* comes into play. The method assumes in principle the impossibility of *knowing* the instant, which equates to the intimate realm: the externals of things are given to knowledge only by dint of their belonging to temporal duration. It thus leaves open a chance to experience that instant: poetry or rapture assume the downfall of knowledge, its elimination, which are not things afforded to us by anxiety. *We have here the sovereignty of poetry.* And at the same time, the hatred of poetry—*since it is not inaccessible.*

1948

Goya

Dessins de Goya au Musée du Prado (text by André Malraux) (Geneva: Albert Skira, 1947), in 8°, *xxix*–213 pp (195 plates).

Goya is not just one of the greatest painters who ever lived, and he is not just the first to herald what we call modern painting, but he foreshadows the complete diremption of the present world.[1] His story belongs only secondarily to the history of art: it may even be said to be a decisive moment—Goya is tangibly the contemporary of Sade—in the history of individuality. The isolated minds that made their mark up until his day were at least part of a continuity of social consciousness. The most rebellious of them did not figure as aliens among living humanity: subversion and attunement to the impossible had not carried the disintegration of the individual to the point of a moral rupture. Or, if that did happen, it happened in silence, and the silence was not communicable.

This side of Goya's personality is the less well known for his painting itself remaining generally so unfamiliar. One can barely get to know it any-where else than at the Prado: and even then the significance of such a strange *oeuvre*, to which reading provides a poor introduction, often remains closed to the visitor.

The publication (in exceptionally accomplished form, leaving nothing to be desired) of 195 drawings held at the Prado (reproducing all those which are not sketches for paintings that are otherwise known) works to reduce the distance that still remains between Goya and ourselves. They differ from his painting and even from his engravings by an exceptional harshness of technique, which has perhaps the failing of lending the whole

---

1 The term *déchirement* here relates to Hegel's concept of *Zerrissenheit*, meaning bad conscience, anxiety or internal conflict. Common English translations, such as 'dis-jointedness', seem to fall a little short of the mark in this case. [Trans.]

collection a certain monotonous starkness, but has the advantage of alerting us to what is essential. The choice of subjects is significant. If we leave aside the oldest of them, it is pretty much exactly the *impossible* that these drawings attempt to represent: the degradations of poverty, infirmity and old age; madness, stupidity, killing, terrifying dream figures and, as a dominant obsession, life savagely persecuted by the Inquisition's tortures. Nothing is clearer than the appositeness of the technique to these subjects. That technique is *hurried*: the anguish, the unhappy, hasty tautness of movement is a response to the impossibility of the subject: it not only goes as fast as possible, but as far as possible, never swerving from the goal, always pressing on further. It is *free*, one cannot conceive a freer technique, and its freedom is a freedom in awakening us a little more to what produces anguish, to what we do not at all have the strength to bear.

Goya had reached his fifties when he arrived at this extreme attitude, which actually coincided with his assuming a rationalist, liberal attitude. His deafness and his ideas contributed to his isolation. But, as Malraux rightly says, rationalist protest against the atrocities he painted does not eliminate his deep complicity, if not with the degradation of the torturer, then with that of the victim: it is complicity in the anguish associated with some impossible situation. At the end of *The Disasters of War*, 'a strange puppet', writes Malraux, 'will bring into a glorious Jesuit sunburst a symbol of pacification. At which point, he will move on quickly to engrave *The Old Man Wandering among Phantoms* . . . ' And in the admirable paintings he did not sell but kept in his dining room, there is a scene in which soldiers are shooting down a heavenly apparition. Similarly, the series of drawings on the Inquisition ends in *Lux ex Tenebris*. But if Reason liberated Goya from the order established by the Church he so hated, if it wrested him from the land he was born into, it does not, for all that, reign over the world to which his spirit awoke. The degradation in the prison cells of the Inquisition, which seem to have been the equal of the German concentration camps, is not just set as a negative value against the mindlessness of the torturers: *it is there because it fascinates*. And if, depicting it, Goya's work is fascinating in its entirety, that is because it expresses, as if by a cry that knows no limits—indeed, that knows nothing—the positive value of an excessive absence of meaning. This is a terrifying thing, no doubt, but it dominates. On this condition: that it is not subordinated to anything. Goya, on the one hand, officially painting the group portrait of the royal family, exploited the fascination produced by profound stupidity. And if he showed a man cry out as he was being shot by a firing squad, the cry—down the ages—of a humanity still not done with dying goes up with an implacable intensity that has the fullness of silence.

I do not know whether Malraux's text effectively conveys these facts *that cry out to us*. There is a continual slippage in Malraux's thought, compensated for by some brilliant little insights. Such a form of thinking breaks out in advance from what, to others, seems to confine it. We have here the servitude of a skittish individual freedom. Malraux was doubtless never a Communist and he is not a Gaullist. And nor is it without some unfortunate slippages that he tries, above and beyond politics, to occupy an indefinable humane position.

There is a faithful attention here, captured wonderfully, to the shared destiny of human beings, but one might have imagined it with fewer individual digressions.

Psychoanalysis

Gratifyingly, a little book in a French collection of encyclopaedic intent has introduced psychoanalysis into the current field of established knowledge. This is not the first time psychoanalytic material has been included in a compendium of scientific knowledge, but the *Encyclopédie française* gave an account of matters at the extreme forefront of research rather than solidly established findings. Despite everything, then, the quiet transition of Sigmund Freud's ideas from scandal to banality merits our attention for a moment. It was not so long ago that the theory of sexuality enjoyed only very ill-famed success.

However, from the moment psychoanalysis was introduced into France it was easy to judge it: Sigmund Freud's writings had from the outset a magisterial authority at the level of experimentation, and consensus among the best minds of the younger generation made up for the sterile incomprehension of those paralysed by age. The way psychoanalysis has been introduced has, moreover, been exemplary: it is emblematic of the ordinary march of human progress. The public is not yet entirely au fait with it, but Freud's revelation as a whole is no longer controversial. One may quibble with details, and the restrained but insignificant philosophical constructions with which those details are linked in Freud's mind (constructions inspired by those of [Wilhelm] Wundt and [Ernst] Mach) may be rejected out of hand. But some facts are fundamental: the determination of what we are—of our thoughts, feelings and behaviour—lies, in large measure, beyond the scope of consciousness; it is modified by a conflict between that consciousness and a whole order of violent urges for release, of which sexuality is only the most obvious aspect; this being the case, it leads to those partly mysterious forms that we observe in myths, art, dreams and neuroses; the methodical analysis of those forms may, in favourable cases, bring their deep determination into the field of consciousness and modify, once again, what we are.

All this, which is quite clearly and distinctly established, seems from the outset laden with implications. We are not speaking of the knowledge required for action on objects but on the subject of knowledge. It is the immediate transformation of human beings that is at issue, not the transformation of nature; the transformation of man's intimate being, not his milieu. Doubtless we transform ourselves by transforming nature, but we do so indirectly. By revealing a new, scandalous reality that had not been accessible to consciousness, psychoanalysis introduces the possibility of rapid, radical change.

It may, in the first instance, effect that change in individuals, having emerged precisely out of a concern to cure patients. To the neurotic it reveals the determinations of pathological behaviour, the product of the—itself unconscious—repression of impulses that had found themselves during earliest childhood in conflict with the various established forces of society and family. Once the accidental causes of conflict have been removed, patients, having acquired full awareness of themselves, can stop conforming to unconscious habits (habitual reactions) contracted in conditions that no longer pertain. Such is the practice, common today (particularly in the US) of the psychoanalytic treatment of the neuroses.

Naturally, there is on the face of it no reason why psychoanalysis should limit its ambitions to changing individuals. Might not the whole of human nature and society be changed by bringing into the field of consciousness habits that have formed themselves into institutions and legal apparatuses? Those habits have meaning only in relation to conditions that no longer exist. Could we not, if society achieved a full consciousness of the outdated element in the determination of an institution, reshape or revamp it in a way that would rid us of obvious defects?

We have to say that this second possibility runs up against a seemingly insurmountable difficulty. If a social class benefits from established institutions, it is futile to hope to make it understand that all its behaviour is merely a bad habit. And it has been said, thinking along these same lines, that the only social psychoanalysis is the class struggle. But this is not the only difficulty. Even at the level of individual therapy, Freud's methods have not always achieved the expected outcome. This is because, first of all, the necessary investigation, the analysis, may be done poorly: there is, inevitably, always scope for error on the part of practitioners and even in the precise exactness of the directives the theory offers them. But, above all, bringing material to consciousness is an operation of a very peculiar nature—which we must now examine at some length to grasp distinctly what is at issue in the problem of consciousness and the Unconscious.

It is not enough, through the analysis of the neurotic's automatic associations of images, to spot the links between an inferiority complex (and the pathological behaviours deriving from it) and a father's threat of castration in earliest childhood that has been taken too seriously. The patient still has to re-live the scene during which he contracted the habit of behaving in the grip of terror. By definition, the primal scene was contradictory in character to the way consciousness registered the event. And the cause of the conflict continues to operate while one is attempting to resolve it. Now, there is in principle no form of human life which does not involve a general conflict between violent urges for release and conscious activity. This may not be remediable: a solution presupposes perhaps both diminished drives and a rather vague conscious activity. But, at any rate, the problem must be addressed.

Freud's discoveries at the level of analytic methods are not lacking in sureness of touch, but he did not frame the most general questions clearly. This may perhaps be a reservation worth considering with regard to the relatively many failures of treatment, but it is crucial if we are looking, in a theoretical way, at the nature of consciousness, to which the Unconscious sets the limits. Neither consciousness nor the Unconscious have been subjected to sufficiently deep research. Freud based his thinking on experimental findings relating, quite rightly, to cases in which pathological behaviour made the conflict very obvious. He did not look into what it was in the nature of consciousness that underlay the general incompatibility of certain drives with their registration in consciousness. At the level of therapeutics, he proposed only rickety empirical syntheses (partial resolutions of the incompatibility). On the theoretical plane, where the object of his studies was concerned, the division between the Unconscious and the conscious, he left only definitions that were hasty responses to the needs of experimentation.

This failing shows up very perceptibly in M. Filloux's otherwise well-crafted little treatise. It is underscored by the title *L'Inconscient*—the Unconscious—which is backed up, in a necessarily deficient way, only by the range of the findings of psychoanalysis (complemented by the earlier or contemporary findings of the failed French efforts of Charcot, Bernheim and Janet). In short, the revelation of a basis of human nature is confined to fictitious glimmers of insight, lacking in cohesion. The crucial question for therapy, of a synthesis of the conscious and the Unconscious at the moment of the harsh efficacy of the analysis, is left in the dark. M Filloux is attuned to current fashion: he speaks of a '*prise de conscience*' that is 'of the order of existence'; 'the unconscious elements', he says, 'must become, existentially, conscious'.[1] This terminology has the virtue of brevity, but it can cast no light on what could probably be defined, initially, as a possibility of the impossible. And, indeed, the elaboration of the notion of Unconscious is so undeveloped that it is difficult to pin down its meaning. One says of an act or a motive that they are not conscious, but that does not mean they are not represented by anything in consciousness. It means that one has no discriminative consciousness of them. For example, when I was eating lunch just now, I drank a glass of wine without noticing I had done so (no doubt because of the interest I was taking in what I am writing now), having originally intended to drink a glass of water. The act of drinking was represented vaguely in my consciousness but not the act of drinking wine. Even in sleep there is a form of consciousness; I am conscious in a way of an alarm clock ringing at the point when it makes me dream of bells, but I do not have a discriminative consciousness of it. Now, every unconscious element has some form or other of consciousness corresponding to it, and it is improbable that that form should not be differentiated to some degree. Given this, it is distinctly odd to introduce a notion of the Unconscious that would operate as a perfectly alien mechanism, in the same way as might a silent alarm clock beside my sleeping body. This way of seeing things probably cannot lead towards that synthesis—both decisive and impossible—of the conscious and the Unconscious that is perhaps the ultimate possibility of 'what is'.

---

1 The reference is clearly to the post-war vogue for existentialism, which was at its height, particularly in the fashionable artistic quarter of Saint-Germain-des-Prés, at the time when Bataille was writing. [Trans.]

Jean-C. Filloux, *L'Inconscient* (Paris: Presses universitaires de France, 1947), in 16º, 128 pp.

This clearly written little work, which does the job of bringing a difficult science to a wider public, has the merit of situating psychoanalysis within the totality of research into the Unconscious. In reality, however, psychoanalysis in fact takes up almost all of the account.

It is strange in a work on the Unconscious to find the following error, which it is hard, given its repetition, to attribute to inadequate proofreading: the name of *Gradiva* is given as *Gravida* . . .

Félicien Challaye, *Freud*, Les Philosophes (Paris: Éditions Mellotée, 1948), in 16º, 387 pp.

This biography is, first and foremost, an account of the doctrine of the master, just as clear but less cursory than the foregoing. Its literary quality is pleasing, but it lacks the advantage that work possesses of being a textbook on its subject.

Tavern Drunkenness and Religion

PHILIPPE DE FÉLICE, *Poisons sacrés. Ivresses divines. Essai sur quelques formes inférieures de la mystique* [Sacred poisons, divine intoxications: An essay on some lesser forms of mysticism] (Paris: Albin Michel, 1936), in 8°, 397 pp.

——. *Foules en délire. Extases collectives. Essai sur quelques formes inférieures de la mystique* [Crowds going wild, collective ecstasies: An essay on some lesser forms of mysticism] (Paris: Albin Michel, 1947), in 8°, 403 pp.

Attempting to describe the state of a drinker in 'the final stage of alcoholic intoxication', Philippe de Félice—strange as it seems to him—can see only one appropriate epithet: it is, he says, a *mystical* state: the emphasis is his own (*Poisons sacrés*, p. 13). And he repeats William James's assertion to the effect that drunkenness 'makes . . . [a person] for the moment one with truth'.[1] It is not only out of depravity, wrote the American, that human beings seek drunkenness. For the poor and the illiterate, it stands in for music and literature. It is one of life's disturbing mysteries that, for many of us, the only moments in which we have some taste of the infinite are the first phases of stupefaction. Drunkenness should, nonetheless, be ranked among the mystical states: it is one part that must be taken into account in judging the whole.

The oriental or Christian mystics comparing the ecstasy in which they lose themselves with tavern drunkenness are ordinarily such ethereal thinkers that one hesitates to take them literally. It is clearly a weakness on our part that we don't find it easy to take seriously—and not just as meaningless cliché—the words of Saint Teresa of Avila when she says: 'I regard the centre of our soul as a cellar' (*Poisons sacrés*, p. 22).

---

1 William James, 'Lecture 16' in *Varieties of Religious Experience* [(London and Bombay: Longmans, Green and Co, 1902) (available online: https://bit.ly/3hVsDjP; last accessed: 24 December 2022). Cited by de Félice, *Poisons sacrés*, p. 32.

That weakness is, of course, unavoidable, but I have reason to stress my point here: it is of the essence of cliché to substitute for the strong impression that is amazing, stunning and profoundly unsettling, the neutral image over which our attention slides without entering, as though the thing in question had to be *skilfully concealed*. As our mind tracks over the cycle of thoughts, images and emotions that pass through it all day long, it is as though it were searching for the word which we say we have 'on the tip of our tongue', which eludes us, tempts us and then slips away, which we do not have the strength resolutely to grasp if it is there, and which is no longer there if we lunge out for it. In this constant mental errancy, the cliché marks the moment when we are *as close as can be* but have no one there to say to us 'You're getting very warm!', as we tell the child hunting the thimble: and we pass on by without discovering the secret that would have bowled us over.

If it comes to an image that brings together the perfect instant of ecstasy—a spiritual, pure instant—with the obscene dulling of the mind in drunkenness, then our clumsiness is so strangely deft as to deserve our devoting some thought to it. 'I regard the centre of our soul', writes Saint Teresa boldly, 'as a cellar into which God admits us when and as it pleases Him, so as to intoxicate us with the delicious wine of His grace.' Or again:

In saying that her Husband brings her into this cellar filled with heavenly wine, she (the Wife) shows that he allows her to drink it until she falls into a happy, holy drunkenness. For this great king does not honour a soul with such extreme favour to render that soul useless to him. He allows her to drink as much as she likes of these delicious wines and to become intoxicated with these inconceivable joys which enrapture her with wonderment at his greatness. This holy rapture raises her so far above the weakness of nature that instead of fearing to lose her life in the service of her divine Husband, she would wish to die in this paradise of delights [...] (*Poisons sacrés*, pp. 22–23)

These humble phrases, to someone who would suddenly awaken, as perhaps on our deathbed we might awaken with a cry, would no doubt vouchsafe the 'secret'. And yet they are there only to conceal from us what they have to offer.

*

I could not go on at this point without in some way offending against decency (and not just the decency of Christians): that is because decency is the expression of an anxious recoil by which we attempt to distance ourselves from the source of anxiety. Reading the saint, we have an impression of transparency and purity, but she was able to express her thought only by using images that are themselves impure and that she would have regarded as demoniacal if she had not immediately transfigured them, if she had not from the outset given them divine meaning. These images refer, in their transparency, to the unmentionable areas of life. But their use detaches them from the reality they evoke. In the comparison, they have a merely neutral sense; they have the blandness of conventional poetry. They attempt to describe a divine rapture by equating it with earthly raptures. But the rapture deprives these latter of their dark quality: it reduces ecstasy smoothly to the pettiness of a lie, of an intoxication that is simultaneously fear of intoxication, a sensual delight that is fear of sensual delight. Doubtless this outcome failed to live up to the intention. What forced the comparison on the saint was not fear but desire: it was the awareness that disorderly acts of debauchery alone matched up to the violence that had set her aglow. But the happy advance itself prompted the need for retreat, and scarcely had the unabashed truth appeared than a veil was immediately drawn over it. In a suspect, rapid movement, a kind of intimate horror was going to tear through the opacity and let the lightning explode out: but that intimate reality is whisked away as soon as it appears; suddenly it is there only in the mode of the word 'on the tip of one's tongue', which a disempowered obstinacy tries in vain to recall to memory.

*

For this sort of derisive irony, which seems as though it must forever conceal us from ourselves (conceal from us what we are *intimately* and leave us with only prosaic reality, the *exteriority* of things), it would be pointless to blame Christian purity. 'To sort all this out', it would not be enough simply to escape the laws that govern excess. It must at least be said that morality is liable to veil the deeply unified nature of an *intimate reality* whose various aspects often seem to us to be separated. We come to an *intimate* awareness of ourselves in states of drunkenness, sensual delight or pure ecstasy that have been caused neither by toxic substances nor sexual ardour. But we conventionally ascribe a spiritual sense to ecstasy, whereas intoxication and sensual delight are assigned to the material realm. If we confine ourselves to superficial impressions, Saint Teresa's language itself opens up a gulf between the two worlds: the demonic world of matter and the divine world of spirituality. But it refers, in fact, to the instant when the gulf is bridged and has its full sense only in the unity of the opposing forms of fiery passion.

It is to Philippe de Félice's credit that his works posit the unity of the inner man and do not separate things which moral judgement alone has styled diversely. The intoxication of alcohol, of opium and other toxic substances cannot be regarded as distinct from a mental intoxication that has no recourse to anything material. The same is true of the general sense of intoxication often achieved when crowds get excited. The field of religion is defined by intoxication in general, which we rightly associate with reaching beyond the self, with leaping beyond the limits of the *real*. Philippe de Félice describes the 'genuine drinker' as someone who drinks alone 'more happily than he does in company', who commits to drinking with an almost ritual seriousness:

> With a vague look in his eyes and sunk in blissful serenity [...], he watches a dream unfold at great length, with no beginning or end, as it transports him to somewhere far from his worries or woes. For him, at that moment, it is the great anaesthetic, an obscure sense of deliverance, of an indefinable but total happiness. He has stopped being himself. He overflows the bounds of his poor existence, enslaved to the harsh necessities of the daily grind. He has escaped beyond the narrow confines of his own personality to lose himself in some ecstasy or other, which allows him to commune with an immense, mysterious unknowable realm. (*Poisons sacrés*, p. 13)

Freed from objects—which are useful to him but demand that he service and attend to them—privately lost in the thousand and one nights of life's profundity, the human being finds himself, at last, at one with himself, in an infinite rapture. It is not exactly *himself* that he finds, but the general truth of human beings, as we might speak of the truth of the sea or air. The recognition of an identity between the mystic who is drunk on God and the drinker intoxicated by wine (and, by extension, between contemplation and debauchery) completes man's return to this intimate truth: it re-establishes the friendship (or love) that man has for the truth of man (a truth detached from the objects from which the individual expects to derive benefit).

*

The Christian world itself has always had in one form or another the sense of a connection between evil and sanctity, between religious purity and sin, but the attachment it maintained was that of the rich for the poor: it expected the sinner's fate to be one of weeping and wailing. Christians were not enslaved to this real world, but they conceded to the world the right to condemn excess. The Christian law is defined, from the standpoint of religion, by an *execration of sacred excess*. Within Christianity what is cast out from divinity is the dubious, violent or crazed element of the divine: intoxication produced by substances alcoholic or other; sensual delight; collective excitation; war-like violence; the bloody sacrifice of human beings or animals. Christianity is in no way a renunciation of the truth of man, but it completely assents to the movement preserving us from that truth, insofar as that truth destroys its patient implementation, something we may call the 'order of things' or 'real order' and which is, in the last analysis, the *profane* world of utility. Obviously Christianity (or, more generally, any dualist form of thought) has, in a sense, separated humanity from its truth, since it has defined as a lie the immediate manifestation of the sacred that was present in archaic societies. Christians can no longer recognize that truth in all the places where it presents itself and, as their beliefs then invite them to regard it as deceptive, depression alters the awareness they have of it. Clearly that depression is more conducive to life in the real order: though it continues to uphold the sovereignty of the divine world, it tends in spite of itself and with increasing sadness to subordinate the whole of Man. But this depressive swerve towards *things*, this anxious aversion to intoxication, can only mistakenly be regarded as an error, as human beings wretchedly running away from themselves. For things to have been that way, it would have been necessary for *consciousness*, in the strong sense, to have *first* been given to them. But consciousness came to them only gradually *as part of this movement*. Clear consciousness is discriminative; it is full human consciousness only insofar as, from being an indistinct sense of self, it became a clear distinguishing of the objects it contemplates. That is why we have simply to say that consciousness developed within us precisely as a result of turning itself away from our intimate truth. But if we speak now of no longer being separated from the truth of the human being, it is the clear consciousness we have become that is at issue: this still has to become conscious of its own truth, since it is the same thing as the human being, but once again, it would not be the consciousness that it is, if it had not first turned away towards objects that lack intimacy.

Moreover, far from having distanced us from our intimate truth, the spiritual movement of which Christianity is the most conspicuous form has constantly brought back towards that truth this very consciousness whose essence it was to be doomed to move away from it. In the most difficult conditions, tacking with unrelenting obstinacy against an adverse headwind, the *Christian consciousness* was akin to a stammering of the *consciousness of self*. It was not *consciousness of self* and could not be, but not for a moment did it abandon the disheartening quest. There was no opportunity for distortion that it did not turn to its advantage to open up what its own movement had closed down. And extreme difficulty has such great virtues for human beings that that consciousness attained at times to a dazzling lucidity. The writings of the mystics bear the noblest testimony to this, even though the light in them is more a memory that a dazzling vision leaves in the blackness of night. We have here perhaps, in a sense, the sole form of intimate truth accessible to consciousness, but we also see the impotence of the 'cliché', which strove to point to an incongruous insight wrested from darkness, but left only a conventional truth and the external meagreness of a thing.

*

Beyond Christianity, the movement of the spirit is borne towards an increasingly clear consciousness of objects, an increasingly precise discrimination. Consciousness then abandons the disorienting quest for its own intimate reality, but it also takes as its object the external forms and manifestations that the intimate life of human beings has assumed historically. The history of religions is the most apparent result of that quest, for the reason that religion *manifests* the concern that human beings have to endow themselves with their own intimate truth (beyond a profane world, a world of things *external* to 'divine' intimacy). Thus, the consciousness of objects, which is originally produced by the human being anguished by his own intimate reality, leads, at the extreme point of its development, to destroying the effort of dissociation that made it possible. In the beginning, clear consciousness was born of an execration of drunkenness or violence and an attention redirected to the world of useful activity. In the extreme case, science (developed, clear consciousness) contests the value of the dissociation effected in the past between the truth of the human being and intoxication.

The works of Philippe de Félice are noteworthy in this sense. They take as their subject *the lesser forms of mysticism*: intoxication through the ingestion of substances on the one hand and, on the other, the ecstasy produced by the excitement of a crowd, achieved by its moving in unison. His works keep to the idea that these forms are inferior in character. But the difference asserted is a difference of degree: de Félice emphasizes the identity of which he has, if not a consciousness (this is what an external analysis does not reach), then at least a clear, justified notion. He sees distinctly, that, whether we are speaking of profane forms of intoxication and secular crowds or ritual forms of intoxication and religious crowds, what is obtained is always an annihilation of relative lucidity and, in that process, a going-beyond oneself at the instant when distinctions fall away, when an undifferentiated truth is unveiled. He is definitely right to compare the state that follows the absorption of a toxic substance with the state that applies in the formation of a crowd, and to compare both with the ecstasy of the saints. The common characteristic of these different states—more precisely, of these different movements—is that an unshackled violence is substituted for the calm concatenation of consciousness and reason. They are all so many kinds of intoxication—of various origins—in which it took only the paralysis of the higher faculties to unleash a movement of rapid consumation. At times, the violence is exerted inwardly and the resources consumed are those of the group or individual carried away by the intoxication, at times it is exerted outwardly and it is the lives and possessions of strangers that fall victim to it. It is entirely as though the higher faculties had energy saving as their function or, generally, the economizing of available resources, the use of which needs to be subordinated to beneficial operations, such that the sum of those resources is, if possible, increased, and at all events never diminished. But this role of consciousness and reason is never easy; barely is the tension relaxed and it is all about destroying or consuming the accessible wealth to no profitable end. In a word, the floodgates simply have to be opened and the waters crash through noisily. The only question that still remains hanging is the direction of flow. Water, which in its movements consumes nothing, simply flows freely out, whereas the flow of energy is consumed and used up in several different ways.

It is a violent movement capable of destroying what it touches, incapable of orderly productive activity: all that it brings in the immediate term is disorder or death; it normally expresses itself in a multitude of actions that have only their frenzied nature in common. The external movement—dancing or rushing about—may be simply a pure internal consumption, but it may translate into action destructive of objects—objects which may at times be the frenzied individual's possessions or members of his close circle, at others, strangers or their belongings. But the object is only yielded up to the frenzy to be negated in some way. Other human beings may be caught up in its movement: but, once that happens, they are no longer others, but become part of the unified frenzy. All that is given is then called upon to be destroyed in the blaze of deep life coming back into its own in this way: the autonomy of any external reality is now denied and this unbridled violence smashes what cannot be absorbed into it.

But it is not necessary—it is even superfluous—for the energy freed up by the suspension of the normal order that binds us to the objects of the useful world to be translated into bodily movements: it is even a good thing about alcohol or drugs that they give us back, from the outset and without the slightest agitation, the blaze in which there is no longer anything but an indistinct radiance filling us with wonderment. The ecstatic meditation of the mystic is doubtless more powerful, but only in terms of method—or in the arbitrary interpretation of emotions—does it contribute something new. Alcohol and meditation both permit of a simple—very rapid—consumption, an extreme intensity by the fact of living reduced to contemplation.

The virtues of these two books, in which Philippe de Félice has provided a sort of monumental panorama of humanity fallen *entirely* prey to the madness of its own rediscovery, cannot be overemphasized. Yet it is no doubt necessary to express some secondary reservations about his detailed analyses. It is touching that he should have finished a book like this in France during the Occupation—a book in which he wanted to show the dangers of the crowd phenomenon that makes enormous releases of energy available for the unhappiest of purposes. But his arguments are not very convincing. Though he may have felt intensely the agonizing nature of the parallels he draws, the escape routes he offers us from that agony fall short. He presents the crowd as an entity that is clearly distinct from society and, though he bases himself on the distinction a biologist like Rabaud[2] makes between animal societies and crowds, he is not in the least able to maintain the clear-cut character of that distinction. By comparison with society, the human crowd can be said, in his view, to be something pathological. In reality, that is meaningless: it would be only too easy to draw from these very works examples in which society presents features no less pathological than those of the crowd. But in hardly any way does this detract from a vision. To see, *in its unity*, the intense movement that is ceaselessly withdrawing deep life from an objective reality in which it was becoming hollowed out, is the contribution de Félice's *oeuvre* makes, an *oeuvre* which could no doubt be improved upon, but the essential point of which is ultimately the *image* that humanity has managed to form of itself.

*

2 Étienne Rabaud (1868–1956) was a prominent French biologist and zoologist. [Trans.]

But the *image* only, something that is still external.

Of course, the fresco Philippe de Félice paints for us is not that of *self-consciousness*. Or rather, it can give us only the *external aspect* of self-consciousness. On all sides and in the maddest, most futile, cruellest forms we see human life manifesting the furious determination it feels to take a grasp of itself, to stop slipping through its own fingers and to fulfil itself. But that doesn't enable us to grasp anything. Of the inner world, we have only the outer shell. But if we cannot get a grip on anything, at least we know where to find what we are looking for. Perhaps at some point we shall even get to see the reason why, once we have found it again, we shall not be able to grasp it. How could we not, in the end, sense that we cannot both be intoxicated and conscious of our intoxication? In that way, we would have recovered what we are looking for, only to know that it is forever lost . . .

We would have struggled in vain: and we would remain condemned, only ever having 'on the tip of our tongue' the word, the last word that would yield up the secret to us. This is a possibility (unless that condemnation itself *were* the word: for, ultimately, without it, how would we stay *awake*? we would fall asleep *if we knew*).

Political Lying

Nowadays lying and the indignation it arouses have become an important part of the political scene. Action resorts as little as possible to the arbitrament of weapons; the aim is to convince rather than to coerce and there is an advantage in distorting—and sometimes in hushing up—the truth.

No one is particularly surprised by this, but the cause of freedom and justice would not be well served, we are told, by lying. It might be said to be the natural weapon for the oppression of the weak and abuse by the strong. Does someone who is not trying to coerce need to lie? It is no doubt easy to argue that coercion can easily dispense with lying; that slaves were not lied to; that the history of politics is a history of progress in the art of lying. (Hasn't Christianity proved the inviolability[1] of a world in which each participant sees the harshness of institutions for what it is, without mitigating factors? Did it not decidedly set the progress of *mores* on the path of a necessary dissimulation?) But the debate on lying is taking place in the world of intelligent thought, among those who are speakers by profession and whose *raison d'être* lies in the use of language. Political lying may, in fact, be a necessity: it nonetheless destroys the edifice of free speech, the space of free discussion in which the 'intellectual' moves and to which he is confined. Hence the insistence on protesting against the political realism of the Communist leaders.

---

1 It may be that the word *inviolabilité* here is a typesetting error, possibly for the less common word *invivabilité* denoting unliveableness or unbearableness. There are a number of obvious typographical errors in the article by Jean Piel on the Marshal Plan that precedes this article in *Critique* 25. [Trans.]

I do not wish to imply that I regard the very edifice to which I am currently contributing as pointless . . . But the question of lying arises in a debate that exceeds the legitimate concerns associated with the exercise of thought. There is a conflict today between the Communist and capitalist worlds. That conflict is not in a violent phase and, for the time being, it takes the form of a moral debate: it may, no doubt, even be said to be the keenest debate in the moral history of humanity, since it raises the ultimate questions in a completely open way (it is to man engaged in life-and-death struggle, not abstract man whose life is already assured, that the questions are addressed). Surely, perched on the heights of moral questioning that we have with some difficulty attained, we cannot find it a bad thing to come up against the oppressed, crushed, human beings, stirred by anger, who, not having had the leisure to engage in reflection, call us to account—we who, without the aid of their toil and sweat would have had to toil and sweat in their stead. The encounter with Communism, which is not just a system of ideas but, generally, the irruption of genuine force into the systems of ideas, might have been welcomed by the world of thought as a piece of good fortune. Most of those who pursue within themselves the long and venerable tradition of human reflection take a different view of the matter, but it is not to disparage them—far from it—if I call on them to think more deeply, to forget concerns that are peculiarly their own and leave the majority of human beings indifferent.

Might they not tell themselves that, if the laws on which the particular existence of the intellectual world are based have been infringed, it is incumbent on them, first, in their thinking, to seek out the reasons for that, rather than meet passion with passion, and the surge of force which they regard as blind with a surge of indignation which they know can only be blinding in its turn?

I do not wish to examine here the question of whether Communists lie, or to what extent they do so. But supposing that they do, and that their lying exceeds the 'permitted' margin (and that arguable opinion at least has a semblance of reason on its side), I ask whether it is not frivolous, contradictory and deleterious to the vigour of intelligence to go no further in the thinking about Communism than the issue of lying.

'Lying,' we are told, 'is the leprosy of the soul' (Marc Bloch, quoted by Roger Stéphane in his questionnaire on Communism). I believe I am driven as much as anyone by the love of truth; and I am not at all insensible of the debt we owe to the memory of Marc Bloch. But that assertion, made as a general point, is unreasonable. For if that is how things are, then the whole of action is leprous. I must say that the interest I take in action is not all that great; the supreme value attributed to it seems highly questionable to me (whatever may be said of it afterwards, action is, in a sense, just a necessity, of the same order as taking a bitter pill or paying a debt). But I cannot regard a man of action as leprous. Quite clearly, lying is no less necessary to him than speaking. And I might even say that, if he denied himself the right to lie, I could not look on him without an astonishment tinged with irritation: I should have to ask myself whether hypocrisy or foolhardiness were the stronger force within him. Those who *speak* of action *speak* of not lying. But those who act, and know how to act, lie insofar as lying is effective. Action is *struggle* and, insofar as there is struggle, there is no limitation on the various forms of violence; there is no limitation, other than effectiveness, on lying. Any other way of seeing is idealist and, as such, is the true leprosy of the soul: it is the inability to look things in the face, the weakness that diverts the eyes for fear of not being able to bear what they see.

The point cannot be over-emphasized: to act is to struggle on a rational basis. Strategy is the rational rule of combat: it is the opposite of the naïve practices of savage warriors who wished first and foremost to show their valour; it is the art of gaining additional effectiveness from a use of force by exploiting or provoking the opponent's mistakes. Transposed into the field of ideological struggle, the principle of strategy dictates that one say no to the truth and, instead, embrace those things that will conquer the resistance of the hesitant or overcome the weariness of supporters. Of course, it is by no means certain that lies are not counterproductive if told too often. The lie is bad if the hearer wearies. Ideological expression does not aim for isolated results; it has to create a lasting connection between speaker and hearer. In particular, if it is clearly a case of combatting oppression and bringing justice, the effectiveness of lying is limited. *But it is, all the same, about effectiveness: the moral question cannot be at issue.*

These remarks will no doubt be seen as a way of dragging down a debate which some keep on a lofty plane of naïve sentimentalism. But there is no doubt that, despite appearances, the detestation of lying aroused by Communist propaganda is a little narrow. 'Intellectuals' are very unhappy with the idea of words, which are their *end*, being treated in propaganda merely as a *means*. It must be said here, in precise terms, that the use of words for propaganda purposes—for purposes of ideological strategy— throws into question the foundation of the intellectual edifice. If effectiveness takes precedence over all other considerations, the conditions are no longer present for the relative autonomy of thought. This is among the most serious of problems; the role of autonomous thought in human development cannot be denied; that autonomy, often achieved at the cost of cruel sacrifice, cannot be dissociated from human development: as a general rule, human beings identify their destiny with the destiny of the human spirit. But if the question of Communism has the scope I ascribe to it, is it not to belittle it to limit it to a particular problem of the intellectual world? The question of Communism lies elsewhere and is a far more intimate matter: to confine oneself to railing naïvely against lying is to substitute an *external* concern. Moreover, I think that formal protestation against principles lethal to the movement of thought paralyses that movement no less deeply than would a rigorous application of those principles themselves.

The thinking that calls naively on reality (on the play of political forces) to respect the laws governing thought—without which it would not exist— is comparable to the prudish mother racking her brains to solve a hot-blooded son's problems for him. The human spirit is no doubt atrophied if forced to concern itself directly with effectiveness. Thought cannot be subordinated: the thinking of men of action who live in the realm of necessity is only ever embryonic (Marx's thinking is derivative, if not from Hegel, then from his own development before *The Theses on Feuerbach*). But inaction, ineffectiveness, and—if one likes to call it that—*freedom* are not necessarily any less harmful to it. In the end, are prudishness and verbal diarrhoea any less alien to thought than coercion?

But let us leave the problems of thought there: it has always developed in very unfavourable conditions; the greatest danger we could pose to it would be to afford it conditions it had chosen itself. We can say nothing of Communism and its methods that is not beside the point unless we get to the bottom of things. If we are looking at methods, it soon becomes apparent that they are effective. It may be that they traduce an initial intention: that is another matter. But if one condemns that betrayal, one takes upon oneself the responsibility of finding an effective response oneself. It is not good enough to say: existing Communism has moved away from true Communism . . . One cannot say anything of the kind unless one acts oneself—*unless one devotes one's whole life* to effective action. Failure on that level will serve as a negative demonstration. Marxism is not a pure theory: it is the implementation of possibilities afforded in history. But no one has to be Marxist (even in the USSR, where you can remain silent or lie). No one has to speak about true Communism. I do not believe it is necessary here to look at the ever-contestable consequences of a doctrine. I am concerned only to define clearly the unavoidable problem Marxism and the USSR pose today for humanity.

There is undoubtedly oppression in the world and we are partially enslaved. Insofar as we are oppressed and enslaved, we are no longer human beings but things. We cannot clear-sightedly accept being things. Insofar as we feel reduced to things, we are *committed* to destroying what it is that is reducing us.

We can escape this reduction individually, but always in a questionable way. To do this, we have in effect to integrate ourselves into a world in which 'the man in the street' is treated as a commodity. We must ourselves, at least by our collusion, turn our fellow human beings into commodities. If we are truly to escape, we shall continually have to be destroying the effect of our integration by behaving other than as things, by violently asserting our individuality. But we shall cease to be things only in this assertion which separates us from the general run of humanity. It is our individuality that is aggressively professed (*against others*) which is not treated as a commodity; the simple humanity in us is never recognized for what it truly is— *something wholly different from a thing*. We assert only a repudiation of common humanity. We become insidiously involved in a betrayal.

But if we reject individual escape and assert our shared humanity—if we accept not being things only at the same time and on the same basis as others—*we have first to accept being things*. It is only when the whole of humanity has stopped oppressing, when there are nowhere any commodity-human-beings for sale, that we shall ourselves escape reduction to thingness. Until then, it is at the level of useable thing, as members of a debased humanity, that we have to contribute, in a disciplined way, to an immense work of liberation.

We may even have to contemplate some painful refinements. The development of science is likely to make it much more possible to reduce human nature to the status of thing. 'Political lying' is itself a first application of the science that will, generally, have to make human beings an experimental field on which it will act rationally. Moreover, pedagogics and biology are likely to eliminate human resistance to the state's actions in an ever more complete way. It is crucially important then that the state itself does not in any way exceed the principles of thinghood, that it is sovereign only in name, that it is unreservedly subordinated to the individuals it subordinates, being itself merely an instrument and object without its own driving principle.

At that moment, man will be free! . . .

And we can no longer speak about him.

But it is at the point where it becomes a pure object in a limitless functioning of operations that the question of humanity is posed in a sufficiently rigorous way. From that point on, the repudiation by human beings of their shared humanity takes on a quite other meaning; it is no longer the cowardly repudiation of the weak by the strong, nor the mind engaging in puerile escapism. The *individual* distances himself, unseeing, from those crushing him (and is prepared to crush them in his turn). By contrast, the man of objective society must grasp his own humanity in the consciousness of his reduction to a thing and in the consciousness of the limits of that reduction.

Naturally, it is a pity in a sense that everything should take place in darkness, that Communism can give no assurances and that it seems at first to be radically moving away from the goal it should, by its very essence, be pursuing. This is not likely to put an end to errors, misunderstandings or wars. Admittedly, only in appearance is this dependent on Communism. It is a particular pity that the outcome can be hoped for only after a conflagration—in that case, it is certain that we shall not escape horror, but to be doubted whether we shall not see the hoped-for outcome slip from our grasp.

This cannot absolve us of seeing the reductionism laid at Communism's door as anything more than a disturbance of intellectual tranquillity: the posing—in a radical, tiresome, but maximally stimulating way—of the fundamental problem.

Man cannot be regarded as a thing. And it is for that reason that he is a Communist. (But we must add: Communism can, at first, only render this reduction to a thing complete and general, and it is also for that reason that man fights Communism to the death.)

CLAUDE AVELINE, JEAN CASSOU, ANDRÉ CHAMSON, GEORGES FRIEDMANN, LOUIS MARTIN-CHAUFFIER and VERCORS, *L'heure du choix* [Time to choose] (Paris: Éditions de Minuit, 1947), in 8°, 177 pp.

Not being members of the Communist party but mere sympathizers, the authors of the studies in this collection take issue with certain political positions. They make clear that in their eyes the USSR is an *example*, not a *model*. French Communism could take independent paths and recognize limits to the necessities of propaganda. And the basic political fact of the present period has to be taken into account: namely, that it is now futile to look to undertake anything on the other side of a war. Whatever the obstacles, on the one hand, and however far removed, on the other, these essays may be from political realism, it would be pointless and at odds with *political realism* itself, to ignore the fact that these are the positions taken by most of the followers of the French Communist Party.

ROGER STÉPHANE (ed.), *Questions du communisme*, special issue of *Confluences* 8(18–20) (contributors: R. Aron, J. Beaufret, J. Benda, R.-P. Caillois, M. Collinet, J. T. Desanti, J. Domarchi, I. Dorgot, J. Kanapa, H. Lefebvre, S. De Madariaga, J.-J. Marchand, G. Martinet, R. Maublanc, E. Mounier, A. Patri, P. Pia, G. Picon, D. Rousset, A. de Soros, S. Spender, R. Tavernier, Tran-Duc Thao, R. Vailland, Vercors) (Paris: Éditions Confluences, 1947), in 16º, 344 pp.

The rare Communists who responded to this survey did so rather testily. Roger Stéphane's questionnaire cites Malraux and Sartre and speaks, of course, of mendacity and freedom; it orients discussion towards individualistic, moral concerns that underscore the sense of disarray generated by contradictions between Communism's actions in the immediate present and its remote aims.

The Sexual Revolution and the Kinsey Report

ALFRED C. KINSEY, WARDELL B. POMEROY and CLYDE E. MARTIN, *Sexual Behavior in the Human Male* (Philadelphia: W. B. Saunders, 1948), in 8°, *xv*–804 pp.

'By virtue both of its intrinsic nature and its dramatic reception, the Kinsey Report, as it has come to be called, is an event of great importance in our culture.'[1] In so saying, it is not Lionel Trilling's intention to express excessive admiration for this voluminous product of American science, but to address it appropriately. We know that in more than 800 pages, 162 tables and 173 graphs and charts, it expresses the sexual life of the US (at least of its male, white population). 'It is right,' observes Trilling,

> that the Report should be sold in stores that never before sold books and bought by people who never before bought books, and passed from hand to hand and talked about and also snickered at and giggled over and generally submitted to humor: American popular culture has surely been made the richer by the Report's gift of a new folk hero—he already is clearly the hero of the Report—the 'scholarly and skilled lawyer' who for thirty years has had an orgasmic frequency of thirty times a week.[2]

I don't know whether the translation of this book will produce an equally strong impression in France; on a certain matter we think we have not much more to learn. No doubt series of tables showing the degree to which each sort of male individual—bachelors, married men, divorcees or widowers; farmers, unskilled labourers, manual and 'white collar' workers, the upper

---

1 Lionel Trilling, 'Sex and Science', *Partisan Review* 15(4) (April 1948): 460. [In the original French text, the page number is given as p. 325, but this appears to be an error. (Trans.)]
2 Trilling, 'Sex and Science': 463–64.

classes; adolescents, adults and old men (divided into 10 or more categories of various ages, from 8 to 60)—relates, on a weekly basis, to each sexual possibility (masturbation, nocturnal emissions, foreplay leading to orgasm, conjugal relations, extra-conjugal relations, relations with prostitutes, homosexuality, bestiality) cannot fail to arouse curiosity. Moreover, the thoroughness of the methods and cross references, combined with the impression of common sense undeniably conveyed by the authors, is such as to overcome an inevitable scepticism: though approximate, these numerical data nonetheless provide a picture we had never before seen with such precision.

The interest of the book is, however, an intimately American affair: the picture it paints is an American, not a European or French one, which, though veiled, is familiar to us. Besides, even if these figures were to provide solutions to the puzzles we face personally, they would not be of such interest to us as they have visibly been to the average reader in the US. What struck American public opinion was suddenly learning that, from adolescence onwards, around 95% of the male population could properly be indicted for some sort of sex crime. To degrees that vary from state to state, American law actually punishes the various forms of activity referred to above, with the exception of conjugal relations and masturbation (this last-mentioned is not entirely clear, the law of some states allowing for the prosecution of teachers who convey to their students the—probably true— notion that masturbation is not harmful). By dint of their involuntary nature, nocturnal emissions also earn the indulgence of the law, though the dreams accompanying them are often far from innocent. This state of things not only has far-reaching implications (which particularly affect children, who are threatened with being sent to special institutions): it reveals a dominant mentality which the Kinsey Report rightly challenges by way of an appeal to the higher authority of science.

This prevailing blindness actually points up the significance of the Report. It has led many readers to *discover* something they were unaware of: that almost the whole of humanity was wicked, that human beings almost all indulged, as they did themselves, in a range of sinister activities.

Where there is a threat of punishment, it is difficult to speak or confess—and, therefore, knowledge is hard to come by. Thus the Report revealed a picture that was concealed by general hypocrisy, and at the same time rendered untenable the system of values founded upon that hypocrisy.

For these reasons, in America this book marks a significant moment in the *sexual revolution* that is raging in a world whose moral stability has been undermined by wars. We might say, in a sense, that it is an effect, before being a factor of that revolution. The countless personal interviews (12,000 at the time of publication of the first volume of a collective work that will run to some ten or so) would not have been possible if the Americans who confided the particularities of their sexual lives to the researchers had not come round to the idea that they were in no way too shameful to mention. But, when translated into statistics, the hesitant freeing of minds assumes the scale and distinctness that belong to the social order and to science. So that the Report is the outcome, conclusion and completion of all the isolated efforts: with the inevitable sniggers and giggles, in this report the whole of America can at last know itself to be free.

At first blush and in spite of everything, this is of rather a minimal interest for French people. If they have really carried out—if they have had to carry out—their *sexual revolution*, then, one way or another, it is over. Those who are likely actually to read the book will either draw from it a general knowledge they already possessed or information about America that cannot affect them deeply.

But, if the reader will linger over these matters for a moment, they are not so clear cut. It is in the nature of sexuality to be subject to fleeting notions that are always rather uncertain. Without rigour and critical attention, it is not possible to make sense of all this; we are not dealing here with a cold truth like a triangle or a weight: in this particular case, the truth is itself a passion. And so, as we pursue it, we are not so much like scientists in their laboratories but more like the heroes of legends, like Oedipus confronted with the Sphinx.

*

First of all, it is difficult even to speak, as I am doing, of *sexual revolution*. The men of my generation, born in the latter years of last century have doubtless witnessed, particularly since the first war, the apparent transformation of *mores*. Even clothing has changed and there has been an appreciable decline in modesty. Relations between boys and girls have become much freer. With varying levels of resistance, literature has ceased more or less everywhere to be so timid and psychoanalysis has instilled a habit of facing up to things as they are. There is, however, nothing openly revolutionary in this and one might even say that it actually represents a restoration.

Without going back to the freedom that prevailed before Christianity, it is clear that prudishness is of recent date, that it is largely a nineteenth-century phenomenon. The licentiousness of the Elizabethan theatre is well known. Only the dominant influence of the bourgeoisie established that asexual, prudish, arrogant world which the term 'Victorian' evokes for an Anglo-Saxon. *Even in its churches*, the Christianity of the Middle Ages had not known this blatant denial of the body and the frenzied forces that drive it. Aggressive modesty is not so much the product of a culture of remorse, based on sin and shame, as of an economy that reserves its wealth for industrial accumulation, rather than for the festivities and exuberance of medieval life. Remorse and the recognition of sin as such carry us less far from *self-consciousness*: hatred was still a sort of pact and, in it, men did not attain to that fulfilled desire for their own truth which made Victorian humanity such a pale *absence of humanity*.

Thus, if there is a *sexual revolution*, it is less about a conquest of new territories than the recovery of a recently lost domain.

Nor is it the revolution of one class against another. It is within the bourgeoisie that change has taken place. On this point at least, the Kinsey Report provides detailed findings that should be seen as having general value. Research into the past of mature males and the present of young people shows, in a remarkable chapter devoted to the change in types of sexuality (pp. 394–447), that neither the working nor the middle classes (those with a level of education not extending beyond high school) have changed, and sexual emancipation is limited to college students.

Yet, the social class enjoying college-level education—hence the ruling bourgeoisie—was more hypocritical than the others. It was and still is to the greatest extent ravaged by solitary masturbation.[3] It was that class that largely still had to liberate itself.

And it was that class which, intellectually, had the possibility of doing so. Sexual behaviour is everywhere governed by *taboos* that are the basis of our human life and which are no doubt inviolable in their essentials: the taboos on incest, on child sex, on nudity and on public sexual display seem difficult to erode. But the mode of life that depends on them seems ultimately grounded in reason and if it is beyond interfering with, that is because it seems rational. In fact every form of irrational sexual behaviour has been questioned as soon as it has appeared to have no rational goal. When the bourgeoisie found the old system of prohibitions *sensible*—that is to say, useful—it reinforced it. But insofar as sufficient accumulation (already even excessive in certain respects—at least at certain moments) reduced the dangers of a costly activity, the bourgeoisie without hesitation contested the value of the traditional rules. It was prepared in advance to do so: it was the bourgeoisie that set the apparatus of reason in train and it is the bourgeoisie that controls that apparatus (the oppressed classes which have traditionally been less inhibited have the time to control that apparatus for only one end: to escape the state of subordination in which they live).

Undoubtedly, this *sexual revolution* of the affluent had nothing particularly heroic about it: it is fundamentally bourgeois and sensible. It has not even arrived at a greater freedom than existed before the wave of prudishness. It might even be seen as insignificant if it did not have about it the character of *consciousness.*

What differentiates today's sexual freedom from that of past periods— and this is why there has been a revolution—is that, at the same time as it is a freedom of the body, it is a freedom of the minds that reflect it, which are not simply free in the bedroom but in sustained thought, which finds

---

3 According to the report's authors, masturbation accounts for around 80% of orgasms for adolescents of 15 years in that class (as against an average of around 50% in the others), 65% between the ages of 16 and 20 (as against 30%), 50% between 21 and 25 (as against 25%) and 45% between 26 and 30 (as against 22%).

expression, ultimately, in books. Proust's licence isn't the expression of a rough and ready simplicity: it works itself out in the infinite twists and turns of thought. It is license enlisted in consciousness. Proust is indeed the contemporary of Freud and the period they lived in saw the accomplishment of the efforts of a lucid consciousness to focus its attention on sexual freedom— in a word, on vice. Sade had obviously lived more than a century before, but his work only effectively assumed meaning for others in that time when consciousness made its descent into hell. The term *sexual revolution* does not refer to some vague debauchery, but to the recognition, in the universal debauchery of all the ages, of a fundamental human truth.

*

Elevation of the debate to this level leaves the very American character of the Report in no way less clear (it might even in a sense be accentuated), but America will find itself linked in with the development of the mentality of the Western bourgeoisie as a whole.

In this world so laden with avarice, power and tempestuous change, there is a profound unity which secondary differences cannot prevent us from seeing. And what is true generally is true of the *sexual revolution*. The path the Americans have followed no doubt differs from that of the French. They have perhaps moved slower and our morals have always been freer, but we ought not to forget the sex education given to French children of the affluent classes at the beginning of the nineteenth century. Among individuals of the male sex, the effect of this seems to have been less weighty, but it was just as much based on terror as in the English-speaking countries. This quotation from a treatise for use by priests doubtless gives a good idea of what went on: 'The poor unfortunate!' it is said of the person who, according to the Report, corresponds to 96% of the population:

> has sinned against nature and against himself . . . He has even reduced himself to a level below the beasts and, like them, his eyes are now fixed solely on the ground; his stunned, doltish gaze can no longer raise itself to the heavens; he no longer dares to raise his ignominious brow, which already bears the mark of the reprobate.

He is gradually sinking into death and a final convulsive crisis at last precipitates the violent ending to this strange and horrible drama. Doubtless not all onanists are so harshly dealt with . . . but there is none who does not display some of the features we have just outlined. All are already punished, all receive punishment proportionate to their crime; and those who come through it feel its effects virtually for the rest of their days.[4]

Such a strange reaction sets the tone for the general attitude to sexual problems. The general thrust of that attitude was methodically transmitted to children, particularly 'well brought-up' children. They responded to it sketchily but were marked by it. They might—and usually did—do what had been prohibited. But they could not prevent it from being unhealthily forbidden. It is curious to compare the French theologian's opinion with this passage from the American report:

In the present study we have examined the histories of 5300 males of which about 5100 record experience in masturbation. It would be difficult to show that the masturbatory activities have done measurable damage to any of these individuals, with the very rare exception of the psychotic who is compulsive in his behaviour. On the other hand, the record does include thousands of cases of boys living in continual conflict, fearful of social disgrace, oftentimes disturbed over the effect of such behaviour on their ultimate sexual capacities, occasionally attempting suicide—as a result of the teachings concerning masturbation. (p. 514)

This precise parallel clearly shows how arbitrary it would be to regard the old and new worlds as entirely separate. The Old World experienced with the New—and doubtless at the same time—the revolution by which common sexual behaviour, including a large swathe of alleged vice, ceased to appear pernicious and contrary to reason.

---

4 Pierre Jean Corneille Debreyne, *Essai sur la Théologie morale* (Paris, 1842). Cited by Antoine Bonal, *Tractatus de Virtute Castitatis ad Usum Seminariorum*, 9th EDN (Paris, 1904), in 8°, p. 124.

It is even a certainty that the two worlds shared a single experience, that each benefited from the other's moves towards freedom: news about lascivious habits crosses the seas easily. At any rate, books passed from one continent to the other: not to speak of Freud or Proust, the Americans have at last read Joyce and D. H. Lawrence (Miller himself is not by any means unknown: since the pre-war years when they were published in Paris, a large number of individual copies of his *Tropics* have found their way into America). American novels have not had the same meaning for us, though at least they taught us that the *mores* of the New World were not so different from our own. But today the Kinsey Report brings Europe an entirely novel contribution to the general revelation of sexual truth.

Beyond banal curiosity, given the local character of the *mores* described in it, and despite the fact that in France such a book will not be performing the positive task of bringing the authority of science to bear against that of the law, the Kinsey Report will no doubt play an appreciable role. If we have to be fully aware of a reality whose very nature is to be as hidden as possible from consciousness, nothing can more precisely remedy the general lack of information that flows from the universal taboo on discussing that reality in public. In itself, the desire to apply a scientific method of investigation to sexual matters already represents a rebellion on the part of consciousness against the effects of a way of acting that necessarily keeps them in the dark. In fact, Alfred Kinsey, the prime mover and director of the study, uses a method he previously tested in his work on insects: his exact intention is to study human behaviour with the same cold objectivity as if he were dealing with bees.

*

The fact of having studied human sexual behaviour with the cold—virtually detached—interest of the scientist observing the action of a lamp on a wasp means something very particular. Let us say no more of an immediate, sensational effect, which, we can only repeat, remains confined to America: the scale of the survey and the results have, however, made this book, for anyone prepared to see it, the source of a memorable change in the very structure of a shifting *historical* reality that we ourselves represent.

It is doubtless not at all new for human behaviour to have become the object of science and to be viewed as inhumanly as if it were animal behaviour; but sexual behaviours seem to have a special importance.

Those behaviours are, as a general rule, precisely those in which human beings are reduced to the level of animals. It is even for that reason that they are hidden and not spoken of and, more generally, that they have no properly assured place in consciousness. At first sight, there cannot be any difficulty with this: why not treat these genuinely animal behaviours like any other that zoologists will research into?

It is worth lingering over this question.

However far a human being may have fallen, he is doubtless never, like an animal, a thing. There remains in him an eminent dignity, a fundamental nobility and a sacred truth which means that he is not to be reduced to a servile state (even if such servility exists). A human being cannot simply be made a means to an end; even if he were momentarily such, he always retains to some degree the sovereign importance of an end in himself; he remains inalienable in himself (even in the worst of cases), which means that he cannot be killed—nor even less eaten—without a sense of horror. This taboo, this sacred character of human life is no less universal than the fundamental sexual taboos (relating to nudity, public display, childhood and incest). Only animals, by contrast, are reducible to thinghood. A man can do what he wants with animals, without the least limitation and without ever having to account for his actions. He may know, at bottom, that this animal he is slaughtering does not differ in any profound way from him, but a furtive recognition of that fact is immediately countered by a denial that never seriously falters. Whatever the varying beliefs, the truth that sees mind in human beings and body in animals only ever meets with ineffective opposition. And the body is a thing, it is base—and servile—like a stone or a bit of wood. The mind alone, the truth of which is an intimate—subjective—matter, cannot be reduced to a thing. It remains profoundly sacred within a profane body, which is sacred only at the point when death reveals the incomparable value of the spirit.

But having said this, which is clear at first sight—and which underlies everyday life from the cowshed to the dining room—still, in the long run, we notice the following point, which is less simple.

We are, come what may, animals. However much we are human beings—and minds—we cannot prevent animality surviving within us and, often, overwhelming us. At the opposite pole from the mind, exuberant sexuality represents the persistence of animal life within us. It might, in consequence, be viewed as a thing: the sex organ is a part of the *body*, which is a thing, and sex is the functional activity of that thing. A sex organ is, all in all, a thing in the same way as a foot is (at a pinch, we might say that a hand is human and that the eye expresses one's spiritual life, but we possess sex organs and feet in an entirely animal way). And, in fact, we say, when our senses prevail in a disorderly way, that we lower ourselves to the level of animals . . .

If, however, we wish to conclude from this that sexual facts are things—in the same way as animals are—we run up against a fundamental difficulty. If we are in the presence of a thing, we can always have a clear and distinct consciousness of it. We may even assert in principle that the contents of consciousness are clearly distinct for us insofar as we have reduced them to things. In fact, every time those contents are not things—but acts which concern us intimately—we have first to place them outside ourselves and look at them as something external, like things.[5] But there is precisely nothing less easy to look at from the outside—to view *as a thing*—than a sexual fact.

There is not one page of the Kinsey Report on which that difficulty is not implicit. So far as I can see, its authors have never actually observed from the outside any of the countless facts they report. They were observed from the inside by those who experienced them. If the reality of these facts is methodically established, it is by way of confessions and stories that have had to be relied upon. I do not say this to cast doubt on the value—at least, the general value—of the findings: the authors took considerable precautions (repetitions of the survey at long intervals, third-party verification, comparison of the graphs obtained by different researchers in the same

---

5 I speak of *myself*, for example, by taking my existence as an isolated reality, similar to the existence of other human beings, which I see from the *outside*; and I have only been able clearly to distinguish other human beings insofar as they have, in their apparent isolation, that perfect identity to themselves which I ascribe to things.

conditions etc.). But these very efforts precisely show that the facts had not been presented as things before the immense machinery of the survey went into action. In reality, sexuality had not existed as a thing before the Report and that is what constitutes its novelty: it is in this respect that it introduces a memorable change into our nature. And this is why we cannot reduce its meaning to a mere episode in American life.

One's first impulse is naturally to protest against such a strange reduction, which often seems so ponderous as to be absurd. But an intellectual operation can only ever establish a theoretical principle; it is even possible that the deep meaning of the Report lies in something that it demonstrates to be impossible: we would then have to read it against the grain and thereby see only a truth that its authors could not or would not see: they have put together an enormous piece of work, the very principle of which requires sexual acts to be regarded as things, but the clearest outcome of their research has been to show without a doubt that ultimately *sexual acts are not things*. Now, it may be that the working of consciousness properly requires the following twofold operation: that its contents are viewed, so far as is possible, as things, but that they are never more fully vouchsafed to us than at the point where the effort of consciousness seems futile. But this deserves to be more precisely set out (particularly as, looking at it overall, this latter truth doubtless comes most clearly into view when we are considering sexual disorders).

The reasons against observing sexual facts from the outside are not solely material. There is, further, a moral impossibility that has to do with their *contagious* character. What we are considering here is not in any sense of a nature comparable to a microbial disease; it is rather an *intimate* form of contagion, analogous to yawning or laughter. That contagion, which puts a halo around sexuality, clearly indicates that it can be known ordinarily only *from within* (and the disgust it quite often produces is simply an inverse effect of that contagion). Ordinary knowledge of sexuality, if I may put it this way, takes the form that Lévy-Bruhl described as *participation* (conversely, our knowledge of sexuality can serve as a tangible illustration of the idea of participation). What we know in an act of participation (of communication) is, in fact, what we know *intimately*: we know the laughter of another person by laughing, the sexual excitation of another person by sharing it. It is precisely in this sense that laughter or excitation are not things: we cannot ordinarily participate in a plank of wood or a stone: we do participate in nudity. The man Lévy-Bruhl dubbed 'primitive' could participate in stone; but the stone was not then a thing, it had no identity with itself and did not exist as something given independently of the subject. Lévy-Bruhl was doubtless wrong to associate this mode of thinking with 'primitive' humanity. All we have to do, through the medium of poetry, is to deny the stone's identity with itself, to speak, for example, of the *moonstone*: from that point on, it exists as part of my intimate life, as I slide, in speaking of it, into intimacy with the *moonstone*. But if nudity or orgasms are not things and if their nature is the same as *moonstone*, some remarkable consequences ensue.

It is odd, in fact, to be demonstrating here that sexuality, which is normally reduced to the level of butcher's meat, has the same privileged status as poetry. Admittedly, we are in a time when poetry, for its part, is keen to prove that it is itself disreputable, and, at a deep level, scandalous in nature. It is nonetheless striking to note that, in the case of sexual matters, it is not necessarily the body in man that bears the burden of the servility of things and that, in a word, his *animality* is *divine*. This is what the scope and incongruousness of the Report's methods bring out by showing their powerlessness to pin down their object *as an object*: so far as the survey's necessary resorting to subjectivity is concerned, it is possible, by examining such a large volume of data, to eliminate the aspect that is contrary to scientific objectivity, but the immensity of the effort required to do so happily underscores an irreducible element in sexual life: the *intimate* aspects (the nonthings) which, beyond the graphs and charts, the Report's data allow us to glimpse have remained entirely inaccessible, alien to the external considerations that relate to frequency, modality, age, profession or class and never go to the essence of the matter. There is, even, a distinct need to pose the question: is this book about sexuality? Can we be said to be speaking about human beings if we confine ourselves to providing numbers, measurements, classifications based on size, age or eye colour? What we know of the human being would undoubtedly appear to lie outside of these notions; they would merely add inessential detail to an already given knowledge. Similarly, authentic knowledge of sexuality could not be drawn from the Report; it is vouchsafed to us by other means and these statistics, frequencies and averages have meaning only insofar as we already know what sexuality is. Or, if they do enrich our understanding, they do so in the direction I have already described, if, in reading them, we experience the sense of something irreducible—for example, if we *laugh* (if we react as we would before something that is theoretically impossible, but nonetheless exists) to see, beneath a ten-column table, this title: 'Sources of orgasm for total US population' and the divisions it introduces: masturbation, 'petting to climax', marital or extra-marital intercourse, 'animal contacts', homosexuality etc. There is a deep incompatibility between these mechanical forms of representation, which ordinarily convey facts about *things* (such as steel or copper and their production . . .) and the intimate realities they are referring to. At least on one occasion the authors themselves realized this: the surveys, the 'sexual stories' on which their analysis is based, appeared to them, in spite of everything, in their intimate dimension. This was not what they were concerned with, but they recognize nevertheless that these stories 'often imply the memory of deep wounds, frustrating pain, unsatisfied desire, disappointments, tragic situations and utter catastrophe' (p. 42). It probably does not take unhappiness to show up the irreducibly intimate nature of sexual matters, but it is at least a mark of the intimate sphere in which they take place and from which they cannot be excised without misrepresenting them. But it is not with this thought, but with the little regard they pay to it, that the authors underscore—through the inevitable reactions of the reader— the nature of sexuality. And they never reveal it better than in an exception to the method of recourse to subjects' own accounts which they had to follow. No doubt without having carried out the observation themselves, they publish data on one matter that derives from objective observation (third parties were able to provide it to them). They studied the—very short—masturbation time required for young children (between six months of age and one year) to arrive at orgasm: these times, they tell us, were observed in some cases using the second hand of a watch and at others with a stopwatch. It seems to me that here the incompatibility between the observation and the act observed, between the method which is valid for things and what is always a *fearsome* intimacy, reaches a level where laughter no longer comes easily. I know that the ordinary affection of human beings for children and the awareness of their weakness enter into this pained reaction. Nevertheless, in spite of the authors, the essential point emerges from these disarming measurements: that one cannot, without altering its true character, present as a thing that which is *something else entirely*—that which is *sacred*—and that the secret animality of the human being or the child cannot, without a gnashing of teeth, be registered in the profane world.

*

I come back again to the fact that animality is, in principle, precisely what is ordinarily reducible to a thing. This is a point that can hardly be stressed enough and I shall try to elucidate the problem that arises here by pursuing my analysis with the aid of the Report's own data.

In this connection, it should be said very clearly from the outset that these data, plentiful as they are, are far from being properly worked up. This is an enormous collection of facts, a remarkably well carried-out survey, whose methods, reminiscent of the Gallup Institute, have been admirably perfected, but one cannot admire the associated theoretical conceptions to the same extent.

As the authors see it, sexuality is 'a normal biologic function, acceptable in whatever form it is manifested' (p. 263), but religious restrictions have been placed on this natural activity.[6] The most interesting series of numerical data in the Report relates to weekly frequency of orgasm. Varying by age and social category, that frequency is, overall, very much lower than 7, which number marks the beginning of what the authors term a high rate. However, the normal frequency of the anthropoid is in fact once per day. The normal frequency for human beings, the authors assert, might be no lower than that of the great apes if there had been no religious restrictions placed upon it. The authors base themselves on the findings of their survey.

---

6 Lionel Trilling (in 'Sex and Science') is right to stress the naivety of the authors who think they can settle the question by asserting this *natural* character.

They have classified the responses of the adherents of various religious denominations, comparing those who actually practise the religion with those who do not. 7.4% of active Protestants, as against 11.7% of inactive ones, reach or exceed the weekly rate of 7, as do 8.1% of active Catholics, as against 20.5% of inactive ones. These figures are remarkable: the practice of a religion clearly curbs sexual activity. But we are dealing here with impartial, indefatigable observers, who didn't just content themselves with establishing the data on which they rely. The statistics for these rates are also broken down by social category: day labourers, skilled and semi-skilled workmen, 'white-collar workers' and professionals. Overall, the working population shows some 10% at the high rate. Only 'the underworld' reaches a level of 49.4%. These numerical data are even more remarkable than the foregoing. But the factor they refer to is less uncertain than religion (let us recall the cults of Kali or Dionysus, tantrism and other erotic forms of religion): that factor is, precisely, *work*, the essence and role of which have nothing ambiguous about them. It is, indeed, by work that the human being is reduced to a thing; it is work that makes the worker a means to an end. Work, something human by its essence and essential to human beings, alone stands unequivocally opposed to animality. The numerical findings separate a world of work and workers, reducible to things, excluding sexuality, from a world of animality that is entirely intimate and irreducible.

This opposition, established by the figures, is rather paradoxical. Among the various values, it implies unexpected relationships, combining with those I have just pointed up, which paradoxically underscore the irreducibility of animal exuberance to the status of a thing. All this requires the greatest attention.

What I said at the outset showed that the basic opposition between human beings and things could not be formulated without implying the identification of the animal with the thingly. There was, on the one hand, this external world, the world of things, of which animals were a part and, on the other, the world of human beings, conceived essentially as internal, as a world of the mind (the subject). But if an animal is merely a thing, and if that is a characteristic that separates it profoundly from the human being, it is not a thing in the same way as an inert object—a cobblestone or a spade—is. Only the inert object—particularly if it is manufactured, if it is a product of work—is *the* thing par excellence, shorn of all mystery and subordinated to ends that are external to it. That which is nothing on its own account is a thing. In this sense, animals are not in themselves things, but human beings treat them as such: they are things insofar as they are the object of work (e.g. cattle rearing) or instruments of work (beasts of burden or draught animals). If they form part of the cycle of useful acts as means rather than ends, animals are *reduced* to things. But that reduction is the negation of what, in spite of everything, the animal is: it is a thing only insofar as the human being has the power to deny its actual character. If we no longer have that power, if we are no longer able to act exactly as though animals were things (if a tiger knocks us to the ground), it is clear that the animal is not, in itself, a thing: it is not a pure object but a subject with an intimate truth of its own.

Similarly, the surviving animality of human beings, their sexual exuberance, could only be regarded as a thing if we had the power to deny it and to live our lives as though it did not exist. In fact, we do deny it, but we do so in vain. Sexuality, described as sordid and bestial, is even what stands most opposed to the reduction of human beings to things: a man's innermost pride attaches to his virility. That pride does not in any way correspond to the denied animal element within us, but to what there is in the animal element that is intimate and incommensurable. It is in that pride even that we cannot be reduced like oxen to mere labour power, to an instrument or thing. There is, without a doubt, in *humanity*—in the sense opposite to *animality*—an element that is irreducible to a thing or to work; without a doubt, the human being absolutely cannot be enslaved and ground under to the same degree as an animal can. But this is only clear secondarily: man is, first of all, an animal who works, who submits himself to work and must, for that reason, give up part of his private exuberance. There is nothing arbitrary in sexual restrictions: every human being has a limited amount of energy available to him and, if he assigns part of it to work, it is not there to be consumed in erotic activity, which is correspondingly diminished. Thus *humanity* in the *human, anti-animal* time of work is that within us which reduces us to things, and animality is then what preserves within us the value of an existence of the subject for himself.

This deserves precise formulation.

'Animality' or sexual exuberance is the element within us which prevents our being reduced to things.

'Humanity', on the other hand, in its specificity in working time, tends to make us into things, at the expense of our sexual exuberance.

*

To these first principles, the numerical data of the Kinsey Report correspond in notably minute detail. Only the members of the underworld, *who do not work, and whose behaviour overall amounts to a negation of 'humanity,'* present a percentage of 49.4 at the high rate. On average that figure corresponds, as the Report's authors see it, to the normal rate occurring in nature—in the animality of the anthropoid. But it stands out, in its uniqueness, from the whole of specifically human behaviour which, varying between groups, displays proportions of high rates ranging from 16.1 down to 8.9%. The spread of the indices is, in fact, noteworthy. Overall, the index varies according to whether *humanization* is greater or lower: with the greater humanization of human beings comes a reduction in their exuberance. To be more precise, the proportion registering high rates stands at 15.4% among day labourers, 16.1% among semi-skilled workers, 12.1% among skilled workers, 10.7% among the lower ranks of 'white collar workers' and 8.9% among their upper ranks.

There is, however, one exception: in moving from the upper echelons of 'white collar workers' to the professions, which correspond to the ruling classes, the index rises by 3.5% to reach 12.4%. If we think about the conditions in which these figures were obtained, there is no reason to take negligible differences into account. But the fall in the rates from the labourer to the upper ranks of white collar workers is rather steady, and the difference of 3.5 between this latter and the professions represents a rise of about 30%: that makes for an increase of around two to three orgasms per week on average. The sense of an upturn in the figures when we move to the dominant class is clear enough from the outset: by comparison with the preceding categories, it enjoys a modicum of leisure, and the middling wealth it enjoys is not always matched by an exceptional amount of work performed; it obviously has available to it greater excesses of energy than exist among the working classes. This compensates advantageously for the fact that it is more *humanized* than any other class.

Moreover, the dominant class's exceptional situation has more precise implications. In pointing up a divine aspect of animality and a servile aspect of humanity, I was led to express one reservation: there nonetheless had to be some element in humanity that is irreducible to thingness and work, so that man is, in a word, more difficult to enslave than animals. That element is found at all levels of society, but it is mainly present among the ruling class. It is easy to see that reduction to thinghood is only ever a *relative* matter: there is no meaning to being a thing except in relation to the person whose thing one is: an inert object, an animal, a human being may be things, but they are necessarily the things of a human being. In particular, human beings can only be things if they are the things of other human beings. Others may themselves perhaps be the things of third parties and so on, but not *ad infinitum*. The moment comes when humanity itself—even if it were, to a degree, to have given the impression of being ground down—has to fulfil itself; when, with one human being no longer depending on any other, the general subordination assumes a meaning in that person to whom it subordinates itself—a person who cannot be subordinated to anything. This kind of terminal point is, in theory, reached in the dominant class, which is generally tasked, in itself, with freeing humanity from being ground down to thinghood, with elevating the human being, in its own form, to the instant when it is free.

Normally, with that end in view, that class has liberated itself from work and, if sexual energy is measurable, it possessed it as a general rule in quantities that made it very much the equal of the underworld. American civilization has moved away from these principles, in that its bourgeoisie, which from the beginning was the sole dominant class, is almost never idle: it nonetheless retains the privileges of the upper classes. Even so, the— relatively low—index that defines its sexual vigour requires interpretation.

The Kinsey Report's classification system, based on frequency of orgasms, is a simplification. It is not entirely meaningless, but it does neglect one appreciable factor. It does not take account of the duration of the sex act.[7] Yet the fact is that the energy expended in sexual life is not limited to the energy represented by ejaculation. The simple fact of sexual activity also consumes quantities of energy that are not negligible. The expenditure of energy on the part of the anthropoid, whose orgasm required only some ten seconds, is obviously lower than that of the cultivated human being whose sexual activity extends for hours. But the art of keeping up the activity is itself unequally apportioned between the different classes. On this point, the Report does not provide details commensurate with its usual meticulousness. Nevertheless, it emerges that the prolongation of sexual activity is the prerogative of the upper classes. Men from the disadvantaged classes confine themselves to rapid encounters which, though less short than those of animals, still do not allow their female partners to reach orgasm themselves. Almost alone, the class with the rate of 12.4 has taken foreplay and sustainment of sexual activity to extreme levels.

I am not at all driven here by the intention of defending the sexual honour of 'well-brought-up' men, but these considerations enable us to make clear the sense of the general data laid out above and to show what the intimate thrust of life ultimately demands.

What we call the human world is necessarily a world of work—that is to say, a world of submission. But work has another sense than travail and tribulation. Work is also the path of *consciousness* by which man emerged from animality. It was through work that the clear and distinct consciousness of objects was given to us, and science has always remained the handmaiden of technology. Sexual exuberance, on the other hand, distances us from consciousness: it diminishes our faculty of discernment; moreover, a freely surging sexuality lessens the aptitude for work, in the same way as sustained work lowers sexual appetite. Between consciousness, which is closely linked to work, and sexual life, there is, then, an undeniably rigorous incompatibility. Insofar as human beings defined themselves by work and consciousness, they had not only to moderate, but to disown and condemn their sexual fervour. In a sense, that condemnation turned human beings away, if

---

7 Lionel Trilling (in 'Sex and Science') points out the inadequacy of the Report in this regard.

not from the consciousness of objects, then at least from self-consciousness. It committed them, at one and the same time, to a knowledge of the world and an ignorance of themselves. But if they had not first become conscious by working, they would have no knowledge at all and there would be nothing but an animal darkness upon the Earth.

It is, then, only on the basis of the disavowal—the condemnation—of our sexual life, that consciousness can be given to us. Sexuality is not alone in that regard: of the whole of our intimate lives, of everything in us that is irreducible to a thing, we are unable to have immediate consciousness. Clear consciousness is, first of all, consciousness of things, and what does not have the external distinctness of a thing is not perceived by consciousness in the first place. Even retrospectively, it is difficult for us to attain clarity.

It is afforded to us first, in principle, as we find it is in the Kinsey Report: in order to discern distinctly what is not reducible to a thing and is, nonetheless, mistaken for one. That is the only path by which intimate truths enter our discriminative consciousness—and that is why we have to say in general that intimate truths elude us. If, in fact, we take them for what they are not, we simply fail to know them the more. We turn away from a truth that is proclaimed by our sexual life if we see it as a natural function, if, before having even grasped its meaning, we denounce the stupidity of the laws opposing it.[8] In this reduction to the innocence of a thing, consciousness, far from assimilating the object it gives itself, ceases completely to take account of an aspect incompatible with itself. Condemnation at least kept that aspect in the obscurity to which disgust consigned it. Science, by declaring it innocent, stops seeing it altogether. At the same time, it declares consciousness innocent. It does not grasp the machinery within clear consciousness that reduces all its contents to the empty exteriority of things, which excludes or distorts those things whose intimate status slides them towards a dangerous mobility and towards a violence which, in any event, destroys the limits of things.

The awakened consciousness of intimacy obligatorily begins with this effort: in order to discover it, one must first to try to see it as a thing. But it is when the effort comes to seem futile that intimacy, if such a thing is

8 I do not wish to defend these laws but to understand their meaning.

possible, reveals itself to consciousness. From that point, intimacy reveals itself precisely to the extent that we come to see its accursed side. Intimacy itself cannot enter, as such, into the clear part of consciousness. But consciousness has the power to distinguish clearly the mechanism that opposes it to what it condemns. It is, thus, in the form of condemned possibility that intimate truth appears to it. *It therefore maintains—and cannot but maintain—a horror which is its essence and which is inalienable within it; but it has the power in these conditions to recognize in that horror, which it cannot fail to feel, its own subordinate character.* This so precious lucidity—in which man locates his superiority, which sexual fervour eliminates and which eliminates sexual fervour—is actually nothing if it does not co-exist with the truth of the creature on whom it is casting light: it has meaning only if it illuminates without destroying, just as the human being itself, in order fully to *be*, needs not only not to be destroyed, but to be in the light, to recognize itself. This resolution demands the *slowing* of the fervour, not a diminution of intensity, but slowness. Herein lies the sense of the evolution of our sexual life, which is diminished first by work and is excluded by consciousness, which subsequently integrates itself in being, in the slackening of work, and in slow voluptuous reflection, in which there persist—with difficulty—both lucidity and the sense of a contradiction between clear consciousness and a vertiginous sense of intimacy.

It is remarkable that the enormous statistical labours of the Kinsey Report support this interpretation, which does not accord with their principles and which may even be said necessarily to negate them. The Kinsey Report is a naïve and at times moving protest against civilized humanity. But, conversely, it comes as no surprise to see justified in it the long evolution which, on its winding path, has elevated humanity to self-consciousness. No doubt the various forms of human life have been sur-passed one by one, but we can, in the end, see the sense of what we have passed beyond. In particular, we would not truly get beyond the man of work, of reduced sexuality and of the consciousness of external things, if we did not see in ourselves the forces that played out in him. This is what, thanks to a long intensity, following on the brief bursts of violence of a simpler humanity, it is open to us to experience slowly and lucidly today:

the sex life of America's most cultivated classes (which the Kinsey Report enables us to imagine, and which mustn't be appreciably different from that of Europe's most cultivated classes) is not itself that maximally awakened consciousness, but it provides the physical pre-condition for it. The Report itself does not deflect from matters being resolved in this way: in fact, it necessarily prompts opposition to its own principles; it spurs consciousness, in a rapid movement of negation, to become clear sighted; it forces it to awaken.[9] And it is in this way that it contributes to the 'sexual revolution' of our age.

---

9 I could have said the same thing about the work of Freud. In a sense, it would have been even better placed for this: psychoanalysis provided a revelation of far greater importance than the Report's statistics. But Freud is much more nuanced, less ponderously scientific, and the development I was set on demonstrating shows up more clearly from a more formal piece of work. Moreover, the Report provides numerical data that form the basis of precise interpretations.

Jean Paulhan - Marc Bloch

Jean Paulhan, Literary Revelry and Politics

JEAN PAULHAN, *De la paille et du grain* [On the wheat and the chaff] (Paris: Gallimard, 1948), petit in 16°, 183 pp.

We remember the polemic that pitted the Comité National des Écrivains against Jean Paulhan, one of its first members. It was a dispute over two issues successively. Jean Paulhan regarded the post-war *épuration* measures towards writers, the moves to ban some of them, as too severe. But the discussion veered into questions of principle after Paulhan asserted that, during the 1914 war, Romain Rolland had betrayed the cause of France.

I do not wish to rehearse the arguments again here. Polemic often clouds problems and that effect, which was definitely achieved in the present case, was perhaps Jean Paulhan's intention. That intention is, in fact, only apparently political—or is so only in the minds of those who felt the need to respond to it. The intention is, indeed, so literary that we are told from the outset that, when it comes to words, they are devices of concealment—at the masked ball that is literature. Let us be clear that this book exists to tell us that politics is the world in which there is no place for Jean Paulhan, but also for much more than just Jean Paulhan—for literature.

One cannot express more precisely, in particular one cannot express in direct language the subtle intention of the author: if that intention reveals itself by way of artlessness (false no doubt, but deliberate . . .), that is because it cannot reveal itself any other way. But it would be wrong to conclude that this were an accusation—even a deliberate one—against literature. I actually believe, taking a rough look at this—or perhaps a myopic one—that an apologia is detectable. The sentiment governing an elusive attitude here is perhaps a sense of terror that the writer feels towards words (we are not speaking now of the terror he is himself tempted to inspire). That is because words command, and we may even be said to live constantly under the command of politicians' words. This isn't always noticeable if we are dealing with the words of a revolutionary party, but nevertheless all politics ultimately has the aim of commanding human beings by laws, and command is implied in words as soon as they are taken up by politics. Literary usage is very different: it gathers words together the way a gardener gathers flowers; and what is the gathering of flowers if not a disregard for the law of labour? Literature is always to some degree the mockery of politics (that is the reason why, if literature has some political meaning, it is revolutionary; but in that case the relationship is not a lasting one). It is always the mockery of morality too, at least of the *self-seeking* morality of the state—and Fourier's appeal to literature was on the basis that it founded a *counter-morality*. Literature is the *play* that inhabits words, that makes them slimy and treacherous. It means that man in society must, admittedly, be led, but he does not himself wish to be conflated with a leadership *of which he makes use.*

Admittedly, this cannot be to the politicians' liking and it is natural that it should anger them. But if politicians exist, they do not exist for nothing; if they exist, it is because they are necessary, being the expression of an imperative human truth, like hunger. Similarly, against *littérateurs* politicians are necessarily in the right: party here does not matter; since each one expresses a particular truth that exists on Earth. If *littérateurs* allow themselves the indulgence of being right, then the fact is they are fighting one type of politics with the aid of another. But, fundamentally, they are in the wrong: their true party is revelry and such levity is of no concern to the nation's housewives. Admittedly, language itself (which politicians necessarily use) is not always 'a punishment'; it is rather, as Paulhan happily notes, 'a great public rejoicing'. But the language of rejoicing, which is 'public revelry'—a revelry to which all are invited and which is literature—is always *wrong*, since, when it expresses itself as something right and reasonable, it immediately loses its specific virtue, since it ceases to express rejoicing.

All it can do then is show up the failings of politics. A thing at which Jean Paulhan excelled, basing himself on an initial paradox (Romain Rolland's betrayal: a paradox is a truth made visible by way of a proposition not easy to uphold). Overall, in fact, the weakness, clumsiness and errors of his opponents are disconcerting, since, as expressions of a political force, they are right. For the force which they are expressing, the fatherland does indeed have the meaning they accord it, which governs the word and thereby governs things. All in all, a fatherland may, like a human being, have its political face: in both cases, this entails contradiction; to varying degrees, but constantly, that face is contested by opposing forces, but no matter ... The political force cannot let words slide, unless they slide to its advantage: what it does is determine, command and rule. And it is the virtue of Paulhan, standing up to a command, that he shows how words are, in themselves, alive and how they scoff at commands. But, for all that, we cannot forget that, beyond the inevitable irony, a command will shape the reality that demands it: the fatherland—and every word—will receive their meaning, on which the 'Little People', among whom Paulhan counts himself, will decide in the same way as a brake decides speed. But the 'Little People'—or literature—perhaps have the better of it.

The Serfs and Slaves of the Middle Ages

Marc Bloch, 'Comment finit l'esclavage antique' [How ancient slavery ended], *Annales (Économies, Sociétés, Civilisation)* 2(1–2) (1947).

In modern philosophy, at least insofar as it repudiates a naïve tradition, the very notion of humanity, to which all thought necessarily refers, is seen in terms of the historical categories of freedom and servitude. The human being is not always a *person*, but may be a *thing* or a *talking instrument* (the *'instrumentum vocale'* of the Romans). And even if, being free himself, he keeps his fellow man in servitude, he removes from the general mass of humanity the underlying meaning that bestows on him his personal life as a free man. Marxism is based, to some extent, on these considerations. There is no humanity so long as a man denies the humanity of his fellow human being. Many people forget this sense of present history. They often find a very inhuman, over-harsh aspect in it. They are upset and frightened to see the *person*, as they conceive it, easily negated. But the person in themselves negates the person in colonialism. The defence of the rights of the person, if it is made by individuals who oppress others—even from a great distance—dooms human thought to the deep ironies of dialectics.

The painstaking construction of *humanity*, which is essentially the respect of man for man, is nonetheless the sense of a *history* that is obviously not at an end. What we are, insofar as we belong to humanity, has depended on the hard-won prohibition on reducing our fellow human beings to servitude: *turning a man into a thing* is a possibility that must absolutely, at all costs, be eliminated. This is to such an extent what drives history that the opposing parties today, each giving different explanations for their attitudes, both struggle to prevent their adversary *turning a man into a thing*. Never, indeed, has there been such a perfect sameness of goals: and should we not regard that sameness as admirable at a point when war, in which *humanity* is at stake, threatens to annihilate what surely must either be free or not exist at all . . . ? Should we not, in the end, see it as very human that the whole of humanity should go down fighting, on each side, for freedom . . . ?

The fact remains that the potential conflict, when highlighted in this way, lends a very topical interest to the slow process by which present society has freed itself from its slave-owning form. The facts are well known: it is a long time now since we believed that Christianity eliminated slavery. But no clear account has emerged in the wake of that simplistic interpretation and Marc Bloch's remarkable clarification of the question, published by *Les Annales*, deserves to be widely known. (We cannot overemphasize here the exceptional value of a publication that has re-emerged from the old *Annales d'Histoire Économique et Sociale* which Marc Bloch and Lucien Febvre founded in 1929.)

Marc Bloch, who died fighting for freedom, has undoubtedly left us the best French-language overview of the genesis of our imperfect freedom. It is especially valuable, since it would be hard to imagine anything more difficult to pin down precisely. How the slaves of antiquity, who really were treated as things and bought and sold like cattle, became the serfs of the Middle Ages, whose servitude was limited by law—and who were in fact themselves descended from the emancipated slaves, the freed men of the Late Roman Empire—is something decidedly difficult to follow. And a shifting vocabulary makes our sense of disarray complete: the very word *servus*, which referred to slaves in the ancient world, was used to refer to the medieval serf.

Marc Bloch emphasizes the key factor in the process: the material factor. Even in the Roman period, alongside the gangs of slaves whose labour was boundlessly available, there were slaves who were settled tenant farmers paying ground rent, able to live more or less well, depending on the product of their labour. From the end of the Empire onwards, some free tenant-farmers, the *coloni,* differed little from these enslaved tenant-farmers, since, though they generally had the legal attributes of free men, they were nonetheless bound to their land, which they could not leave, and to the owner of that land. Overall, at a late stage, the holdings of small-scale farmers, free or otherwise—though in neither case able to give up their tenure—held an economic advantage over the large holdings worked by groups of slaves. In the ninth century, the greater number of these small farmers appear to have had the status of free men. It is unimaginable that the slave families should have completely died out, so there is every reason to suppose that a great many slaves had been freed. This was because it was in the interest of the local lord to 'group around him a large number of dependents, not slaves but free men, capable of sitting on juries and serving in his army. That was the price to pay for power and prestige.' The fact is that when slaves were emancipated, the duty of *obsequium*—'obedience'— most often did not disappear. In this way, there was a gradual transition from the animal condition of ancient slavery to the human condition of serfdom.

It is easy to be clear, above and beyond questions of utility, about both the moral implication of this development and the—secondary—role of Christianity and the Church. On the one hand, the Church regarded emancipation as a charitable deed, liable to bring about the salvation of souls, but it forbade slave-owning bishops and abbots to free them: that was seen as an easy way to save one's soul at the expense of property that was not one's own to dispose of. Thus Christianity, though opposed to the principle of slavery, kept it firmly in being, even to its own advantage. At a pinch, the ecclesiastic could proceed to free slaves, but he had to compensate for the harm he was thereby doing to the Church with a payment out of his own assets. The moral sense and value of emancipation can thus be seen to go, to some degree, beyond the self-interest assigned to them by Marc Bloch.

It was, in a sense, a glorious gift, probably of little importance, but a gift nonetheless. This development, which was economically favourable to society, presupposed a leap on the part of the lord, a leap from which prestige and power were also to be had.

The most tangible effect of Christian morality concerned the source of slavery. The Church in fact prohibited the enslavement of free Christians. The supply of slaves, based on capture in war, was certainly thereby reduced. If slavery disappeared, it was not just because of the emancipation of former slaves but the increasing scarcity of new supplies. The change of vocabulary underlines this important factor. Only non-Christians, such as Slavs, could be captured and sold in Europe. Thus the name for the slave condition was that of the people that was raided as a source of human labour—the Slavs. *Slave* and *Slav* are, in fact, two forms of the same noun. But this latter source itself petered out: from the ninth to the twelfth centuries, slaves properly so called were very few in number and of no economic significance. They were practically unknown in France at the time. And they disappeared quite quickly from Europe, despite a slight upturn due to the resumption of large-scale Mediterranean trade.

These facts have much to teach us, but first and foremost they show the dramatically disjointed state of history, in which Man can never pretend to human dignity unless he prefers death to the loss of freedom.

On the Meaning of Moral Neutrality
in the Russo-American War

RAYMOND ARON, *Le Grand Schisme* (Paris: Gallimard, 1948), in 8°, 347 pp.

'We are living,' writes Raymond Aron, 'through one of the most tragic, but also one of the most prestigious periods in history' (p. 343). Nothing is more urgent, of course, than to understand such a remarkable period; nothing is more urgent than to define its problems and perspectives; but nothing is more difficult either. To see its prestige and its tragedy is of no great importance. The essential thing is to strip down its hidden drivers and analyse its workings. To that end, it is necessary first of all to raise the description to the level of *political theory*, which isn't content just to say 'there is . . .', but elucidates the sequence of causes and effects and locates that sequence within the range of human possibility, within the perspective of action.

It may be that, where that endeavour is concerned, there is no one better equipped to succeed today than Raymond Aron. Not only is he the most comprehensively informed on the world's political realities, but he is equally familiar with the economy and economic theories. He has, moreover, an acknowledged competence in sociology and the philosophy of history[1] (in particular, he knows the Hegelian Marxist tradition well). His knowledge of Marxism goes way beyond that of most theorists who undertake critiques of it. Let us add also that Marxism, rightly or wrongly, does not weigh heavily on him, that he is in no way burdened by a concern to reduce the workings of the world to some pre-established schema. Quite the contrary, Marxism for him is merely an incitement to produce a dynamic description of current human affairs (such is, all in all, the subject of *Le Grand Schisme*)

---

1 The works that made his reputation before the war were entitled: *La Sociologie allemande contemporaine* (Paris: Alcan, 1936) and *Introduction à la philosophie de l'histoire. Essais sur les limites de l'objectivité historique* (Paris: Gallimard, 1938).

in the form of classical analyses in which each element is considered in relation to the whole range of origins and possibilities. And let us make this clear right away: the breadth and, at the same time, the limitations of his work are given in the fact that, seeing the necessity constantly to meet these exigencies, he immediately realizes that it is impossible to do so completely. If Raymond Aron escapes, in a sense, the narrowness of a system, if he is able continually to establish rich perspectives, to multiply points of view, he cannot combine with that description the overall resolution of the difficulties analysed. Though he has not the narrowness of the Marxists, he does not, as they do, provide a programme, a therapeutics commensurate with the sickness described. He admits 'humbly, the limits of our knowledge'. The mass of knowledge he has accumulated forces a reticence upon him: he confines himself to the pluralism of viewpoints.

Raymond Aron is right to stress the point: our age is that of the 'great schism'. The 'schism' tearing it apart is its major feature: two parts of a single world, sharing the same civilization, the same culture, the same technologies, have separated. Not the way war quite commonly separates identical neighbours. War often highlights differences and, in war, it happens that the parties wish to point up a deep opposition that exists between them, thus justifying their antagonism. But much more is involved on this occasion. The separation has occurred without being caused by war: and it is tending to divide two vast regions of Western civilization as deeply as once Christianity and Islam were divided. But the exclusion from humanity of each half by the other is taking place 'coldly'. The 'iron curtain' is the image invoked to convey this spectacular division whose scale and sharpness are dismaying.

There can, of course, be no peace in such a world. But that does not mean—at least it does not yet exactly mean—war. 'Impossible peace, improbable war' is Raymond Aron's formulation. In that expression, he encapsulates a situation in which, as it were, the war-fighting powers of all the ages are amassed, a situation slowly accumulating, in an infinitely active peace, all the explosive forces that everywhere and at all times have governed the clash of armies. But 'improbable war' is to be understood here, principally in this sense: the phrase points up the virulent, unremitting character of the antagonism.

It is, if I may put it this way, in the extreme flourishing of civilization, freed from diplomatic and military contingencies—or, at least, elevated above them—the capacity humanity has to oppose itself, to find within itself the fundamental opposition between two irreconcilable possibilities.[2] As in tragedy, the antagonism comes to a high point of intensity; as in tragedy, we find an *exposition* of that moment. The present time seems, in fact, to share the tragic author's concern not to rush to the *dénouement* but first express the irreconcilable violence of the colliding forces.

Raymond Aron does not bring out this spectacular aspect so markedly: his book is not a vision, it is a detailed analysis, but would the description of such a massive diremption be of any value if it were not based on the vast plethora of precise details? Above all, the author, who is distrustful of the rousing, all-encompassing imagination, excels at showing a succession of narrow effects playing themselves out in the spheres of diplomacy, domestic politics, ideology or economic interests. Even the 'End Note', in which he wishes to point out the difference between his world view and Spengler's pessimistic vision, variously dispels the German ideologue's arguments but does not respond by reductively assigning some determinable direction to the multiplicity of developments. Equidistant from fear and hope, this is the

---

2 We should probably clarify the sense of this especially important opposition. In passing, Raymond Aron rejects the meaning Marxism accords it, but he does not propose any other. The criticism he levels at Marxism is perhaps generally misguided in relating to particular points rather than to method. It seems to me that the difficulties of the Marxist schema would partly disappear if it were seen that the opposition could not entirely unfold unless the spirit of *revolution* were separated from the spirit of *rebellion* [*révolte*]. An enormous misunderstanding ensues from this. Rebels are at times thrown back on to a will to conserve and at times continue a fight against the capitalists, who tolerate them, alongside Communists, who would kill them if they won the day. But the sense of the opposition would perhaps emerge distinctly if it were realized that at the height of its development, the spirit of rebellion inevitably becomes *neutral* (without any doubt at the extreme of despair). It may in fact be that the full unfolding of the opposition, which alone permits the opposing terms to confront each other as equals, ultimately represents a move towards the point where the difference between the terms is at least attenuated. In that case, the spirit of rebellion (which is alone in authentically achieving neutrality: Could someone who were not a rebel both understand the Communists completely, and suffer its consequences in all their severity?) has the only possibility of resolving the opposition, but *that is the only possibility that remains to it.*

book of a man dominated by awareness of the naïveté—or rancorousness—
of the mind that needs to aspire to far-sightedness.

It is this modesty which, with steadfastness, produces rigorous studies
that attempt to account, openly and without hostility, for Communist policy
in particular, which they condemn. No doubt Raymond Aron thinks that
one cannot combat an evil adeptly without first knowing it. And spoken
polemic, which contents itself with peremptory opinions inspired by hatred,
is at times inimical to the effectiveness of genuine polemic, of political and
military *struggle*. Along these same lines, Aron ascribes some rather dark
features to the regimes he defends, but whose shortcomings he is also eager
to expose. It is pleasant to see a 'partisan'—he refers to himself as such—
strive first and foremost for lucidity. But a concern with objectivity is not
the only reason for this modesty. Aron refuses honestly to claim scientific
status for his book; though he is wary of hatred, insults and 'political
Manicheism', he is nonetheless conducting a *battle*: if, however, that battle
leaves the author calm and clear sighted, there is another reason. The book
ends on a significant statement: 'Let us stop dreaming and return to the
daily task'. Aron is attached, above all, to a clear, limited way he has of considering things. If he is constantly preoccupied with the relation between
the facts he writes about and general notions, he is even more concerned
to restrict the scope of the relations one is tempted to imagine. His political
theory is almost entirely negative. It aims ultimately to underpin the
decision he has made to apply his activity to limited problems—problems
limited both in space and time. He expressly narrows down his examination
of the current world to short-term and French problems. If he has chosen
to be fully conscious of all possible generalizations, he has done so to lend
greater meaning to the act of close examination; to give, if one may put it
this way, a depth to the act of remaining superficial. Naturally, to point to
this characteristic of an author's work is, in no sense, to reject it. This attitude
is perhaps the only valid one, the only one at least that does not produce
the exhausting sense of futility of bold predictions. It does, however, have
some demonstrable disadvantages.

If the author speaks of the Marshall Plan, he does so mainly to assert
that it is not contrary to French interests in the scope it grants for German
recovery (that recovery, in fact, if one looks at the current situation in

Germany, is in no way likely to threaten France: Aron presents some decisive detailed arguments on this point). On the other hand, he envisages it being difficult—without drawing any great consequences from this—to maintain a system of international trade in the future. Yet it is that difficulty which the Marshall Plan is attempting temporarily to mitigate. It has to be said that it is a paramount issue for the future of the capitalist world. This is not the place to go into the long argument that would be required, but is it not crystal clear that a capitalist world without trade would bring down on itself the very catastrophe it seems to fear? America will speak of peace, will hate war with a vengeance, but *how will it be able to eliminate a threat on which its existence will depend?* If no other way out is found, war alone can provide an outlet for an expanding industry that is forbidden to export. As of now, the worrying attitude of Russia is playing a part in postponing the possibility of a new crisis. But in any event, analysis of the current capitalist world cannot avoid highlighting this problem of impossible trade, which is exposed as acute by the Marshall Plan. The fact that such a problem cannot be raised in the sphere of French politics does not prevent it from being a predominant one at the global level. The 'daily task' of the French politician diverts him here from a concern that is anything but fanciful.

This necessarily brings in another consideration (or, in a sense, another form of the first), which cannot remain on the back-burner either: the 'great schism' points to war, unlikely today but in all probability unavoidable tomorrow. One can accept that a man who is suffering from cancer, left ignorant of his illness or the rapid course it will take, should have no other horizon, as he has always had, than the daily task: this is often the desirable solution. But if he knows the situation, he cannot carry on like that. At the very least, it is right he should first try to overcome the disease and give the doctors' efforts priority over more immediate concerns. The situation is doubtless bleak: but he must do all he can. Let us even imagine that the cancer patient is not averse to dying, that existence quite often seems futile to him. Insofar as he cannot, for all that, cease to be a human being, he will still put the curing of his cancer ahead of other personal concerns. Now, we know (Raymond Aron knows better than anyone) that the 'schism' from which our world is suffering is like a cancer within it, that it is the 'mortal illness' beyond which action will have no effect. The war it heralds would ineluctably bring down the whole industrial edifice.

What would be the sense, in the case of a Russian victory, of a world largely in ruins where the United States, far from aiding other nations, would be more profoundly devastated than Germany is today? At that moment, the USSR would be barely less ravaged for its part, and the Marxism dominating the world would bear no relation to the radical new order demanded by the development of the productive forces. What would be the meaning of a destruction of capitalism that would at the same time be a destruction of capitalism's *works*? Clearly the crudest rebuttal that could be given to Marx's lucidity. The humanity that would have destroyed the work of the industrial revolution would be the poorest of all time: the memory of recent wealth would put the finishing touches to making life unbearable. Lenin defined socialism as 'the Soviets plus electrification'. Socialism actually requires not just popular power, but wealth. And no sensible person would imagine it being based on a world in which the civilization symbolized by the names of New York and London had crumbled into shanty towns. That civilization may well be detestable; it is also, in a sense, a nightmare; it produces the sort of boredom and exasperation conducive to a slide into catastrophe. But no one can be drawn to a solution whose appeal is simply nonsensical.[3]

Of course, it is still open to us to imagine a US victory over Russia that would not have devastated the world so completely. But the low cost to the winner would mean the 'schism' was correspondingly the less reduced. Doubtless in appearance universal domination would belong to the sole possessor of the decisive weapons, but in the same way as the victim belongs to his persecutor. This persecutor role is so unenviable, and the awareness that such a bloody solution would definitively poison social life is so strong, that there is no coherent faction in the American camp arguing for war in the near future. Whereas it is clear—or at least probable—that time is on Russia's side.

---

3 This does, of course, imply my agreement with Albert Camus on the fact that currently revolution can spread in the world only through war. Camus's stance on this is decisive. The point has not yet gained general acceptance, but people are not blind and simply need time to admit it.

In these conditions, can the 'daily task' (which for us, generally speaking, means the resolution of French problems) reasonably take precedence over the—more remote—concern to reduce the 'schism' that brings death in its wake? Doubtless the idea of the schism being 'healed' is fanciful, but the idea of death is not . . .

Admittedly, for Raymond Aron, it is not the 'schism' that is the mortal illness, but the USSR, which has a tentacular reach through the Kominform. The only salvation, as he sees it, would be the defeat of Communism. But that is the despairing solution. If only he could see another way out . . . And, in fact, he does see a glimmer of one.

'An internal transformation of Russia is unlikely,' he writes (p. 93), 'it is not impossible'. In fact, this hypothesis defines future humanity's dilemma. Russia's leaders seem currently to believe in the inevitability of war. As a result, the concern to avoid war has apparently only negligible value in their eyes, by comparison with the desire to win one. If that is how things are, there is no likelihood of avoiding war unless their attitude changes or their successors take a different stance. The current dilemma is therefore: either the Kremlin changes, or the destiny of humanity is finished. But is the struggle against Communism currently such as to bring about change?

There are two aspects to this question which need to be clearly distinguished. If war is to be avoided, there is nothing more dangerous than one of the enemies flagging or flinching. That makes for a situation in which it is in the other's interest to seize the moment immediately. Even if it hated the very idea of war, that interest could bring it, by some fateful rigidity, to do something irremediable. Even if one were appalled by American civilization, if concern about war takes precedence over all others, then a policy of abandoning the US would not be desirable.

However, the risk of responding to the Kremlin's hesitancy by prostration isn't remotely capable of bringing about a change in its policy. It is, then, only a means of temporarily avoiding an irreparable act.

That being said, a change in Communist leadership is conceivable on only one condition: that the awareness emerge on the other side—and gradually win out—that something other than an inhuman will is responsible for the adversary's attitude; that its hard-line stance reflects something other than a wicked nature; that, in short, the 'schism' is not the creation of one of the parties, so that *change by the one calls for change by the other*. How can we not in fact see that, on the capitalist side, the unfettered development of the economy leads no less inevitably towards war than the rigid attitude of Moscow? Thus, as long as the US directs its economic surplus into no other channel than war, as long as it is driven blindly by economic dynamism, as long as it goes on accumulating industrial productive force with no other end than impossible profit, there is no true security for Russia. And the problem is actually unavoidable—and would still be there for a victorious America. Profit cannot be infinite and those who accumulate energy, if its peaceful use cannot be indefinitely profitable, condemn themselves to expending it in wars. Raymond Aron denies this inevitable connection between the development of industry and war, but all that his arguments show is that war had other causes in the past: they do not in any way demonstrate that enormous industrial growth *without easy trading relations* is not, in the absence of war, a catastrophic absurdity. Doubtless this can, at a pinch, be remedied. But the 'schism' cannot be healed if it is not. *The condition that must be fulfilled if humanity is to be saved from imminent demise is the viability of American growth.*[4]

Now, this material condition first requires the development and the *moral* predominance in the world of a *neutral* consciousness.[5] Of a moral consciousness disentangled from the 'schism'.

---

4 The necessary condition, obviously not the sufficient condition.

5 It will, without doubt, be objected that neutrality is impossible. No nation, no party can genuinely have *self-awareness*. The opinion of a French national on Indochina necessarily differs from that of a Vietnamese national: even if both were calm and lucid, they would not say the same thing. But in reality the positions I have just laid out are linked to the *action* implied in a particular stance. Neutrality undoubtedly means the rejection of any action, a determined distancing from any political undertaking, the sense of an inevitable pause, an inevitable moment when the onward rush of the driving forces of history ebbs (it is impossible, obviously, to know whether that ebbing will be the product of war itself or of fear of war). The deep sense of this paradox is that, in action there can be no *self-awareness*.

The Divinity of Isou

ISIDORE ISOU, *L'Agrégation d'un nom et d'un messie* [The aggregation of a name and a messiah] (Paris: Gallimard, 1947), in 8°, 451 pp.

A biographical note informs us that Isidore Isou Goldstein was born on 31 January 1925 in Romania; that he arrived in Paris on 23 August 1945 after a six-week clandestine journey; and that he founded the Lettriste movement there in November of the same year. *L'Agrégation*, an autobiographical novel, relates to the war years in which the author, in Bucharest, dreamt of going to Paris and becoming 'the greatest man of his times'.

It is in a sense a private diary, but a mythical one. And since, as it goes along, it progressively erects the enduring statue of the novelist, it is also an 'aggregation' or, in other words, a construction. A frenzied statue if ever there was one, but primarily a statue pronouncing—or, more accurately, screaming or booming out through a loudhailer—an immense, risible panegyric to itself. The life of young Isou is the life of any adolescent addled by literature (and by boundless knowledge), but driven through the world by a disruptive—deliberately disruptive—brazenness: Isou is infinitely crude and lacking in manners and reason. His story is often superb: one would cry genius if the word, according to Isou, were not superfluous.

L'Agrégation can be described in any way you like: touching, awful, stupid, failed, puerile, a work of genius, as risible and embarrassing as a bare backside. The stupidity that leads a young man to scream at the top of his voice that he is sublime is clearly a source of some sorrow. But that is how it is: putting myself in Isou's place, I can see nothing that should legitimately have stopped him. Is it offensive to human dignity? Yes, but, after all, dignity tells lies, just as Isou's lack of dignity tells lies.

Yet I should not like to say anything that would be in danger of *satisfying* a man who is, let us say, so unlucky—a man who has, it seems, been reduced to clownishness of this kind *to make a living* (the clownishness is not confined to this adulation of Isou; the book boasts a panegyric of Stalin and Isou combined, and an Isouian system of world judaization that would stand Hitlerism on its head . . .). That this offensive book should be written, published and read (read?) is satisfactory only from a rather devious point of view. It lends the human condition the sense of an unacceptable mystification. *Everything* can, in fact—or even inevitably must—be said. The figure of Isou is not an empty space in a full world, unless, that is, it is the empty space that allows us to glimpse something . . . What it allows us to glimpse is the most tiresome of things. 'Every solitary is imperfect,' says Isou. 'He must find a face that can respond to his own (towards which he moves) and in which he can find confirmation of his own truth, as God does in the believer . . . We shall call the divine Reader the one who makes him complete by sanctifying him through the comparison with other gods (saints) . . . This integral part of God that is the reader . . . ' and so on. This passage, the veiled character of which is exceptional in the book, is nonetheless bolder than some others in which the author confines himself to claiming to be the Messiah. The fact is that the story, despite all the clangour, actually ends in a climb-down. Though he seems driven by boundless aspirations, this young man, his intelligence so acute that it is pure disorder, still only goes half-way. This is because it is agreeable to be the Messiah, but depressing in the extreme to be God.

The idea that God is the shadow cast by Man is not at all a new one (it is, indeed, a Marxist idea). But one does not normally see the consequence of it: even as a child, it is commonplace to imagine that being a human being is to have had a mean trick played on one, but let us imagine now that to be a human being is to be God (and that is how it is, in fact, if the above idea is correct and God is the shadow cast by me). That means that worlds are founded upon myself and there is nothing more profound than me in the depths of the worlds. If God is man's shadow, he is the shadow of the 'remotest' (most chilling) man. But the 'remotest' man cannot really differ from the most familiar one, the 'closest'. The 'depths of the worlds' are vouchsafed to us equally in this 'touching, awful, stupid, failed, puerile, genius . . . ' Isou only half-knows the messiah, but he can glimpse him: it is a question of corrupt lucidity, of a lubricious understanding acquired from behind a thin dividing wall. It might even be said that the whole charm of the book consists in the absurdity into which the author inevitably descends in a swirl of crazy comedy: he is fond of exploiting a horrible potential to project what is 'closest' into the 'remotest' category and what is 'remotest' into the 'closest'. But it is a slippery game in which the author, as he falls, steadies himself by catching hold on himself, as he might on a banister, catching hold on his adolescent's genius-level superiority . . . (No surprise if he then lacks mastery—or, to put it another way, talent.)

The Mischievousness of Language

Raymond Queneau, *'Saint-Glinglin', précédé d'une nouvelle version de 'Gueule de Pierre' et des 'Temps mêlés'* (Paris: Gallimard, 1948), in 16°, 271 pp.

——. *L'instant fatal* [poems] (Paris: Gallimard, 1948), in 16°, 139 pp.

Among the literary projects of a period fertile in bizarre endeavours, there is perhaps none more disconcerting than the one to which *Saint-Glinglin* apparently puts the final touch.

The literary life of Raymond Queneau began with a bang: *Le Chiendent*. But it was possible to see that quite astounding comic portrait of sordid suburban existence as having nothing deeper behind it. An attentive, waggish reader—one perhaps even possessed of a gift of prophecy—could doubtless have hailed the book as a first exercise in existential philosophy in France. Within the history of thought, *Le Chiendent* would deserve that label: for the first time, attentive thinking, schooled in the refined methods of German phenomenology, open—as a result of Heidegger's questioning—to metaphysics, trained its lens on the most pitiful, degraded forms of life. There was no reforming intent here; the author simply had the intention of *seeing* those forms, of *experiencing* them. *Le Chiendent* placed Raymond Queneau among the ranks of cheerful authors. For a philosopher of existence, that is perhaps the proof of the authenticity of his work: could that philosophy indeed be any more than an awakening to the existence *that is*, precisely as it is? But, like most books, *Le Chiendent* had few 'attentive' readers, never mind 'attentive, waggish' ones. The agenda behind *Gueule de Pierre*, which Queneau published in 1934 immediately after *Le Chiendent*, is by contrast, if not clear (it is decidedly difficult to grasp the author's precise intention) at least perceptible in a variety of ways.

From the beginning, *Gueule de Pierre* might have been termed existentialist (if the word had existed). But the crimes of *psychoanalysis, sociology* and *mythology* could also have been laid at its door. With a large measure of pedantry, one would have had to describe it as the mythological transcription, in the mode of lived experience, of scholarly findings from collective (psychoanalytic) psychology. I doubt that any work of fiction exists that is so deliberately manufactured out of science.

It is not usual for the author of *Exercises de style* to be seen as the scholar, mathematician, the philosopher. Nevertheless, from a body of work in which fantasy is generally left to run free without any apparent counterweight, *Gueule de Pierre* stands out by its surprising mix of skilful, ambitious construction and comic shambolicness: 'it is life itself that is the source of all my activity: it is towards Its understanding that the whole of my intelligence strains' or, 'how can we bring the universe under a series of linked concepts?'—this is how the hero of *Gueule de Pierre* speaks. And, further on, the lyrical tale takes flight like Zarathustra:

'I have not come into these mountains because I love them, said Pierre. —I have not come to your part of the world because I was led here by a dream. I have not come to spend time here because I would not know what to do in the city down below. —My brother came this way, I know not why. Because he could breathe better? —I go into the mountains because my Truth must triumph.'—'And what is your Truth?' asked Nicomedes and Nicodemus [. . .]

To tell the truth, Pierre's answer is enigmatic and the book ends with the words that would yield its meaning still unsaid, but we learn at least that, through one of the most fantastical of stories, the most far-reaching quest that man can undertake is at issue. The story itself is decidedly disconcerting.

Pierre is one of the three sons of the Mayor—which is to say, the ruler—of Home Town. The state his father rules over has awarded him a grant: he is staying in Foreign Town to learn its language. But his study of that language proves futile. Pierre spends his time in Foreign Town deciphering the puzzle of Life, a quest which takes him to aquariums to meditate on the existence of fish. Convinced that he has solved life's secret and resolving to give up the study of the foreign language, he returns to his own country before the agreed period is up. He arrives back on the eve of Saint-Glinglin, Home Town's national day of celebration.

Home Town, governed by Pierre's father, the all-powerful Mayor, has two noteworthy institutions. The first is the cloud chaser, which affords the town eternally fine weather. The second is the Feast of Saint-Glinglin, at which the prominent figures of the town display piles of fine crockery to be smashed on the stroke of noon. This latter institution is lifted quite faithfully from the *potlatch* ritual of the Indians of the American Northwest. Like the acts of destruction by the Kwakiutl, the breaking of crockery by the notables of Home Town provided a mark of wealth and distinction. The Mayor's acts of destruction are, naturally, the most extravagant and the massacre he inflicts is made possible only by the use of a machine gun.

But in the life of the Mayor's family there lurks a mystery. He is hiding his daughter in a mill at the foot of the mountains. And this explains the anxiety-laden comings and goings of Pierre's youngest brother Jean through these mountains. And so, beneath an exterior of extreme vulgarity—a genuine 'shitshow' even—the celebrations of the Saint-Glinglin of the story are a prelude to the most lyrical drama. Pierre has notified the Home Towners that he will make a speech at the end of the afternoon. And at six in the evening, to his many listeners, including his father, he reveals the Truth of Life, the fathomless Truth of the cave-dwelling fish, the skate, the lobster and the sea bream. The crowd fails to understand, bursts out laughing and the Father himself, at the very height of his power that day, mocks him affectionately but publicly.

Pierre immediately procures a revolver. The Father learns of this and runs off into the mountains and, from that point on, the tale shifts from farce to epic. The old Mayor joins up with his daughter, imprisoned at the foot of the mountains, and carries her off with him: they flee together helter-skelter across arid, rocky country. Jean is already out looking for his sister and Pierre, searching for his father, meets up with him. They scurry off after the fugitives, having spotted them in the far distance. Pierre is intent on killing the man who refused to understand him and slighted him, while Jean wants to free his lost sister. Hunted down and cornered, the Father refuses to be captured: brandishing the weapon he took with him as he fled, he takes aim at his sons but does no more than that. By the time they reach their sister, she is standing over the petrifying spring in which the Father has drowned himself. Pierre feels thwarted in his murderous frenzy, but he takes the block of human mineral produced by the petrifying action of the waters back to Hometown: he will erect this strange statue of the Ruler-Father and attempt to establish a cult around the great 'Stone' that the corpse has become in the water.

This surprising amalgam of philosophical reflections, 'psychoanalytic' farce and 'sociological' epic had a sequel: it appeared in 1942 as *Temps mêlés*, subtitled *Gueule de Pierre II*. First of all, *Les Temps mêlés* adds to the story a meditation on nature by Pierre's younger brother Paul: Paul loathes the countryside, trees and earth, and sees the seductive object that is a revealingly half-dressed (and, subsequently, completely naked) pretty woman as man's triumph over vile nature. There follow a series of burlesque scenes, during which Paul meets in the flesh the scantily clad American film star he had adored on the silver screen. She is there as a tourist and becomes his mistress. However, Pierre, who has become mayor, has reform on his mind: for the established customs of the town he wishes to substitute scientific institutions, a set of myths and a form of worship that are the product of his own personal genius (rather than collective creations on the part of the people), aided by scholarly notions from the sociology of religion. A foreign anthropologist, on a field trip to this strange country, initially offers his support and considers for a brief moment proposing that 'some puberty rites' be established, to be followed at a later point by 'human sacrifices and totem meals'. However, he changes his mind, ashamed at having contemplated these artificial creations, robbing Pierre of the faith he still had in the town's old institutions. Convinced that these are inane, Pierre goes all out to provoke catastrophe: he forbids the celebration of Saint-Glinglin and closes down the cloud-chaser. Rain immediately falls on the town, the population stirs, Pierre is ignominiously driven out and Paul is elected mayor.

Les Temps mêlés begins with a series of poems, most of them relating to the history of Hometown, though this poetic section is not in any sense a response to the one in *Gueule de Pierre*. With this, Raymond Queneau provided a first example of that spirited, unsettling, demotic poetry to which *Les Ziaux*, published shortly afterwards, gave free rein (particularly in the admirable 'Explication de Métaphores'). Between *Gueule de Pierre I* and *II*, there was an appreciable lowering of the tone. The first part ended in epic mode. Burlesque comedy predominated from the outset in the second. One is even tempted to regard this second part as mocking the first, as its sardonic, negative conclusion.

But the hypothesis of a two-phase plan on the part of Queneau isn't necessarily correct. All this is confused from the outset because of the language used. Right from *Gueule de Pierre I*, demotic language knocks the intention off course—or, if one prefers, the intention is only admitted on one condition: that irony distort it. It is style that is naturally the agent of this distortion: this is the moment to remind the reader that *the style is the man*. The thrust of demotic language mischievously undermines, as it were, the realities the sentence sets before us. In everyday life, that undermining happens every time a vulgar expression is substituted for straightforward denigration. The substitution in the text of *Saint-Glinglin* of coarse (or comical) words for those of the first version of *Gueule de Pierre* will provide us with an illustrative example of such a conventional literary operation.

Saint-Glinglin, which completes Raymond Queneau's extraordinary mythological novel, reprises *Gueule de Pierre* page by page; then takes up, in a rather different form and with variants regarding the facts, the events reported in *Les Temps mêlés*. A final chapter, itself entitled 'Saint-Glinglin', adds a third, relatively short, part to the work. In it we see Home Town swept by constant rain, after they have got rid of the cloud-chaser. Paul is the mayor and his filmstar wife disports herself in her swimsuit, to the great excitement of Home Town's males. Pierre has returned to the town, on condition that the rain-drenched statue of his Father be sculpted in marble. The mysterious Jean and the no less mysterious—and very beautiful— Hélène, who after being reunited in the mountains on the death of the Father had disappeared together without any further ado, have returned to Home Town. They are all burying the grandmother, who was formerly Hélène's jailer (taking her to 'the Pits'[1]). At the end, the act of putting up an

---

1 Raymond Queneau, *Saint Glinglin* (James Sallis trans. and intro.) (Normal, IL: Dalkey Archive Press, 1993), p. 157.

eel-basket[2] and erecting Pierre's statue chases the clouds away again and the characters in the story dissolve, simply die or go away.

A decidedly strange development, itself new, links this new part to the old. For once, the silent Hélène is allowed to speak. At the beginning, Pierre was lost in meditation on the existence of the cave-dwelling fish, the fact that the cave-dwelling fish *exists*, that it contemplates and constructs the world in its own way. It is, directly, the existence—that is to say, the world-view—of tiny animal life that is expressed in Hélène's meditation. Hélène says what a microbe would say, according to Queneau, or rather her words attempt to convey the supposed thoughts of the microbe. In this way, the author tries to level out living beings in general and that levelling necessarily brings man down to the lost depths of a cave-dwelling fish, to the simplicity of a living particle too small to be visible to the naked eye. There is a degree of arbitrariness in this, but that has little impact on the sad and breezy, detached and passionate flippancy characteristic of Queneau. All things considered, Hélène's meditation might actually be the key to the total deprecation in which *Saint-Glinglin* culminates. But it does seem as though the author's language—its deep existence and its truth—had taken things to that point more decidedly than any—apparently altered—initial intention.

The changes from *Gueule de Pierre* to *Saint-Glinglin* show up clearly this dominant role of language. In this connection, *Gueule de Pierre* had, in the first instance, fallen short of unity: an uneven, clumsy, indecisive aspect prevented complete assent and gave the impression that an—in itself fascinating—effort had produced only a flawed work. In *Saint-Glinglin*, Raymond Queneau restores unity to *Gueule de Pierre* (second version), a unity based on a deprecation effected by language. The philosophical meditation at the beginning and the epic poem at the end lose some of their initial seriousness and high-mindedness. No doubt the intention of combining the philosophy and the epic with farce is palpable from the outset, but as philosophy, as epic. In *Saint-Glinglin*, philosophy and epic both take a hit. Language corrodes them and tends, surreptitiously, to destroy them as such.

---

2 Queneau, *Saint Glinglin* (Sallis trans.), p. 168.

A la fin de la fête, le père s'était enfui comme un voleur. [At Festival's end, the father had run off like a thief.]

So spoke the poet of *Gueule de Pierre* in a text often elevated in style (which one might wrongly, though conveniently, describe as resembling the work of Paul Claudel). For that plain sentence, the author of *Saint-Glinglin* substitutes:

A la fin de la fête, le fazeur f'était enfui fel un foleur.[3]

In this way the tone is set from the third line, in such a way as to undermine the very subject of the poem. In *Gueule de Pierre* what the author had to say was dominant: from the outset, the mischievousness of *Saint-Glinglin* beats down the ghosts that are conjured up and ridicules them. Their value is not truly eliminated, but it is set at the level of the valueless.

There would be no point in regarding this definite deprecation as an abandonment of the initial intention. But the levelling-down of *Saint-Glinglin* did not, at first, have the same resolute character. It is the force, or rather the exigence, the unity, of the language, of the style that produce that resolution retrospectively. There was, in the initial plan, a complexity of intentions, some elevated and others deprecatory, which apparently remained unresolved. The author was meeting the concern to respond with sufficient fullness to the scope, depths and possibilities opened up for thought by sociology, psychoanalysis and phenomenology. But he had, in the end, some fifteen years later, to reduce everything to the requirements of poetic deprecation. This is because richness of thought cannot survive richness of poetry, since poetry breaks down the well-founded simplicity

---

3 It is well known that Raymond Queneau likes to write English words as though they were French: hence *father* becomes *fazeur*.

[The distortion Queneau has applied to this line plays on the resemblance between the old typographical form of the letter 's' and proceeds to set up an alliteration on the initial consonant 'f'. Beneath the text, the French reader can 'see': *A la fin de la fête, le* father *s'était enfui tel un voleur. Quite reasonably* sidestepping these untranslatable elements in his version of *Saint-Glinglin*, James Sallis writes: 'At Festival's end, the old faker had flown like a thief' (p. 59). (Trans.)]

of intellectual facts: it moves to a deeper truth. At that level, things no longer have their use-value. Each one is an object of desire or aversion, of mirth or dread. In a sense, this is what psychoanalysis (speaking of *libido*), sociology (of the sacred) and phenomenology (of existence) teach us, but they tell us these things on a plane where each word is carefully attuned to the distinctly defined object. There is ultimately nothing sadder than their insistence on speaking to us of *libido*, the *sacred* and *existence*; they have to modulate their sentences ponderously, and often expend their energies twisting themselves into contortions or descending into sustained susurrations that lack poetry's rushing wind and crackling fire. They can never manage what genuine poetry achieves with ease: to clean up, as it goes along, the messy debris that is the discursive articulation of thought; and to reach, in plain language and beyond airy notions, the simple—*formless, modeless*—truth of poetry, that truth to which the window of the hovel that is *Saint-Glinglin* is thrown wide open.

Where that truth is concerned, a 'coherent' philosophy knows that discourse only accedes to it, in a final resolution, at a point beyond discourse. This is the meaning of *Saint-Glinglin*, which sparks the scrap iron of notions into life with its lightning flashes of irony. It has to be said that this book (and this is true of Queneau's work as a whole) cannot be mistaken for ordinary comic literature (with all due respect for the latter). The fact is that great poetry turns humour into its opposite. If it pitches itself at the lowest possible level, then, far from flirting with the petty treatment of trivia, it nullifies things more completely, in a sense, undermining all high-flown notions.

In this regard, Queneau's last collection of poems, *L'Instant fatal*, often reaches a level of accomplishment that had previously been achieved almost exclusively by 'L'Explication des métaphores' in *Les Ziaux*). I cannot more tangibly convey a truth expressed with so much effort in these few pages than by free-loading on Queneau's easy mastery and quoting the end of the wonderful poem with which the book opens:

you have a good job you live and thrive
    by profiting from the dead

there you are developing a paunch growing grey fat father
    you abhor the dead

then it's illness and then poverty
    the dead trouble you

coughing and trembling you gently degenerate
    you look like the dead

until the day when, done for and diving down
    all awry among the dead

trying to snatch at the initial sensation
    which is not for the dead

wishing to forget the arbitrary term
    that designates the dead

you want to relive at last the fulsome memory
    that removes you from among the dead

praiseworthy effort! worthy task! exemplary awareness
    At which the dead smile because

Always will come the fatal moment to distract us.

Marcel Proust

If the non-Christian world some day defines the forms of its spiritual life ('spiritual' in the religious sense of the word); if, in other words, it should happen that a humanity no longer requiring the aid of Christianity finds fulfilment, recognizes its own face and stops wandering off into a multiplicity of forms associated with poorly defined, dishonest representations, and based on a desire for blindness—on fear—that spiritual face, whose features would then harden, might resemble Proust's. This is, assuredly, a paradoxical proposition. The tradition that goes back, through Lautréamont and Rimbaud, to Romanticism, and through Romanticism to the esoterism of all ages, is much more alive and is the only one to have developed self-consciousness. Moreover, if it is true that spiritual truth demands fully rounded thought, Nietzsche alone has shown the extent of the enormous effort—the exhausting effort—that devolves on those no longer able to draw on Christianity for their assurance. Compared with these two paths, the poetic and the Nietzschean, Marcel Proust's experience seems fragile, uncertain, and attached to trivial concerns.

As regards the face it has left to show to the world, I shall willingly admit that its features remain hazy, and even that they leave no clear stamp on our thinking from the outset. But does not the determined, assertive, clearly interpretable character that one might range against it from other quarters precisely signify the treacherousness of that which is deliberate, assertive and perhaps a little hastily interpreted? What lends the things Proust teaches us a special character all their own is undoubtedly the rigour with which the object of his *quest* reduces, in his hands, to an *involuntary* discovery. What is disappointing in the other possible paths is, by contrast, the decisiveness, the deliberate shaping, the resolute discourse that carry on the Christian attitude within us. The object of Proust's search is so well defined by immanence that, in it, a method limited to the search for transcendent objects loses all meaning. If, in fact, one abandons that use of our resources which is directed towards salvation, we need look for nothing beyond the present instant and we can no longer involve in our search this deliberate shaping, this mobilization of resources, and this painful imitation of a piece of work (whose *raison d'être* lies in the future) that enable us to speak discursively. Admittedly, Proust never stopped discoursing, but arguably the discursive component in his work is something of a foreign body; at a pinch, we may say that it points clumsily, like sick people struggling to make themselves understood, towards what matters. At the very least, what matters is placed out of the reach of the will. For it is no longer about changing the world, but about grasping it (or perhaps letting the world freely grasp us).

At that point the world's spectacles cease to be an object of moral concern for us. *This* world is no longer presented as matching up poorly with some truth existing beyond its this-worldness, its present time. It has not been clearly recognized that, once it is no longer offered up to be forgotten by those who look beyond it—offered up to the reformer's pity or the revolutionary's scorn—then the world-as-it-is offers itself up to whoever is willing to grasp it in the moment, in its indelible truth, as the screen through which we have to see, a screen which our passion will suddenly render transparent. In this way, spiritual life has fully withdrawn from the heavens and from 'worlds beyond' [*des arrière-mondes*][1]: its field of force is the shabby realm of the 'here below': of the street, the bedchamber, the drawing room. We can no longer withdraw into a cleansing solitude, we are here, surrounded by actual human beings, more completely than a fish is surrounded by water: as though the water the fish swims in were an immense extension of the fish's being. We live amid an infinite play of hidden desires and reticences, a game in which we are constantly losing, since time is constantly stealing us from ourselves. But all we can do is transfigure the enormous disaster to which we belong body and soul. It is not by chance that the second volume of *Time Regained* transformed the spectacle of salon society into a slow descent into the grave. But *within* that wretched, useless

---

1 The notion of *arrière-mondes* translates Nietzsche's concept of *Hinterwelten*. [Trans.]

fading into the mist, there still remains something like a tiny sound to which we attend, trembling (though Proust was an inept philosopher and he is doubtless wrong to imagine that *that* lasts: it is nothing truly graspable)—which is truer than any object we employ for a useful purpose.

Proust's weakness, no doubt, is the contempt in which he held that object. It was at the same time his strength, but that contempt was based on the wealth he had received by chance. There is, thus, in this perfect experience something premature, something painfully privileged. It is doubtless the experience to which humanity is boundlessly called, but humanity cannot respond to that call. Humanity necessarily accords priority to action and cannot generally enjoy Proust's privilege, his distress at the height of the possible, without which the ultimate truth escapes us since, having some means of battling against distress, we have no chance of rendering the opacity of things transparent.

Marcel Proust, *A un ami. Correspondance inédite,* [To a friend: Unpublished correspondence] *1903–1922* (Georges de Lauris pref.) (Paris: Amiot–Dumont, 1948), in 8°, 270 pp.

These are letters to Georges de Lauris. Here is a passage from a letter probably dating from 1908: 'I like hardly anything (at this moment, as you may suppose, I like nothing) but girls . . . You're going to tell me that they invented marriage for that, but those are no longer girls. I understand Bluebeard, he was a man who liked girls.'

Marcel Proust, *Lettres à Madame C.* [Letters to Madame C.] (Léon Daudet pref.) (Paris: J. B. Janin, 1947), in 8°, 215 pp, illustrated with eight plates.

Madame C. was a friend of Proust's mother. This correspondence begins around 1885 with a letter from the author to his grandmother and continues from 1899 to 1921. It is particularly copious during the war.

FRANÇOIS MAURIAC, *Du côté de chez Proust* [Proust's way] (Paris: La Table Ronde, 1947), in 8°, 155 pp.

Built around two letters sent to him by Proust, this memoir begins with a first meeting in 1910 at the home of the duchesse de Rohan. Mauriac recognized Proust's talent as soon as he read the Preface to his translation of Ruskin:

> From that point on, I never stopped asking people about Proust and they told me the tale of his strange reclusive life into which I never had any hope of penetrating. If I possess a copy of the first printing of *Swann's Way*, that is because as soon as I had made out the name Proust in a bookshop window I rushed to acquire the book.

ÉLISABETH DE GRAMONT, *Marcel Proust* (Paris: Flammarion, 1948), in 16°, 286 pp.

E. de Gramont, who has already devoted a first, precious book to Robert de Montesquiou and Marcel Proust, here relates all the memories she has of a life partly spent in Proust's own milieu. To *In Search of Lost Time*, this book adds a view of the same world and the same facts seen by other eyes. In this way, the landscape transfigured by Proust's work is presented to us—additionally, as it were—in the simplest light.

FLORIS DELATTRE, 'Bergson et Proust. Accords et dissonances' [Bergson and Proust: Harmony and discordance] in *Les Études bergsoniennes*, VOL. 1 (Paris: Albin Michel, 1948), pp. 7–127.

In 1891, Bergson married Mademoiselle Neuberger, Madame Proust's cousin. Marcel Proust was best man at his wedding. Proust admired Bergson, read little of his work and denied being influenced by him. The unavoidable parallel, based on the importance accorded to memory, runs up against this major difference between the two, perhaps insufficiently emphasized by the author: Bergson subordinated the truth of memory to action. Proust, stressing *involuntary* memory, took as his object only a *non-utilitarian* grasp of what is.

JEAN MOUTON, *Le Style de Marcel Proust* (Paris: Corréa, 1948), in 8°, 240 pp.

An in-depth analysis, discovering the man (his inner truth) through his style. It stresses the preciosity of his metaphors and underscores their demoniacal character, through which he shows an affinity with 'automatic writing'.

Bibliography and Notes

Georges Bataille's complete works in French have been published by Gallimard in 12 volumes (1970–88). *Critical Essays: Volume 1, 1944–1948* presents a selection of 41 articles in English translation from volume 11 (*Articles I, 1944–1949*) of his *Œuvres complètes*.

Unless otherwise stated, all bibliographic notes in this section are translations of notes supplied by the editors of the original volume, Francis Marmande and Sibylle Monod. The lists of works cited also contain references made in the footnotes by the editors of the original volume and the translator, as well as English translations, when available, of texts discussed by Bataille.

BATAILLE, Georges. *Œuvres complètes*. Paris: Gallimard:

Volume 1 (1970): *Premiers écrits, 1922–1940* (Denis Hollier ed., Michel Foucault pref.).

Volume 2 (1970): *Écrits posthumes, 1922–1940* (Denis Hollier ed.).

Volume 3 (1974): *Œuvres littéraires* (Thadée Klossowski ed.).

Volume 4 (1971): *Œuvres littéraires posthumes* (Thadée Klossowski ed.).

Volume 5 (1973): *La Somme athéologique I*.

Volume 6 (1973): *La Somme athéologique II*.

Volume 7 (1976): *L'économie à la mesure de l'univers – La Part maudite – La limite de l'utile (Fragments) – Théorie de la Religion – Conférences 1947–1948 – Annexes*.

Volume 8 (1976): *L'Histoire de l'érotisme – Le surréalisme au jour le jour – Conférences 1951–1953 – La Souveraineté – Annexes* (Thadée Klossowski ed.).

Volume 9 (1979): *Lascaux, ou La naissance de l'art – Manet – La littérature et le mal – Annexes*.

Volume 10 (1987): *L'érotisme – Le procès de Gilles de Rais – Les larmes d'Eros*.

Volume 11 (1988): *Articles I, 1944–1949* (Francis Marmande and Sibylle Monod eds).

Volume 12 (1988): *Articles II, 1950–1961* (Francis Marmande and Sibylle Monod eds).

Is Nietzsche Fascist? (pp. 3–5)

'Nietzsche est-il fasciste?', Œuvres complètes, VOL. 11, pp. 9–11.

First published in Combat 113 (20 October 1944) under the section 'Les Lettres et les arts', preceded by the headline 'On a Centenary'.

A (less nuanced) rough draft of this article appears in Œuvres complètes, VOL. 6, pp. 418–20. The first formulation goes back to the article 'Réparation à Nietzsche' in Acéphale 2 (Œuvres complètes, VOL. 2, pp. 447–65), in which the quotation 'Have no truck with anyone mixed up in this shameless fraud of race' already appears.

For Combat, to which Bataille will also give 'Letter to Merleau-Ponty' [published in this volume, see pp. 168–69] and 'Le paradoxe du don' [The paradox of giving] (Œuvres complètes, VOL. 11, pp. 432–33), he prepares two articles that will remain unpublished: 'Sur le communisme' [On Communism], in which he announces a short book (Nietzsche et le communisme) to be published in May (?), and 'Communisme et liberté' [Communism and freedom]. They are to be found in folders 78 and 156 of Bataille's papers (see Œuvres complètes, VOL. 8, pp. 399–404, 615 and 667–78). [The two unpublished and unfinished articles are reprinted in the editorial endnotes to Œuvres complètes, VOL. 11, pp. 557–59. (Trans.)]

Is Literature Useful? (pp. 6–7)

'La littérature est-elle utile?', Œuvres complètes, VOL. 11, pp. 12–13.

First published in Combat (12 November 1944).

The Will to the Impossible (pp. 11–15)

'La volonté de l'impossible', Œuvres complètes, VOL. 11, pp. 19–23.

First published in Vrille (issue entitled 'La peinture et la littérature libres'), 1945.

Other contributors to this issue included Georges Hunier, Robert Desnos, Marcel Béalu, Pierre Mabille, Jean Arp, Henri Michaux, Michel Butor. There was also a translation of a work by William Blake and illustrations by Dominguez, Max Ernst, Labisse, Cocteau, Valentine Hugo, Picasso, Delvaux, Dali, de Chirico, Tanguy etc.

Picasso's Political Paintings (pp. 16–17)

'Les peintures politiques de Picasso', *Œuvres complètes*, VOL. 11, pp. 24-25.

First published in the first and only issue of the journal *Actualité*, 'L'Espagne libre' (published by Calmann-Lévy, fourth quarter, 1945).

Bataille had conceived *Actualité* with Pierre Prévost, Jean Cassou and Maurice Blanchot. This first issue published, at his direction, a group of texts (by Jean Camp, Jean Cassou, José Quero-Molares, André Camp, Robert Davée, Roger Grenier, Federico García Lorca, Albert Olivier, W. H. Auden and Maurice Blanchot), prefaced by Albert Camus: 'For nine years now, the men of my generation have had Spain in their hearts. For nine years they have been carrying it like a nasty wound.'

The second issue of *Actualité*, though half-prepared for publication, never appeared.

On Ernest Hemingway's *For Whom the Bell Tolls* (pp. 18–20)

'A propos de "Pour qui sonne le glas?" d'Ernest Hemingway', *Œuvres complètes*, VOL. 11, pp. 25-27.

First published in *Actualité*, 'L'Espagne libre' (1945): 120-26.

Bataille's article on Hemingway is preceded by a text 'L'odeur de la mort' [The smell of death] translated by Diane Koutchoubey (whom he will marry at Nantua in eastern France on 16 January 1951).

Works cited:

BATAILLE, Georges. *L'histoire de l'œil*. Paris: Pauvert, 1928.

HEMINGWAY, Ernest. *Death in the Afternoon*. New York: Scribner's, 1932.

———. *Mort dans l'après-midi* (René Daumal trans.) (Paris: Gallimard, 1938).

Klee (p. 23)

'Klee', *Œuvres complètes*, VOL. 11, p. 34.

First published in *Cahiers d'Art*, 1945-46.

Miller's Morality (pp. 24–39)

'La morale de Miller', *Œuvres complètes*, VOL. 11, pp. 41–55.

First published in the first issue of *Critique* (June 1946): 3–17.

'La morale de Miller', like 'Le sens moral de la Sociologie', the article which follows it directly in *Œuvres complètes*, VOL. 11, was published in the first issue of *Critique* in June 1946 (pp. 3–17 and 39–47).

Bataille was the director of this 'General Review of French and Foreign Publications', which was originally due to be called *Critica*, Pierre Prévost was its chief editor and Maurice Girodias was the publisher (at Éditions du Chêne). The magazine's editorial and administrative address was 16, place Vendôme, Paris 1. The editorial committee consisted of Maurice Blanchot, Pierre Josserand, Jules Monnerot, Albert Ollivier and Éric Weil.

Apart from the two articles by Bataille, the table of contents includes the names of Jean Maquet, Alain Girard, André Sénéchal, Pierre Prévost, Pierre Germain, Jean Chauveau, Éric Weil, Alexandre Koyré and Georges Ambrosino. On its back cover, future articles by Raymond Aron, Maurice Blanchot, Roger Caillois, Georges Friedmann, Georges Limbour, Jacques Prévert and Denis de Rougemont are announced.

Critique will publish studies of works and articles published in France and elsewhere.

Those studies extend beyond the scope of mere review articles. Through them, *Critique* would like to provide the least incomplete insight that it is able into the various activities of the human mind in the fields of literary creation, philosophical inquiry, and historical, scientific, political and economic knowledge. The authors of the articles freely expound an opinion for which they alone are responsible; they seek to ground that opinion in reason and not to content themselves with facile polemic.

It is still difficult at the present time to accord appropriate importance to the analysis of foreign publications. *Critique* will develop this part as exchanges with foreign countries return to normal.

Lastly, the unsigned editorial announces that, from issue no. 4 onwards, a series of 'Brief Notes' will complement the studies published. In an interview, Bataille links the creation of *Critique* to his experience of some ten years in the Periodicals department of the French National Library: 'Reflecting on what might be the significance of periodicals, I thought about how useful it would be to have a journal representing the essentials of human thought taken from the best books. One of the oldest magazines, *Le Journal des savants*, which dates from the seventeenth century, ran along those lines.'

In May 1947, *Critique* left Éditions du Chêne and was taken over by Calmann-Lévy, from issue no. 13 to no. 40.

In 1948, the journal won the prize for 'journal of the year'. In September 1949, it closed. The hiatus lasted a year: issue no. 41 is dated October 1950 and was published by Éditions de Minuit.

In 1963, for the issue 'Hommage à Georges Bataille' (August–September, 195–96), Bataille is listed as usual as its founder, Jean Piel as the director and the editorial committee is made up of Roland Barthes, Michel Deguy and Michel Foucault (who will supply the preface to volume I of Bataille's complete works).

That issue contained contributions from Alfred Métraux, Michel Leiris, Raymond Queneau, André Masson, Jean Bruno, Jean Piel, Maurice Blanchot, Pierre Klossowski, Michel Foucault, Roland Barthes and Philippe Sollers, together with a letter from Bataille's childhood friend Dr Georges Duteil.

Works reviewed (in order of their appearance in the essay):

MILLER, Henry. *Tropique du Cancer* (Paul Rivert trans., Henri Fluchère pref.). Paris: Denoel, 1946, 381 pp.

——. *Tropique du Capricorne* (J-C. Lefaure trans.). Paris: Éditions du Chêne, 1946, 508 pp.

——. *Printemps noir* (Paul Rivert trans.). Paris: Gallimard, 1946, 271 pp.

Works cited:

MILLER, Henry. *Obelisk Trilogy: Tropic of Cancer, Tropic of Capricorn, Black Spring*. Paris: Olympia Press, 2008.

——. *Tropic of Cancer*. New York: Grove Press, 1961.

Dionysos Redivivus (pp. 40–42)

'Dionysos Redivivus', *Œuvres complètes*, VOL. 11, pp. 67-69.

First published in 'Voyage en Grèce', special issue, *Messages de la Grèce* (July 1946): 32-33.

The combined issue 3–4 of *Acéphale* (July 1937) is devoted to Dionysus (with texts by Bataille, Caillois, Klossowski, Masson and Monnerot). See Bataille, *Œuvres complètes*, VOL. 1, pp. 477–90).

Mystical Experience and Literature (pp. 43–46)

'Expérience mystique et littérature', *Œuvres complètes*, VOL. 11, pp. 83-86.

First published in *Critique* 2 (1946): 117-19.

Work reviewed:

PAUWELS, Louis. *Saint Quelqu'un*. Paris, Éditions du Seuil, 1946.

Works cited:

ROLLAND, Romain. *La Vie de Ramakrishna*. Paris: Stock, 1930.
——. *La Vie de Vivékânanda*. Paris: Stock, 1930.

The Indictment of Henry Miller (pp. 47–52)

'L'inculpation d'Henry Miller', *Œuvres complètes*, VOL. 11, pp. 107-12.

First published in *Critique* 3-4 (1946): 380-84.

Work cited:

MILLER, Henry. 'Obscenity and the Law of Reflection'. *Kentucky Law Journal* 51 (4).

Gide – Baranger – Gillet (pp. 53–55)

'Gide - Baranger - Gillet', *Œuvres complètes*, VOL. 11, pp. 113-15.

First published in *Critique* 3-4 (1946): 367-68 and 372-74.

Works reviewed (in order of their appearance in the essay):

GIDE, André. *Journal 1939–1942*. Paris: Gallimard, 1946, in 16°, 215 pp.

BARANGER, William. *Pour connaître la pensée de Nietzsche*. Paris: Bordas, 1946, in 8°, 127 pp.

GILLET, Martin Stanislas. *La Mission de sainte Catherine de Sienne*. Paris: Flammarion, 1946, in 16°, 262 pp.

Work cited:

GIDE, André. *The Journals of André Gide, Volume 4: 1939–49* (Justin O'Brien trans.). London: Secker & Warburg, 1951.

The Last Instant (pp. 56–65)

'Le dernier instant', *Œuvres complètes*, VOL. 11, pp. 116-25.
First published in *Critique* 5 (October 1946): 448-57.

An English translation of this article by Thomas Walton appeared in *Transition* 48(1) (January 1948): 60–69. In preparing the present version, the corrections Bataille made to the copy of *Critique* have been taken into account.

Work reviewed:

DEGUY, Madeleine and Gabriel Marcel. *'Les Condamnés précédé' de 'La Parole est aux saints'*. Paris: Plon, 1946, in 16°, 177 pp.

Works cited:

CATHERINE of Siena, *Le Lettere di S. Caterina da Siena*, VOL. 4 (Niccolo Tommaseo ed.). Florence, 1860, in 16°.

———. *The Letters of Catherine of Siena*, VOL. 1 (Suzanne Noffke trans.). Tempe, Arizona: ACMRS, 2000.

Gide – Nietzsche – Claudel (pp. 66–69)

'Gide - Nietzsche - Claudel', *Œuvres complètes*, VOL. 11, pp. 126-29.
First published in *Critique* 5 (October 1946): 463, 466-68.

Works reviewed (in order of their appearance in the essay):

GIDE, André. *Thésée*. Paris: Gallimard, 1946, in 16º, 115 pp.

NIETZSCHE, Frédéric [Friedrich]. *Pages mystiques* (A. Quinot trans. and ed.). Paris: Éditions Robert Laffont, 1945, in 8º, 297 pp.

CLAUDEL, Paul. *Les Sept Psaumes de la pénitence avec un examen de conscience. Le Buisson ardent* (Pierre Legris series ed.). Paris: Éditions du Seuil, 1945, in 16º, 70 pp.

Work cited:

GIDE, André. *Oedipus and Theseus* (John Russell trans.). London: Secker and Warburg, 1950.

Take It or Leave It (pp. 70–71)

'A prendre ou à laisser', *Œuvres complètes*, VOL. 11, pp. 130-31.

First published in *Troisième convoi* 3 (November 1946): 24-25.

Works cited:

GIDE, André. *Souvenirs littéraires et problèmes actuels. Avec deux présentations de G. Bounoure.* Beirut: Les Lettres françaises, 'Publications de l'École supérieure des lettres de Beyrouth', 1946.

The War in China (pp. 72–85)

'La guerre en Chine', *Œuvres complètes*, VOL. 11, pp. 132-45.

First published in *Critique* 6 (November 1946): 540-51.

Works reviewed (in order of their appearance in the essay):

GELDER, Stuart. *The Chinese Communists*. London: Victor Gollancz, 1946, in 16º, 290 pp.

FORMAN, Harrison. *Ce que j'ai vu en Chine rouge* (Sabine Bernard Derosne trans.). Paris: Éditions Pierre Seghers, 1946, in 8º, 277 pp.

NOLDE, André. *La Chine de Chiang Kaï Chek*. Paris: Corrêa, 1946, in 16º, 199 pp.

Cossery – Robert Aron (pp. 86–89)

'Cossery – Robert Aron', *Œuvres complètes*, VOL. 11, pp. 146-50.

First published in *Critique* 6 (November 1946): 565-66, 568-69.

Works reviewed (in order of their appearance in the essay):

COSSERY, Albert. *Les Hommes oubliés de Dieu*. Paris: Charlot, 1946, in 16°, 134 pp.

ARON, Robert. *Retour à l'éternel*. Paris: Albin Michel, 1946, in 16°, 251 pp.

Work cited:

COSSERY, Albert. *Men God Forgot* (Harold Edwards trans.). Berkeley: Circle Editions/George Leite, 1946.

Marcel Proust and the Profaned Mother (pp. 90–101)

'Marcel Proust et la mère profanée', *Œuvres complètes*, VOL. 11, pp. 151-61.

First published in *Critique* 7 (December 1946): 601-11.

Works reviewed (in order of their appearance in the essay):

FRETET, Dr André. *L'Aliénation poétique. Rimbaud, Mallarmé, Proust*. Paris: J.-B. Janin, 1946, in 8°, 333 pp.

SAURAT, Denis. *Tendances. Idées françaises: De Molière à Proust*. Paris: La Colombe [Éditions du Vieux Colombier], 1946, in 16°, 152 pp.

Work cited:

PROUST, Marcel. *Remembrance of Things Past*, VOL. 2 (C. K. Scott Moncrieff and Terence Kilmartin trans). London: Penguin Books, 1989.

———. *Sodom and Gomorrah* (John Sturrock trans.). London: Penguin Classics, 2003.

Adamov (pp. 102–3)

'Adamov', *Œuvres complètes*, VOL. 11, pp. 162-63.

First published in *Critique* 7 (December 1946): 654.

Work reviewed:

ADAMOV, Arthur. *L'Aveu*. Paris: Éditions du Sagittaire, 1946.

The Friendship between Man and Beast (pp. 107–11)

'L'amitié de l'homme et de la bête', *Œuvres complètes*, VOL. 11, pp. 167-71.

First published in *Formes et couleurs* (special issue on the horse) 9(1) (Lausanne, 1947), unpaginated.

Illustrated article: Parthenon frieze; drawing by Bellini (Horseman jumping over a tomb, Louvre Museum), Domenico Tiepolo (Centaur carrying off a Female Faun, École nationale des Beaux-Arts, Paris); Kohler (Bedouin Camp); Jacques Thévos (Small White Wooden Horse, photograph); J. Fouquet (The Conversion of Saint Paul, page from the illuminated *Livres d'heures d'Étienne Chevalier*, Musée Condé de Chantilly); Bellini (Knight on Horseback, drawing, Louvre); Apocalypse Scene (French School, 13th century, Cambrai Library); André Masson (Diomedes's Horses, 1934); Bellini (Faun and Cupid on a Horse led by a Satyr, drawing, Louvre); Van Dongen (Little Horses, oil on card); Jacques Thévoz (Dead Horse, photograph).

Bataille's text is preceded by a presentation, in the style of *Documents* (in whose first issue Bataille published the article 'Le cheval académique', *Œuvres complètes*, VOL. I, pp. 159-63) in the name of the magazine's editors:

> Where does the horse come from? From China probably, for everything turns out to be from China in the end. Though decorative and, overall, very elegant, and wild, Alfred Jarry did not like it. He liked neither its snarling nor its galloping, and even less its shape. He saw it merely as an outsized grasshopper, just one more apocalyptic monstrosity. But Jarry was a born cyclist. Hence his hatred.
>
> In reality, the conquest of this mettlesome animal, strangely elastic and chockfull of electricity, was a noble one; the conquest of this galloping pride, this power with foaming nostrils, its hooves spangled with sparks, which our ancestors already appreciated in the form of rare steaks, long before they had put a halter round its neck or calculated its energy mathematically [. . .]

Giraud – Pastoureau – Benda – Du Moulin de Laplante – Govy (pp. 112–21)

'Giraud - Pastoureau - Benda - Dumoulin de Laplante - Govy', *Œuvres complètes*, VOL. 11, pp. 188-97.

First published in *Critique* 8-9 (1947): 171-72, 175-76, 181-86.

The last two notes are signed N.L., but in December 1947 they appear in the Index under Georges Bataille's name.

Works reviewed (in order of their appearance in the essay):

GIRAUD, Victor. *La Critique littéraire. Le problème. Les théories. Les méthodes.* Collection L'histoire littéraire. Paris: Aubier (Éditions Montaigne), 1946, in 16º, 208 pp.

PASTOUREAU, Henri. *La Blessure de l'homme.* Paris: Robert Laffont, 1946, in 16º, 179 pp.

BENDA, Julien. *Exercice d'un enterré vif (juin 1940 – août 1944).* Paris: Gallimard, 1946, in 16º, 179 pp.

LAPLANTE, Pierre du Moulin de. *Histoire générale synchronique. I. Des origines à l'Hégire.* La Suite des temps, VOL. 15. Paris: Gallimard, 1946, in 8º, 325 pp.

GOVY, Georges. *Sang russe.* Collection 'Esprit': La condition humaine. Paris: Éditions du Seuil, 1946, in 16º, 238 pp.

Work cited:

BRETON, André. 'What is Surrealism?' in Franklin Rosemont (ed.), *What is Surrealism? Selected Writings.* New York: Monad, 1978.

On the Relationship between the Divine and Evil (pp. 122–31)

'Du rapport entre le divin et le mal', *Œuvres complètes*, VOL. 11, pp. 198-207.

First published in *Critique* 10 (March 1947): 227-34.

This long reflection on the *sacred* may be compared with an (unpublished) project drawn up for the radio programme 'Le sacré au XXe siècle', to be found in *Enveloppe 37* of Bataille's papers, though we have no other material on that programme. [The unpublished text is reprinted in the editorial endnotes to *Œuvres complètes*, VOL. 11, pp. 568–69. (Trans.)]

Work reviewed:

Pètrement, Simone. *Le Dualisme dans l'histoire de la philosophie et des religions.* La Montagne Sainte-Geneviève. Paris: Gallimard, 1946, in 16°, 132 pp.

Works cited:

Durkheim, Émile. *The Elementary Forms of the Religious Life* (Joseph Ward Swain trans.). Mineola, NY: Dover Publishers, 2008.

Herz, Robert. 'La Prééminence de la main droite. Étude sur la polarité religieuse'. *Revue philosophique* 1 (1909).

Smith, W. Robertson. *Lectures on the Religion of the Semites. First series: The Fundamental Institutions.* Edinburgh: Black, 1889.

Pierre Gordon (pp. 132–33)

'Pierre Gordon', *Œuvres complètes*, VOL. 11, pp. 208-9.
First published in *Critique* 10 (March 1947): 281-82.

Work reviewed:

Gordon, Pierre. *L'initiation sexuelle et l'évolution religieuse.* Bibliothèque de philosophie contemporaine: Psychologie et sociologie (Maurice Pradines series ed.). Paris: Presses universitaires de France, 1946, in 8°, 274 pp.

What Is Sex? (pp. 134–45)

'Qu'est-ce que le sexe?', *Œuvres complètes*, VOL. 11, pp. 210-21.
First published in *Critique* 11 (April 1947): 363-72.

Work reviewed:

Wolff, Étienne. *Les Changements de sexe.* L'Avenir de la Science, VOL. 23 (Jean Rostand series ed.). Paris: Gallimard, 1946, in 8°, 307 pp.

A New American Novelist (pp. 146–49)

'Un nouveau romancier américain', *Œuvres complètes*, VOL. 11, pp. 222-25.
First published in *Critique* 12 (May 1947): 387-89.

Work reviewed:

PROKOSCH, Frederic. *Les Asiatiques* (Max Morise trans.). Paris: Gallimard, 1946, in 8°, 300 pp.

Work cited:

PROKOSCH, Frederic. *The Asiatics*. London and Paris: The Albatross Modern Continental Library, 1947.

Sartre (pp. 150–52)

'Sartre', *Œuvres complètes*, VOL. 11, pp. 226-28.

First published in *Critique* 12 (May 1947): 471-73.

Work reviewed:

SARTRE, Jean-Paul. *Réflexions sur la question juive*. Paris: Paul Morhien, 1947, in 16°, 199 pp.

Work cited:

SARTRE, Jean-Paul. *Anti-Semite and Jew* (George J. Becker trans.). New York: Schocken Books, 1965.

A Morality Based on Misfortune: *The Plague* (pp. 153–67)

'La morale du malheur: *La Peste*', *Œuvres complètes*, VOL. 11, pp. 237-50.

First published in *Critique* 13-14 (June-July 1947): 3-15.

Works reviewed (in order of their appearance in the essay):

CAMUS, Albert. *La Peste*. Paris: Gallimard, 1947, in 16°, 339 pp.

———. *'Le Malentendu' suivi de 'Caligula'*. Paris: Gallimard, 1947, in 16°, 215 pp.

———. 'Remarque sur la révolte' in *L'Existence*. La Métaphysique, VOL. 1 (Jean Grenier series ed.). Paris: Gallimard, 1945, in 8°, pp. 9–23.

———. 'Ni victimes, ni bourreaux'. *Combat*, 19–30 November 1946.

Works cited:

CAMUS, Albert. *Caligula and Three Other Plays.* New York: Vintage Books, 1958.

———. *The Plague* (Robin Buss trans.). London: Penguin Classics, 2020.

DE SADE, Marquis. *Philosophy in the Boudoir, or The Immoral Mentors* (Joachim Neugroschel trans.). New York: Penguin, 2006.

Letter to Merleau-Ponty (pp. 168–69)

'Lettre à M. Merleau-Ponty', *Œuvres complètes*, VOL. 11, pp. 251–52. First published in *Combat* 930 (4 July 1947): 2.

This letter, dated 24 June 1947, on the position taken by Sartre on Surrealism in *Les Temps modernes* of May 1947, is preceded by the following text:

> Georges Bataille asks us to publish the letter below which was sent to the editor of *Les Temps modernes*. It tells how Georges Bataille was invited to contribute to that journal, but declined on account of Jean-Paul Sartre's recent article on André Breton and Surrealism. Our literary editor has taken a position on that attack which came out of a clear blue sky [*que rien ne laissait pressentir*] (in these very columns, Breton himself spoke very courteously of Sartre and existentialism). We are therefore publishing this letter for your information; we would also like to point out another—equally vigorous—reply to Sartre from Max-Pol Fouchet in the latest issue of *La Gazette des Lettres*.

Transition 48 carries a partial English translation of this letter ('Marx, Lautréamont or Heidegger', *Transition 48* 2 (June 1948): 122–23).

Triggered by the sarcastic review Sartre had produced in 1943 of *L'Expérience intérieure* [translated into English as *Inner Experience*] in an article published in three parts by *Les Cahiers du Sud* ('Un nouveau mystique', 260, 261, 262; October, November, December 1943; pp. 783–90, 866–86 and 988–94; reprinted in *Situations I* (Paris: Gallimard, 1947), pp. 143–88 [Jean-Paul Sartre, 'A New Mystic' (1943) in *On Bataille and Blanchot* (Chris Turner trans.), The Seagull Sartre Library, VOL. 10 (London: Seagull Books, 2021), pp. 1–61], Bataille's reaction to the work of the man he refers to elsewhere as 'the philosopher' runs through and informs a number of his articles and other writings. In 1944, Bataille held long conversations with Sartre.

At the end of *Sur Nietzsche* [translated into English as *On Nietzsche*], he outlines a defence of *Inner Experience* (*Œuvres complètes*, VOL. 6, pp. 195–99) and returns to the attack with 'Le surréalisme et sa différence avec l'existentialisme' (p. 70), then 'Baudelaire "mis à nu". L'analyse de Sartre et l'essence de la poésie' (*La littérature et le mal* [translated into English as *Literature and Evil*], *Œuvres complètes*, VOL. 9, pp. 189–209 and 441–49).

The fact that Bataille was sometimes ranked among the 'existentialists' by commentators he regarded as superficial, did nothing to help the situation.

Is Lasting Peace Inevitable? (pp. 170–75)

'La paix durable est-elle fatale?', *Œuvres complètes*, VOL. 11, pp. 253–58.

First published in *Critique* 15-16 (August-September 1947): 230-35.

Work reviewed:

MORICE, Lucien. *Vers l'empire du monde*. Liberté de l'Esprit (Raymond Aron series ed.). Paris: Calmann-Lévy, 1947, in 16°, 215 pp.

Joseph Conrad (pp. 176–81)

'Conrad - Breton', *Œuvres complètes*, VOL. 11, pp. 268-73.

First published in *Critique* 18 (November 1947): 463-67.

Works cited:

CONRAD, Joseph. *Sagesse de Conrad* (Georges Jean-Aubry ed.). Paris: Gallimard, 1947, in 16°, 143 pp.

JEAN-AUBRY, Georges. *Vie de Conrad*. Leurs Figures, VOL. 3. Paris: Gallimard, 1947, in 8°, 304 pp.

Preface to the Gaston-Louis Roux Exhibition (pp. 182–83)

'Préface à l'exposition Gaston-Louis Roux', *Œuvres complètes*, VOL. 11, pp. 277-78.

First published as the preface to a Gaston-Louis Roux exhibition catalogue (Kahnweiler, 1947).

Born at Provins on 24 January 1904, Gaston-Louis Roux was initially a student of Maurice Denis and Raoul Dufy. Vitrac published an article on him in the seventh issue of *Documents*. In 1932, Roux joined the Dakar-Djibouti mission [an ethnographic expedition financed by the French government (Trans.)] and would design the cover of the issue of *Minotaure* which related to that mission.

From Existentialism to the Primacy of the Economy (pp. 184–216)

'De l'existentialisme au primat de l'économie', *Œuvres complètes*, VOL. 11, pp. 279-306.

First published, in two parts, in *Critique* 19 and 21 (December 1947 and February 1948): 515-26 and 127-41.

Despite the difference in dates (1947–48), we present the two parts of this article as one continuous piece.

In the interim, Bataille published 'Le sens de l'industrialisation soviétique', *Critique* 20 (January 1948): 59–76, which is included in *La Part Maudite* (*Œuvres complètes*, VOL. 7, pp. 7–179).

Two copies of the article, corrected by Bataille, are to be found in his papers for 1947 (*Enveloppes* 146 and 147). One is entitled 'corrected proofs' and the other 'corrected copy'. We have therefore incorporated all these corrections and we point out in the notes the variants published by *Critique* in 1947.

Works reviewed (in order of their appearance in the essay):

LEVINAS, Emmanuel. *De l'existence à l'existant*. Exercice de la pensée (Georges Blin series ed.). Paris: Fontaine, 1947, in 16°, 176 pp.

WAHL, Jean. *Petite histoire de 'l'existentialisme', suivi de Kafka et Kierkegaard. Commentaires*. Paris: Éditions Club Maintenant, 1947, in 16°, 132 pp.

DE RUGGIERO, Guido. *Existentialism* (E. M. Cocks trans.) (Rayner Heppenstall ed. and intro.). London: Secker and Warburg, 1946, in 8°, 52 pp.

BENDA, Julien. *Tradition de l'existentialisme, ou les Philosophies de la vie*. Paris: Grasset, 1947, in 16°, 125 pp.

Works cited:

BLANCHOT, Maurice. *Thomas l'obscur*. Paris: Gallimard, 1941.

JANET, Pierre. *De l'angoisse à l'extase*. Paris: Librairie Félix Alcan, 1928.

KELLENBERGER, Hunter. ' "Consummation" or "Consumation" in Shakespeare?'. *Modern Philology* 65(3) (February 1968): 228–30.

LEVINAS, Emmanuel. *Existence and Existents* (Alphonso Lingis trans.). The Hague: Martinus Nijhoff, 1978.

LOEWITH [Löwith], Karl. 'L'achèvement de la philosophie classique par Hegel et sa dissolution chez Marx et Kierkegaard'. *Recherches philosophiques* 4 (1934–35).

SARTRE, Jean-Paul. 'A New Mystic' (1943) in *On Bataille and Blanchot* (Chris Turner trans.). The Seagull Sartre Library, VOL. 10. London: Seagull Books, 2021.

WAHL, Jean. *A Short History of Existentialism* (Forrest Williams and Stanley Marron trans). New York: Philosophical Library, 1949.

Goya (pp. 219–21)

'Goya', *Œuvres complètes*, VOL. 11, pp. 309-311.

First published as 'Note: Dessins de Goya au musée du Prado (texte d'André Malraux)' in *Critique* 21 (February 1948): 181-82.

Work reviewed:

Dessins de Goya au Musée du Prado (text by André Malraux). Geneva: Albert Skira, 1947, in 8°, *xxix*–213 pp (195 plates).

Psychoanalysis (pp. 222–26)

'La psychanalyse', *Œuvres complètes*, VOL. 11, pp. 317-21.

First published in *Critique* 24 (May 1948): 466-69.

Works cited:

CHALLAYE, Félicien. *Freud*. Les Philosophes. Paris: Éditions Mellotée, 1948, in 16°, 387 pp.

FILLOUX, Jean-C. *L'Inconscient*. Paris: Presses universitaires de France, 1947, in 16°, 128 pp.

Tavern Drunkenness and Religion (pp. 227–36)

'L'ivresse des tavernes et la religion', *Œuvres complètes*, VOL. 11, pp. 322-31.
First published in *Critique* 25 (June 1948): 531-39.

Works reviewed (in order of their appearance in the essay):

DE FÉLICE, Philippe. *Poisons sacrés. Ivresses divines. Essai sur quelques formes inférieures de la mystique.* Paris: Albin Michel, 1936, in 8°, 397 pp.

———. *Foules en délire. Extases collectives. Essai sur quelques formes inférieures de la mystique.* Paris: Albin Michel, 1947, in 8°, 403 pp.

Works cited:

JAMES, William. 'Lecture 16' in *Varieties of Religious Experience*. London and Bombay: Longmans, Green and Co, 1902. Available online: https://bit.ly/3hVsDjP (last accessed: 24 December 2022).

Political Lying (pp. 237–44)

'Le mensonge politique', *Œuvres complètes*, VOL. 11, pp. 332-38.
First published in *Critique* 25 (June 1948): 561-66.

Works cited:

AVELINE, Claude, Jean Cassou, André Chamson, Georges Friedmann, Louis Martin-Chauffier and Vercors. *L'heure du choix*. Paris: Éditions de Minuit, 1947, in 8°, 177 pp.

STÉPHANE, Roger (ed.). *Questions du communisme*. Special issue, *Confluences* 8(18–20). Paris: Éditions Confluences, 1947, in 16°, 344 pp.

The Sexual Revolution and the Kinsey Report (pp. 245–66)

'La révolution sexuelle et le "Rapport Kinsey" ', *Œuvres complètes*, VOL. 11, pp. 339-60.
First published, in two parts, in *Critique* 26 and 27 (July and August 1948): 646-52 and 739-50.

The second part of this article is reprinted in *Eroticism*, though in a sufficiently altered form that its publication is justified here in its totality and with its first part.

Work reviewed:

KINSEY, Alfred C., Wardell B. Pomeroy and Clyde E. Martin. *Sexual Behavior in the Human Male*. Philadelphia: W. B. Saunders, 1948, in 8°, *xv*–804 pp.

Works cited:

BONAL, Antoine. *Tractatus de Virtute Castitatis ad Usum Seminariorum*, 9th EDN. Paris, 1904, in 8°, p. 124.

DEBREYNE, Pierre Jean Corneille. *Essai sur la Théologie morale*. Paris, 1842.

TRILLING, Lionel. 'Sex and Science'. *Partisan Review* 15(4) (April 1948).

Jean Paulhan – Marc Bloch (pp. 267–72)

'Jean Paulhan - Marc Bloch', *Œuvres complètes*, VOL. 11, pp. 361-66.

First published in *Critique* 27 (August 1948): 756-57, 761-63.

Works reviewed (in order of their appearance in the essay):

PAULHAN, Jean. *De la paille et du grain*. Paris: Gallimard, 1948, petit in 16°, 183 pp.

BLOCH, Marc. 'Comment finit l'esclavage antique'. *Annales* (*Économies, Sociétés, Civilisation*) 2(1–2) (1947).

On the Meaning of Moral Neutrality in the Russo-American War (pp. 273–80)

'Du sens d'une neutralité morale dans la guerre russo-américaine', *Œuvres complètes*, VOL. 11, pp. 367-74.

First published in *Critique* 28 (September 1948): 832-38.

See also *Œuvres complètes*, VOL. 7, pp. 159–63.

Work reviewed:

ARON, Raymond. *Le Grand Schisme*. Paris: Gallimard, 1948, in 8°, 347 pp.

Works cited:

ARON, Raymond. *Introduction à la philosophie de l'histoire. Essai sur les limites de l'objectivité historique*. Paris: Gallimard, 1938.

——. *La Sociologie allemande contemporaine*. Paris: Alcan, 1936.

The Divinity of Isou (pp. 281–83)

'La divinité d'Isou', *Œuvres complètes*, VOL. 11, pp. 379-81.

First published in *Critique* 29 (October 1948): 943-45.

Work reviewed:

Isou, Isidore. *L'Agrégation d'un nom et d'un messie*. Paris: Gallimard, 1947, in 8°, 451 pp.

The Mischievousness of Language (pp. 284–92)

'La méchanceté du langage', *Œuvres complètes*, VOL. 11, pp. 382-90.

First published in *Critique* 31 (November 1948): 1052-56.

Bataille formed 'a close friendship' with Raymond Queneau at the time of the polemic against André Breton (the pamphlet *Un cadavre* of 15 January 1930). Later, they attended Alexandre Kojève's lectures on Hegel together and worked together on *La Critique sociale*. 'La critique des fondements de la dialectique hégélienne', a long study written by Bataille alone which the journal published in its fifth issue (March 1932, *Œuvres complètes*, VOL. 1, pp. 277–80) is the product of in-depth discussions between the two. This article (which Bataille always refers to as having been written 'in collaboration with Raymond Queneau') is reprinted in *Deucalion* 5 (October 1955): 45–59.

They also worked together to assemble material for a book on 'literary madmen', which would lead to the publication (by Queneau [in 1938]) of *Les Enfants du limon*.

Works reviewed (in order of their appearance in the essay):

Queneau, Raymond. *'Saint-Glinglin', précédé d'une nouvelle version de 'Gueule de Pierre' et des 'Temps mêlés'*. Paris: Gallimard, 1948, in 16°, 271 pp.

——. *L'instant fatal*. Paris: Gallimard, 1948, in 16°, 139 pp.

Works cited:

Queneau, Raymond. *Saint Glinglin* (James Sallis trans. and intro.). Normal, Illinois: Dalkey Archive Press, 1993.

Marcel Proust (pp. 293–97)

'Marcel Proust', *Œuvres complètes*, VOL. 11, pp. 391-94.

First published in *Critique* 31 (November 1948): 1133-36.

Works reviewed (in order of their appearance in the essay):

PROUST, Marcel. *A un ami. Correspondance inédite, 1903–1922* (Georges de Lauris pref.). Paris: Amiot–Dumont, 1948, in 8°, 270 pp.

——. *Lettres à Madame C.* (Léon Daudet pref.). Paris: J. B. Janin, 1947, in 8°, 215 pp, illustrated with eight plates.

MAURIAC, François. *Du côté de chez Proust.* Paris: La Table Ronde, 1947, in 8°, 155 pp.

GRAMONT, Élisabeth de. *Marcel Proust.* Paris: Flammarion, 1948, in 16°, 286 pp.

DELATTRE, Floris. 'Bergson et Proust. Accords et dissonances' in *Les Études bergsoniennes*, VOL. 1. Paris: Albin Michel, 1948, pp. 7-127.

MOUTON, Jean. *Le Style de Marcel Proust.* Paris: Corréa, 1948, in 8°, 240 pp.